Values for the Environment

A Guide to Economic Appraisal

This illustration by Neil Bennett is reproduced from ECONOMICS OF THE ENVIRONMENT, THE CONSERVATIONISTS RESPONSE TO THE PEARCE REPORT written by John Bowers and published by the British Association of Nature Conservationists, 69 Regent St., Wellington, Telford, Shropshire, TF1 1PE

OVERSEAS DEVELOPMENT INSTITUTE

Values for the Environment

A Guide to Economic Appraisal

J. T. Winpenny

LONDON: HMSO

ISBN 0 11 580257 6

James Winpenny is a development economist of 25 years' experience, gained in academic, government advisory, private consultancy and research work which has taken him to most parts of the world. He is currently a Research Fellow at the Overseas Development Institute, London. This is his fourth book. His previous publications include Planning Development Projects, also published by HMSO. He is married with four children and lives in Esher.

Front cover: the effects of acid rain in the Harz Mountains of Germany. Acknowledgements to the Robert Harding Picture Library.

Contents

Foreword

This Guide was commissioned and funded by ODA as a companion to our 1989 Manual of Environmental Appraisal. It aims to give economists working in developing countries a single volume which summarises the state of the art on the methodology and practice of economic appraisal of environmental effects. It also provides a wide range of case studies. ODA economists will take full account of the principles set out in the Guide in their work and we will require consultants working on ODA commissions to use it similarly. We hope it will also be helpful to developing country economists.

The art of environmental appraisal is in a very fluid state and we expect more work on this topic to be undertaken in Britain in the next year or two as well as in the international agencies and elsewhere. We hope this will build on and refine the practical techniques set out in this Guide. We are confident that the Guide will provide a useful map for this further work as well as a comprehensive summary of existing best practice.

J. B. Wilmshurst
Chief Economist
Overseas Development Administration

Preface

This book deals with the increasingly important and topical question of how environmental concerns can be taken into account in choosing and appraising projects. It targets development practitioners of various sorts - officials, consultants and other professionals - who have to ply their craft in the face of serious practical constraints - of data, time, cost and credibility. It sets out, for each of a number of representative sectors, a role for environmental economics which is intended to be feasible, plausible and useful.

There are a number of good textbooks available on the methodology of project appraisal, and a swelling stream of writing on environmental economics, including methods of economic valuation. This book parts company with some writing on environmental economics in laying as much stress on what is not feasible, as on what can be done. As Socrates may have said, the admission of one's ignorance is the beginning of knowledge.

The book starts with the notion of 'sustainable development', and what it is likely to imply in practice. The case for putting economic values on environmental assets and effects is then made, with due recognition of the problems this involves (Chapter 1). Chapter 2 describes the environmental problems of a number of different habitats and identifies the main functions of the environment for mankind. Chapter 3 introduces the main economic techniques available to value these functions, and Chapter 4 goes on to review how far they have been tried in practice.

Chapter 5 is laid out for the benefit of project planners and appraisers. It gathers together, sector by sector, environmental effects to be aware of, and a judgement about which of them can be valued, and how. A broader and more general picture is presented in Chapter 6, which is concerned with the impact of various kinds of policy on how projects perform.

The discussion should be comprehensible to readers with an economics background. Technical jargon is avoided wherever possible, and no use is made of mathematics. The text contains plentiful reference to the literature, and there is a full Bibliography in Appendix 1.

The book is mainly addressed to practitioners in, or concerned with, developing countries, from which most of the illustrative material is drawn. However, the problems and methods are of universal interest, and the discussion is particularly relevant to East European and the so-called Newly Industrialising Countries. The book is complementary to the Manual of Environmental Appraisal of the UK's Overseas Development Administration, to which the author also contributed. But whereas the Manual's aim was to inform a non-technical readership about environmental effects and how to deal with them as part of the typical 'project cycle', this Guide addresses the specific responsibilities of economists.

The author wishes to acknowledge the financial support of the ODA for the work on which the Guide is based, and to Alan Coverdale, whose initiative this was, for providing encouragement and advice throughout. Many detailed comments were received from ODA Advisers, including those not mentioned separately below.

An Advisory Committee helped to shape the contents of the book, and its time and interest is gratefully acknowledged. Members of the Committee were: Prof. Dennis Anderson, John Corkindale, Alan Coverdale, Prof. John Howell, Prof. Edith Penrose, Prof. Ghillean Prance and Peter Prynn. In addition the following people read and commented on draft sections: Martin Adams, Mike Arnold, Roy Behnke, Martin Birley, Elizabeth Cromwell, Jon Moris, Gill Shepherd, John Tarbit, Mary Tiffen, Linden Vincent and Geoff Walduck. Colleagues in the Overseas Development Institute were an abundant source of material, advice and comments. Patsy de Souza lent efficient and uncomplaining practical support in preparing the text.

Many others contributed their time, advice, comments or written material to this venture, proving the great depth of interest and professional generosity that the subject evokes. The following people have, in various ways, left their mark on the book:

Yusuf Ahmad, Jaap Arntzen, Edward Barbier, Scott Barrett, John Beddington, Malcolm Beveridge, Robin Bidwell, Jan Bojo, John Bowman, John Browder, Art Bruestle, Nigel Burdett, Ajay Chhibber, Charles Clift, David Cope, Herman Daly, John Dixon, Paul Driver, Chris Finney, Tony Garvey, John Goldsack, Robin Grimble, Maria Bernadete Gutierez, Ian Haines, Lawrence Hamilton, Jill Hanna, John Horberry, Ron Kemp, Pat Koshel, Prof. A. Kuyvenhoven, Jerome La Pittus, Jeffrey Leonard, Ralph Luken, Jeffrey McNeely, Prof. Karl-Goran Maler, David Norse, Prof. Tim O'Riordan, Prof. Hans Opschoor, Prof. David Pearce, Michel Potier, Michael Redclift, Robert Repetto, Richard Sandbrook, D.W.Sanders, Hartmut Schneider, Prof. Gabriele Scimemi, Iona Sebastian, Salah el Serafy, Gill Shepherd, Julian Sondheimer, Walter Spofford Jr., Michael Stocking, Peter Street, Kerry Turner, David Turnham, Harmen Verbruggen, Michiel van Pelt, Roy Waller, Maggie Walsh, Tom Walton, Jeremy Warford, and Michael Wells.

The UN's Food and Agriculture Organisation kindly agreed to the use of the diagram appearing as Figure 4.1. Dr Edward Barbier consented to the reproduction of Table 4.2.

On behalf of the reader, I would also like to thank Margaret Cornell for her usual invaluable editorial advice.

Finally, I must acknowledge my family, who have supported and inspired this venture: Lyndsay, for environmental services and life support; Diana and Dominique, who have eroded our natural habitat; Guy and Helen with best wishes for sustainable development. Harold Wilson is supposed to have said to a lady who dragged her noisy child out of one of his Election meetings, 'Bring that child back, madam, this Election is about his future'. So is this book.

J.T.W.

1

Introduction. Why Value the Environment?

The purpose of this Guide is to provide advice to economists and other economically literate professionals in applying economic values to the environmental effects of development projects. Its frame of reference is a system of decision-making about projects and policies based on cost-benefit analysis (CBA), a method which estimates the net effects on the economy from the activity being appraised. Until recently a project's impact on 'the environment' was overlooked by this method: either these effects were not recognised; they affected other parties outside the ambit of the project; or it was not judged possible to value them. The development of environmental economics as a specialised branch of welfare economics holds out the possibility of rectifying these shortcomings of traditional CBA.

This opening chapter introduces the terminology and the elementary concepts of environmental economics, including the notions of 'sustainable development' and national resource accounting, and some operational implications of these ideas are considered. It sets out the general arguments in favour of the valuation of environmental effects, and considers some objections to an extension of this practice. Finally, it offers a short User Guide to the book's contents.

1.1. Definitions and concepts

The term '*environment*' has been defined as follows:

> The conditions, circumstances and influences under which an organisation or system exists. It may be affected or described by physical, chemical and biological features, both natural and man-made. *The* environment is commonly used to refer to the circumstances in which man lives. (Brackley, 1988).

In contrast, a *habitat* is:

> The locality in which a species or community of plant or animal naturally lives and grows (*ibid.*).

The distinction is important to the use of this book. Chapter 2 is organised according to a number of *habitats* which are important, in different ways, to mankind. Within a particular habitat, however, various *environmental* effects arise, which are common to a number of different habitats. The economic treatment of a dozen major environmental problems forms the basis of Chapter 4.

It is customary to distinguish three fundamental kinds of *environmental services* (also sometimes called 'functions'):

i) general life support. The environment contains ingredients essential for life, health and human welfare. Some of these are being lost or modified by the present course of development (e.g. the ozone layer, the composition of the atmosphere, natural beauty), while others are 'finite' and subject to irreversible loss (biodiversity). The life-support service is shorthand for a large and complex range of environmental functions which we currently only partly understand.

ii) supply of raw materials and energy which are physical inputs used up in current production and consumption and which may be either renewable or finite. Finite resources are always depleted when worked, whereas renewable resources (e.g. soil, forests) can either be worked sustainably or depleted from excess use and insufficient maintenance.

iii) absorption of the waste products of economic and social activity, through the air, soil or water - sometimes called the 'sink' function. Up to a certain level, the environment can safely assimilate waste - which can be regarded as a sustainable level (though certain materials are not safely assimilable in any quantity - e.g. heavy metals, radioactive substances, certain chemicals). Beyond that level, however, natural systems become saturated and overloaded; this is tantamount to the unsustainable use of the environmental waste function.

Environmental economics has been authoritatively described thus:

> Environmental economics is a new field, essentially the creation of the present generation of economists. But its roots are in the externality theories of Marshall and Pigou, the public goods theories of Wicksell and Bowen, the general equilibrium theory of Walras, and the applied field of cost-benefit analysis . . . the essence of environmental issues is that they involve externalities and public goods. (Kneese and Russell, 1987, p.159)

In turn, *externalities and public goods* have been respectively defined as follows:

> An external effect arises when the utility or production function of one person is dependent upon the activities of other persons. (Hufschmidt *et al.*, 1983, p.45).

> . . . goods are called public goods because their units are not divisible and distinct. Their services are available to many persons at the same time, including those who do not pay for them, and unlike private goods the use of their services by one person does not diminish their availability to others. (Kneese, 1984, p. 13)

Market failure is the underlying rationale of environmental economics. The workings of markets do not always achieve the most efficient allocation of resources due, for instance, to the existence of monopolies and imperfect information among consumers. In environmental economics, externalities and public goods are two of the main reasons for market failure. Another is the failure to take the interests of future generations fully into consideration in taking present decisions (for further discussion, see Bojo, Maler and Unemo, 1990).

1.2. Sustainable development and environmental capital

The realisation that much economic activity may damage the environment is one important tenet of environmental economics. Another basic notion is of the environment as a form of natural capital, analogous in some ways to physical or financial capital assets. Damaging the environment is therefore akin to running down capital, which sooner or later reduces the value of its recurrent services (or income stream). Economists have sought to identify a level of environmental use that is in some sense 'sustainable' and consistent with preserving environmental capital.

A satisfactory definition of 'sustainable development' has become the Holy Grail of environmental economists. A recent paper lists almost 60 suggested definitions

(Pezzey, 1989), while the Pearce Report exhibits 30 in its Gallery of Definitions (Pearce *et al.*, 1989). Although the concept is much older, recent discussion has crystallised around the Brundtland Commission's notion that development is sustainable when:

> . . . it meets the needs of the present without compromising the ability of future generations to meet their own needs. (Brundtland, 1987)

Sustainable development reverts to the theoretical distinction between capital and income. According to one classic formulation:

> . . . we ought to define a man's income as the maximum value he can consume during the week and still expect to be as well off at the end of the week as he was at the beginning. (Hicks, 1968, p. 172)

By analogy, sustainable development is that which leaves our total patrimony, including natural environmental assets, intact over a particular period. We should bequeath to future generations the same 'capital', embodying opportunities for potential welfare, that we currently enjoy.

There are many problems in interpreting and applying this admirable precept. Future generations, being unborn, cannot be consulted about the kind of world in which they wish to live. Future society may accept, and even prefer, a life-style which makes very different demands from our own on material resources and the environment. In any case, the number of people to be satisfied out of our 'capital bequest' will be much larger than at present, and fine-tuning natural capital will be futile.

The value and nature of the capital stock to be passed on 'intact' into the future is therefore problematic. The very idea that the stock of natural resources should not diminish has been criticised in the following terms:

> . . . there is nothing sacrosanct about the stock *levels* we have inherited from the past. Whether or not policy should be directed at expanding environmental resource bases is something we should try and *deduce* from considerations of population change, intergenerational well-being, technological possibilities, environmental regeneration rates and the existing resource base. (Dasgupta and Maler, 1990, p.10)

It is also a moot point whether we should be concerned with passing on a constant physical level of capital, or one that preserves its value in economic terms. As resources become scarce they become more economically valuable. The last piece of coal mined on earth will no doubt have a high rarity value, but that is no consolation to people dependent on burning coal.

For such reasons it may be more appropriate to treat the concept of natural capital as a suggestive metaphor, rather than something which can be defined and measured with any precision. This is not, however, to deny the relevance of attempts to measure the stock of particular environmental resources, for the purpose of deriving management and policy conclusions (see section 1.4). In addition, as this Guide argues later, certain environmental effects are capable of being measured and valued.

Environmental economics distinguishes three broad types of capital. *Man-made capital* (factories, roads, houses, etc) can be increased or decreased at our discretion (ignoring, for the moment, the sacrifices and demands on the natural environment that are entailed). *Critical natural capital* (ozone layer, global climate, biodiversity, wildernesses, Antarctica, etc) comprises natural assets essential to life that cannot be replaced or substituted by man-made capital. The third category - *other natural capital* - includes renewable natural resources and some finite mineral resources that can be wholly or partly replenished or substituted by man-made capital.

This distinction implies that there are some kinds of natural capital that are vital, irreplaceable, and beyond price. The preservation of such assets should be an absolute constraint on all activities. It also implies setting safe minimum standards (e.g. for water and air quality, preservation of biodiversity) and ruling certain kinds of development out of bounds.

Other types of non-critical natural capital should, in principle, be valued. If activities lead to a reduction in natural capital (by using up resources in production, or destroying them through pollution or other externalities), these 'costs' should be measured, and debited to the activity responsible for them. They can either remain notional (shadow values) or become actual charges to the project (e.g. by building in compensation or specific environmental protection measures).

The use of finite resources (e.g. minerals and fossil fuels) is by definition non-sustainable. Environmental economics has only very general precepts to offer about the production and use of such resources, e.g. to improve the efficiency with which such resources are extracted and used, to promote the use of substitutes, etc. (e.g. Barbier, 1989b, p. 188).

1.3. Implications of sustainability for development projects

The implications of sustainable development are potentially wide-ranging. The principle does not imply avoiding all exploitative projects like mining or hardwood timber felling. Nor does it require projects to continue indefinitely. The following are some of its more certain operational implications:

i) avoid damage to critical natural capital, such as biodiversity, the ozone layer, etc., and be wary of starting processes that are irreversible;

ii) where possible put economic values on environmental costs and benefits as a reminder to decision-makers that these resources are not free, with the aim of moderating the use of environmental services;

iii) in certain cases, 'internalise' the costs of a project to the environment, either by requiring compensation to be made (to society, or to parties damaged) or by building a 'compensatory project' into the scheme being appraised (e.g. planting to replace trees destroyed during road building);

iv) for man-made and non-critical natural capital, aim to recover at least the initial capital by the end of the project. For man-made capital (e.g. a steel mill) this entails applying the normal rules of CBA, namely fully recovering the initial cost of the project over the life of the scheme, leaving the original outlays for reinvestment or redeployment in the future. For renewable natural capital, e.g. agriculture, forestry, fishing, it implies maintaining the resource and limiting exploitation to sustainable levels. For finite resources, such as petroleum extraction and mining, it implies using the sales proceeds for conversion into man-made capital, or more generally setting aside and investing enough proceeds to produce a permanent income stream (El Serafy, 1989);

v) in project design, and as part of project negotiations, aim to incorporate as many of the environmental costs (and benefits) as possible through the adjustment of *actual* prices, taxes and subsidies. This is another example of the attempt to 'internalise' such costs, and takes the analyst into the realm of policy dialogue and conditionality, explored further in Chapter 6.

There are many other practical implications of sustainable development, especially in the areas of national and international policies (e.g. Repetto and Pezzey, 1990).

1.4. National resource accounting

Ideally, work to achieve sustainability at the project level should be complemented by the adjustment of national accounts to reflect true resource use, in order to produce more accurate measurement of real economic performance.

Environmental economics asserts that growth, as measured by changes in GNP, fails to allow for the depletion of natural capital (analogous to the depreciation of physical capital). Many resources that can be considered environmental assets such as forests, farms, and fisheries, are being worked at unsustainable rates, often because not enough is being spent on maintaining the asset. In such cases, capital consumption is being treated as income. This gives the wrong signals to policy-makers in their respective countries, and produces misleading measures of their comparative international performance. For producers and exporters of primary products, allowing for capital depletion can drastically change their measured growth rates. For example, a recent attempt was made to rework the national accounts of Indonesia allowing for the depletion of its natural assets (Repetto *et al.*, 1989). Taking account of estimated real depletion of Java's hill farming, forestry and petroleum reserves, it was estimated that national income in 1984 would be lower by around 17%, and the rate of growth for 1971-1984 nearer 4% rather than the 7% with which it is normally credited.

Furthermore, services provided by the environment are frequently omitted from national income because they are not priced or marketed. Nevertheless, when these services are lost, society is forced into 'defensive expenditure' to replace them, (e.g. cleaning up after pollution, dredging eroded soil from water courses) and this spending is counted as part of national income. Thus the degradation of environmental resources appears to raise, rather than lower, national income.

In principle, there is a good case for netting environmental depletion out of income when drawing up national accounts. However, a number of problems would have to be overcome before environmental accounting became widespread and comprehensive:

i) conceptual disagreements need to be resolved, such as whether sales of minerals represent asset sales or income, and in what proportion;

ii) there is the vexed question of how to treat 'defensive expenditure'. Spending on measures to protect against the effects of environmental deterioration (e.g. double glazing against aircraft and traffic noise) is no different in principle from other kinds of spending to preserve or replace the quality of life: longer commuting journeys, repair costs from vehicle accidents, domestic burglar alarms, industrial and personal security, costs arising from drug, tobacco and alcohol abuse, and even the national defence budget. It is difficult to draw the dividing line between these 'defensive' cost items and outlays for more positive and agreeable purposes, and netting all such items out of national income would leave the accounts in tatters;

iii) there is disagreement about whether or not to tackle the issue head-on, by seeking reforms to the System of National Accounts, which has been the basis of national accounting worldwide since the 1960s. The alternative would be to complement the existing system with a parallel set of 'satellite' accounts to illustrate the state of the environment and give pointers to sustainable growth. France and Norway have gone furthest in developing environmental accounts, and both rely heavily on physical measures which are hard to integrate into conventional national accounts (Pearce *et al.*, 1989).

Adjusting national accounts in the ways suggested would be easier for countries relying on natural resource exploitation than for industrial and semi-industrial countries (e.g. in East Europe, East and South-East Asia, Mexico, Brazil) where there are formidable problems of urban and industrial pollution. In a sense the latter are 'running down' their environment for the sake of current output, and will have either to curtail future development of the same kind, or spend heavily on pollution abatement and control. Yet measures of industrial and urban environmental depletion are far less developed than those available for agriculture, forestry and mining.

1.5. The importance of valuing the environment

It should be clear from the above discussion that valuation is only one item on the agenda of sustainable development. It is nevertheless an important and fundamental task, for the following reasons:

i) It is a reminder that the environment is not 'free', even though there may not be a conventional market for its services. It measures the rate at which environmental resources are being used up, and signals the growing scarcity to their users.

ii) It helps to redress the balance between quantifiable and non-quantifiable effects in cost-benefit analysis, or between monetary and non-monetary values. For that large class of decisions that are taken on financial or economic criteria, quantifiable effects may weigh more heavily in the mind of the decision-maker. Hence the importance of identifying potential effects, and valuing them as far as possible (and plausible) in order to arrive at a better and fairer decision.

iii) In the context of a cost-benefit decision, valuing as many effects as possible narrows the field remaining for 'pure' judgement. There will always be a need for judgements between non-comparable factors. However, the difficulty (and arbitrariness) of making this judgement will be reduced the more environmental effects can be expressed in common economic terms.

iv) Valuation can provide a truer indication of economic performance.

v) Quantification, carried out carefully and recognising its limits, can provide a more secure basis for policies to induce more careful environmental use, e.g. taxation, charging, subsidies. To implement the policy of 'Polluter pays', we need to know 'how much' the polluter should pay. To introduce a carbon tax presupposes that we know the 'right', or even an approximate, level for the tax. Valuation can inform such decisions.

There are a number of common objections to using economic valuation in environmental appraisal:

a) Trying to put economic values on environmental effects which are inherently non-quantifiable merely devalues the debate. Certain things do have an absolute value which makes them essentially non-quantifiable - life itself, beauty, the diversity of species. However, there are many instances of apparent 'non-quantifiables' to which the economic measuring rod is already being partially applied - e.g. health, an unobstructed view, air and water quality, etc. The approach taken in this Guide - spelled out in Chapter 3 - is to restrain valuation to the limits of good sense and plausibility, and not just to the receding boundary of what is technically possible. True non-quantifiables are treated as 'off bounds'.

b) CBA is cynically manipulated by parties interested in producing a certain result. The argument has been expressed thus:

> . . . the agencies that are carrying out the CBA are in a position of power to manipulate the analysis to achieve the answers that they want. They do so because requirements of objectivity underlying CBA are in practice not met. Those who carry out the analyses are fully committed to the projects that they are appraising and use CBA to attain their ends. If they are required to value environmental effects this would not alter the outcomes. (Bowers, 1990)

There is no denying that CBA is often abused, and its objectivity bent in order to justify a pre-conceived outcome. In judging the worth of an appraisal, the institutional pressures bearing on the analyst must always be borne in mind (Little and Mirrlees, 1990). But this is a criticism of any objective decision criterion. In the last resort the criticism amounts merely to the statement that CBA is irrelevant to the outcome in such cases. There *are* honest appraisers and sincere decision-makers, and the refinement of CBA to include environmental factors can be helpful to such, not yet endangered, species.

c) Valuation requires a great deal of technical and economic data, which are generally lacking in developing countries. Urgently needed projects cannot wait until such data are generated. Furthermore, the production of the required data, and the conduct of sophisticated appraisals, commits extremely scarce resources in developing countries, with a high opportunity cost. These are perfectly valid objections, which influence much of the discussion in subsequent Chapters.

d) The valuation techniques on offer in standard texts are those that have evolved to deal with environmental problems characteristic of developed societies. They are of much less applicability in countries with different problems, different economic systems, and a different scale of relative environmental values. This is also a valid objection, the importance of which is further assessed in Chapters 3, 4, and 5.

1.6. A brief User Guide

This book's main aim is to be of operational value in project appraisal and, ultimately, policy formation. Its secondary objective is to provide elementary information on environmental issues and processes to non-specialists. For those readers unable to work through the whole book in its present order, various short-cuts are available. Let us take the part of the target reader, an economist with project responsibilities working in, or for, a spending agency.

Suppose the project in question is a new road, to be built in a tropical country through forested, hilly terrain. The analyst may wish to focus directly on the relevant part of Chapter 5, namely the Roads and Railways part in 5.3.2. This will remind him/her of the range of likely environmental effects in this sector, and suggest focusing on those effects which are more capable of being valued, or on which there is valid comparative data. Case studies are summarised, where they are relevant.

Chapter 5 draws on Chapter 4 as a quarry for material on the treatment of particular environmental problems. Thus, if the road is likely to lead to a significant loss of forest cover and some soil erosion, sections 4.1 and 4.2 should be consulted. If biodiversity were substantially at risk, section 4.11 would also be relevant.

Economists unfamiliar with some of the physical environmental processes at stake should also find material in Chapter 2 helpful - in the example chosen, section 2.2 on watersheds and 2.3 on tropical rain forests. This chapter is organised around the notion of environmental services to be found in various habitats.

Economists familiar with CBA but who are newcomers to environmental economics should find Chapter 3 useful in deciding which techniques to use in tackling a particular environmental problem. It may also be interesting to economists familiar with the basic techniques but who wonder about their relevance to developing countries. The same chapter may also be useful, and should be intelligible, to officials and other professionals with basic economic literacy, who have to work with environmental economists and understand their output.

Finally, Chapter 6 is necessary reading for all parties involved, including the 'decision-maker' - that legendary being about whose wisdom, aptitudes and behaviour we make so many assumptions, and the ultimate consumer of this Guide's contents.

2

Environmental Problems of Major Habitats

The preceding chapter introduced the notion of the environment as natural capital, providing a stream of services, which, if used sustainably, provide a level of income or welfare to their users. However, if the environment is used excessively or is damaged this will sooner or later affect its ability to continue supplying its services.

Economists need to be able to understand what is lost to national income and welfare when environmental capital is depleted. As a prelude to considering how such valuation can be made (Chapters 3 and 4), this chapter discusses the importance of the environment in a number of typical habitats vital to the developing world's population, and indicates the main ways in which they are being threatened. The main environmental services are identified.

The scale of the respective issues can be illustrated by the following very approximate estimates of numbers (in millions) affected or potentially at risk from current environmental trends (from Leonard, 1989): living in, or dependent on, tropical forest: 200, affected by dryland degradation: 850, dependent on irrigation for a livelihood: 1,000, occupying degrading watersheds: 500, threatened by downstream soil erosion: 400, dependent on diminishing supplies of fuelwood: 3,000 (by year 2000), squatting on badly-serviced urban peripheries: 100. In addition, 335 million are living in cities of over 1 mn. people (1980) (Hardoy and Satterthwaite, 1989).

Populations in these categories will frequently overlap - e.g. urban squatters depending on fuelwood gathered in the hinterland, irrigation farmers menaced by sedimentation, hill farmers running short of fuelwood, etc.

2.1. The aquatic environment

The scope of this section includes the oceans themselves, large inland seas and largely enclosed bodies of water like the Black and Mediterranean Seas, small islands, and sensitive coastal systems like reefs and beaches. The special case of coastal wetlands is covered in section 2.6.

2.1.1. Vital issues and problems

Some of the main problems in the aquatic environment are the following:

i) A rise in sea level is threatened by global warming, which would lead to a thermal expansion of ocean waters, possibly followed by a further addition to sea volume as terrestrial icecaps melted. Low-lying coastal areas would be inundated, certain small islands submerged, and everywhere the severity of coastal storm damage would increase. This grave threat is further discussed in section 4.12.

ii) In selected inland seas, however, a fall in sea level is a more pressing problem. One of the best publicised cases is the Aral Sea in Soviet Central Asia whose volume has been drastically affected by the massive diversion of the waters of its main feeder rivers for irrigation of the surrounding cotton-growing areas. Since 1960 its level has fallen by 13 meters, its area has shrunk by 40%, its volume has fallen by two-thirds, and its salinity has tripled. All its native fish have disappeared, and salt from its dry bed is blown inland and ruins agriculture. (Brown *et al.*, 1990; Medvedev, 1990). Lake Chad in Africa has also shrunk over the last 30 years, from 28,000 to 10,000 square km., and its volume of water has fallen by 60%. The latter is an example of the variability of shallow tropical lakes mainly owing to natural causes. (Part-time fishermen are better able to cope with such fluctuations.)

iii) Pollution can damage fish, wildlife, human health and amenity, depending on whether it occurs on the high sea or in coastal waters. The main risk of pollution in open waters is from oil slicks owing to accidents to tankers, cleaning and discharge of tanks on vessels, or the clandestine dumping of hazardous waste at sea. The worst effects of such pollution are experienced if and when it reaches coastal waters. If it occurs close to shore, it can foul shorelines and beaches and add the destruction of amenity to its other costs - most vividly exemplified by the *Exxon Valdez* accident in Alaska in 1989. Inshore pollution is less dramatic but more insidious. Raw sewage, industrial waste, and agro-chemicals routinely foul the world's coastal waters, and the costs are borne by fishermen, aquaculturists, swimmers and tourism operators. Sea creatures also suffer.

iv) The over-exploitation of aquatic resources is already occurring in some heavily fished areas, and may become an increasing problem. Fish stocks are also being depleted locally by inappropriate fishing techniques and inshore pollution.

v) Small, low-lying islands, especially coral atolls, are at risk from storms, loss of fresh water from saline intrusion, and eventually from rising sea levels. Their vulnerability to storm damage is heightened by the destruction of reefs by fishing or construction. Their drinking water is derived partly from rainwater collection and partly from the underground fresh-water 'lenses'. The latter tend to become more saline and diminish with the encroachment of the sea (Roy and Connell, 1989).

vi) Reefs and beaches are being lost as a result of dynamiting, pollution, and the excavation of sand for construction purposes. Reefs often serve as coastal protection, are popular with tourists and divers, are important in the food cycle of fish, and harbour a great deal of biodiversity. Beaches are increasingly at risk from pollution (from oil, sewage, industrial and agro-chemical discharges) and physical destruction from wave action and quarrying, with consequent losses to amenity and tourism. Algae bloom ('Red Tides') from industrial and agro-chemical effluent has started to become a problem to tourism adjacent to areas of industry or intensive agriculture (e.g. on the Adriatic in 1989).

vii) The sea, and the reefs and wetlands on its fringes, are rich in biodiversity, much of which is unexplored and little understood, and has a wider interest for students of evolution and lovers of wildlife. Of more direct and immediate interest to human economies are the role of marine organisms, especially in reefs and wetlands, in the life cycle of fish, the potential value of sea plants and creatures as medicines, and their role in tourism and leisure, and in assimilating waste products.

2.1.2. Environmental services

The sea provides a host of environmental services, many of which are not under any serious or immediate threat (though see section 4.12 for the possible effects of global warming on sea levels). The sea regulates the earth's climate, supplies a major source of food and provides the medium for navigation, which is only reaching its limit in certain busy channels. The sea bed is a major source of oil and natural gas, and potentially of minerals. Some of the sea's minor products (seaweed, shells, live tropical fish) are of considerable local economic importance. This section examines three of its more important functions, all of which are of major economic importance, and are under actual or potential threat from human agency.

a) **Fisheries** are highly prone to natural variability in their environment, in ways which can be complex and unpredictable, and may interact with human interventions to produce serious consequences (cf. the impact of the El Nino current on the Peruvian fishing industry). There is a vital role for oceanographers in work on the fisheries environment. This section concentrates on factors more within human control.

The world's fishing grounds are coming under growing pressure from exploitation. This brings the risk that their future *sustainable yield* will be reduced, and at the limit wiped out, that certain species will be eliminated, and that competition between different types of fishing operators will cause serious economic and social distress to the losers. As one survey concludes:

> Stocks of fish not fully exploited are decreasing, and are mostly found in less accessible areas, or include species which are less easily marketable. Industrial fisheries are finding it increasingly difficult to find fresh, unexploited stocks, and those within the range of artisanal fishermen are now mostly fully or overly exploited. (DANIDA, 1989)

It has been estimated that 99% of the world's fishing catch is taken within 200 miles of land, i.e. within actual or potential Exclusive Economic Zones. The EEZ is an example of the creation of fishing property rights vested in the Government with jurisdiction over the Zones, and provides the means of regulating commercial exploitation, provided quotas are judiciously fixed and effectively policed. Even so, the formerly large anchovy industry of Peru has been severely depleted.

In principle, the sustainable yield of the main commercial species of fish should be estimated, and the annual catch limited to that level. This is a very elusive concept in practice (see section 4.5). Where recorded catches over a number of years give clear signs that total yields are declining, this is evidence that sustainable yields are being exceeded. In these circumstances, projects to invest in more or improved vessels and gear should allow for their likely negative effects on other parties. Many aid-funded projects in artisanal fisheries have merely led to a given catch being spread over more fishermen, with more costs and effort expended all round (DANIDA, 1989).

The *species composition* of fish stocks may also change. The introduction of the Nile perch into Lake Victoria in the 1950s has been a mixed blessing. One school of thought holds that the carnivorous perch has been responsible for the decline in smaller indigenous species, which are more popular with the local people. Fishing the perch has concentrated the industry into the hands of fewer, wealthier, individuals, while smoking the fish has led to deforestation around parts of the lake. These effects have to be balanced against the social and economic benefits resulting from exploitation of this fish. In the Gulf of Thailand and other heavily fished tropical waters the species composition has also changed, with an increasing preponderance of smaller and shorter-lived species, including shrimp and squid, which have helped maintain the total catch.

Some of the obvious reasons for the pressure on fish stocks are over-fishing, indiscriminating fishing methods, and pollution. *Overfishing* is fundamentally a product of growing demand and has been the impetus for the development of better catching and preserving techniques, such as the mechanisation of artisanal fishing. It has also been helped by population growth providing surplus labour which sees fishing as a residual activity.

Indiscriminate fishing methods destroy the habitats used by young fish, kill juvenile and immature fish, and catch and kill many more fish than are actually sold. Dynamiting (blast fishing) is widespread in some communities (e.g. in the Philippines) as a profitable and labour-saving, though short-sighted, method of catching fish - but one which destroys coral. The use of sodium cyanide, to catch fish living in coral for aquarium use, also kills living coral as well as non-target fish. The 'muro-ami' method using a large number of swimmers with vertical weighted scare lines damages coral and captures many non-target species (World Bank, 1989). Using nets with a fine mesh (say, below 5-6 cm., depending on species) captures small and immature specimens, at the cost of future catches.

On a larger scale, the use of drift gill nets 10-15 meters deep and 35 to 60 kilometers long ('wall of death' fishing) kills many non-target species while aiming to catch target species by the gills. The practice occurs both on an artisanal scale, and in international waters, where it is difficult to control. It depletes the fishery of the target species, is wasteful - since much of the catch drops out on hauling or escapes injured - and kills non-target species including mammals, birds and reptiles. Nets which break loose from their ships carry on 'ghost fishing' for years afterwards, at great cost to fish and other vessels that get entangled in them.

The third major cause of fish depletion is *siltation and pollution*. Siltation due to forest denudation is, for example, one of the greatest factors in the degradation of coral reefs in the Philippines (World Bank, 1989). Soil washed down from unprotected watersheds causes turbidity, which stunts coral growth, and in large volumes can entirely bury the coral. The tailings from mining are particularly damaging. A study of the effect of siltation in Bacuit Bay, Philippines, caused by logging and road construction, came up with the following results: each extra 400 tonnes per sq.km. of sediment deposited in the Bay reduced coral cover by 1% annually; each 100 tonnes/sq.km. of sediment deposition led to the extinction of one coral species per year; for every 1% annual decrease in coral cover fish biomass decreased by 2.4%; and for every coral species lost fish biomass decreased by 0.8% (Hodgson and Dixon, 1989).

Pollution is caused by various kinds of effluent, accidental discharges of oil and hazardous substances, and atmospheric deposition. Much of the world's sewage enters the sea untreated. The volume of sewage, the length of the sewer outfall, and the depth of the water and prevailing currents will determine whether the waste is disposed of harmlessly or accumulates in coastal waters. Some fish species thrive on a certain level of organic matter in the water (e.g. eels, sharks), though that safe limit is soon exceeded.

Industrial effluent is potentially more harmful: oysters caught in Hong Kong waters in 1988 were found to contain levels of cadmium and lead that made them unfit to eat. Lake Laguna near Manila in the Philippines is an important fishing resource providing a livelihood for 70,000 people, but it is being depleted by uncontrolled effluent from over 400 industrial operations surrounding the Lake (*Development Forum*, 15, 1989). The catch in the Azov Sea in the USSR has been reduced to 5% of 1950 levels because of industrial waste, untreated sewage and agro-chemical effluent. The value of the fish lost over a 25-year period has been put at 2 billion roubles (Medvedev, 1990).

Oil spills also cause serious damage. The loss to commercial fisheries from the *Amoco Cadiz* accident in 1978 was estimated to be $45m (in 1981 prices - Cohen, 1986), while the 1989 *Exxon Valdez* spill is so far thought to have cost $12 m. in lost fishing earnings and another $7 m. in damage to hatcheries (*Washington Post*, 6 February 1990). Even the solvent used to clean up oil pollution may have harmful effects on fish, humans and wildlife. The long-term effects of oil pollution on biomass are little understood . Less publicised are the leaks and spillages that occur around marine oil drilling rigs and in busy shipping lanes used by oil tankers.

A sizeable amount of marine pollution is also thought to originate from the atmosphere, for instance as acid rain. It is, for example, possible that the regular burning of savanna grass in West Africa is a major contributor of 'greenhouse' gas, and that the acid rain it causes falls in Lake Victoria with deleterious effects on the fish population.

b) **Biodiversity and wildlife.** Marine wildlife is threatened in various ways by current economic development. Coral reefs have the highest species diversity of any biome in their respective environments. They are the marine equivalent of tropical forests. The Australian Great Barrier Reef supports 8% of the world's fish species. In the Philippines, more than 2000 fish species live in or near coral reefs. The waters of the Indo-Pacific region are especially rich in species (Reid and Miller, 1989). These biodiverse resources are being lost as a result of destructive reef fishing, construction, siltation and pollution.

Accidental oil spillages are the best documented cases of the effect of pollution on wildlife. It was estimated that the *Amoco Cadiz* accident killed between 19,000 and 37,000 sea birds, and disabled many more (Cohen, 1986). The *Exxon Valdez* spill in 1989 killed at least 725 sea otters and 20,000 sea birds (*The Siren*, July 1989). There was a massive clean-up operation to save 350 sea otters - of which only 180 survived, and 35 were released into the wild.

A number of the larger sea creatures are threatened with extinction from various causes. Particular species of whale (e.g. sperm, minke, humpback) have been greatly depleted by commercial hunting. Dugongs (sea cows) are also seriously depleted from drowning in gill nets and aboriginal hunting. Porpoises and turtles are threatened by hunting and, in the latter case, egg collection and habitat destruction. Other species - dolphins, otters, seals, etc.- while more plentiful, suffer in various ways from human activities.

c) **Amenity and recreation**. Coastal waters, and their associated beaches, reefs and cliffs - a vital ingredient in leisure, amenity and tourism - are being degraded in many ways. Marine pollution has caused problems in such popular holiday areas as the Adriatic, Mediterranean and Black Seas. The massive oil spill from *Kharg-5* came close to devastating Morocco's tourist beaches in December 1989. Coral reef destruction is threatening snorkelling and diving ,both rapidly growing sports.

On a global scale, the loss of the ozone layer is likely to increase the risk of skin cancer in those who expose themselves to the sun. The rising sea level in the wake of global warming could overtake the regenerative capacity of coral reefs and the rate of beach formation, leading to net loss of both. One observer has noted the irony that, as a result of future global warming, the UK could enjoy sub-tropical weather yet lose many of its finest beaches.

The Maldives is the epitome of several of these problems. Tourism provides around one-fifth of GDP and government revenue. However, the international airport is a mere 1.2 metres above sea level, and most settlements, industry and infrastructure lie within 0.8-2 m. above sea level. These islands could be the first victim of global warming (Commonwealth Secretariat, 1989). Meanwhile, the mining of coral for construction (including the airport) has ruined many reefs, and blasting is harming the reef life forms. The continued discharge of untreated household waste, sewage, and industrial effluent into the shallow waters around the main settlements is starting to exceed the sea's natural assimilative capacity, and the water around the main islands is now unfit for swimming. Added to this pollution is the waste from the burgeoning tourist industry, which includes non-biodegradable items like tins and plastic bags, and is dumped close offshore (*Orbit*, Summer 1989).

Tourism is a cause, as well as a victim, of marine pollution and reef destruction. This is further analysed in Chapter 5, section 5.6.

2.2. Watersheds

A watershed is the total land area that drains to some point on a stream or river. However, it may be more useful to refer to the area drained by a river as a catchment area or river basin, while the high ground separating adjacent catchment areas is the watershed (Pereira, 1989). Whatever definition is used, the degradation of watersheds affects production on the land within their boundaries and activities carried out downstream in river basins.

Watersheds are threatened by the encroachment of farm populations, livestock grazing, firewood collection, commercial logging, road construction into virgin areas, major civil works such as dams and highways, and the conversion of forest to plantations, amongst other factors. In assessing the results of these processes the economist depends on receiving clear and quantified information on the biophysical effects of a particular land use or intervention, to which economic values can readily be applied. This presumes good data on cause and effect applied to such processes as soil erosion, water retention and run-off, and sedimentation. The relation of physical and hydrological changes to biomass also needs to be specified. A review of the scope for measuring erosion, and establishing its on- and off-site effects is postponed for Chapter 4, section 4.1. This section introduces the processes involved in watershed degradation and some of their causes.

2.2.1. Problems of watershed degradation

About half the world's population are potentially affected by watershed degradation - the 10% who live on the slopes concerned, and the 40% who occupy the adjacent lowland areas. In the tropical regions of the Western Hemisphere, for instance, between a quarter and a third of the population live in hillside zones, and half these farms are on slopes greater than 20 degrees. Likewise the mountainous slopes of South-East Asia, the Himalayas, East and Central Africa and elsewhere are of vital agricultural importance to their respective countries.

Although there is mounting evidence of local watershed degradation and its effects, there is controversy over its global extent, as well as its causes (Belshaw, Blaikie and Stocking, 1991). For instance, there is dispute over the extent of land degradation in the Himalayas, its contribution to downstream siltation, and the respective influences of natural and human agencies (Blaikie, 1989).

However, there is serious degradation in many areas. Many tropical hill areas contain low productivity subsistence agriculture carried out amidst rapid population growth, poverty, and economic marginality. These farm populations may be difficult to reach with normal public services. Those that are better integrated with the national market (e.g. in Java) frequently respond to policy and market signals which encourage degrading farm practices. Even for communities that appear to be beyond the reach of government measures, some aspects of national policies and institutions (e.g. land distribution, farm development) can impinge on their behaviour (Jagannathan, 1989). The basic predicament has been summarised as follows:

. . . environmental degradation is so widespread in hillside areas because the social and economic factors associated with underdevelopment are there combined with a land resource subject to rapid deterioration under improper human use. (De Boer, 1989)

A change in vegetation or land use in a watershed (e.g. deforestation, ploughing up steep slopes, grazing animals) can unleash a number of interrelated processes:

a) increased exposure of the earth to the mechanical effects of rain and run-off, leading to soil erosion, and reduced soil fertility from the loss of nutrients and soil structure;

b) greater run-off of water, leading to gully erosion and flooding;

c) less retention of water locally, leading to reduced local groundwater levels, and water shortages in local wells and springs;

d) the transport of sediment, producing silting in rivers and irrigation works, deposition in reservoirs and lakes, and changes in river courses. This increases the risk of flooding, affects fisheries, and reduces the capacity of dams and irrigation systems.

Not all these effects are wholly negative. Farmland lower down the catchment may benefit from the deposition of fertile silt during floods. Systems of domestic and irrigation water may depend on high rates of run-off, and, conversely, suffer from anything that causes greater upstream moisture retention. Nevertheless, the balance of effects from the encroachment of uncontrolled development on watersheds is more likely to be negative than positive.

This section examines three important processes in watershed degradation:

a) **Soil erosion.** The three main types of erosion are surface erosion, gulley erosion, and soil creep. Surface erosion involves the loss of soil particles from exposed land areas. Its severity depends on a number of local factors, such as the erosiveness of rainfall (force, frequency), the erodibility of the soil, topography, vegetation, etc. A certain level of erosion results from 'natural' causes and can be tolerated without significant effects on soil fertility. But more serious erosion normally results from a change in vegetation cover, e.g. from deforestation, conversion from perennial to annual crops, grazing by livestock, etc.

Gully erosion and soil creep have more dramatic effects; they are always a danger on marginal slopes in high rainfall areas. Gully erosion follows from the action of unrestrained run-off from slopes, e.g. stormwater on bare earth. Soil creep, or mass soil movements, tends to occur on steep slopes on which soil bodies are subject to unbearable 'shear' stresses. Typical causes include road building across slopes, careless forest logging, and a change in cropping from deep- to shallow-rooted varieties. Landslides are an extreme form, risking damage to property and loss of life and livestock as well as agricultural and sedimentation costs.

b) **Water flows and yield.** Soil erosion and sedimentation are most directly affected by the movement of water down a slope, and the more rapid and unconstrained this movement is, the worse, in general, will be the erosion and deposition. However, the converse of run-off is water yield, which has a different connotation for downstream water users. Where watershed management causes water flows and yields to diminish, which is not uncommon, a conflict of interest could occur between the different groups of people affected.

One important negative aspect of increased water yield is greater liability to flooding. Changes in land use that increase water yield and run-off will increase the risk of floods, especially in the common case where peak flows are greater. (The incidence of flooding also needs to be assessed in the light of sedimentation discussed below.) However, land use in a watershed will make little or no difference to flooding arising from exceptionally severe storms (say, a one in a 100 years event), and will not therefore obviate the need for *some* flood defence works.

The quality of water in a catchment has important economic effects, and is affected by land use. A forested slope with little human or animal population and no erosion will produce the best quality water. Erosion and contamination (e.g. by animals, chemical additives to the soil) will tend to cause pollution. This, in turn, will have adverse effects on drinking water, fisheries and recreation.

c) **Sedimentation** is the product of erosion and water flow. The build-up of sediment ('aggradation') may occur in rivers, in which case it would cause flooding, navigation problems, and changes in river channels which could leave offtake works high and dry. Equally, sedimentation could occur in irrigation systems or reservoirs. In the first case, this would call for dredging, cleaning and clearing, while in the latter case the value of the combined reservoir/hydroelectric scheme could be drastically reduced. Apart from lowering the net storage capacity of a reservoir, siltation can damage hydroelectric turbine blades and fill access pipes.

Sediment carried all the way down to the sea can reduce the productivity of coastal fisheries. Where it contains soil nutrients and artificial fertiliser its effects on fisheries and recreation through 'eutrophication' or turbidity are magnified.

The major sources of sediment are surface and gully erosion, pre-existing sediment in channels, mass soil movements into a reservoir or channels, and the effect of specific works in the vicinity. The siltation of reservoirs is a particularly serious problem. In practice the most common causes are: the abrasive action of changes in reservoir level on its banks; careless construction of roads in the neighbourhood, causing slope failures; and the creation of borrow pits for dam construction, which become instantly erodible.

Anything that reduces peak discharges (e.g. tree planting) can have a disproportionate effect in reducing sediment transport, and therefore silting and deposition (White, 1989).

2.3. Tropical rain forests

The principal frame of reference in this section is humid tropical forests. Trees growing in semi-arid conditions are covered elsewhere in the following sections. Readers are also referred to section 2.2 where forests are located in watersheds.

2.3.1. Environmental threats

Since 1950, the forested area in North America and Europe has stopped shrinking, and in some countries is increasing thanks to the growth of commercial plantations. The main problems this poses for the environment relate to the encroachment of certain dominant species (e.g. pine, eucalyptus) into formerly deciduous forests or mixed wildland to the detriment of diversity in animal and plant life. Temperate forests sufficiently close to industrial areas are also becoming susceptible to damage and stunting from industrial and urban emissions ('acid rain').

By contrast, the virtually universal problem in tropical regions is the destruction and loss of natural forest, which is running far ahead of new planting and the growth of secondary forest on cleared areas. Tropical moist closed forest currently covers about 1.2 billion ha., half of it in the Amazon area (WRI/IIED, 1988). It is being removed at an average rate of almost 14 million ha. per year (Houghton, 1990).

The weight of the primary causes differs between regions. In South Asia deforestation is mainly due to fuelwood gathering and overgrazing. In continental South-East Asia trees are lost mainly because of the expansion of agriculture from heavily populated rice-growing areas, and shifting cultivation by hill tribes. In Malaysia, Indonesia, the Philippines and parts of Thailand uncontrolled commercial logging is the prime culprit, together with pioneering settlement (Watanabe, 1989). In Africa, deforestation is primarily due to the expansion of agricultural areas, the practice of shifting cultivation in areas of plentiful land, the uncontrolled grazing of livestock, and the collection of fuelwood, especially for urban use. In the tropical parts of Latin America the activities of shifting cultivators and clearances by land-hungry peasants have been superseded by government-inspired programmes of highway construction, frontier settlement, cattle ranching and commercial timber concessions.

In practical terms, the loss of mature tropical hardwood forests is irreversible since trees take 50-100 years to mature, and the original balance of species is unlikely to be recaptured by the growth of secondary forest on cleared areas. The impoverishment and loss of soils and destruction of biodiversity could be permanent, as well as leading to the dispersal (and death) of indigenous animals and people.

2.3.2. Environmental services

a) **Climatic and atmospheric**. In equilibrium, a natural forest has a neutral effect on atmospheric oxygen supplies, consuming in plant respiration as much as is given out during photosynthesis. Hence the loss of forest in itself does not affect the world's oxygen balance. Nor does a stable mature forest act as a 'sink' for atmospheric carbon released elsewhere from industrial or motor emissions.

However, *changes* in forest cover can upset this equilibrium, in two offsetting ways. Burning trees releases the stored carbon into the atmosphere, where it may add to the 'Greenhouse Effect' on global climate. Trees and forest soils hold 20 to 100 times more carbon than the crops and soils that replace forests. Methane is also released into the air from burning trees and grass and from decaying vegetation, and is further liberated from some of the land uses that supersede forests, such as cattle, rice production and flooding forests for hydroelectric reservoirs (Houghton, 1990). If the cleared land is ultimately allowed to revert to secondary forest, then during its growth phase the latter will be a net absorber of carbon, but this is only a partial and gradual offset to the sudden and large-scale carbon release during deforestation.

Scientific evidence about the scale of these effects and their impact on climate is still being assembled. The burning of tropical forest on the current massive scale is thought to contribute 25-33% of the global emission of carbon dioxide, which in turn is responsible for half of the world's 'greenhouse gases' (*ibid.*). It is unlikely to be offset in the foreseeable future by the growth of new trees, given current patterns of land use.

The equatorial forests of the Intertropical Convergence Zone are also thought to play an important part in the recycling of heat from tropical to temperate zones (Molion, 1989).

Deforestation can also result in local micro climatic effects. The large-scale removal of trees is likely to raise ground ambient temperatures and cause increased evaporation by sun and wind. Studies in Nigeria and Amazonia show that deforestation can raise soil temperatures by 5°C and between 2°C and 5°C, respectively, and increase day air temperatures by 3-6 and 1-3 degrees C (*ibid.*).

On a larger scale, forests contribute to the cycle of rainfall and transpiration. It is estimated that 50% of the rainfall in Amazonia has its source in the evapo-transpiration of the trees themselves (quoted in Prance, 1986). Thus deforestation *could* start an irreversible movement towards greater aridity. However, scientific evidence on the local effect of forest cover on rainfall is inconclusive (Hamilton, 1988).

b) **Watershed effects**. Forest cover helps to preserve the stability of slopes, inhibits soil erosion, regulates water flows and moderates downstream deposition and silting. These effects are described more fully in the previous section.

Undisturbed forest cover is superior to most other land uses in safeguarding watersheds. However, it is possible to exaggerate its benefits, especially where forests are modified in various ways. (Hamilton, 1988, gives a balanced and suitably qualified account of what forests can and cannot achieve.) The 'rain-making' power of forests has not been properly demonstrated, except in special circumstances (such as in cloud forests at high altitudes, or in very large systems like the Amazon). Likewise, the ability of forests to control flooding is limited in respect of major floods, or where the topsoil under the forest is thin and saturated.

The ability of tree cover to prevent soil erosion is compromised where leaf litter or low undergrowth (understorey) is removed, e.g. by cattle or fire. Logging, even on a selective basis, can aggravate soil erosion through the construction of tracks and clearings.

In the case of sedimentation, although the chain of cause and effect between changes in forest cover and downstream siltation is well established, the size of the effect and the lags in the chain are more difficult to predict. For example, silt washed out from temporary storage *en route* may cause flooding, rather than a change in forest cover. Hamilton (1988) cautions:

. . . the full effect of soil erosion reduction measures through a practice such as reforestation may not show up for many years, even decades, in terms of a realizable downstream benefit in sediment reduction.

c) **Local soil protection and conservation of fertility**. Forests help to retain tropical soil and nourish it in various ways. Certain tropical volcanic soils are very fertile, but many other types are thin and barren. The apparent luxuriance of tropical forests is often due to the storage of a high proportion of total nutrients above ground, in the trees' own biomass. Such forests are an efficient way of creating biomass from unpromising soils. Their removal to make way for crops or pasture often causes rapid soil degradation and the failure of these alternative land-use regimes.

d) **Biodiversity and genetic store**. Tropical forests contain enormous species diversity. Sample surveys of single hectares of Amazonian forest typically reveal 200-300 different species of trees alone (Prance, 1986; Repetto, 1988b). The majority of their plant and animal species are practically unknown, yet where they have been analysed important gains to science, medicine, and agriculture have been made. For example, a quarter of all prescribed drugs sold in the United States are based on tropical plants. Most of the 1300 or so medicinal plants known to Amazon Indians remain unknown to outside scientists. They constitute a potentially rich store of genetic material for pharmaceuticals and other medical products, as well as products and pest-control methods for agriculture (Repetto,1988b; McNeely, 1989). Two dozen major world crops have already been improved with wild germplasm, mainly to make them more disease-resistant (Prescott Allen, 1988).

e) **Life-support system for forest-dwellers**. For millions of indigenous forest-dwellers and aboriginal people, the forest is their habitat and satisfies practically all their needs. For the many people with no regular contact with official or commercial society the loss of their forest can cut them off from their means of livelihood. Many fail to make the adjustment to a new way of life, and either die or are pauperised.

To such people, the tropical forest is an extraordinarily rich store of products for living. In an inventory of trees on a hectare of forest carried out for each of four indigenous Amazonian groups, between a half and four-fifths of all the species were found to be useful to the local people, whether for food, construction, other materials, remedies or trade (Prance *et al.*, 1987).

Tree products can be important to household food security. They diversify the diet, provide minerals and nutrients, fodder for livestock and fuel for cooking. They help provide seasonal balance in food supplies, and represent assets which can be liquidated in hard times (Falconer, 1989; Chambers and Leach, 1989). In South-East Asia there are almost 30 million forest-dwellers who are vitally dependent on non-timber forest products (de Beer and McDermott, 1989).

f) **Source of commercial products**. Hardwood is the most obvious product of tropical forests. However, the value of tropical timber exports has stolen the limelight from the many other forest products that are collected and sold, often for export. This list includes, *inter alia*, essential oils, resins, medical substances, rattan, rubber, flowers, bamboo, tannin, gums, honey and beeswax (FAO, 1978). The export of such 'minor' forest products is a major foreign exchange earner in several Asian countries. In Amazonia half a million people earn a living as rubber tappers, using wild trees. In the Acre region alone, the annual value of extracted products, of which rubber is a major item, is around $US 26m., twice that of livestock (and can be sustained) (McNeely, 1988). The growth of nature-based tourism could also be an important alternative income-earner in certain regions.

There is growing evidence of the value of retaining tropical forests, both for their sustainable timber yield, and as sources of a range of other commercial products. In the Amazon, for instance:

> The value of the standing forest is matched by very few alternative systems such as intensive cultivation of tropical floodplain forest and a few well-designed agro-forestry systems . . . (Prance, 1989)

More generally:

> The capacity of the natural forest to supply a perpetual stream of valuable non-wood products that can be harvested without cutting down trees has been overlooked. (Repetto, 1988)

g) **Ecological links**. Stands of forest harbour plants, birds, insects and other forms of life that interact with neighbouring agricultural systems. They may be fish-spawning areas, sources of seeds, and refuges of birds, bats and insects which control pest in the vicinity (and can be hunted for food). The cultivation of Brazil nuts depends on the proximity of forest habitat for certain kinds of bees, rodents, insects and humming birds (Ledec and Goodland, 1986, quoted in McNeely, 1988).

h) **Aesthetic, spiritual and existence value**. Forests have a capacity for inspiring artists, writers, poets and musicians which is ample testimony to their aesthetic value. To millions of forest-dwellers trees are vested with spiritual values (e.g. the 'holy hills'in Xishuangbanna, China, quoted in Hamilton, 1988). Many people who are unlikely ever to see a tropical forest value the fact that it exists, quite apart from any conceivable direct and indirect benefits it may confer.

2.4. Drylands

'Drylands' include arid and semi-arid areas with a mean annual rainfall in the range of 300-1500 mm.(DANIDA, 1988; Heathcote, 1983). Within the developing world, 'drylands' cover the Sahelian zone of Africa, parts of East and Southern Africa, the North-East Indian subcontinent, Central Asia, and parts of Thailand, Mexico, Argentina, Bolivia and North-East Brazil. Within the dry areas thus defined, the spectrum runs from areas where one rain-fed arable crop per year can be expected, to areas on the fringes of desert where supplementary sources of water would normally be needed to sustain regular farming. In 1975 it was estimated that the population of arid areas was 132 million, while that of semi-arid areas was 314 million. Most of these people are very poor (Stryker, 1989).

In desert areas, receiving less than 100 mm. of rainfall per year, rain-fed farming is not normally feasible. Deserts cover large parts of North Africa and the Arabian Peninsula, with pockets elsewhere. Although even deserts sustain some wildlife and nomadic peoples, they are less important than drylands as life-support systems. Our focus in this section will be on semi-arid areas as defined above.

The political and strategic importance of drylands is belied by the poverty of their indigenous populations. Drylands tend to act as buffer zones between areas of greater fertility and population density. They are often on the geographical frontiers of their countries, and are the scenes of migrations, resettlements, armed conflicts and skirmishes, and refugee movements. The presence, or the promise, of oil and mineral wealth magnifies political interest in these areas.

2.4.1. Environmental threats and problems

Drylands are at risk from a number of sources, which can be conveniently summarised as 'desertification' (where this is understood as land degradation). Degrading factors tend to reinforce each other, hence a downward spiral can easily be set in motion. Although there is agreement that desertification exists and on its possible causes, there are different schools of thought about its current extent and on the relative weight of its different causes. There is, however, a dismal consensus that policy and project interventions to halt desertification have had little impact (DANIDA, 1988; Nelson, 1988; ODI, 1987).

The evidence of desertification is still under debate (Nelson, 1988; Mortimore, 1989; Warren and Agnew, 1988). It is not obvious that the world's major deserts are expanding into former dryland areas. But it is clear that certain concentrations of population have caused local degradation which is spreading outwards from them. The 'advance of the Sahara' by sand invasions seems to be a localised phenomenon, associated with man-made degradation.

Climatic changes have been responsible for some desertification. By historical standards the last two decades have been unusually dry in Africa's Sahel. It is too soon to conclude that this is the start of a long-term trend towards greater aridity, though the continuation of secular fluctuations might have similar results if the dry periods lead to degradation which is difficult to reverse later (the 'ratchet effect').

Population growth and migration is another potent cause. In the past population has adjusted to the carrying capacity of the land by temporary or permanent migrations, and by use of the bush-fallow system. Recently, this process has been affected by large refugee movements, especially in the Sahelian belt, and by projects to stabilise populations in unsuitable areas.

The encroachment of arable cultivation into marginal areas has often resulted from population pressure and the resettlement of farmers on land really only suitable for livestock. The inappropriate introduction of mechanised farming exposed land to the risk of wind erosion in Eastern Sudan, Iran, the USSR and the US 'Dust Bowl' region (Warren and Agnew, 1988).

The behaviour of livestock is commonly blamed for desertification, destroying young trees, overgrazing sparse pasture and treading down vegetation around water points and along trails. This no doubt accounts for much local degradation. Whether excessive livestock numbers have caused desertification on a major scale is debated. One school argues that livestock numbers tend to adjust to carrying capacity (Sandford, 1983). There is evidence of long-term increases in numbers in some countries (e.g. Western Sudan, Zimbabwe, Lesotho), though the impact of numbers can be masked by changes in the species composition of herds. Control of the rinderpest disease has also tended to increase livestock numbers in previously infested areas. What is certain is that many well-intentioned livestock projects have had undesirable local environmental effects, due to the temporary concentrations of stock.

The destruction of trees for fuelwood for urban use is a major explanation of degradation in many regions (see Shepherd, 1989, for an analysis of this process in Somalia). As fuelwood becomes scarcer, a vicious downward spiral of events ensues (Nelson, 1988). Crop residues and animal dung are diverted from use in fertilising soil, and are increasingly used for fuel. The yield of soil declines, leading to less vegetation, and the use of crop residues to feed livestock. Soil fertility declines further and erosion sets in. The above factors are sometimes caused, and are always aggravated, by a breakdown in traditional methods of conservation and adaptive husbandry. The decline of the bush-fallow system is a case in point, which might result from population pressure, war, drought, refugee movements, etc. Policy measures (discussed further in Chapter 5) may have perverse effects, as when governments remove powers and responsibility from local hands, causing a management vacuum (e.g. Pearce, 1987, 1988 for Sudan; Shepherd, 1989 for Somalia).

The 'Tragedy of the Commons' is a suggestive notion for understanding overgrazing and destruction of trees for firewood and charcoal (Hardin, 1969). This is certainly a major reason for the over-use of 'open access' areas, but much common property is actually managed and regulated by local users, and it is wrong to think that the private selfish motive is always allowed to proceed untrammelled. The Tragedy of the Commons often occurs when local communal control breaks down, for instance when the Government presumes to take it over.

2.4.2 Environmental services

Drylands can provide a livelihood for well-adapted social and economic systems. However, they are essentially fragile environments, which can easily be disturbed. The equilibrium established at any moment between the natural environment and its human and animal population can be overturned by sudden shocks or gradual encroachments. If balance is not recovered, 'desertification' will set in. The millions of people regularly exposed to the risk of drought in dryland areas are witnesses to their natural instability.

To understand what is lost when a dryland turns into a desert, we need to consider the various services it provides to its inhabitants, and to the wider environment. These can be divided into direct and 'ecological' benefits. This is an artificial distinction in practice, however, since the continued supply of direct benefits depends on the ecological effects being preserved.

a) **Direct benefits**. Dryland peoples draw their livelihood from crops, trees and livestock, or more usually from a combination of these. Although different groups may specialise in, say, cropping, tree harvesting, or pastoralism, their survival in times of hardship depends on their flexibility, and their capacity to draw on whatever life-support system is available. While recognising the separate strands making up the dryland economy, the system should be considered as a complex and changeable whole.

Adaptability is a necessary condition for survival. This can be illustrated by examining the ways in which the population of the Sahelian zone of Africa traditionally survive periodic droughts (ODI, 1987). Pastoralists adjust the composition of their herds between different kinds of animals, and move to more distant grazing areas. Temporary or permanent migration takes place. Pastoralists and sedentary farmers engage in trade. Farmers and pastoralists resort to wild food from the bush, or hunting and fishing. Herds temporarily shrink, and usually expand again when conditions permit.

The direct economic services of drylands can be summarised as the provision of crops, livestock, tree products, fuelwood and wildlife for tourism.

Crops. Where soils are sufficiently fertile, annual crops are grown in rain-fed conditions. In the Sahel, sorghum, millet and groundnuts are popular; in semi-arid parts of Asia, sorghum, millet and pulses are more common. In Africa the bush-fallow system is widespread, where cultivated land is left to recover for several years before being replanted. In certain areas, rain-fed cultivation is supplemented by irrigation schemes, prevalent in semi-arid parts of South Asia, and in a few major schemes in Sudan, Nigeria, Senegal, Mali, etc. Elsewhere in the Sahel small-scale schemes using flood water, surface flows or shallow wells are more common. These all rely on rainfall.

Livestock. Most dryland farmers keep some livestock as an integral part of the production system (Jahnke,1982). In Africa camels, cattle, sheep, goats, and poultry are typical. In areas of Africa where rainfall exceeds c.800 mm. per year cattle are vital for ploughing. For this reason, the numbers and well-being of livestock are closely correlated with the yield of grain and other foodstuffs.

Pastoralism is a more important lifestyle for most dryland people. The carrying capacity of the typical semi-arid grassland and bush is low and variable, hence the pastoral economy often depends on movement of herds over large distances. In the past livestock numbers have adjusted, over a number of years, to variations in rainfall. Attempts to stabilise numbers by improving pasture, delimiting rangelands, providing veterinary services, or improving water points have had poor results. However, the 'natural' methods of adjusting animals to carrying capacity have their own costs to herders and to governments and aid agencies who take responsibility for their welfare.

Pastoralists help to spread their risks by 'species diversity', where different kinds of animals have different nutritional needs. Their different products are another cushion against hardship. The larger animals provide draught power around the farm and for working wells. Other livestock products include blood, milk and eggs to supplement and vary diets, dung to fertilise soils and provide fuel, and meat, skins, hair and wool.

Animals are a store of wealth, and can be traded or sold to cover cash outlays or in emergencies. Many pastoralists attach significant non-monetary value to their livestock, and the size of a herd is widely regarded as an index of social status.

Tree products. Trees and bush - strictly any kind of woody biomass - prevailing in semi-arid areas have a variety of uses for knowledgeable local people, either for subsistence use or sale. They include firewood, building materials, poles, fencing and roofing material, fruit, nuts, fibres, medicines, animal fodder, etc. Less tangible, though important, direct services also include shade for households and crops, protection from the wind, organic matter for soil fertilisation, etc. (see section 5.2.2 on agro-forestry for a more complete discussion).

Woodfuel. Firewood is cut and often transported long distances for sale in urban markets. Poorer developing countries, including most of those in semi-arid zones, rely predominantly on wood for fuel in heating and cooking, even in urban areas. Because tree cover in drier areas is usually sporadic, urban requirements have pushed supply sources of wood well into the hinterland of towns and cities. With appropriate tenure, management and pricing arrangements, the supply of fuelwood for urban use could be a sustainable activity and a profitable business for the drylands. In the absence of these conditions, it becomes a source of environmental degradation and long-term impoverishment for the local communities. The process accelerates in drought years when trees are one of the few resources available for exploitation.

Wildlife and tourism. Many important animal habitats are situated in the semi-arid areas and attract sizeable tourist numbers. Although tourism is not an unmixed blessing environmentally (see section 5.7) it is an important source of income for the target countries, and - if properly managed - can provide a powerful motive for nature conservation. In principle, the controlled culling of game can also be exploited as a tourist attraction, as a more environmentally benign form of big game hunting. Commenting on a scheme in Zimbabwe, McNeely says:

> The proper use of wildlife offers one of the best opportunities for redressing the socio-economic and environmental plight of much of the drier parts of Africa. (McNeely, 1988)

However, successful culling depends on strict control and disciplined policing. Too often, it can degenerate into unofficial poaching.

The co-existence of wild animals with domesticated livestock and settled farming is problematic, and may be resolved only by setting aside certain areas as protected nature reserves. Whether as reserves, or as controlled 'recreational hunting', the management of wildlife may be the most profitable form of land use in many areas, allowing all the direct and indirect revenues from the tourism trade.

Nor should the value of 'vicarious tourism' be overlooked. The consumption of books, films, and TV programmes about wildlife is another indication of the value of drylands (amongst others) to society at large, some of the benefits of which might be captured by the host communities.

b) **Ecological effects**. In theory, there is a level of human and animal activity which is 'sustainable' in the long term by dint of careful farming and husbandry. In practice, drylands are never in a static equilibrium state, but rather in the constant throes of adjustment to natural shocks of various kinds. They tend to undergo 'boom and bust' cycles, with a corresponding ebb and flow of populations. Achieving sustainable development in drylands depends on recognising and promoting the interdependence of the system's component parts.

Within individual cultivation systems, the growth of trees or other forms of permanent vegetation helps to retain soil and prevent erosion by water or wind action. They also contribute to soil fertility through leaf litter and root activity. By providing mulch and browse for livestock, they indirectly provide dung for fertiliser or fuel. They also provide shade for other crops and wind shelter, which can prevent physical damage and increase soil moisture.

Taking a wider (off-site) perspective, trees and bushes can help preserve slope stability and arrest landslides, control water run-off and lessen the risk of flooding and siltation. Trees, bushes and permanent grassland also act as buffers to invasion by sand.

Underlying many of the causes of desertification is the growth of markets for the animal products of drylands - the 'monetisation of the pastoral economy' (Stryker, 1989). This has led to an increase in commercial animal raising at the expense of subsistence pastoralism, and the ownership of livestock by people (e.g. farmers, traders, officials) outside the traditional means of control.

2.5. Irrigated lowland farming areas

A large proportion of the developing world's food, and an important share of its export crops, are grown under intensive farming conditions in fertile valleys, basins and alluvial plains. Much of this land is irrigated, by natural (e.g. seasonal flooding) or human-assisted means. The techniques for getting water to the fields vary. Leaving aside simple methods of conserving rainwater, there is a basic distinction between surface diversion (from reservoirs or rivers) and groundwater extraction (e.g. by tubewells). Application can be by inundation or sprinkling. Irrigation permits the growth of high-value crops and takes much of the risk out of using bought-in inputs, such as improved seed varieties, fertilisers, pesticides, and irrigation water, in some cases supplemented by farm machinery, such as tractors and motor-powered pumps, funded by farm credit programmes.

This section will take irrigated farming as the paradigm for intensive lowland tropical farming. It can be regarded as a representative habitat for hundreds of millions of people in the developing world. Irrigated agriculture extends over some 250 million ha. Over the last two decades the agronomic package made possible by irrigation has been largely responsible for the ability of the developing world to supply food to its growing populations. It has been estimated that over the next twenty years the growth of world demand will require a 40% increase in the irrigated area and a 60% increase in the average yield of irrigated crops (FAO, quoted by Yudelman, 1989).

Important as irrigation is to food supply, its continuation and expansion will have serious environmental consequences unless there are radical improvements in its management and maintenance. Apart from such wider economic problems as cost and time overruns in construction, waste of water, massive operating subsidies, unequal appropriation of benefits, underperformance, etc. (Repetto, 1986), irrigation may be responsible for a range of environmental risks.

2.5.1. Environmental effects

The sheer extent of irrigated farming implies a major interference with the environment. The phenomenon is not new, since irrigation has existed in certain parts of the world for two millennia or more, but the extension of the irrigated area has gathered pace over the last few decades. The creation of *new* schemes and command areas - especially where diversion is achieved by building major new dams and reservoirs - alters the physical environment, habitat and economy of large areas, and often involves displacement and new concentrations of people and animals. The operation of *existing* schemes has a different set of effects which also, where badly managed and neglected, have the potential for serious degradation of their environments.

Not all irrigation schemes are guilty of the same environmental infringements. Schemes that are well-designed, adequately funded, properly maintained, well managed and responsibly used are perfectly sustainable. Schemes that are small and privately or co-operatively owned and managed tend, other things being equal, to be more successful than large ones, which are publicly owned and managed (though there are notable exceptions - e.g. the overuse of privately owned tubewells). Schemes in semi-arid areas tend to be more problematic than those in more humid conditions. Rice systems in semi-humid areas can operate sustainably at lower levels of technology and management than those in semi-arid areas. The worst problems are not necessarily found in the developing world. US irrigated farming graphically displays many of the risks discussed here (Repetto, 1986).

This section concentrates on the environmental risks posed by the operation of irrigation schemes. The once-and-for-all consequences of building the schemes are dealt with in Chapter 4 (though it should be realised that a finite act of investment can trigger forces that have continuing effects - e.g. erosion caused by resettlement). In assessing the effect of irrigation schemes the likely consequences of *not* building them should also be fairly addressed - the 'without project' scenario contains its own possible environmental risks.

The common distinction between on-site and off-site effects (or 'internalities' and 'externalities') is blurred in the case of large schemes. In large irrigated regions like the Gezira in Sudan or the Indus Valley in Pakistan, 'external' effects on public health and water pollution immediately affect other people in the same command area, and become the concerns of the same management unit.

The possible effects are grouped under five headings.

a) **Fertility, salinity and waterlogging**. Irrigation permits the growth of two or even three annual crops on the same soil. Sustaining the yields from this intensive regime depends on continuing fertilisation, either by silt deposition from natural flooding (as in the Nile Valley before the construction of the Aswan Dam) or by applying chemical and organic fertilisers, or by rotating crops. Any failure to replenish the required soil nutrients can quickly lead to a decline in crop yields. The repeated cultivation of particular crops often leads to the build-up of pests peculiar to them - e.g. tomatoes encourage nematodes.

The related problems of salinisation and waterlogging affect large areas of irrigated land in arid areas, and seriously reduce their fertility. Surface-water bodies and groundwater contain salts dissolved from soil and rocks which become concentrated through evaporation. If the water table is close to the surface, soil moisture can rise to the surface by capillary action, and its salts are deposited in the topsoil. At certain concentrations, these salts kill normal plants. The safe level of the water-table is about 3 meters or more below the surface (Pereira, 1989), due allowance being made for the type of soil.

Salinisation is affecting crop yields in parts of the most important arid irrigated farming areas - amongst others, the Indus Valley in Pakistan, the Nile Delta in Egypt, parts of Iraq, Peru, Mexico, and the interior of North-East Brazil (Yudelman, 1989). The rise of the water-table is caused by a complex of factors. The design of schemes and the way on-farm development is carried out may make it difficult for farmers to control the optimal application of water. There is excessive application by certain farmers with privileged access to supplies. There is widespread leaking during distribution, and inadequate drainage. The lack of financial autonomy suffered by many public schemes, with the Treasury siphoning off whatever revenue is collected, is a common reason for the neglect of maintenance on irrigation structures.

The excessive use of water can be partly blamed on financial factors such as low and subsidised charges, poor cost recovery, and lack of metering. In a survey of irrigation finances in six countries, it was found that actual receipts amounted to less than 10% of the full costs of services, including capital recovery. In all but one country, receipts were even less than the costs of operation and management (Repetto, 1986). Where water is so cheap, its use becomes highly profitable, and there is no incentive to use it sparingly on the part of farmers with plentiful access. (Equally, many farmers do not get enough.) Other factors explaining excessive water use are poor management and control by the irrigation authorities, and deficient extension advice.

The waste of water on its way to farmers is excessively high on many schemes. Less than 50% of the water diverted from the Indus reaches farmers' crops; some of this is lost from evaporation or seepage from unlined canals, and the rest leaks from village watercourses (Pereira, 1989). Water lost to the water table can recharge aquifers, to the benefit of tubewell owners and users, but this is usually an unintended benefit, and not necessarily the most cost-effective way of doing it. The main causes of waste are the design of irrigation systems, the failure to line canals in porous soils, and poor maintenance and clearing of banks and structures. These are aggravated by the absence of financial incentives to the authorities to husband their water, and their inability to retain revenues for further development and maintenance.

Inadequate drainage can usually be traced to the low priority given to this problem when the original irrigation works are designed. Major drainage works are often not required until some time after the work is completed, but the situation needs to be carefully monitored so that drainage is installed when needed, and financial provision made for it. Agro-chemicals used as pesticide or the control of weeds may also accumulate in the topsoil, and harmfully affect plants.

b) **Water flow and quality.** Irrigation schemes divert water and interfere with the previous flow through a catchment area. Some of it is taken up in plant growth. Some is lost to evaporation - for instance the various upstream dams on the Euphrates increase the salinity of the river lower down, as well as lessening its volume. Some irrigation water enters the ground. What is returned to the river system will have a different flow pattern, and is likely to be polluted by chemical, agricultural and human wastes. Downstream from the irrigated area, the altered flow of water may cause movements in the river channels, erosion of banks, and reduced silt deposits (the latter having both positive and negative aspects). Changes in the quality of water will affect downstream consumers, other irrigation users, and the yield of fisheries. The use of fertiliser, especially soluble nitrates, can contaminate drinking water drawn from aquifers (Yudelman, 1989).

Changes to the flow and quality of water in major river systems on which millions depend have serious consequences, and become international political issues (e.g. between Turkey and Iraq over use of the Euphrates, between India and Pakistan over the Indus waters, or Sudan and Egypt over the Nile). Irrigation fed by tubewells (common in Bangladesh, for example) may run the risk of lowering the groundwater level. Excessive pumping in parts of Saudi Arabia and the United States has lowered the water table to the point where the aquifer is permanently depleted.

The impact of irrigation on the volume of water used by others is not always negative. In the Indus Basin, the massive leakage from public irrigation systems negative. In the Indus Basin, the massive leakage from public irrigation systems recharges the aquifer, and benefits the large number of farmers with their own tubewells. In this case, the public supply is akin to a 'base load', while farmers' tubewells meet the 'peak' demand for water (quoted in Repetto, 1986). In one Indian village the construction of irrigation tanks raised the water level in local wells and allegedly made it easier for the tribal men to obtain brides! (Saha, Kaul and Badrinath, 1989).

c) **Health**. Irrigation has a positive contribution to make to human health, since it increases the supply and variety of food and creates opportunities for work, income, and recreation. The following remarks are not intended to detract from these benefits.

There are three main kinds of risk to public health from irrigation schemes. The first is from the application of agro-chemicals, especially the misuse of dangerous chemical pesticides, which farmers apply to insure against the loss of their crops and the cash outlay they have made in seeds, fertiliser, water, etc. The immoderate use of dangerous pesticides causes occupational diseases to the workers handling them, and to their families. Local atmospheric pollution from spraying affects a wider circle of people. The build-up of chemical residues in the soil and on plants may then enter the food chain, and thence to all consumers of the foodstuffs. The use of fertiliser can also cause the appearance of algal blooms on surface water, which reduces its appeal for household use, though it may not be dangerous.

It is estimated that 10,000 people die and 400,000 suffer acutely from pesticide poisoning every year in developing countries - though not all these are on irrigation schemes (Repetto, 1985). Most are farmworkers handling the chemicals, who suffer skin, eye and respiratory complaints, but the contamination easily spreads to their families and other villagers. Deformities in unborn children and breast-fed infants have been traced to the intake of pesticides by their mothers (UNEP, 1988). In the USSR it has been alleged:

> In Uzbekistan and Moldavia, chemical poisoning with pesticides has led to such high rates of mental retardation that the educational curricula in secondary schools and universities have had to be modified and simplified. (Medvedev, 1990)

Many countries ban the use of the more dangerous chemicals, but such bans are widely evaded by farmers and plantation companies concerned to protect their investments. Their use is encouraged by government subsidies. A survey of pesticides in nine developing countries showed an average subsidy equivalent to 44% of retail costs, in some countries over 80% (Repetto, 1985). Pesticide requirements tend to increase over time, as their targets develop resistance, but individual farmers locked into their use dare not desist. The vicious circle can, however, be broken by various forms of Integrated Pest Management, which are much gentler in their environmental effects.

The second risk arises from water-related tropical diseases encouraged by the pressure of so much surface water. The first category, water-borne or water-washed, are spread by direct human contact with water and affect large numbers of tropical people causing death in some cases, and sickness and debilitation in many more. Diarrhoea, typhoid fever and guineaworm result from people using water in canals, drains and reservoirs for drinking and washing. Workers in flooded rice fields multiply their chances of acquiring these diseases.

The second type of disease is passed on to humans by insects or snails, likely to be found in irrigated areas with large water surfaces. Malaria and schistosomiasis (bilharzia) are the most widespread. In certain areas, lymphatic filariasis (elephantiasis), onchocerciasis (river blindness) and Japanese encephalitis are the main dangers (Tiffen, 1990). Malaria is the most widespread disease, causing death, debilitation and suffering affecting several hundred million people. Schistosomiasis is another debilitating disease affecting some 200 million people and is spreading rapidly in newly irrigated areas. Filariasis is not normally fatal, but is severely disabling. Onchocerciasis, prevalent in West Africa, causes blindness if untreated. Japanese encephalitis, prevalent in East and South-East Asia, is an acute condition leading to death in around half of all cases. Children are especially at risk, and can carry the diseases all through their lives. Such diseases are more likely to spread on irrigation schemes where one or more of the following conditions hold: soils are badly drained; drainage channels are neglected; rice or sugar cane is cultivated; reservoirs are constructed or borrow pits left with stagnant water; or canals are unlined or have unchecked vegetation growth (Tiffen, 1990).

These public health problems can be controlled by a combination of modifications to design and water management, provision of public health services and medical centres, education of the populations at risk about safe behaviour, and the supply of safe water, sanitation and sewerage. Some of these measures properly fall to the project authorities - such as draining marshy areas, keeping ditches clean, straightening banks, adding molluscicides to the water, encouraging predatory fish to kill snails, etc. (Pereira, 1989).

The third source of health risks arises from the concentrations of people and animals associated with irrigation schemes. In the absence of adequate clean water, sewerage and sanitation, cholera and yellow fever can be added to the other potential disease risks mentioned. Rodents, especially rats, tend to congregate around irrigated settlements.

d) **Wildlife and genetic diversity**. The creation of the irrigation network, involving river diversion, flooding, destruction of vegetation, etc., destroys previous habitats and creates new ones. There are losers and gainers from this. Animals and woodland birds would tend to be losers, while fish and aquatic birds would benefit. Of closer direct interest to farmers, the typical irrigation 'package' entails interference with natural controls on pests and predators, and the substitution of plant varieties that are more vulnerable to natural risks. These are examples of the environment striking back at its despoilers.

The widespread and indiscriminate use of chemical pesticides kills a wide range of insects and small animals along with the pests that are its real targets. These other creatures are part of a complex chain of predators and victims; if some are destroyed, their victims multiply and may themselves become pests. The natural predators of pests are destroyed along with the pests themselves. Over time, the use of pesticides in South-East Asia has led to the revival of the brown plant hopper as a threat to the rice crop. This insect had previously been controlled by natural predators that had been destroyed by pesticides (UNEP, 1988). Useful insects such as bees and other pollinators are innocent victims of this chemical warfare.

Over time, the pests develop resistance to the pesticides, hence a given application runs into sharply diminishing returns. A given level of pest control requires a progressive increase in the required amounts of pesticide, with all the other environmental risks that this entails.

Plants grown under intensive irrigation are becoming less resistant to disease and pests. The diffusion of new, genetically uniform, high-yielding plant varieties has reduced genetic diversity over large areas, and made crops more susceptible to pests and diseases. There is a trade-off between yield and risk. Meanwhile research continues into plants with greater disease resistance which, if successful, would reduce the above-mentioned dangers.

e) **Climatic effects**. Major schemes entailing the creation of extensive new surface water bodies could temper local climates, since water moderates extremes of temperature, and the vegetation associated with irrigation provides welcome shade in arid conditions. On a global scale, methane from irrigated rice fields is believed to be a minor contributor to the 'greenhouse effect' (adding 5% or less to greenhouse gas emissions).

2.6. Wetlands

'Wetlands' is an elastic term including a great variety of landforms. Certain wetlands that appear in temperate or cold climates (e.g. tundra) have no tropical equivalent, and *vice versa* for tropical forms (e.g. mangrove). One definition of wetlands is '. . . lands transitional between terrestrial and aquatic systems, where the water table is usually at or near the surface, or the land is covered by shallow water' (Turner, 1988). So defined, wetlands can be permanent, temporary or seasonal, with static or flowing water, which may be fresh, brackish or salt. Wetland ecosystems can be marine, estuarine, riverine, lacustrine or marsh, bog, or swamp (Maltby, 1986; Turner, 1988). In developing countries three forms of wetlands are of particular economic note - mangroves, seasonal wetlands in dry areas (e.g. along rivers) and deltaic environments.

2.6.1. Threats

Wetland areas suffer in many ways from developments elsewhere. They are commonly taken over or encroached upon for other uses, and are damaged or destroyed indirectly by pollution or other forms of interference. Sometimes the damage is an unavoidable result of pressures on land, but in many other cases it happens because the value of wetlands is misunderstood and unappreciated. Thus one of the underlying threats to wetlands is ignorance. Following Turner's (1988) classification, the main threats can be classified into five groups.

a) **In-filling**. This may be inadvertent, as in siltation from upstream erosion, but is more often deliberate, where there is a land-use conflict with various kinds of commercial development and recreation. Some wetlands are in or close to cities, and are swallowed up in urban expansion, which may be of the 'spontaneous' kind, where squatters move onto wetlands as the only realistic housing option (e.g. Manila, Bombay, Guayaquil), or part of planned housing development (e.g. Hong Kong, Singapore).

Coastal wetlands are obvious targets for building industrial plants, especially the polluting kind that need to be sited away from population centres. Roads and causeways are often planned through wetlands to avoid conurbations, or because of the lower and more level relief. Regions or islands with little flat land reclaim coastal wetlands for development or to relieve congestion.

Wetlands often become dumps for spoil, refuse and hazardous waste, usually because they are seen as having little alternative value. Agriculture may also encroach, e.g. swamp rice, or through full-scale drainage and conversion to arable or livestock production.

b) **Excavation**. Large-scale peat extraction disfigures wetland landscapes (e.g. in Ireland) and limits their value for other uses. Other examples of extractive industry are oil and gas (e.g. Nigeria, Cameroon), sand (Nigeria), bauxite and iron ore (Ivory Coast). The extraction of salt, involving boiling brine, can devastate wetlands through the use of firewood (e.g. Benin). Alternatively, excavation may be incidental to construction projects or navigational improvements, (e.g. dredging ports and marinas, widening shipping channels, laying pipes).

c) **Changes in hydrology**. Wetlands are very sensitive to anything that alters the characteristics of the water flowing in, or changes its level. Hence they are disturbed by such things as upstream river basin development (damming, irrigation, drainage), coastal works (canals, levees) or the construction of impediments to surface run-off (roads, or radical changes to land use).

d) **Chemical changes.** The delicate ecosystems in a wetland suffer from changes in the chemical content of its water intake. These can arise from industrial and municipal pollution (discharges, untreated sewage, hazardous waste, etc.) or from farm chemicals and irrigation water. A reduction in freshwater intake will cause increased salinity.

e) **Biological effects.** Any of the above changes will have repercussions on the wetland biomass. For instance, eutrophication may result from the nutrients contained in farm chemical run-off. The removal of trees, or alternatively afforestation schemes, will set off a biological chain-reaction. Over-hunting or over-fishing of certain species, or the introduction of exotic fauna, will also upset the previous balance. Agricultural or other land-use changes in the vicinity will spill over and affect the wetlands biomass, often in ways that are hard to predict.

2.6.2.Services

The true value of wetlands, for long disregarded and abused, has increasingly been recognised by science. Wetlands are diverse and complex ecological systems that contain many species, occupy a key position in food chains, perform vital cycling and filtering tasks, and provide natural protection to coastlines. They regulate water flows, provide a habitat for wild animals and birds, and offer a rich variety of products to people living in their vicinity.

Their environmental services can be divided into products and functions. (Tropical coastal wetlands are particularly rich and multi-functional; for a more complete categorisation of their products and functions see data quoted in Dixon, 1989.)

Products (sometimes called 'components') are the tangible output of a wetland, and can usually be used directly or sold; functions (or services) are what the wetland contributes to the wider environment, and their value must be inferred in indirect ways. Alternatively, the functions of wetlands can be broken down into on-site and off-site goods and services, each of which can be either marketed or not (Dixon, 1989). Here we shall retain the separation of products and services, it being understood that these can arise both on- and off-site (e.g. fish) and be either marketed or not.

The balance of uses is likely to differ between temperate and tropical regions. In temperate areas the direct products are likely to be of relatively less importance to local inhabitants, whereas their recreational and 'existence' values will be greater. In developing tropical countries, the reverse is likely to be true (Barbier, 1989a).

(i) *Products*

The harvest from wetlands varies enormously according to climate (temperate or tropical), location (coastal or inland) and specific features of the locality (soil, vegetation, site configuration, water supply, etc.). Properly managed, a wetland can provide a continuing stream of products to local people. If the resource is over-exploited, the harvest will not be sustainable, and the wider environmental functions of the wetland may be impaired.

a) **Fish and shellfish.** At the interface between land and sea, wetlands are rich in nutrients, which provide a variety of ecological riches making for a wealth of aquatic life. They are therefore important for fishing, shellfish and aquaculture, while mangroves can also furnish a number of materials vital for fishing, such as poles, floats, tannins for nets, etc.

b) **Birds, animals and other wildlife.** Meat and other products (eggs, skins, furs, honey, wax, etc.) are important supplements to the diets of local people in many areas.

c) **Wood and other tree products.** Mangroves, typical of many tropical coastal areas, are striking examples of adaptation to shifting and unstable ground and constantly varying water levels. In the process they develop large and complex root systems. This extensive biomass is useful for fuelwood, timber, fodder, and many local construction purposes (boat-building, fencing, furniture, flooring, etc.).

d) **Agriculture and livestock.** Irrigated rice (e.g. in West Africa) is one of the farm systems compatible with wetlands. Foodstuffs produced in wetlands include sugar, alcohol, cooking oil, vinegar, fermented drinks, sweets, vegetables, fruit, etc., as well as medicines. Livestock can use wetlands for seasonal grazing and benefit from the year-round supply of fodder and browse.

e) **Peat**. This is an important energy source in the highland bogs of East and Southern Africa and elsewhere. Although by definition non-sustainable, peat extraction can be justified where it substitutes for wood or charcoal in countries with serious deforestation (e.g. Burundi, Lesotho).

f) **Miscellaneous products**. Reeds are widely cut for roofing, utensils and hand-icrafts. Salt is another valuable product (though the wood cut for the evaporation may cause local environmental harm). Sand and gravel are other products, though they need to be exploited in a manner that avoids environmental damage .

(ii) *Functions*

Some of the natural functions of wetlands are only imperfectly understood. Until scientific enquiry has made further progress the real long-term significance of wetlands may be appreciated only long after they have been destroyed, when the consequences on the environment start to appear. There is much uncertainty about the nature of their environmental role, the strength of cause and effect, and the time period involved. The irreversibility of their loss, and the uncertain state of knowledge of their contribution, makes them a prime case for caution and postponement of drastic action. It has even been suggested (Turner, 1988, writing of temperate wetlands) that the onus of proof or persuasion should rest with those proposing *development* of wetlands, rather than their *preservation*. With these ca-veats, some of their more obvious functions can be identified.

a) **Water supply and regulation.** Wetlands act as reservoirs and sponges for holding water, and help to even out its release. They regulate groundwater stor-age and recharge. They help to arrest siltation (though in coastal sites they often have the positive role of trapping silt and building up land mass). Away from the coast, they help to purify water through natural filtration. By acting as natural brakes on river flow they reduce flood risk. (In a classic study, it was shown that the wetlands along the Charles River in the United States reduced the peak river flow by 65% and delayed the peak flow from a particularly violent storm by 3 days; quoted in Turner, 1988).

b) **Coastal protection.** Coastal wetlands act as a buffer between the sea and coastline. Mangrove vegetation protects land from erosion and helps to build and consolidate silt, while coastal shallows, such as lagoons and salt flats, can take the sting out of tidal waves accompanying hurricanes and storms. Civil engineers often find the need to provide man-made substitutes to replace the coastal defence function lost with the destruction of mangrove and other wetlands (Farber, 1987).

c) **Habitat for wildlife.** Apart from the creatures caught for local consumption, wetlands provide an important seasonal habitat for migratory fish and birds. Their international importance led to the signature of the Convention on Wetlands of International Importance, the Ramsar Declaration, in 1971. Wetlands provide a great variety of biological niches and evolutionary adaptations, and are consequently rich in fauna and flora. This makes them of great interest to science, and of potential value to agriculture, medicine, etc. A number are listed as of international importance under the Ramsar Declaration. Many others are national conservation areas.

d) **Tourism and recreation.** Some of the more notable wetlands have become important tourist assets (e.g. the Everglades of Florida, the Okavango in Botswana, the Sundarbans in Bangladesh, and South-West Tasmania). Others are valued for local recreation (bird-watching, boating, rambling, shooting, fishing, hunting).

e) **Transport.** The creeks and channels of coastal wetlands offer a sheltered network in areas where other means of transport (such as roads) are lacking and difficult to provide. This is notably the case in parts of West Africa and the Gulf Coast of Central America.

f) **Biophysical externalities for fishing, etc.** Wetlands occupy an important slot in the food chain, though the exact processes at play are only dimly understood. They provide a rich source of nutrients for all forms of life, including fish, and are favoured breeding grounds for certain kinds of marine life. Thus, they provide crucial life-support for activities going on elsewhere, especially fishing, which might not register as the direct harvest of the wetland itself. Quantifying this externality is difficult, and its true size may become apparent only some time after the wetland is lost or impaired.

g) **Climatic effects.** Under natural conditions organic soil wetlands act as net carbon sinks for atmospheric gases. Their conversion to agriculture has resulted in a loss of these sinks and their replacement with carbon sources. It has been estimated that over the last 200 years the carbon sink capacity from wetlands in Central Europe has been eliminated (Turner, 1988), with significant effects for climatic change and global warming. Extensive wetlands also have local micro-climatic effects, though these are difficult to isolate, let alone measure.

2.7. Wildlands

Wildlands can be defined as: '. . . natural land and water areas which have been only slightly, or not at all, modified by modern society' (Ledec and Goodland, 1988). The term includes all relatively undisturbed ecosystems, whether terrestrial, or linked to inland water bodies, and coastal or marine areas.

There is obviously a large overlap with other habitats considered in earlier sections of this chapter. Wildlands differ from these other habitats, however, in that, by definition, they do not contain sizeable numbers of people. They are nevertheless important to humanity, partly because of the vital biodiversity they support, partly for their direct products, and partly for the range of environmental functions they serve.

The International Union for the Conservation of Nature and Natural Resources has designated a number of Exceptionally Endangered Wildlands (reproduced in Ledec and Goodland, 1988), which are either biologically unique, ecologically fragile and vulnerable, or of special importance to local people or for the environmental services they provide. They include a number of tropical forests, high mountain forests, Mediterranean-type brushlands, mangrove swamps, coastal marshes, coral reefs, and small oceanic islands. Arctic, Antarctic, and high mountain regions can be regarded as special cases, though a number of the general problems discussed here would also apply to them.

2.7.1. Problems and threats

Since wildlands span the whole range of habitats, it is difficult to generalise about their problems and the reasons they are threatened (see, however, the respective sections above). A number are of strategic importance. Interested governments occupy them for geopolitical reasons (Antarctica), to settle their population (Amazonian countries, the outlying islands of Indonesia), or as theatres for intermittent warfare (the Himalayas). The natural wealth of the jungles of South-East Asia and Central America, and the nature reserves of Southern Africa, has been extensively pillaged by rival armies for cash and sustenance. Deserts and remote islands are used for testing nuclear devices.

More common, however, are demographic and economic pressures, as in Amazonia, West Africa, and South-East Asia. Road construction has abetted these trends by improving access to previously remote areas. Mining, ranching, and agricultural schemes have been responsible for much conversion of former wildlands. Many wetlands have been lost to the growth of industry, agriculture, housing and infrastructure. Fragile marine ecosystems have been degraded by oil pollution. In virtually every case, the conversion of wildlands has been explained or justified by the view that the land is 'free', worthless, or under-exploited in its current use.

2.7.2. Environmental services

The main economic interest of wildlands lies in their contribution to biodiversity, in the supply of direct products, and in a range of environmental services. Since these have all been discussed in the respective earlier sections of this chapter, suffice it to summarise them in Table 2.1. It is also possible to classify these functions in a different way, according to the economic sectors that they benefit (Ledec and Goodland, 1988).

Table 2.1: Functions and products of wildlands

i) Biodiversity:

ecological base-line studies
preservation of crop germplasm
source of new species for crops, fish, livestock, trees, etc.
material for medical research and drugs
natural laboratory for pure science

ii) Products

game for consumption or trophy
fodder and grazing
timber
minor forestry products
fuelwood

iii) Functions

protection of watersheds and soil:

reduced sedimentation of irrigation, reservoirs, rivers
prevention of flooding, landslides
maintaining seasonal water flow and quality for farming and
household use

arresting of coastal erosion by coastal wetlands

climatic regulation, local and regional

habitat for wildlife

ecological externalities:

habitat for pollinators, pest control
feeding grounds for fish and shrimp

basis of tourism, vicarious consumption

2.8. Industrial and urban concentrations

Urban and industrial areas are not synonymous; their demands on the environment and their problems and solutions are quite different. However, it is convenient to deal with the two types of development together. Many of the largest developing cities are also major industrial centres (e.g. Mexico City, Bombay, Calcutta, Sao Paulo, Bangkok, Shanghai, Manila, Lagos). This is no accident, and is the outcome of economies of scale and agglomeration, as well as the result of the industrialisation policies followed (Leonard, 1988, Harris, 1989).

In cities the environment is used, and often abused, by millions of individual agents. The city is a large Commons, where pollution is not always perceived by those responsible for it. Nor is there much incentive for individual agents to change their behaviour in the absence of collective incentives or sanctions. The environmental effects of particular projects or programmes are hard to disentangle from those due to everyone else's. The attribution of environmental costs (and benefits) is thus very difficult.

It is easy to condemn the development of cities on account of their environmental impact, and to seek to restrict their growth and achieve a more dispersed pattern of settlement. This reaction would not necessarily be appropriate. City development confers important gains in productivity and economies in providing public services (Harris, 1989) and these have to be set off against the environmental effects of conurbations.

2.8.1 Environmental effects

There is a useful distinction to be made between urban environmental concerns at local, city-wide and regional levels (Hardoy and Satterthwaite, 1989).

a) **The locality.** The rapid growth of cities in an unplanned fashion forces poor people into close proximity with each other, in bad housing conditions, and lacking elementary public services. The problems are worst on the urban peripheries of the developing world, where up to 100 million very poor people are at risk from various kinds of environmental calamities (Leonard, 1989). The living conditions of many other urban dwellers, including those in well-established central locations, are deteriorating because of overcrowding, and the failure of public services to keep up with needs.

The combination of crowded and cramped living conditions, inadequate water, sewerage or refuse collection, and insufficient primary health care produces a milieu in which disease is endemic - diarrhoea, dysentery, typhoid, intestinal parasites, and food poisoning, to name the most common. The absence of decent sewerage is especially serious:

> Most cities in Africa and many in Asia have no sewers at all - including many cities with a million or more inhabitants . . .. Around two-thirds of the Third World's population have no hygienic means of disposing of excreta and an even greater number lack adequate means to dispose of waste waters. (Hardoy and Satterthwaite, 1989)

Overcrowded conditions encourage the spread of infectious diseases. Tuberculosis, influenza, meningitis, mumps and measles are widely prevalent, especially among children. In Kanpur, India, 60% of slum children are believed to have TB. Accidents in the home are also common because of overcrowding, lack of storage space for dangerous substances, and dangerous cooking and heating methods. Women and children are particularly at risk.

Much small industry and trade is conducted from the home, or in premises interspersed with low-income housing. Although the so-called 'informal sector' is a thriving and vital part of the urban economy, it often has harmful effects on the household and neighbourhood environment. Accidents, fumes, leaks, noise, dust, contamination, pollution and fire are added to the list of environmental hazards in poor settlements.

Larger industrial plants may be guilty of employing dangerous machinery, hazardous materials, and lax safety standards, to the detriment of their workers. Apart from death and disablement from accidents, workers are liable to acquire illnesses which cause long-term suffering and premature death. A survey of workers in Bombay found that one-third of those in asbestos factories had asbestosis, many cotton workers suffered from brown lung, while a quarter of those in the Gas Company had chronic bronchitis, TB or emphysema (quoted in Hardoy and Satterthwaite, 1989).

b) **The city.** Some of the main symptoms of a worsening city-wide environment are air and water pollution, the accumulation of refuse and harmful waste, noise, congestion, landslides and land subsidence.

Air pollution. The main forms are excessive amounts of carbon monoxide, airborne lead, ozone, nitrogen dioxide, sulphur dioxide and particulates (dust). It may lead to reduced visibility, e.g. industrial 'smog', photochemical smog (caused by the action of strong sunlight on vehicle pollution), and acid fog (where industrial emissions occur where fog is prevalent - e.g. in certain Middle East Gulf states). Its four main sources are industrial emissions, fuel burnt for heating or power generation, the burning of solid waste, and the exhausts from motor vehicles (especially diesel-powered). The worst pollution is found in Third World cities with a heavy concentration of industry (e.g. Bombay, Seoul, Sao Paulo); heavy and congested motor traffic (Bangkok, Bombay, Tehran, Lagos, Manila, Calcutta, Mexico City); widespread burning of solid fuels for domestic cooking and heating (e.g. Ankara, Tehran); or local physical or climatic factors trapping the pollutants (e.g. Mexico City, Ankara, Tehran, Beijing).

The most obvious effect of air pollution is on human health. There is strong circumstantial evidence that excessive pollution causes various respiratory diseases (bronchitis, TB), skin and eye complaints, lung cancer, etc. Airborne lead, which settles as dust or dirt is held to be responsible for bone disease, and retards children's mental development. The majority (60%) of Calcutta's residents are thought to suffer from respiratory diseases related to air pollution. From time to time, the pollution in Mexico City is deemed too bad to expose children to it: schools were closed during January 1989. The Mexican Government warned that rapid breathing, e.g. during exercise, could damage health, and some Mexican doctors argued that regular breathing of the city's air was equivalent to smoking 40 cigarettes a day.

Air pollution has costs that are more directly economic, such as corrosion damage to buildings and structures, the stunting and spoiling of crops and trees, and the extra costs and loss of public services. The quality of urban air also has an obvious effect on amenity, aesthetic enjoyment, and recreation. These various kinds of cost sometimes arise simultaneously where important national monuments are at risk. The Taj Mahal in Agra is suffering surface deterioration as a result of the air pollution from industrial and power plants in the vicinity. The Egyptian Sphynx is threatened on two counts - firstly by sewage from squatter settlements corroding its foundations, and secondly by chemical pollutants increasing weathering on the face of the monument.

Water pollution. This is caused mainly by the discharge of untreated, or inadequately treated, sewage, industrial effluent, waste-water run-off from storms and households, and agricultural residues (mainly the run-off of agro-chemicals). The absence or deficiency of sewerage and refuse-collection services causes water courses to become grossly polluted. A shortage of fresh water can aggravate the situation where there is insufficient volume to dilute pollutants to safe levels.

Less than 7% of India's 3119 towns and cities have sewerage and sewage treatment facilities, and only 8 have full services. The Ganges, which is used by millions of people for washing, is the receptacle of untreated sewage from 114 towns and cities, as well as effluent from chemical, fertiliser, rubber, paper and pulp, and tannery complexes. The Hooghly River estuary receives untreated industrial effluent from 150 major factories in Calcutta, and raw sewage from 361 outfalls (quoted in Hardoy and Satterthwaite, 1989). The situation is just as bad in some other countries. A number of important rivers are biologically 'dead' (e.g. the Huangpu in Shanghai), and there are cases of badly polluted stretches actually catching fire.

Polluted water can spread diseases amongst people who use it for washing, cooking, or bathing. The presence of hazardous wastes (e.g. heavy metals) is particularly harmful. As major water courses become polluted, there is a risk of contamination to groundwater, and a whole new class of users become exposed to danger (e.g. those with piped water supplies from wells, agricultural users). Another kind of pollution is saline intrusion, caused by excessive abstraction of groundwater coupled, in some cases, with subsidence (e.g. Jakarta, Bangkok).

Water pollution has its most immediate effect on human health, through water-borne diseases. Most of these register as private costs, though public health provisions are also affected. There are direct effects on production - most notably of agriculture, fisheries and tourism, but also industry insofar as extra costs of treating water intakes are incurred. The longer-term damage to productivity from widespread chronic dysentery, diarrhoea, etc. is a major hidden cost to the economy.

Toxic and noxious waste. Household garbage and refuse, the residues of public markets, and sometimes even wastes from hospitals, public utilities and industry are left in areas without adequate public collection services. A high proportion of solid urban waste is not collected, and is dumped on empty land, in streets, or into rivers. It causes congestion, can block drains and sewers, is a fire risk, attracts insects and rats, is hazardous to children, and eventually contaminates ground-water (Campbell, 1989).

Solid waste disposal tends to be given low priority by hard-pressed city authorities. Moreover, there are vested interests in the present disposal arrangements from the organisers of unofficial scavenging that occurs on the waste tips of the Third World. These tips are a danger to public health and safety, especially to the people who work on them. The garbage can also disrupt public services (transport, sewerage) and damage property (fire risk, accidents).

Toxic waste is more obviously dangerous to health. The most common toxic wastes are heavy metals, nitrogen and sulphur oxides, hydrocarbons, PCBs (poly-chlorinated biphenyls), cyanide, arsenic, solvents and asbestos. Radioactive waste is especially lethal. The chemical industry is the main source, together with metal processing and fabrication, petroleum refining, pulp and paper, electrical equipment, leather and tanning, and scrap merchants (see UNIDO, 1988, for a more comprehensive list of dangerous materials and industries).

The safe handling and disposal of these dangerous wastes is expensive, hence the motive for illegal and dangerous dumping. Toxic substances make their impact on humans through direct handling, contamination of soil and water, or by entering the food chain though cattle, fish or crops. Amongst many possible examples of damage to life and health are the effect of mercury on the nervous system, cadmium on kidney damage, asbestos on cancer, and chromates on the skin. Most toxic substances have compound effects.

Animals cause additional waste. In the Indian subcontinent, the Middle East and elsewhere in the Third World large animals (camels, bullocks) are used in transport, and in Hindu societies cows are left to wander or lie in the streets, attracting flies and depositing dung. Stray dogs are also a health risk.

Noise is perceived as a public nuisance mainly in the context of aircraft movements. But most large cities have a high ambient noise level from traffic, and there is a high decibel level in the vicinity of power stations, railway lines, certain industrial processes, and construction sites. Excessive and chronic noise can cause deafness to those directly exposed (e.g. workers in factories, power stations or building sites), and tension and irritation to those with high levels of indirect exposure. It may interrupt certain activities sensitive to noise, and require structural adaptations in houses, public buildings, factories, etc. The fact that much Third World urban housing is in noisy locations (next to airport runways, on the edge of highways, even between railway tracks) should not be taken as indifference to noise, but rather a sign of a shortage of housing space for the poor and their lack of choice over location.

Congestion is a feature of most large cities and is related to population density, the number of employers in central areas, the efficiency of public transport, and the planning, layout, and zoning. The heavy and largely unregulated use of private transport, as in Mexico City, Lagos, Tehran and Bangkok, can be a contributor to congestion, but even a well developed public transport system, as in Bombay, will not relieve congestion if services are over-used. Rio de Janeiro and Hong Kong have expanded in the spaces between mountains and the sea, while central Bombay is confined to a narrow peninsula. Transport in these cities is inherently problematic. Calcutta has a different problem in that it is under-provided with road space (which takes up only 7-8% of its central area), and has a large number of animals on its streets. In Dhaka the ubiquitous cycle rickshaws cause blockages and delays to other modes of transport in the central areas.

The effects of congestion partly feed back through additional air pollution and noise (e.g. through stationary and idling vehicles). But there is also a pecuniary impact on commerce and industry (greater time spent in transport and distribution) and on public services (more vehicles, fuel and wages required to provide a given service). Congestion also encroaches on people's leisure through the longer time they take to get to and from work and other urban destinations.

Landslides and subsidence are increasingly common hazards in many cities. In Rio de Janeiro up to 3 million people occupy steep slopes in and around the city and hundreds have died and thousands have lost their homes from landslides during storms (Leonard *et al.*, 1989). The North-Western part of Mexico City has expanded onto a former lake bed, and the weight of development combined with extraction of groundwater has caused a sizeable amount of subsidence (Schteingart, 1989). This affects the stability of existing buildings. In coastal cities, e.g. Bangkok, subsidence increases the incidence of flooding, and causes saline intrusion into groundwater (Phantumvanit and Liengcharensit, 1989).

(c) *The region*. As cities grow, they make increasing demands on their hinterlands for land, water, energy and food. The growth of Mexico City is estimated to use up 700 ha of farm land every year. Cairo has expanded onto some of the most fertile agricultural land in Egypt, which is now no longer available for food production. Most large cities have ceased to be self-reliant for water needs and draw water from increasingly distant locations. The combined requirement for water and electric power leads to environmentally momentous dam and reservoir projects, such as Brazil's plans for exploiting the Amazon's water power.

The growing demand for foodstuffs causes the intensification of agriculture and ploughing up slopes and marginal areas, both of which could harm the rural environment. In poorer societies the use of wood and charcoal for urban heating and cooking causes devastation to forests in the interior (e.g. Mogadishu, Delhi). These effects may be irreversible (e.g. on wetlands, unique natural areas). Some of these effects are treated elsewhere in this chapter in the context of watersheds, forests, drylands, wetlands, or intensive agriculture.

There are many examples of long-distance pollution by cities on their regions, e.g. destruction of fisheries in downstream rivers and estuaries, acidification of farmland and acid rain damage to trees, the effect of water pollution on coastal communities, etc.

This chapter has identified some of the main environmental services present in different habitats, and the reasons why some of them are threatened. The following two chapters consider how these functions can be valued, in theory and practice.

3

The Techniques of Economic Valuation

The most common methods of project appraisal are cost-benefit (CBA) and cost-effectiveness analysis (CEA). The former is used where benefits can be valued, and the latter where the exercise is one of selecting the best (i.e. lowest-cost) method of satisfying a given objective. This chapter will take as common ground the use of CBA/CEA as the normal decision-making method used in project appraisal, and will assume an elementary understanding of these techniques (see ODA, 1988; Bridger and Winpenny, 1987). Its purpose is to consider how, within the CBA framework, environmental effects can be measured and added in alongside conventional benefits and costs.

CBA has made relatively little headway in treating the environmental impacts of projects or programmes. There are several reasons for this: i) *ignorance* of the effects; ii) difficulties in assessing their importance, or *quantifying* them in physical, biological, medical, or other relevant terms; and iii) problems in *valuing* them, even where they are known and quantified. These problems arise where markets for the effects are absent, imperfect or incomplete. Items (i) and (ii) are the province of scientists and researchers in a number of professional areas. A common device for assembling such information is the Environment Impact Assessment (EIA), now increasingly required to accompany major proposals, or those in environmentally sensitive areas (see the ODA *Manual*, 1989, for an EIA outline). Economists should not hesitate to call for EIAs, or specific data collection, where important information is lacking. Valuation (item iii) is already controversial enough, and its problems are compounded if the underlying environmental data are weak.

The following two sections of this chapter introduce CBA and CEA as they are used in environmental project appraisal. Section 3.3 then discusses six of the principal techniques developed to value environmental benefits, with particular stress on their applicability to projects in developing countries. Finally, section 3.4 explores some general methodological problems and how they can be handled by the practitioner.

3.1. Cost-benefit analysis (CBA)

If properly applied, CBA can combine rigour with comprehensiveness in a way that few other techniques can match. The need to balance the costs of an action against its benefits is intuitively appealing, and provides an important discipline with which to approach decisions. CBA has by now been applied to most sectors of interest to developing countries. On the scope for this, one leading practitioner states:

> . . . the most useful approaches for valuing environmental effects, especially of projects, have frequently been the simplest . . .. The more experimental techniques, or those that require extensive data sets . . . have had much more

limited applications to date. In developing countries the most useful approaches have been those that require the fewest assumptions and the least amount of data . . .. It has proved much harder to 'sell' the results of more hypothetical or abstract techniques. (Dixon, 1991)

CBA needs to pay adequate attention to questions of risk, uncertainty, sustainability and distribution, if it is to carry conviction in environmental appraisal (see section 3.4). The criterion of choice is also important. Although a positive Net Present Value (NPV) is, in theory, the most satisfactory criterion, other measures (Internal Rate of Return, Benefit/Cost Ratio, etc.) should also be included if they are more meaningful to the decision-maker. For instance, the Benefit-Cost Ratio may be more appropriate where the choice is to be made amongst a cluster of projects of different sizes and with different NPVs.

Sensitivity analysis has a particular value in approaching uncertainty. The 'switching value' of a variable is a useful refinement, enabling the decision-maker to see how much a particular item (of cost or benefit) needs to change to reduce the NPV to zero. Because environmental appraisal brings together benefit and cost items that are often varied and dissimilar, it is important not to conceal this variety by collapsing it into one or a few aggregate numbers (like a single NPV). Although the results of an analysis obviously need to summarise and simplify the detailed data used in the CBA, they should not discard and waste important information. It should be standard practice to display the contributions of the main cost and benefit items to the overall result, and to show by sensitivity analysis which of these are more important.

3.2 Cost-effectiveness analysis (CEA)

CEA comes into its own where benefits cannot be measured. It is applicable in such circumstances as: devising the most efficient (least cost) method of meeting a given environmental objective (e.g. achieving a certain level of clean air and water); determining the best use of a fixed budget in achieving certain stated aims (e.g. how the optimise the use of a fixed budget for conservation); or assessing the cost of meeting different alternative goals, as a way of deciding which goal to adopt. The decision criterion of CEA is to select the most cost-effective option, namely that which meets the objective at least total cost. Costs can include forgone environmental benefits. As with CBA, CEA needs to be adaptable to meet environmental concerns about sustainability, distribution, risk, uncertainty, etc.

In practice, the main problems in the use of CEA revolve around the definition and satisfaction of the project's objectives. Where objectives cannot be precisely specified, where their attainment cannot be exactly measured, or where the alternatives being compared would not attain the project's aims in precisely the same manner, CEA becomes ambiguous. Where a project has several objectives, and the different options satisfy certain aims more fully than others, CEA would not yield one clearly superior solution. The Beijing water project (5.4.3) was, for example, assessed on four different measures of water quality (two measures in each of two rivers) as well as on benefits, where they could be measured. In this case, eight options had to be compared according to how they fared on each of five criteria. (This case study also illustrates how CBA and CEA can be combined in a project where some benefits are measurable, and others not.)

Rejecting all options which failed to meet all the aims, however narrowly, might be justified for certain matters of public health and safety. But such perfectionism could be very costly, if there were other options which, although narrowly failing to meet one objective, could satisfy others much more cheaply than the first. There are various possible decision rules in these circumstances. Options could be ranked for each aim (cost, duration, quality, ease of implementation, etc.) and the one with the best aggregate score selected. Or more complex trade-offs could be used, depending on the decision-maker's preferences. An option which narrowly missed satisfying one objective might be preferred because it fulfilled another by a great margin.

CEA can provide useful feedback on the cost of setting environmental standards. Few such standards have absolute status; they tend to be raised as nations can afford them. It is unwarranted to assume that standards should be met whatever the cost (ADB, 1986).

3.3. Environmental benefit estimators

An environment confers benefits on users, and those who, while not using it directly, are glad that it is there. User benefits are derived by two types of consumer: i) all who make actual use of the environment - farmers, fishermen, recreationists, polluters, etc., ('actual use value') and ii) potential users of the environment in the future, either in the present or the unborn population. This element is the 'option value' of the environment, which has been defined as: 'a willingness to pay for the preservation of an environment against some probability that the individual will make use of it at a later date' (Pearce, Markandya and Barbier, 1989, p. 60).

A different type of benefit is the 'existence value', which has been described as follows:

> Even if the individual himself does not consume the services . . . he may still be concerned about the quality or existence of the asset. For example, he may derive satisfaction from the pure fact that the asset is available for other people - living now or in the future. (Johansson, 1990, pp. 37-8)

These 'armchair' friends of the environment have a mixture of motives - altruism, sympathy for the natural world, vicarious pleasure, a sense of responsibility, a desire to pass on natural resources for future generations, etc. Existence benefits are also referred to as 'intrinsic'.

In environmental economics, the Total Economic Value (TEV) is the sum of all three values. In practice, the actual use value is the concept which most commonly appears, but where the other two elements arise, e.g. in the preservation of rare species or cultural property, contingent valuation methods may be appropriate estimators.

Six different methods are considered in this section, each sub-section setting out the general principle behind the method, how it is carried out, its data requirements, an assessment of its overall usefulness, and a judgement of its applicability to developing countries. It is appropriate to stress the fluid state of valuation methodology, and the rapid strides that have been taken in recent years. As one authority notes:

. . . valuation methodology has undergone a tremendous development during recent decades and many values that twenty or so years ago were classified as intangibles can now be measured in monetary terms. If development continues in the same rapid way, one would expect many of the remaining problems to be solved within a decade or two. (Johansson, 1990)

3.3.1. The Effect on Production (EOP) approach

Principle. An activity may affect the output, costs and profitability of producers through its effect on their environment, and the welfare of consumers through changes in the supply and price of what they consume, thus altering their consumer surplus. Where there is a market for the goods or services involved, the environmental impact of an action can be represented by the value of the change in output that it causes - e.g. the reduced value of fish caught as a result of river pollution. The party responsible for the effect may or may not bear its economic consequences. Where the effect is felt by other parties (e.g. farmers and fishermen lower down the watershed, foresters in the neighbouring country) this effect is an externality. However, the effect could equally well be experienced by the party responsible for it, e.g. a decline in soil fertility eventually affecting the hill farmer responsible for the soil erosion that causes it. A number of the studies of soil erosion (see 4.1) are concerned with these 'internal' environmental effects.

Environmental effects are not necessarily negative in their impact on producers and consumers. Bee keepers benefit neighbouring gardens and farms (and vice versa), and reservoirs create major new fisheries, as well as affecting those downstream. But EOP has also been used to trace the impact of such environmental changes as soil erosion, deforestation, wetland and reef destruction, and air and water pollution on agriculture, forestry, fisheries, power, public services and other sectors.

Technique. The EOP method proceeds in two steps: first the physical effects are determined, and then their effect on monetary values.

i) *Determining the physical effects* of the environmental effect needs to be substantiated by such methods as the following:

a) laboratory or field research (e.g. effect of marine pollution on fisheries through its effect on reef ecology; effect of overfishing on fish populations); damage functions can be estimated by observation or controlled experiments (the 'dose-response' method - e.g. observing the effect of air pollution on crops or materials corrosion);

b) controlled experiments, in which the effect is deliberately induced (e.g. agronomic trials on land with different degrees of erosion, or with different applications of pesticide; exposing animals to chemical contamination or air pollution); making observations on receptors with and without the effect by using control groups as the norm;

c) statistical regression techniques that try to isolate the influence of a particular effect from that of a number of others.

Whichever method is used, the estimation of effects should, in principle, eliminate any underlying trend, or the influence of exogenous forces. The effects should be those solely attributable to the prime cause, i.e. there should be a clear 'with' and 'without' distinction. (This is not always easy to achieve, for instance where there is an underlying natural rate of soil erosion independent of farmers' activities.)

ii) *Estimating monetary values*. In its more straightforward application, EOP uses ruling market prices to value changes in production. This is defensible if the change in output is unlikely to affect prices, and if the price is a market-clearing one. Where the effect is on such a scale that prices are likely to be affected, an attempt should be made to predict the new price level. This would be warranted where, for instance, a large part of national supply came from the area affected by pollution or erosion, or where local markets were badly linked with those in the rest of the country (e.g. local markets for fresh fish). In theory, where price changes occur, effects on consumers' surplus should also be allowed for.

Predicting market responses could become complicated. For instance, producers and consumers are likely to take action to protect themselves against the effects of environmental change (e.g. consumers switching away from foodstuffs they believe to be contaminated, producers growing crops less susceptible to soil erosion, fishermen spending longer at sea). If the appraisal is done *before* such adaptations occur, it will overestimate the value of the effects, whereas if it is done *after* adaptations are made it will underestimate the real impact on producer surplus and consumer welfare. The use of actual prices would also be misleading if markets were seriously distorted by monopoly, price controls, protection, etc. This is a problem in the use of all kinds of CBA and is particularly serious for non-tradables. In principle, prices should be adjusted to their market-clearing, or competitive, levels (see ODA, 1988 for a further discussion).

EOP can also be used for non-marketed output, where an actual market exists for similar goods, or substitutes, elsewhere. For subsistence production it may be possible to estimate a 'border price' from the nearest actual market. Another approach is to take the price of a close substitute. Valuation is a serious problem where there are no close marketed substitutes for the product (e.g. tropical forest products, discussed in section 4.2), or where realised market values are a poor proxy for real values (e.g. dryland livestock, discussed in section 4.3).

The main **data requirements** are: i) evidence of the environmental repercussions of an activity on the output of marketed goods; ii) data on the market prices of the goods in question; iii) where prices are likely to be affected, predictions of production and consumption responses; iv) where the output is not marketed, information about the nearest market for that good, or its closest marketable substitute; and v) an appreciation of the behaviourial adjustments that producers and consumers are likely to make, or have already made, in response to the environmental damage. Illustrations given (amongst others) include soil erosion in Mali (section 4.1), afforestation in Nigeria and Ethiopia, and farm improvement in Lesotho (all in section 5.2).

Usefulness of the technique. The EOP is the most widely used and intelligible valuation technique. Most of the valuation studies done in developing countries rely upon it wholly or in part. The main problems in its use are likely to be where markets are badly developed or distorted, and where the changes in output are likely to have a significant effect on prices.

The main limitations of EOP are as follows:

(a) The physical relationships between activities affecting the environment, and output, costs or damage are rarely well-established. Forging the link between cause and effect usually depends on making assumptions, transferring data on relationships established elsewhere, or taking an eclectic approach drawing evidence from a number of methods and sources.

(b) It is often difficult to disentangle the effect of one cause from that of others in determining the impact on the receptor. This is most clearly true of air pollution, which normally arises from a number of sources. However, it also applies to soil erosion, where there are a number of stages in the transfer of soil to lower down the watershed, which may be influenced by a number of factors. Distinguishing the effect of man-made from natural degradation is also difficult (e.g. for erosion, acid rain damage to crops and trees).

(c) Where the effect on markets is likely to be substantial, a more complex view needs to be taken of the market structure, elasticities, and supply and demand responses. Consumer behaviour needs to be introduced into the analysis. The adaptive response of producers and consumers is also relevant.

(d) Determining the effect of an action on output entails setting up a 'with' and 'without' scenario. Where there is already a degradation process (e.g. serious air and water pollution, on-going erosion of a watershed) it is difficult to attribute precise effects to a particular action, or ascribe benefits to a specific conservation programme. In unscrupulous hands, CBA could easily lead to an overestimation of damage, for instance through exaggerating the losses avoided by conservation programmes.

Applicability to developing countries. The EOP technique is in principle well-suited for use in developing countries since it relies on observed market behaviour, is readily intelligible to decision-makers, and concentrates on output which potentially enters GNP and the budgets of firms and households. There are, however, two ways in which the limitations noted above are likely to apply with even greater force in developing countries:

(a) Causal relationships which have been established in temperate or high-income economies may not apply in tropical or poor environments. Much of the work on the link between soil erosion and crop yields, or between shelterbelts and crop yields, or models of fish populations, has been done in temperate conditions. Almost all the dose-response relationships between air pollution and materials corrosion - which themselves are weak - have arisen from work in OECD countries and make no allowance for tropical climate, humidity, nor the very different range of materials at risk.

(b) Certain markets for produce are absent or underdeveloped in largely subsistence economic systems. This entails roundabout valuation methods, or the use of strong assumptions about comparable products. There are valuation problems for items only a small proportion of which is marketed, e.g. livestock in drought conditions, or widely used natural products for which there is no close commercial equivalent (e.g. medicines from the rain forest).

There are also complications where a change in the output of one good causes its substitution for another, which may replace a third (see the Ethiopia afforestation project in section 5.2 for a valuation of fuelwood based on the value of dung used as fertiliser, which in turn is valued by import savings on chemical fertiliser). Another roundabout valuation method applies to effects on output (e.g. fuelwood) with implications for human time and energy (e.g. time spent collecting it - see the Nepal Phewa Tal project in section 4.1).

3.3.2. Preventive Expenditure (PE) and Replacement Cost (RC)

Principle: The value that people place on preserving their environment is inferred from what they are prepared to spend to prevent its degradation (PE) (sometimes referred to as 'defensive' expenditure) or to restore its original state after it has been damaged (RC). Three important variants should be noted:

i) relocation, a special case of RC, in which the victims of environmental damage 'replace' their environment by moving away from the afflicted area;

ii) environmental 'surrogates', a special case of PE, which are goods and services bought as a substitute for deteriorating environmental services (e.g. private water sources rather than polluted public supplies);

iii) 'shadow' or 'compensating' projects, a special case of RC, in which the expected environmental damage from an activity is offset by the inclusion of a project that would replace the lost environmental services (e.g. planting new trees to replace those cut down to make way for a road). This offsetting project can be real, in which case it is an actual cost to the original scheme, or notional, where it serves as an appraisal device and establishes that there would be sufficient resources generated by the project to provide compensation if desired.

The boundary between PE and RC is not always easy to uphold. Spending to mitigate further environmental damage, once the process has begun, could be regarded as either (e.g. double glazing against aircraft noise could be regarded either as the prevention of further noise pollution, or as an attempt to restore pristine conditions of peace and quiet). PE and RC are useful where a process has physical effects which are well perceived, and for which there is the possibility of prevention or restoration, and are widely used in connection with soil erosion, siltation, noise, air and water pollution and wetland destruction.

Technique. Information can be obtained in three main ways:

i) direct observation of actual spending on safeguards against environmental risks (e.g. terracing to prevent soil erosion, walls to keep out siltation, double glazing to reduce noise);

ii) enquiring of people what they would be prepared to spend to defend themselves against an impending or possible environmental threat. Where the threat is hypothetical, the technique verges on Contingent Valuation (see section 3.3.6).

iii) obtaining objective professional estimates of what it would cost for people to defend themselves effectively against environmental damage, or to replace an expected loss of environmental quality. In practice, consultants are widely used to make such costings during project preparation, in order to decide whether the project to prevent further environmental harm is worth doing, as compared with waiting for the damage to happen and attempting to restore the *status quo ante* (see the Korean project in 5.2).

Data requirements are the values of PE or RC derived from any or all of the three methods above, illustrated by the upland soil and water conservation project in Korea (section 5.2).

Usefulness of the technique. There are a number of limitations to be borne in mind when applying this method:

(a) PE takes for granted that the expenditure is worth incurring. This is a reasonable assumption for well-informed private firms and individuals with a good idea of the relevant benefits and costs of their actions. It is assumed that they will pursue PE until the combined cost of PE and the mitigated level of damage (MD) equals the original level of perceived damage (PD) (ADB, 1986). However, where the risks are novel, or where the scale of risk is increasing, it will not be valid to assume perfect foresight and a rational level of PE.

(b) PE ignores the consumer surplus that parties will enjoy where PE plus MD is less than PD. Thus PE will only provide minimum estimates of environmental quality, except in those cases where parties spend too much on it.

(c) PE and RC are constrained by the ability to pay of the population at risk. In poor communities, this will give the estimates a downward bias. Thus, terracing might be financially profitable and economically justifiable in order to reduce soil erosion, but the level of spending on it may be sub-optimal if farmers are too poor to afford the temporary reduction of income it implies, if rural credit markets cannot supply the required loan, or if farmers do not own the land they work. This is a general problem in using the market as the yardstick for values where the income distribution is highly skewed, and is another reason for expecting PE to give minimum values.

(d) The assumption is that there are no secondary benefits associated with PE or RC. There are many situations where this will be unrealistic, and where - contrary to points (b) and (c) above - these methods will exaggerate environmental values. For instance, tree planting to preserve the stability of watershed slopes will yield fruit, browse and firewood in addition to pure environmental benefits (see Morocco project, section 4.1). Construction of new water supply points to guard against contaminated supplies is likely to improve both the quantity and quality of supply, compared with the original service. Double glazing against ambient noise will improve heat insulation, and the appearance and longevity of the windows, as well as reduce the interior noise level.

(e) RC assumes that full restitution of the environment is possible after damage, in other words, there is no uncompensated loss. This is a strong supposition. Many environmental effects will not be fully perceived, will arise in the long term, or will not be capable of being restored (e.g. replanting trees will not restore the original biodiversity, cleaning up after an oil spill cannot replace all the wildlife destroyed). In this respect, RC will underestimate environmental quality.

(f) Both PE and RC which are based on communities in a particular environment under threat, will fail to take into account people who have already moved in anticipation of the problem. These will include activities that are particularly environmentally-sensitive, and people who value environmental quality most highly. For example, sufferers from bronchial complaints may move out of polluted cities in anticipation of worsening atmospheric conditions. Households

especially sensitive to noise will have moved ahead of any programmes to mitigate the effect of aircraft landings. For such parties, the observed levels of RC will
be insufficient to restore their original environmental quality, and will underestimate environmental values.

Applicability to developing countries. PE and RC should have some intuitive
appeal to decision-makers, who will be able to judge the importance of environmental programmes and projects in the light of what people directly affected are
already willing to spend, or what RCs (including public outlays) will be avoided.
In some instances it will also be useful to make separate estimates of PE and RC
and to compare them, in order to decide whether it is more sensible to try to
prevent degradation, or to risk it happening and try to restore the damage.

Some of the limitations noted above will apply with particular force in developing
countries. The income constraint will limit PE amongst poor communities, and
make such estimates unreliable. Likewise spending on environmental surrogates
like private water supplies or swimming clubs is unlikely to be representative of
the population as a whole, and should not be extrapolated to obtain total environmental values. Where environmental change is fairly recent, and is happening
rapidly (e.g. through rapid urbanisation or massive deforestation), the full consequences of present changes may be only dimly understood by the people affected, and in these circumstances the observed level of PE will be a poor guide to
the damage they may eventually suffer. There are also important sectors or classes
of problem where PE and RC are ill-adapted - e.g. tropical deforestation - or where
lost environmental functions cannot easily be replaced - e.g. damaged reefs and
wetlands.

The above reservations also apply to the technique of the 'shadow' or compensating project, which presupposes that it is feasible to replace damaged environmental services. The design of such projects will be a challenge to professional skill in
the sectors concerned. It is a difficult matter adequately to compensate for the loss
of complex ecological systems or diversified biomass, or to offset complicated
hydrological or atmospheric effects. Compensating projects are, moreover, likely
to have their own environmental effects, which may also not be understood.

Despite all these reservations, PE and RC are likely to count among the more
useful valuation techniques in developing countries, and a number of applications
are noted in Chapters 4 and 5.

3.3.3. Human Capital (HC)

Principle. In the human capital (HC) approach, people are treated as units of
economic capital, and their earnings as returns on investment - a concept familiar
in analysing the social and private returns to education and training. Environmental economics focuses on the impact on human health of bad environmental
conditions, and the effect this has on the individual's, and society's, productive
potential. Although the term 'human capital' is somewhat misleading in this
context, it is commonly used in the environmental literature, and will be retained
here, it being understood to refer to the economic cost of illness. The variant to be
discussed here is that concerned with the loss of earnings which individuals suffer
as a result of environmental factors, plus the resource cost of medical treatment
and health care. It is useful when the following conditions hold (ADB, 1986): i) a

direct cause-and-effect relationship can be established; ii) the illness is be of limited duration, does not threaten life, and has no serious long-term effects; iii) the economic value of the lost productive time is calculable, and the costs of health care known. Where these conditions are present, HC is a useful technique for valuing the effects of air and water pollution, water-related diseases, insanitary living conditions, unsafe or unhealthy working conditions, anti-social industrial activities, etc.

Technique. The basic technique is as follows: identify the feature in the environment which could cause illness; determine its precise relationship with the incidence of the disease; assess the size of population at risk; calculate the probable loss in productive time and the health care resources used up; and place economic values on both of these. Identifying the cause is normally the province of medical science, founded on case histories, laboratory experiments and epidemiological data. Sometimes the causative agent is disputed, as in the responsibility of radioactive exposure for leukaemia. More often, its critical level is uncertain. The presence of the agent in the environment needs to be measured - e.g. x parts per '000, above threshold levels for y hours or z days per year, etc. Section 4.6 discusses this further in the case of air pollution. Even where there is strong circumstantial evidence linking the presence of a harmful element to the incidence of a certain illness, HC requires the relationship to be quantifiable, e.g. the presence of x amount of pollution is associated with the incidence of y cases per '000 of the population at risk. This degree of precision is rarely possible. Relationships established in particular cases tend to be applied outside their context to other cases lacking direct data. This is dangerous where other factors are likely to be present, e.g. data obtained from temperate conditions applied to tropical circumstances.

Assessing the population at risk is a matter of defining the catchment area for the harmful agent, which may involve modelling the dispersal pattern (in the case of air and water pollution), or narrowing down the total exposed population to those especially at risk (pregnant women, young children, old people, asthmatics, etc.). All the data mentioned so far will contribute to predicting the incidence of illness. If the average duration of the illness can be fed in, the total time lost can be estimated. The population affected then needs to be categorised according to whether it is 'productive' or not, and in what degree. In passing, we should note the difficulties of making these distinctions in societies where there is no clear distinction between 'productive' and 'unproductive' work; medical and health care resources then need to be attributed.

The final step is to put economic values on the time and resources taken up by the illness. The crudest methods employ average earnings, though in theory consumption should be deducted to arrive at the worker's net contribution to productivity. In any case, some adjustment needs to be made for those not engaged wholly or partly in productive work. Medical and health care costs will depend on the standard of care customary in each situation (very much less in developing countries than is usual in the United States, where most data have been collected) and on whether health care resources are fully employed. If hospitals, clinics, doctors, drugs etc. are in scarce supply relative to demand, their use by one individual will not affect overall use.

Data requirements. It is evident from the above discussion that HC, even in its simplest 'loss of earnings' variant, needs a good deal of data, of the types indicated. In particular, establishing the relationship between the causative agent and the incidence of disease normally depends on epidemiological studies with very large data sets (for examples see Kneese, 1984 and Freeman, 1979). Illustrations are the health problems of rice farmers in the Cameroon (4.10) and the Ismailia waste water project in Egypt (see 5.4).

Usefulness of the technique. As noted earlier, the 'loss-of-earnings' variant of HC depends on certain conditions being present. *Per contra*, where they are absent the technique is limited. Some general problems are as follows:

(a) The impact of environmental quality on human health is uncertain over important areas. The aetiology is not well-established in many cases.

(b) In typical situations, there are a number of possible causative factors (e.g. in air pollution). It is usually difficult to isolate one agent as an incontrovertible cause of a particular symptom; there are many unknown or interrelated variables.

(c) HC does not do justice to people defined as 'non-productive', or to productive workers near the end of their working lives.

(d) HC overlooks people's willingness to pay to avoid or reduce their exposure to disease. It also leaves out the psychic cost of suffering, and thus provides only a minimum estimate of the costs to health. However, the difficulty of estimating willingness to pay is a serious obstacle. In the words of one authority on US data, 'I am not aware of any empirical estimate of willingness to pay to avoid any category of morbidity' (Freeman, 1979, p.191).

(e) It is difficult to apply where the illness has long-term effects on a person's productivity.

On balance, HC is useful in the fairly narrowly defined circumstances listed above, provided it is understood that it provides minimum estimates of value, from a strictly economic viewpoint. In the two developing country cases quoted, one (Cameroon) enjoyed unusually favourable research conditions, while the other (Egypt) used US epidemiological data in the absence of local information.

Applicability to developing countries. The above limitations show up even more starkly for the use of HC in developing countries.

(a) Medical data are often unsatisfactory, and cannot support the formidable data requirements of serious epidemiological studies.

(b) The prevailing levels of poor health and low life expectancy in poor communities have a number of interrelated causes, and it is difficult to isolate one causative agent.

(c) There are many more chronic and debilitating diseases with long-term effects on productivity and life expectancy, whose economic costs cannot be reckoned simply as a few weeks off work.

(d) The boundary between productive and unproductive time is usually blurred. Most members of poor families contribute some productive time, whether in urban or rural communities (e.g. old people to cottage industries, children to farm work or retailing). Productive time lost by the illness of one person may be offset by extra inputs from other members of the family or community. In the case of farm-work or small industries, it may even be possible to make up lost time by more intensive efforts later.

(e) The assumption that output is constrained by labour inputs will not be realistic in all societies, or in a given society at different times of the year. If another factor (land, machinery, water, etc.) is the binding constraint, the illness of a worker may make little difference to output. In other words, his/her marginal product may be below average earnings.

(f) Where medical resources are scarce - as in many poor countries - their overall use may be little affected by greater illness in certain areas. In extreme cases, an outbreak of disease may simply lead to a redistribution of resources over a larger number of sufferers. Some forms of health care are in any case difficult to cost - e.g. traditional remedies, care of the victim by his or her family.

3.3.4. Hedonic Methods (HM)

Principle. In the absence of a direct market, and price, for environmental quality, the value of the latter is derived from the prices of surrogate goods, the most common of which are property and labour. The Property Value approach (PV) is the most common application, and it consists of observing systematic differences in the values of property between locations, and isolating the effect of ambient environmental quality on those values. The prices of houses or land differ for a number of reasons; if all the major explanatory variables can be statistically controlled, the residual variable can be taken as a proxy for an environmental attribute. Under certain conditions, changes in this value can be regarded as willingness to pay for environmental quality.

Likewise for Wage Differentials (WD), which are assumed to depend on a number of factors - age, skills, education, location, environmental risk, etc. By controlling for these, the residual premium (or discount in the case of a pleasant environment) is derived, and represents the extra wage needed to compensate workers for incurring environmental risk (dangerous, unhealthy or disagreeable working conditions).

These two types of HM obtain their data from actual markets, and use sophisticated statistical methods to infer the influence of environmental factors on actual price differences. PV has mainly been used in developed countries to estimate the implicit damage to the environment caused by air and water pollution and aircraft noise. WD has been mainly used, also in developed countries, to estimate the implicit values that workers place on the risk of death from workplace accidents. It is less reliable, though still potentially applicable, in valuing health risks from pollution.

Technique. The PV method has two stages. First, it identifies, by multiple regression analysis, how much of the observed differences in property values is due to differences in their environmental quality. Secondly, it estimates how much people would be willing to pay for environmental improvements (Freeman; 1979, Pearce and Markandya, 1989) - a procedure fraught with statistical complexities (see Freeman, 1979; Hufschmidt et al., 1983; Pearce and Markandya, 1989). Suffice it to say that the PV method entails considerable data bodies, experience in complex statistical estimation, and the utmost care in interpretation of the results.

Using WD also relies on an assumption that the market for labour is efficient and in equilibrium. Multiple regression analysis is again used to 'explain' wage differences related to the residual environmental variables. As with the PV variant, WD requires a great deal of data and sophisticated statistical estimation, and its results are sensitive to the chosen method.

Data requirements. PV requires a large body of data on the following: a range of different representative environments, with information on all the principal features of properties influencing their values, including such intangible qualities as 'neighbourhood characteristics', 'prestige', or 'exclusivity', and relevant socio-economic data on the households involved - such as income, family size, social class, etc.). The environmental variables also need to be specified and calibrated (e.g. the degree of air and water pollution from a specified agent should be stipulated). For WD the main data needs are for: average total remuneration available in different kinds of occupation in a range of localities; categorisation of occupations, and of the same occupation in different localities, according to key attributes; and some quantification of the environmental risks to which workers are exposed (e.g. probability of industrial injury or death, level of ambient air pollution). The illustration is the valuation of aircraft noise (section 4.7).

Usefulness of the technique. One balanced conclusion is that:

> [PV] is particularly well suited to estimating the costs of air and noise pollution on the residential environment but it works poorly if the form of pollution is one whose effects are unclear to the individuals affected and which cannot be easily measured or quantified. (Pearce and Markandya, 1989, p.30)

More generally:

> The assumptions necessary to interpret the results of the hedonic pricing technique as benefit measures are restrictive and, in many real world settings, implausible. (USEPA, 1988, p.19)

Certain limitations are common to both the PV and WD variants:

(a) There are large data requirements and the need for statistical competence in generating and interpreting results.

(b) The estimating equations are highly sensitive to decisions about specification and estimation. Using the values of a residual as a proxy for a particular variable is inherently problematic.

(c) The environmental variable must be capable of being measured, as for air and water quality or for noise. However, some elements of purity cannot easily be measured (e.g. visibility, turbidity, taste, smell), and levels of pollution below the threshold may not be picked up. The level at which thresholds are set will be critical. Environmental risks to workers may be difficult to measure objectively (e.g. the likelihood of an explosion or leak) and may take a long time to show up in chronic illness, debility or premature death.

Some limitations are peculiar to the PV approach:

(a) The assumption of a well-functioning property market, in which householders are well-informed about the environmental effects in different locations, free to move about, and explicitly prepared to pay more for environmental quality, is unlikely to be universally valid (see 4.6 for a Californian example). Most housing markets are segmented. In many countries the public sector owns housing stock and allocates it at controlled prices. Rent controls further hamper the emergence of market-clearing property prices.

(b) The price of land and property embodies a view about future environmental quality, when what is needed is an indication of how it is valued now.

(c) Not all aspects of environmental quality are perceived, or registered as significant, by households. The presence of some harmful pollutants may not be noticed, and would not therefore enter into willingness to pay for improvements.

(d) Households may take averting behaviour to avoid or mitigate environmental damage.

Other problems apply to WD:

(a) Labour markets rarely function as perfectly as the method postulates:

It assumes that people can make free choices with perfect information in the absence of discrimination, monopsony, union market power, involuntary unemployment or barriers to mobility. (Hufschmidt *et al.*, 1983, p. 215)

(b) The risks of different occupations or locations may be hard to measure objectively, workers may be badly informed about them, and their subjective view may be at variance with that of an objective 'rational' individual. Certain occupations attract people who are less risk-averse than average.

(c) Most WD studies concern the risk of death from industrial accidents. The method is more problematic when it is extended to measure the damage to health from pollution. In certain cases the risks are impossible to avoid, that is, they are not voluntarily incurred (e.g. escaping from heavily polluted industrial areas is not a practical option for most families).

Applicability to developing countries. All the limitations noted above have been levelled against the use of PV and WD in developed countries, especially the United States - the home of the majority of existing HM studies. The criticisms apply *a fortiori* in developing countries, where property and labour markets tend to be more imperfect, choices more constrained by income, information about environmental conditions less widespread, and the data, and their ability to manipulate them, even scarcer.

Markets - for property and labour - are extremely active in most developing countries with market-oriented or mixed economies. But they often do not behave in the ways required by HM. For instance, rent controls in a number of large Third World cities restrict, distort and conceal the transactions taking place. Much property is owned by the state, and does not fetch a market-clearing price. Cities are segmented by class, occupation, tribe, or ethnic origin, which restricts choices and mobility.

Environmental attributes are closely correlated with, and often submerged by, other important features of property. The notion of willingness to pay for general environmental improvement is somewhat far-fetched in poorer communities, though it often surfaces for specific and visible local improvements. Most rapidly growing cities have serious housing shortages, and many poor families have little choice over where they live. The value at which property changes hands may be hard for an independent researcher to establish, and require insights into the informal property sector.

For the purposes of WD, the labour market is likely to be highly imperfect. In many developing countries, and especially in their cities, there is an excess supply of labour willing to work for prevailing wage levels. Poverty makes people disregard environmental risks in their search for jobs and income security. Certain risky or unhealthy jobs are also low-paid. The differential rewards of occupations may be heavily influenced by custom, caste, or law. Workers, many of whom could be illiterate, are unlikely to know the full environmental risks of their jobs, even if their employers do. Some may even take a (macho) pride in the risks of their work.

Notwithstanding such problems, simple versions of PV may be useful in appraising improvements to neighbourhood amenities, provided it is possible to examine property values with and without the project, or before and after the improvement. Schemes to clean up rivers, install proper water supply and sanitation, and provide garbage collection and paving, lighting and cleaning in poor neighbourhoods have been shown to have clear and immediate effects on property values in the vicinity. These changes in values can be used as rough and ready indicators of the scale of possible benefits from such schemes. (Double-counting should be avoided, e.g. separate user benefits from cleaner water should not be counted in addition to the change in property values.)

WD is of less obvious relevance to countries where workers are less able to pick and choose their occupations and locations, and where relative rewards are less sensitive to environmental differences. Even in such cases, however, employers may set environmental weightings. In a highly polluted part of one East European country, the government provides a wage premium and other differential benefits (longer holidays, earlier retirement, better health benefits) to workers willing (or forced) to tolerate the harsh conditions. Although such practices are not widespread in developing countries, where they exist they indicate minimum levels of environmental values imposed on the workers concerned.

3.3.5. The Travel Cost Method (TCM)

Principle. The value people place on a good environmental location is inferred from the time and cost they incur in travelling to it. The method has been applied mainly to public recreation sites with free or minimal admission charges, where it is argued that the cost of travel is analogous to an entry price. The fact that people are observed to 'pay' it enables a demand function for that attraction to be constructed, in which the visitation rate is related to the cost of travel. Once the basic relationships have been established, it is then possible to provide evidence of the value placed on environmental quality, either by examining changes in the visitation rate resulting from changes in the environmental quality of a given site, or by comparing visitation to several sites of different environmental quality but with the same travel cost.

The TCM evolved in the United States to measure the value of public recreation locations. It has also been applied to water quality issues and wildlife sites. There are very few serious applications outside high-income OECD countries.

Technique. In its simplest form, TCM starts by dividing the area surrounding the site into concentric circles, where the 'contours' join points of equal travel distance. Visitors are sampled to determine their zones of origin; for each zone, visitation rates are calculated. A statistical regression is then carried out for each zone relating visitation rates to travel cost and other socio-economic variables such as income, to derive a demand curve for visits to the site which measures the consumer surplus of visitors (for a full account of the method see Freeman, 1979).

Data requirements. Data are obtained by surveys of the number of visitors to the site, their place of origin for the journey, and basic socio-economic features such as income, education, etc. The duration of their journey and direct travel expenses need to be computed, and a value placed on their time. The total population in each travel zone should be estimated.

Illustrations are the Lumpinee Park in Bangkok and the Ismailia waste water treatment in Egypt (both in section 5.4).

Usefulness of the technique. Certain general limitations apply to this method wherever it is to be used.

(a) Formal assumptions are made about individuals' behaviour in order to construct the demand curve - e.g. that all users get the same total benefit from the use of the site, that people in all distance zones would make the same number of visits at a given monetary cost. These are simplications (Hufschmidt *et al.*, 1983)

(b) The method relies on collecting a great deal of data, which are expensive to collect and codify.

(c) Results are sensitive to the statistical methods used to specify the demand relationship and the way estimation is tackled (Pearce and Markandya, 1989).

(d) The shadow value of a recreational traveller's time is a difficult concept. The use of wage rates as a basis for value is problematic, especially where the trip takes place in leisure hours and involves people not active in the formal labour market (the old, young, unemployed, etc.). Nor is it entirely satisfactory to use commuters' observed trade-offs of time and money, since these are invariably taken from travel-to-work situations. In one study of US data on the value of time taken outside working hours, a range of one-quarter to one-half the wage rate was suggested (Cesario, quoted in Freeman, 1979).

(e) Travel may itself be part of the pleasure of the visit.

(f) Some trips are multi-purpose.

(g) Benefits rely on the concept of consumer surplus, which rules out direct comparability with valuation techniques that do not, e.g. contingent valuation (CV). In studies where the TCM is complemented by CV techniques, TCM tends to provide estimates near the upper limit of indications of willingness to pay.

(h) On the other hand, TCM provides minimum estimates of benefits in the sense that it omits option and existence values, as well as benefits enjoyed by people who never actually visit the site (e.g. from cleaner air, good views, observing, or catching, the wildlife it supports).

(i) Changes in environmental quality are difficult to capture and model by this method. The problems are finding objective measures of the environmental change, discovering whether travellers perceive it, and finding out how they value it. Studies have shown wide discrepancies between objective or expert measures of environmental quality, and what users perceive and value. In this respect, a complete loss of the amenity is a more straightforward application of TCM than its mere degradation.

The main virtue of the TCM is that it rests on the observed behaviour of people, which gives it greater credence than methods like CV which depend on people's stated responses to hypothetical situations. One measured conclusion is:

> TCMs are a useful tool for valuing recreational benefits in situations where sites are visited by a broad range of users specifically for recreational purposes and where adequate data on the characteristics of the site and the user are available. (Pearce and Markandya, 1989)

Applicability to developing countries. Much of the application of TCM has been in countries, especially the United States, where motorised access to the amenity is the norm, and where time has a significant opportunity cost. There are unresolved problems in valuing non-work travel time, and the method has never been particularly well fitted for valuing urban environmental quality. In developing countries there are extra complications.

(a) A number of important areas for recreation and amenity that are threatened by encroachment or degradation are located in or close to cities (e.g. beaches in Rio de Janeiro, Bombay and Dar es Salaam, open areas in Calcutta and Nairobi, the Corniche in Beirut, urban parks in Bangkok). In general, in poorer societies with limited access to private transport, people will not travel far to seek their amenities. In such cases, travel costs are small and not a serious disutility, and the journey could be part of the pleasure.

(b) The notion of the value of time is very questionable when visitors use the amenity deliberately to seek a break from work (at mid-day or after work). The strictly 'non-productive' members of the population - especially the unemployed and children under working age - typically form larger proportions of the population in developing countries than elsewhere, making the valuation of non-working time crucial to TCM results. The value of time in the widespread 'informal sector' is also fraught with problems, since incomes are irregular.

(c) In certain societies, and in countries where the motor car is a mark of prestige, motoring itself is a positive source of pleasure, not a disutility. The fact that an attraction is located a certain distance away may make it attractive compared with one closer at hand, which tends to be frequented by people who can not afford to go further. Distance lends enchantment, and fashionability.

(d) Many people in the informal sector use public recreation areas to ply their trade (entertainment, food, petty trading, touting, prostitution, begging, theft). The benefits they obtain and the values they place on the amenity will be different from those of other visitors (more like a rent than a consumer surplus).

(e) Access to sites may be artificially constrained or vary according to the security situation, the availability of public transport and petrol, or the state of the roads. Thus the observed outlays of time and cost may not be a true reflection of what people would really be willing to pay to visit the amenity.

Well-conducted TCM exercises can, nevertheless, provide useful ammunition about the value of retaining amenities in their present use, compared with their 'development' value. TCM may come more into its own with the growth in domestic and international tourism by people highly conscious of time and expense - such as in South-East Asia.

But even if the problems of collecting data and deriving estimates of the demand function for the amenity can be overcome, the result will still exclude option and existence values. With growing populations and increasing interest in environmental quality, this is a serious omission.

3.3.6. The Contingent Valuation (CV) method

Principle. Where actual market data are lacking, CV seeks to discover how people would value certain environmental changes by directly questioning a sample of the population concerned. These changes, and the markets in which they are to be valued, are hypothetical - hence the name of the technique. The two concepts most widely used are willingness to pay (WTP) for an environmental benefit, and willingness to accept (WTA) compensation for a loss of environmental quality. The two are by no means the same. To improve the realism of the declared values, and to eliminate so far as possible various potential biases, CV has evolved a number of variants, some of which use games, outlined below.

CV is potentially widely applicable, either on its own, or in conjunction with other valuation techniques. In many situations it will be the only method available. There is no other way, for instance, of arriving at option or existence values. In principle, it can be used in the majority of circumstances in which environments are threatened, or conversely to value proposed improvements.

Technique. A number of techniques are available, some of which are common to commercial market research. All of them seek to elicit people's preferences for certain environmental states, and the money values they would place on them. The more sophisticated try to eliminate possible biases by simulating real market behaviour, e.g. by asking people to operate fixed budgets, trading off one choice against another, or using alternative ways of producing the same information as a check on consistency.

The most common method is the use of *questionnaire surveys*, some varieties of which include bidding games. The sample should be representative of all shades of environmental opinion, and not confined to those with strong views on the subject or to those best informed. Some check on respondents' disposable income is advisable to rule out clearly unrealistic declarations.

The results from the sample survey are then grossed up to represent the total valuation likely to be placed by the whole population. The accuracy of this process is improved if the declared values can be related (by statistical regression) to personal characteristics such as income, education, etc.

Take-it-or-leave-it experiments entail splitting the sample up into sub-groups, each of which is offered the environmental change at a different price, on a take-it-or-leave-it basis. With *trade-off games*, respondents are offered various combinations of states of the environment and bundles of other goods and/or money. The aim of the exercise is to discover people's rate of substitution between environmental quality and cash. *Costless choice* is similar, except that respondents choose between alternatives, one of which is environmental quality, and the other can be a well-known good whose value is known. Finally, the *Delphi technique* seeks 'expert' opinion rather than approaching consumers directly. Obviously the usefulness of this technique depends on the experts being representative of society in general.

Usefulness of the technique. The underlying weakness of CV is that it does not use observations of actual market behaviour, and does not test consumers' effective demand by requiring them to back up their opinions with cash. The main specific objections are as follows:

(a) Respondents may think that they can influence the course of real events by the shape of their answers, and bias them accordingly - *strategic bias*. There are also various kinds of *design bias* in CV. The way in which information about the problem is put across can be a powerful effect on the answers obtained, for instance by revealing the researcher's bias, or by stressing information known to elicit a certain kind of reaction (see Samples, Dixon and Gowen, 1986 for a discussion of this problem in the context of endangered wildlife). '*Instrument bias*' can also arise where respondents react strongly against any of the hypothetical methods of payment included in the surveys. Another possible distortion ('*starting point bias*') comes from the researcher suggesting starting bids for WTP or WTA which skew the possible range of answers.

(b) There is a large asymmetry between WTP and WTA, for which economic theory does not prepare us. The results of CV studies invariably show WTP to be several *times* (typically, one-third to one-fifth) lower than the WTA amount. In principle, WTP applies to valuing a benefit, while WTA relates to the imposition of a cost. One plausible explanation is that people value more highly the loss of something they already own, compared with the gain of something they do not yet have (Pearce and Markandya, 1989), the implication being that, even in the hypothetical world of CV, there is no unique popular valuation of environmental quality, and the elicited values depend on whether the changes are presented as gains or losses. (And what of avoided losses?).

(c) Grossing-up from the sample survey to the total relevant population is tricky in the case of non-user values such as option or existence values. In the Grand Canyon example (section 4.6), the values from the sample were applied, successively, to all existing 'users' (visitors), to all residents of the Southwestern states, and to the whole of the United States. But why not to Canada, or to all potential international visitors? The correct definition of the appropriate population, to include existing non-users, the unborn, or all potential future users, is vital to the level of total values, and their credibility, but is inherently an open-ended problem.

There is an 'adding-up' problem of a different sort where populations are used (or invoked) for a succession of different WTP questions without reference to each other. Since actual cash payments are not entailed there is no real constraint on the values that people can bid across a range of environmental issues. Yet obviously their actual budgets would be constrained when it came to contributing to various causes. This problem could be addressed by designing surveys incorporating such constraints. Otherwise, the studies will lose credibility, especially where they involve estimates of international WTP for existence values.

Applicability to developing countries. It may be significant that there have been very few examples of CV of environmental issues in developing countries. Apart from the obvious data gathering and processing requirements, CV depends on the respondent accurately perceiving the environmental change at issue, understanding its likely impact on him/herself, and the declared WTP and WTA being realistic in the light of actual incomes. Information about the environment is very uneven in all countries, and in those in the grip of strong vested interests or undemocratic regimes the flow of information about what is going on may be very selective. It was only in 1988, when floods washed felled trees down to wreck settlements, that Thailand's 'green' movement helped to bring about the ban on logging.

Few poor countries, and no undemocratic ones, have any tradition of market surveys amongst consumers. Researchers would have major hurdles of distrust to overcome, or the opposite problem of politeness - the urge to give the desired answer. The uneven distribution of incomes, and the prevalence of much absolute poverty, makes it vital to distinguish the relative scales of values held by different groups, and to gross up from samples to the larger population with great care.

Market research on WTP undoubtedly has a place in planning local environmental improvements, such as water supplies, garbage removal, sewerage, cleaning up heavily polluted rivers or waste dumps, etc. Respondents can understand the impact of such issues on their own lives, and may even have the evidence of improvements elsewhere. Given the more pressing concerns of poorer citizens, it is less likely that they would give serious answers to questions about biodiversity or the preservation of rare species. Existence values for threatened environments may be stronger from abroad than locally, but such values may also be less reliable.

3.3.7. Conclusion: the relative usefulness of different valuation methods

The amount of space devoted to the respective methods in the environmental economics literature is sharply at odds with the extent to which they have actually been used in developing countries (this point is illustrated in Chapter 4). The EOP and PE/RC methods have received relatively little attention in standard texts, presumably because they do not entail novel methodological interest. On the other hand, they are used in the bulk of empirical case studies in the developing world.

At the other extreme, CV, HM, HC and TCM methods receive much more space in methodological writing, partly because of their greater sophistication, and also because they are *potentially* useful in tackling some of the more elusive environmental effects. In any event, this state of affairs reveals a bias due partly to the professional interests of the main exponents, and partly to the types of problems encountered in their host communities.

With the environmental situation of developing countries in mind, the applicability of the various methods can be summarised as follows (where 'applicability' includes relevance to typical effects, need for data, ease of execution by personnel likely to be involved, and intelligibility and plausibility to people taking the decisions):

Effect on Production (EOP): Useful in many situations of environmental degradation where there are actual effects on output, and actual markets for the goods concerned or their close substitutes. Applicable. to soil erosion, deforestation, desertification, loss of wetlands and other natural systems, and for the production effects of air and water pollution. The basis of the majority of appraisals of conservation. Relatively easy to carry out, and intelligible and plausible.

Preventive Expenditure (PE) and Replacement Cost (RC): Widely usable wherever the parties responsible for environmental damage or their victims perceive the costs of that damage, and take steps to prevent or mitigate it or to restore the *status quo ante*. Information can be obtained either by direct observation, or by objective opinion, e.g. consultants' reports. Potentially applicable in many if not most projects with environmental effects, either on their own or in conjunction with other methods. Where data are good, EOP, PE and RC can be used together to determine whether to prevent damage, to allow it, or to allow it and then repair it. Intelligible and plausible.

Human Capital (HC): In its simpler 'loss-of-earnings' variant, HC is the most straightforward way of valuing the economic aspects of damage to human health. The resource costs of medical care can be added in to obtain a more complete account of social costs. Useful for air and water pollution, and health effects of new reservoirs, irrigation systems, etc. Depends on reliable data about the likely health effects (still rather shaky in respect of air pollution), and on assumptions about the local labour market. Can be used to justify particular levels of preventive or curative health care, or modifications to project design. Intelligible and plausible.

Hedonic methods (HM): HM has limited applicability, especially in developing countries. It requires an extensive data set, and the ability to manipulate it in quite sophisticated ways, and rests on assumptions about the way property and labour markets work which do not hold in many situations. Not so clearly intelligible or plausible as EOP, PE/RC, and HC. Changes in local property values may, however, provide useful data on the benefits from local environmental changes (e.g. slum upgrading, provision of piped water, resiting a sewage works).

Travel Cost Method (TCM): TCM is applicable to changes in amenity in developing countries affecting visitors whose travel cost is significant and meaningful, therefore relatively uncommon except for commercial tourism. Relevance to urban amenity is especially dubious. Data collection and manipulation likely to be onerous. Intelligible, but not often plausible.

Contingent Valuation (CV). CV is a perfectly intelligible type of market research, but because the 'product' being investigated is hypothetical, its value depends on the respondents having a good understanding of the issue, some imagination, and the ability to relate the questions to personal circumstances. The way the survey is conducted can bias the findings. There are also difficulties in 'grossing-up' its results, especially determining the appropriate total population concerned. In practice, most useful for valuing changes in amenity, air and water quality, wildlife and biodiversity amongst a well-informed and concerned population.

3.4. Methodological problems and issues

The use of CBA in environmental appraisals has given rise to a number of concerns and criticisms, some of them old problems in new guise. In this section some of them are outlined and an attempt made to give practical guidance on how they might be handled. A number reflect deep-rooted controversies, and it would be idle to pretend that they can be resolved here.

3.4.1. Distribution of costs and benefits

Using actual markets as the basis for valuing the environment, which most of the methods in section 3.3 do in varying degrees, would only give a value reflecting the actual distribution of income and assets in a society. Where that distribution is highly uneven, as in most developing countries, the valuations resulting from the recommended techniques would be biased by the (actual or implicit) market power of the richer elements of those societies. This factor would carry weight in balancing environmental costs/gains accruing to different income groups, or between countries at different levels of affluence. For instance, a proposal to convert a wetland for middle-class housing or office development would entail balancing the existing value of the resource to relatively poor local groups - however the market was simulated - against the market values of the land as affected by commercial interests and the middle classes. Deciding on a tropical timber concession would involve comparing the worth of the timber to affluent overseas furniture buyers, as against the local value of the conserved resource, which would have to reflect the low effective demand of poor local people.

Such dilemmas are unavoidable if the market is to be used to set environmental values, and would apply to normal CBA or any other technique that was based on real prices, costs and incomes. Whatever the injustices in the world in which he/she operates, the project appraiser has little power to change it. The justification for using the market in environmental appraisals is that this would improve decision-making by exposing the real costs and gains from certain courses of action which had previously been carried out in a false belief that the environment was a free good. Poorer groups will often gain from this process.

For appraisal purposes:

the gainers and losers from an action should be identified (see below);

the balance between different socio-economic groups should be clearly indicated;

Market distortions which might bias the decision (e.g. monopoly elements, artificially high or low prices) should be highlighted and, if possible, corrected for;

as part of the policy prescriptions and conditions, actions which encourage sustainable resource use should be promoted (this would normally cater for the interests of local environmental users).

According to the Pareto criterion, an action which makes some people better off should not leave others worse off. Since its literal application would exclude most conceivable activities, which normally create losers as well as gainers, the principle has been reformulated in terms of *potential* welfare, and the *potential* ability of gainers fully to compensate losers. On this criterion, an activity should proceed if it generates benefits for the gainers which are more than enough to compensate those who will lose. This is the principle on which CBA works (Mishan, 1971, p. 316).

One of the standard objections to the notion of 'potential Pareto improvement' is that it is consistent with a lot of people being made actually worse off..Where there is no requirement for the gainers to compensate the losers, inequalities of income are very likely to widen, and many people could actually suffer. This objection has even stronger force when applied to the present as compared with the future generation. The pursuit of present wealth, if it destroys the environment, will be at the expense of the future population, and the present generation may have neither the desire nor the means fully to compensate the future victims.

One solution to the dilemma is to require gainers *actually* to compensate losers fully (Mishan, 1971). This principle is easier to grasp in dealing with transfers at a given moment of time than in dealing with problems of inter-generational equity. But, in principle, gainers in the present generation should *actually* compensate society in the future for any predicted losses, provided a sensible means of compensation can be found. It would not be feasible to expect actual compensation in every case. The losers may be numerous, ill-defined, or more affluent than the gainers. The gainers may likewise be diffuse, hard to predict with precision, illiquid, insolvent, or particularly deserving cases. At an international level, different factors will come into play (e.g. political power, the ability to offset this cause against some other bargaining point).

However, the general principle of 'internalising' environmental damage should be carried through where possible, to bring home the environmental costs (or benefits) of their actions to the parties responsible for them, thus correcting for them 'at source'. This can happen at a notional level, for the purpose of appraisal, or in practice, where prices, taxes or subsidies are adjusted. One way of achieving internalisation is for the gainers actually to compensate the losers. Compensation might be considered where: gainers and losers can be clearly identified; the extent of their gains and losses can be roughly and unambiguously estimated; losers have clear rights which are being infringed; gainers are able to pay; and there is popular support for the principle of compensation.

3.4.2 Discounting

The case for discounting costs and benefits in CBA is clear. Other things being equal, future costs and benefits should weigh less in the decision than those occurring nearer the present time. The capital tied up in a project has potential value in other uses. This forms the 'opportunity cost' of using it for the project in hand rather than for something else. The opportunity cost increases the longer the gestation period of the project. The principle that 'time is money' is an important ingredient in rational decision-making.

The other main strand of the argument in favour of discounting is the notion of time preference. People prefer to have present rather than future satisfaction, unless they receive compensation (e.g. interest). Governments are in a position to take a longer view than individuals, but even they will tend to prefer present values over future ones, even if uncertainty and inflation are left out of account. In other words, the rate of social time preference will be positive. The case for discounting is the mirror-image of the rationale for interest payments.

It has been argued that 'environmental' projects should be subject to a lower discount rate than others (e.g. Foy and Daly, 1989, Repetto and Pezzey, 1990). Lowering the discount rate or dropping it altogether would, however, allow bad projects to proceed, as well as those with long-term environmental benefits. It would favour capital-intensive schemes with long pay-back periods - not, in general, a wise course for countries short of capital and preoccupied with the relief of current poverty. Lowering discount rates would also allow more projects to proceed, assuming sufficient capital would be forthcoming.Unless investment capital could be rationed (not a realistic course in most circumstances) this could lead to the greater use of natural resources and more pressure on the environment.

Manipulating discount rates is in any case a very blunt instrument for picking environmentally sound projects. It would even favour some projects with adverse environmental effects (e.g. hydroelectric power compared with some of the cleaner thermal options, such as gas-fired combined cycle stations). It is worth recalling that US environmentalists used to advocate *high* discount rates for the appraisal of public water and power schemes on the grounds that this would discourage schemes with such major environmental impacts.

One justification advanced for the use of low discount rates for conservation projects is that the value of increasingly scarce natural resources (e.g. biodiversity, wildernesses, etc.) should be assumed to increase over time. Thus any discount applied to the benefits of preserving them would be reduced by the rate at which their values increase - the net effect being the same as the use of a lower discount rate. This approach conflates two issues which would be better considered separately, namely the level of the discount rate and the future value of scarce natural resources. The method has been applied to the value of preserving a wilderness in Tasmania (the Krutilla-Fisher approach, as summarised by Markandya and Pearce, 1988). This may be a reasonable view to take of future prices where there are actual markets for increasingly scarce resources (e.g. tropical hardwoods, nuclear and toxic waste disposal sites). It becomes very arbitrary for non-marketed environmental resources. It would be difficult to justify choosing any specific rate of growth in their value. However, the essential point of the method, to draw attention to the growing scarcity of certain natural resources, is an important one.

For discounting to fulfil its purpose efficiently, the same rate must be applied to all projects considered (ODA, 1988). It is undesirable, and impractical, to create separate criteria for 'environmental' as opposed to all other projects. Nor would it be possible to create a watertight boundary between them. It might even entail applying different discount rates to different effects within the same project (e.g. a loss of income from soil erosion being treated differently from a loss of income due to post-harvest losses). In their private decisions individuals will continue to use market-related interest and discount rates. The use of public discount rates below these would create distortions in capital markets.

Although there is a sound case for retaining conventional discount rates in appraising all projects, including those with major environmental aspects, certain consequences of discounting apply with greater force in the context of environmental appraisal, and may need to be explicitly addressed. Projects such as conservation programmes with a long-term pay-off would find it difficult to compete head-on for funds with projects offering a more immediate return. Their long-term benefits would be more heavily discounted compared with those arising at an earlier date. At a discount rate of 10% benefits are reduced to below 10% of their nominal value by year 25, and to less than 1% by year 50.

The discount rate will also affect the use of both finite and renewable resources. In the case of finite resources such as minerals and oil, high discount rates will tend to increase their rate of depletion in the earlier years and lead to their exhaustion within a shorter period. With renewable resources such as forests and fisheries, the discount rate affects the optimal rate of harvesting. If the rate were to exceed the maximum biological growth rate of the stock, the short-term exhaustion of the stock would be preferred over its 'sustainable yield' harvesting, and the stock could disappear. In practice, in a well functioning market the value of finite resources would rise as they became scarcer.

By the same token, environmental costs arising in the distant future, even if they are grave or potentially disastrous, are reduced to insignificance by discounting. The future effects of deforestation, the risk of catastrophic floods, the extinction of important commercial species, etc. would lose much of their nominal weight in the CBA calculus by the time they were discounted. These are serious problems, but should be tackled explicitly by the following process to be outlined below, rather than by using nil or low discount rates for environmental costs and benefits. In a nutshell:

(a) Environmental costs and benefits of all projects should be identified, valued so far as possible, and appraised using the normal discount rate. In some cases, the real values of finite natural resources can be assumed to increase over time.

(b) Environmental effects that are considered important or critical should be highlighted for the decision-maker's attention. If the NPV is negative at the normal discount rate the size of the shortfall should be indicated, and set against the environmental benefits claimed. Conversely, environmental costs that are too distant to influence the NPV, or which cannot be satisfactorily valued, should also be underlined, to be set against the NPV.

(c) The rate of increase in the value of the natural resource needed to show a positive NPV (its 'switching value') can be identified.

(d) Natural resource projects should, in addition, be subject to the *sustainability criterion*.

Earlier in this section it was noted that discounting encourages the exploitation of both finite and renewable natural resources. For finite resources, the precept of sustainable development requires that sales should be converted into assets yielding a permanent income stream (El Serafy, 1989). The rate of exploitation should also ideally be governed by the prospects for developing substitutes or recycling techniques, though it is difficult to turn this into an operational rule in particular cases.

For natural renewable resources, the recommended approach has been stated as:
   . . . resource using projects should use only the sustainable yield, or should

include as a cost in the project the regeneration of any stock that is otherwise permanently removed. (Markandya and Pearce, 1988, p. 52)

Much work remains to be done in converting this principle into operational guidelines. Translating the concept of sustainable yield into practice in forestry, fisheries, or rangeland projects, for example, is by no means straightforward (see Chapter 4).

The regeneration of renewable resources can in certain circumstances be accomplished via compensatory projects, e.g. replanting forest, something that can happen either within projects or by rebalancing the whole national investment portfolio. The latter would then include environmental improvement projects to compensate for others where it is not feasible literally to apply the sustainability criterion, and which should be subject to different selection criteria. The treatment of one kind of compensatory project - conservation schemes - is dealt with in section 5.2.5.

3.4.3. Future generations

Future generations can obviously have no say in decisions made now, and their interests depend on how the present generation interprets and defends them. The use of any discount rate implies that future costs and benefits are given less weight than those occurring in the present, and the higher the rate the greater the discrimination against the unborn. Keynes was speaking for his contemporaries when he said that 'in the long run we are all dead'.

The view implicit in conventional CBA is that future generations are provided for by maximising the productivity of present investments so as to bequeath them the largest possible stock of economic and financial wealth. However, this attitude will not safeguard the future if it is accompanied by the loss of vital natural capital which cannot be replaced or substituted. The ruination of Banaba's natural landscape by phosphate mining, and the conversion of its mineral wealth into financial capital held on behalf of its former inhabitants, is a viable development option on a small scale, but not for the whole world!

The myopia of the present generation should not be exaggerated. People, both individually and collectively, do take decisions on projects whose benefits they do not expect to reap in their own lifetimes (planting gardens, and in historical times building cathedrals and other public monuments). Sometimes the motive is religious, sometimes the desire materially to benefit one's descendants. The pleasure obtained from doing this is the *bequest value*, which accrues at the time the sacrifice is made, and would not therefore be eroded by discounting. However, although bequest value helps to explain why people invest in projects with very distant yields, it is difficult to give it a precise value which would be of help in justifying a project by CBA.

The issue of justice to future generations is closely bound up with the use of high discount rates in CBA, discussed above in the previous section. In short, it is preferable explicitly to define the rights of future generations, and draw the necessary conclusions for project design, rather than try to accommodate them by adjusting discount rates, with all the complications that entails. What these 'rights' constitute is a difficult question, which is not the subject of this Guide (though they certainly include the survival of critical natural capital). In any event, some definition of these rights would be implicit in any attempt at justice for the future population, including zero discounting.

3.4.4 Irreversible effects

Deciding not to implement, or to delay, a project at least leaves open the opportunity to pursue it in future. A decision to proceed now, on the other hand, removes or reduces the scope for reversing the decision, or its consequences, at a future date. Some decisions are effectively irreversible, if they set in chain cumulative processes or permanently alter the state of nature.

This asymmetry is important in at least two cases. Where there is uncertainty about the future - including the effects of a project on the environment or public attitudes to it - there is a certain value in retaining the option of proceeding with it or not. A decision to proceed in the face of uncertainty leaves out of account the hidden cost represented by this option value. Delaying a decision gives time for new data and evidence to be assembled about the project's impact. The fact that future choices remain open gives such delay an option value. Unlike the situation in commodity and financial markets, options for public investment decisions do not have an objective money value. But postponement is justified where there is some likelihood of more relevant information about a project coming to light.

Secondly, implementing a project may forfeit alternatives which are likely to increase in value. Certain environmental resources fall into this category:

> Unique natural environments are in many cases likely to appreciate in value relative to goods and services they might yield if developed. (Fisher, 1981, p. 133)

In such cases, an irreversible decision carries a cost which increases over time. Irreversibility arises in practice in cases such as flooding a valley to create a hydroelectric scheme, destroying the habitat of a rare species, draining an original wetland, using geothermal energy for power generation, mining in high mountain or arctic areas, etc. As Fisher (1981) points out, the scenic aspects of an opencast mine in an attractive area may be even more exhaustible than the mineral itself, which at least can be replaced from mineral reserves elsewhere.

If a project is likely to set in motion major irreversible processes, serious thought should be given as to whether it should proceed at all. One approach is to measure the cost of not proceeding, in terms of the benefits that would be forgone from abstaining from the proposed development and how large present use values would need to be to offset them. This is the essence of the method used by Krutilla and Fisher (1975) and Fisher (1981). In the Hells Canyon project (Fisher, 1981) it was proposed to dam an extremely scenic river gorge to generate hydroelectricity. The conventional benefits of the scheme were the value of power produced and flood control. But it was argued that the benefits, measured in relation to the alternatives of thermal generation, would diminish over time as technical advances reduced the cost of thermal generation. On the other hand, recreational benefits from the river would tend to increase. Taking this dynamic perspective meant that the current recreational benefits from Hells Canyon needed to justify sacrificing the development benefits were actually quite small. A similar procedure was used for the Gordon River in Tasmania (see section 5.3.1.).

There is thus a good case for delaying projects with important irreversible effects on the environment, justified by the loss of option values. Where the project would irreversibly destroy unique or otherwise valuable natural areas the Krutilla-Fisher approach is a useful framework for quantifying the costs and benefits of not proceeding.

3.4.5. Uncertainty and risk

Decisions about all projects are made in ignorance about the future. Predicting their environmental effects adds an extra layer of uncertainty, arising from: ignorance about basic environmental processes and the long-term environmental effects of the project; uncertainty about the likely public attitude to those effects; and imprecise measures of environmental costs and benefits.

Uncertainty is different from risk. Within a range of possible outcomes, it may or may not be possible to attach a probability to each of them happening. Where it is possible to attach such probabilities, the issue is one of risk, where it is not, we are dealing with uncertainty. Risk has been described as 'measurable uncertainty'. In the context of project appraisal, a risky situation is more tractable than one with a high degree of uncertainty.

The typical CBA uses 'expected values' of costs and benefits (ODA, 1988). These are obtained by weighting their possible outcomes by the probability of each of them occurring - in other words they are dealing with a risky rather than an uncertain world. In a situation of genuine uncertainty there is a strong common-sense case for generating more relevant information before making decisions on projects. This may mean postponing the project and carrying out more specific research into its environment, and its possible impacts. Or it could point to introducing the project in pilot form, and studying its environmental effects in miniature. Unless there is some basis for believing that certain outcomes are more likely than others (i.e. unless some degree of risk can be established) there is little ground for taking a decision.

In many areas of environmental analysis, there is potentially a high pay-off to further research that helps overcome uncertainty. The expected value of having perfect information about a project's future environmental effects is known as *quasi-option* value (Johansson, 1990). Decision Analysis (see below) stresses 'value of information' analysis to guide the project analyst in setting research budgets.

Assuming that uncertainty can be converted into risk, sensitivity analysis can be employed to test the robustness of the base case, or central values, to changes in important variables. The 'switching value' of key variables can be estimated to show how large changes in them would need to be in order to reduce the NPV to zero. In practice, sensitivity tests are usually much too conservative - taking changes of only 10-20% of key variables. In the environmental arena, much larger ranges are called for. In addition, most sensitivity analysis fails to indicate the probability of these changes happening, or how acceptable they would be (Brent, 1990).

Where projects entail major environmental risks, and where the worst outcomes would be a matter of serious concern, the analyst should consider supplementing routine appraisal procedures (described in ODA, 1988, Chapter 6) with techniques that put greater stress on risk, and ways of handling it. A more extensive and imaginative use of sensitivity analysis is recommended (Brent, 1990). The use of 'Certainty Equivalents' (CEs) may also be appropriate.

The CE is the amount that would be just as acceptable as uncertain benefits or costs. For risk-averse decision-takers, the CE would be higher than the expected value for costs, and lower for benefits. Translating the CE into actual values suitable for CBA would be an arbitrary process unless it were based on carefully researched and consistent views on the part of individuals or public decision-makers (e.g. by using WTP/WTA surveys, or expressed preferences).

If decision-makers cannot easily contemplate the 'worst outcome' they may wish to include a 'secondary project' within the preferred scheme (Brent, 1990). These are projects specifically aimed at reducing risk, e.g. strengthening the body of guards on nature reserves, or boosting pollution inspectors. In principle this is a similar device to the compensatory project, and its cost should be debited to that of the main scheme.

Three other techniques are also of interest - risk-benefit analysis, acceptable risk analysis, and decision analysis.

Risk-benefit analysis (RBA) is a way of focusing on the prevention of events carrying serious risks. It can be viewed as the inversion of normal CBA, because it starts by presuming no action. The *cost* of inaction is the likelihood of the risk occurring (e.g. a serious rail accident, an explosion at a chemical works). On the other hand, the *benefit* of inaction is the saving in the cost of preventive measures. If the costs are less than the benefits, no action is justified, and vice-versa. For projects where risk is the paramount consideration RBA is a useful way of bringing out the issues. It does assume that costs (risks) can be fully captured in money values, which is not always the case. Moreover, the use of expected values is unlikely to give due weight to a catastrophic event with only a small probability (Pearce and Markandya, 1989).

Acceptable risk analysis (ARA). The conventional treatment of risk in CBA, taking expected values and subjecting the result to sensitivity analysis, assumes: i) that the various possible outcomes can be defined and specified; and ii) that the economic effects - costs and benefits - of each possible outcome can be attributed and measured. These conditions do not hold for many so-called 'environmental' risks. Many of them are shrouded in uncertainty - about their likelihood, scale and nature - even before admitting difficulties in placing economic values on them. Scientific understanding of important basic phenomena is imperfect, controversial, or subject to 'perception bias' (Brown, 1989).

ARA tries to answer the question, 'How safe is "safe enough"?' (Fischhoff *et al.*, 1981). It takes an eclectic approach, avoiding exclusive reliance on formal methods. Its hallmarks are the following:

(a) There is no definitive method of selecting the most acceptable option. In deciding what constitutes acceptable risk, formal methods (like CBA) need to be complemented by professional opinion, and the lessons of past experience.

(b) There are no value-free methods for choosing the most acceptable option. All parties should try and perceive the value assumptions within their views: 'for most new and intricate hazards even so-called objective risks have a large judgemental component.' (Fischhoff *et al.*, 1981)

(c) The expertise necessary for these decisions is scattered throughout society. Expert opinion should be combined with that of people in all walks of life, including the lay public.

The need for eclecticism, plurality, participation and open-mindedness in dealing with acceptable risk is hard to dispute, but it complicates the task of analysis! It implies, amongst other things: seeking advice on risk from a number of sources, including interested members of the community; becoming aware of where the risks would fall and who would bear the costs of avoiding them; erring on the side of safety, e.g. by including large safety margins, delaying decisions pending more information, insisting on safe minimum standards of environmental use, etc.; treating methods of 'objective' risk estimation (e.g. expected values) with appropriate professional reserve; making maximum use of sensitivity analysis to identify important risks; and introducing flexibility in design, while retaining future options.

Decision analysis (DA) eschews the assumption of risk-neutrality implicit in CBA, and analyses the effect of risk-averseness in decision-makers. As Pearce and Markandya (1989, p. 20) put it, 'It is to decision theory that we owe the idea of transforming the problem into one of 'expected utilities' rather than expected values.'

The main steps in DA are the following (Covello, 1987):

i) Structuring the problem. This includes defining the objectives, identifying alternatives, setting performance measures, identifying critical uncertain variables.

ii) Assessing probabilities, through discussion with specialists, supplemented by the beliefs of non-specialists and decision-takers. Probabilities are treated as statements of belief rather than of objective fact (Fischhoff *et al.*, 1981, p.106).

iii) Drawing up and assessing preferences, judgements and trade-offs, the purpose being to obtain the weights that decision-makers would attach to outcomes differing according to their level of risk. The risk-averse decision-maker would prefer an option which avoided the risk of a particularly bad outcome, to one which offered the chance of greater gain as well as greater loss. In theory, a utility function is drawn up, relating the decision-maker's utility from different outcomes. The revealed preferences may be incorporated into formal decision rules, e.g. MiniMax (minimise the maximum possible loss).

iv) Evaluating alternatives. The expected utility of each possible alternative is obtained by multiplying the probability of its occurrence by its utility. The chosen alternative is that with the highest expected utility.

v) Sensitivity and value-of-information (VOI) analysis. Sensitivity analysis would indicate those variables for which it would be valuable to seek greater information. This would help to set a budget for research, pilot studies, etc. Conceptually, researchers assume a clairvoyant, and estimate how much the decision-maker should be willing to pay for the clairvoyant's services.

DA can be incorporated into CBA at the point where data have been assembled and decision rules are being considered. It would call for a more thorough and explicit analysis of possible outcomes and decision-makers' preferences than is usual in traditional CBA, but this would greatly add to the credibility of CBA where there are significant environmental risks.

3.4.6. Unmeasurable items

Even after the most careful application of techniques such as those outlined in section 3.3, certain effects will elude measurement and valuation. Some of these are measurable in principle, but the state of science does not yet allow them to be quantified (e.g. many potential effects of pollution on health and materials corrosion). Others are inherently non-quantifiable (e.g. much biodiversity, the preservation of obscure rare species, keeping Antarctica inviolate, etc.). Yet others can be captured in money values only up to a point (e.g. the psychic cost of human illness, human life, the value of antiquities, beautiful landscapes, etc.).

It follows that appraisals of environmental effects will inevitably omit a great deal from their attempt to value costs and benefits. Narrowing down the range of non-quantifiable effects to an irreducible core performs a service for the decision-maker, provided it is done carefully, and its assumptions and limitations spelled out. Careful measurement will set the bounds of the area left for 'pure' judgement, intuition, prejudice, or politics, even though these will always be important.

3.5. Conclusions on methodology

A number of the methodological problems raised above are complex and cannot definitively be resolved. The approaches recommended here should not be seen as solutions. They are, rather, defensible and practical steps to take, which avoid some of the pitfalls, pending further theoretical (and philosophical) discussion. Certain practices recommended here are expedients. If all environmental assets and effects were able to be captured in economic values we could have much more confidence in CBA, without the various safety-nets discussed above. The fact that in the present and foreseeable state of the art large areas of the environment cannot be valued (a point underlined by Chapters 4 and 5) means that expedients and safety-nets will continue to be necessary in CBA, unsatisfactory as they may seem to the theorists.

4

Economic Valuation in Practice

This Chapter reviews how far economic valuation can in practice be taken, examining a dozen of the major environmental problems identified in Chapter 2 and illustrating the discussion with summaries of actual case studies of problems likely to be encountered in the appraisal of projects in developing countries.

4.1. Soil erosion, siltation and deposition

The processes described in Chapter 2 section 2.2 can, up to a point, be measured and predicted. The relationships established between, say, soil erosion and the arrival of silt at a certain point downstream, or between erosion and reduced crop yield, provide data which economists can then attempt to value. This section therefore reviews first of all some of the problems and possibilities in providing the physical data which are a necessary input to valuation exercises.

Soil erosion. The best known predictor of surface erosion is the Universal Soil Loss Equation, applicable to agricultural land with slopes of less than 50 degrees. In its basic form, the USLE makes soil loss a function of rainfall erosiveness, soil erodibility, topography and vegetation management (erosion control). A modified USLE has been developed to cater for non-agricultural land with a variety of vegetation on steeper slopes. The collection of the necessary data for the USLE from local farmers is a manageable undertaking, and the Equation provides useful results for a range of typical conditions. The Soil Loss Estimator for Southern Africa is a more refined attempt to develop an erosion predictor for that region (Elwell and Stocking, 1982).

Different types of vegetation can produce startling differences in soil loss rates. Measurements carried out on slopes in Thailand demonstrate average annual loss of up to 10 tonnes per square kilometer under natural forest or flat paddy, over 1000 tonnes for mixed forest, rubber plantations, orchards and paddy, and over 100,000 tonnes for mixed field crops, forest, and unstable shifting cultivation (O'Loughlin, 1985). It should be stressed that these results would not necessarily be valid in a different context. In the Philippines the corresponding soil erosiveness of various kinds of biomass cover is as follows (taking primary forest with dense undergrowth as 100): secondary growth forest with good undergrowth and high mulch 300; degraded secondary growth forest with shrubs and plantation crops 600; industrial tree plantations, up to 6,000. In absolute terms, whereas undisturbed forest may only lose 1 t/ha/year, cultivation of plots in conditions of high intensity rainfall, steep slopes, erodible soil and poor cover can lead to losses of 300-400 t/ha/year (World Bank, 1989).

Erosion-crop yield relationships. It is a large and hazardous step to proceed from physical soil loss to predictions of fertility and productivity. All that is available are experimental results valid for particular situations, of greater or lesser interest elsewhere. Reliable general formulas are not available (though the Soil Changes Under Agro-forestry model is a promising prototype for predicting effects on economic biomass, discussed in Stocking, Bojo and Abel, 1989). The USLE has been criticised for ignoring the quality of soil left behind (in which case its value would be principally for predicting sedimentation).

Some level of 'soil loss' ('T-value') has little significant effect on productivity, depending on the initial status of the soil, organic matter content, parent material, climate, available soil water etc. Suggested 'permissible' levels of soil loss (in tons per ha., annually) fall in the range 2 to 15, depending on initial depth, type of soil, and type of cultivation (quoted in FAO, 1987). However, it is not clear how long these annual losses could continue without eventually undermining productivity, and even the levels quoted would be of concern to downstream areas affected by sedimentation.

The relationship between loss of soil and crop yield has been extensively plotted in the United States and to a lesser extent in other temperate countries. For maize, the decline in yield (kg. per ha., for each cm. of soil loss) ranges from 30 to 268; for wheat from 21 to 54 (Stocking, 1984). The relationship depends heavily on the type of soil, its initial depth, slope, crop, and on temperate or tropical location. Erosion appears to have a greater effect on absolute yields in tropical conditions, starting from a lower average base (Stocking, 1984). Soil loss can be very rapid in marginal areas, and after a while soil depth diminishes to a point at which crop growth is not viable, and the land goes out of production.

Trials have been carried out to estimate the amount of fertiliser required to restore the productivity. For a particular kind of soil in Hawaii, for instance, a loss of 35cm. was associated with a yield of maize stover of only 25% of that on uneroded plots. Restoring the yield required fertiliser applications of 220 kg/ha.of N, 450 of P, and 250 of K (quoted·in FAO, 1987).

One of the best data bases on the erosion/fertility relationship was assembled in Rhodesia from 1953 to 1964. This showed that erosion led to a heavy and selective loss of key nutrients, which caused a noticeable decline in fertility, unless re-medied by applications of commercial fertiliser. This was an incomplete restorat-ive, however, since eroded soil tends to have an inferior structure and is acidified, and therefore less efficient than before in supplying nutrients to plants. For il-lustrative purposes, however, assuming that inorganic fertilisers could replace nutrients lost through erosion, commercial arable farms were losing c. $US20 per hectare (in 1985 prices) in nitrogen and phosphorus, communal arable areas $50, and communal rangelands $80 (the latter figure excluding organic matter) (Stock-ing, 1986). These data would be useful parameters in setting up the 'without project case' for soil conservation projects in comparable parts of Southern Africa.

Suggestive as these results may be, the most reliable method of predicting the effects on soil productivity from a given soil loss is likely to be from a comparison of observations taken from eroded and uneroded land in the same watershed. Both gully erosion and mass soil movements are capable of being measured by aerial photography coupled with field surveys. Such data can indicate what pro-portions the afflicted areas are of various categories of land use, and thence the amount of total product of the watershed that is at risk. Once land has been subject to gully erosion, a high proportion, if not all, of its productivity can be presumed lost. In the case of unstable slopes subject to mass soil movements, restoration of fertility - even for pasture - can take years of careful nurturing and fertilisation (quoted in FAO, 1987).

Water yield. Conventional wisdom is that the yield of water from a watershed will increase with clearing or thinning of forests, a conversion from deep- to shallow-rooted species, or a change in vegetation cover from species with high to those with low interception capacities. Local soils and climatic conditions will also have an effect. Experiments have shown that a given (10%) reduction in the following kinds of vegetation cover could produce the following increases in annual water yield (in mm.): conifer and eucalypt forest 40 (range 20-65); deciduous hardwood 25 (range 6-40); and shrub 10 (range 1-20) (quoted in FAO, 1987). These results illustrate the potential effects on downstream water supply from such actions as afforestation. It should, however, be noted that most of them have been drawn up in temperate conditions, hence the need for due scientific caution in their wider application.

A more direct way of estimating water yield is to build up a water budget from data on rainfall, initial soil moisture, and evapotranspiration. Run-off is derived as a residual, when remaining available moisture exceeds water-holding capacity. Data requirements for this calculation are relatively modest.

An important complication in estimating water yield is that, in its passage from A to B, the water can be 'lost' in various ways. The scope for such losses increases in proportion to the distance travelled. Vegetation along stream courses can account for sizeable losses through transpiration, and water may also leak out. Where large water bodies (e.g. reservoirs) form part of the present or planned watershed system, evaporation should also be allowed for. The converse of increased water yield is, of course, greater liability to flooding (see section 2.2.1).

Sedimentation. Three quotations illustrate the problem of predicting sedimentation:

> The relationship between upland erosion (and erosion control practices) and downstream sedimentation is poorly understood . . . (FAO, 1987)

> . . . it is very difficult to predict upstream-downstream reactions in terms of altered runoff or sedimentation amounts or distributions. This is because the processes involved are extremely complex. Most of the computer models which exist for predicting catchment scale discharges or sediment yields rely on calibration of parameters for an existing situation. To reliably predict the impact of a proposed catchment management change is almost impossible. (White, 1989)

> The problems in interpreting the measurements and calculations for the Magat watershed [in the Philippines], which has been better studied than all but a few watersheds in developing countries, should give us pause in trying to extrapolate to wide areas. The link between upland erosion and downstream silt delivery is especially problematic: clearly in the short term the majority of the soil lost upstream does not reach the dam, much less the sea. Correspondingly, most of the silt reaching the dam today was lost from upstream sites long ago . . . (World Bank, 1989)

A pragmatic approach suggested by FAO (1987) consists of: estimating sedimentation rates from sediment surveys and models; identifying sources of sediment from particular processes and contributing areas; estimating delivery ratios to points of concern; modifying parts of Soil Loss Equations in the light of project practices; and applying the same delivery ratios or routing models to predict the 'with project' effects.

4.1.1. Valuation of benefits

Table 4.1. On-site and off-site benefits from watershed conservation

(i) On-site effects

Avoided losses in crop yields from soil erosion, loss of soil depth and fertility, or loss of land through gulley erosion; alternatively, savings in fertiliser to maintain yields on eroded soil;

Value of wood products from tree planting (timber, poles, fuelwood, forage, fruit, etc.);

Value of enhanced livestock products from rescued or improved pasture, or from fodder from trees (meat, milk, wool, dung)

Increased crop yields from 'ecological' benefits of a managed mixed regime (increased soil organic matter, more soil moisture retention, shading, etc)

(ii)Off-site

Irrigation benefits; value of crops preserved through reduction of sedimentation in reservoirs and channels; alternatively, reduced cost of maintaining and cleaning reservoirs, channels and works; output saved from preserving existing water regime;

Hydroelectric power benefits; by avoiding reservoir siltation, extending the life of a hydropower scheme, especially its ability to generate dry-season power; or avoiding cost of raising level of dam, with all that implies for extra inundation; or avoiding cost of alternative generating capacity; plus savings in repairs and cleaning of turbines and intake works;

Flood damage avoided; alternatively, savings in cost of flood prevention works, or reduced cost of roads and bridge maintenance;

Gains to fisheries; less silting and turbidity in reservoirs and rivers and more even year-round flows. Avoided damage to productivity of coastal waters and mangrove systems;

Navigation benefits from more predictable river channels; or reduced dredging costs, both in river system and in inshore coastal waters;

Benefits to domestic water quantity and quality; avoidance of need to resite intake works through river silting and changes in channels;

Tourism and recreation benefits preserved and enhanced.

Provided that the technical cause-and-effect relationships discussed above are sufficiently clear and robust, certain economic effects can be derived and valued in conventional ways. Some of these effects arise 'on-site', within the boundary of the project, or directly affecting the parties undertaking the activity in question. Others happen 'off-site', usually lower down the watershed, and do not directly impinge on parties responsible for the change. The latter are the true 'externalities'. Certain benefits accrue as direct products, others as environmental services.

The various kinds of benefit are illustrated in Table 4.1 and Figure 4.1.

Certain *costs* of conservation schemes should also be allowed for. These include the opportunity costs of the land taken out of crops or livestock, and in the case of badly threatened slopes, the loss of output until its fertility was restored. Benefits might also be forfeited from the diminished fertility of land lower down the watershed depending on regular inundation and siltation for its fertility, and in some circumstances reduced water supplies for abstraction by irrigation and domestic uses. There is also the possibility that increased agricultural activity on upper slopes may cause chemical fertiliser and pesticide pollution of land and water lower down. There are various available techniques for putting economic values on these effects in such contexts as: the economic costs of allowing watershed degradation to continue; comparison of the economic costs/benefits of alternative land-use regimes; the merits of a watershed conservation programme. EOP and PE appear to be the most relevant methods for economic valuation:

Effect on Production. The most straightforward application of EOP is to value the effect of erosion on the direct on-site products of the land at risk, or, alternatively, the direct products of conservation schemes (wood, fruit, etc.). The case studies in section 4.1.2 rely heavily on valuing these direct products.

Valuing off-site productivity effects is more problematic. The damage caused by siltation to estuarine and offshore fisheries is an example of an effect with tangible results on marketed output. In the Philippines deforested catchment areas have led to a large increase in the amount of silt deposited in estuaries, mangrove systems and coral reefs. The shellfish reared and caught in these waters provide an export income of $100 million p.a., a large part of which could disappear if the siltation continues (Myers, 1988a; Hodgson and Dixon, 1989). Another study of catchments in Palawan Island, Philippines, estimated that up to half the irrigated rice area would be placed at risk from erosion of the catchment, as a result of higher wet season and peak flows, and lower and less reliable base flows (Finney and Western, 1986. See also section 5.2).

If markets are absent, sparse or otherwise imperfect, alternative approaches to valuation are possible. For instance, in valuing gains to fuelwood from conservation measures in Nepal, the market values of wood in the principal town were supplemented by indirect measures, described in the Nepal case study in section 4.1.2.

Preventive Expenditure. In the context of watersheds, PE, necessary to avoid or mitigate damage, includes dredging for river navigation, creation of flood barriers, bunds, resiting water intake works, etc.

EOP and PE are alternative ways of valuing conservation benefits, though they can complement each other in the same appraisal. EOP can be used when the relevant effects can be predicted and valued with confidence, and when they

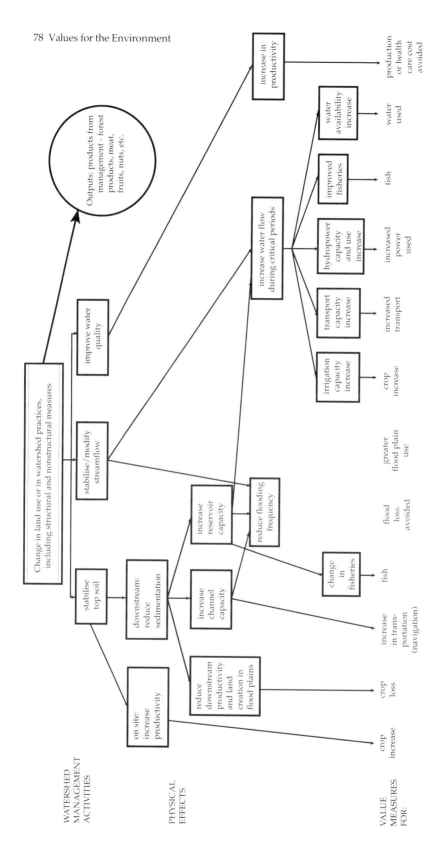

Figure 4.1   Examples of physical effects and measures of benefits from some watershed management practices as compared to conditions 'without' the practices. (FAO 1987)

would be less than the costs of preventive measures. On the other hand, where the effects on production are difficult to predict, but where they are likely to be of a size to justify preventive expenditure *and* there is a good likelihood that the latter would be carried out, it would be more reasonable to use PE.

The application of the two approaches can be illustrated from water supply, flooding, hydro-power and irrigation effects. For *water supply* improvements, the alternatives are to count the investment required to assure the amount of water involved (PE) or to value the increment of water at some economic rate (EOP). The benefits of more and better water for human health might also be tackled using the Human Capital approach, though in practice the health benefits might be difficult to specify with sufficient confidence.

Where a scheme avoided *flooding*, or reduced its frequency and severity, the benefit would be the gross value of crops that would be preserved, adjusted for the probability of flooding. Physical damage to fields, houses and infrastructure could be treated likewise. It should be noted that 'improved' watershed management, such as planting trees on bare slopes, may impose costs on downstream water users, where the trees cause greater local moisture retention (there is a well-known case of this happening in Fiji).

Silting from soil lost from slopes can drastically reduce the storage capacity of *reservoirs*, thus affecting the volume of water available for power generation, irrigation, and domestic supplies, and also limiting the ability to control flooding. The split of benefits/avoided costs between these various functions will depend on the purposes of the reservoir and how it is managed. In principle it is possible to allocate the reservoir's storage capacity to each of these purposes (Briones, 1986). In the tropics, the sedimentation rate for reservoirs linked to hydropower schemes averages 2% p.a., but exceeds this in cases of serious watershed erosion. There are a growing number of examples (quoted in Myers, 1988b) of major hydroelectric schemes whose power-generating lives will turn out to be a half or less of those planned. PE in the form of dredging the reservoir is not feasible in the common case where the dredging costs more than the economic value of the storage .

The benefit to *power* from avoiding siltation can thus be regarded as: i) prolonging the life of the scheme as an all-year round source of power (an extra number of years' power output); ii) the avoided cost of raising the height of the dam, and the associated saving of extra inundated land, plus the avoidance of other effects of dam construction (see section 5.2); or iii) the saved expense of investing in new generating capacity elsewhere, or the saving in fuel that would otherwise have been necessary to operate existing thermal capacity more fully.

The same factors affect *irrigation* water from the reservoir. Sedimentation will cause direct losses to irrigable crops, unless supplementary structures are built. The irrigation of the Indus Basin in Pakistan depends on water stored in the Tarbela and Mangla reservoirs, which only contain five days' supply between them (Pereira, 1989). Meanwhile, they are being gradually filled by sediment from the degraded and heavily-populated lower watersheds. The analysis of output losses will require an assumption about how the reduced amount of stored water would be apportioned between irrigation, power, and drinking uses.

In practice, the above benefits span most of the environmental effects of watershed management. Among those left out of account are effects on local micro-climate, wildlife, recreation and aesthetic pleasure. Most of the case studies (below) concentrate on one or two major effects where these are robust and capable of valuation, rather than attempting to span all the possible impacts. Bojo (1986) provides a more comprehensive discussion of the comparative methodologies of 18 studies of soil and water conservation projects. Other relevant cases appear in section 5.2.

4.1.2 Case studies

The following five case studies seek to quantify benefits from soil or watershed conservation (Nepal, Morocco, El Salvador), or estimate the losses from continuing degradation (Java, Mali). They are all weighted towards the direct on-site benefits of conservation. The other main effect considered is the reduced siltation of hydropower systems, irrigation schemes and harbours.

(i) Nepal: Phewa Tal Watershed Development (Fleming, Hufschmidt et al. in ADB, 1986)

The main interest of this study is that it justifies soil and water conservation measures with reference to their direct on-site products. The basic rationale of the project was to arrest the destruction of natural forest in the middle hills of Nepal by systematically managing hill forests to meet local needs for fuelwood and fodder. The programme was to be complementary with a separate programme to increase agricultural productivity. After consulting the villagers in various wards, the crucial change in land use was to make cattle stall-fed. Nurseries were set up to supply trees for planting on denuded upper slopes, and fodder grasses planted in eroded gullies. Both these sources provided fodder to cattle, and the women who formerly scoured the slopes for dung for applying to the terraces had the easier task of carrying grass from the gullies. The big increase in manure collected from the stalls permitted an extra winter crop of wheat (Pereira, 1989)

Method. The first step was to predict land use, with and without the project, up to the year 2022. For this purpose the areas under agriculture, pasture, scrub and forest with the project were assumed frozen at 1983 levels. In respect of farm land, this assumption relied on increased levels of productivity from the separate farm project.

The products of each of the major land uses were estimated and valued both with and without the project. The 'with project' case also included a new forest plantation element. The main products of grazing land were milk and fertiliser (dung) valued at market prices. The product of pasture was taken to be five times the yield from grazing land. Unmanaged scrubland and forest yielded milk (valued at local market prices), dung (valued at local prices for commercial fertiliser) and fuelwood. For fuelwood, alternative valuation measures were taken. The market values of wood in the principal town were supplemented by two indirect measures, first in terms of its closest substitute, animal dung, and secondly, of the savings in opportunity cost of the labour needed to collect it over a greater distance (Fleming 1983, and Hufschmidt et al, 1983, used in FAO, 1987, Annex 2).

Results. The expense of the project was justified by a comparison of the products with and without it projected to 2022. This showed an economic rate of return of 8.5%, a conservative estimate, since it took no account of benefits from reduced soil erosion, landslides and flooding.

(ii) Morocco: Loukkos Basin Watershed Management (Brooks *et al.*, 1982)

In this study the watershed management costs were justified mainly by the avoided losses in irrigated crops, and to a lesser extent by the value of the direct products of trees planted on the upper slopes. The scheme was for reforestation, pasture management, planting fruit trees, stabilisation of channels and building gulley control structures. This watershed in Northern Morocco drains into an important reservoir used for irrigation and power generation.

Method. Erosion with and without the project was compared using a modified USLE. Without the project, it was estimated that soil loss would amount to 90 tonnes/ha. annually, equivalent to 56 cu.m. A sediment delivery ratio of 39% was taken to indicate how much of this loss would be deposited as silt in the reservoir, and used to predict the rate at which the reservoir would silt up without the project. It was estimated that the 'dead storage' volume of the reservoir (the amount of water at the bottom not available for irrigation or power use) would be filled within five years, and after that the amount available for irrigation would be progressively reduced, with effects concentrated in the dry season. Compared with this scenario, the 'with project' case would have an effect after 5 years, as the physical structures and, later, the vegetation measures became effective. The average crop loss avoided was taken to be the gross irrigation benefit of the scheme. To this was added the direct on-site benefits of the project, consisting of the value of olives, figs and prunes yielded by the project trees, a small part of overall benefits.

Results. The internal rate of return of the whole project was 15.9% on the strength of the above-mentioned benefits. No account was taken of soil fertility benefits in the catchment, which might be approximated by valuing commercial fertiliser needed to replace lost nutrients, nor of the gains to livestock and wood users. Irrigation water was treated as the 'marginal' use of the reservoir's storage, with priority given to drinking water and power generation, hence the latter would not be immediately affected. In the long run, the project would also have power and municipal water benefits, which were not taken into account.

(iii) Java, Indonesia Economic losses from soil erosion (Repetto *et al.*, 1989, Magrath and Arens, 1989)

This was an attempt to draw up a 'soil account' for Java, for the purpose of adjusting Indonesia's national accounts to reflect the depreciation of its main natural asset, erodible farmland.

Method. The extent of physical soil erosion was estimated from soil maps, aerial photographs and topographical data. Five main soil/land-use types were then determined, namely: irrigated ricefields (*sawah*) with low erosion rates; dryland farming (*tegal*) mostly on slopes, with high erosion; natural and planted forest, perennial plantation crops, with slight erosion; degraded forest, including shifting cultivation and degraded home gardens (*pekarangan*) with moderate to high erosion; and wetlands, with low erosion. Actual erosion rates for each type were based on measurements from various aid projects and research schemes, supplemented by expert judgements based on erosion elsewhere under comparable conditions. Average results for the four main soil/land use types were (in metric tons of soil lost annually, per ha): *tegal* 139.5, forest land 6.0, degraded forest 88.3, and *sawah* 0.5.

The calculation of the economic cost of this erosion distinguished between two kinds of rain-fed food crops, those sensitive to soil fertility (maize, soyabeans, groundnuts, green beans and dryland rice) and cassava, which is less sensitive. Yield-erosion relationships were estimated for 25 soil types for each . The results were weighted according to the distribution of soil types and cropping patterns throughout the island.

Results. The results can be illustrated for *tegal* land, where erosion was most severe (it was estimated that soil loss of less than 15 tons/ha./year had negligible effects on yield). For the whole of Java, there was an average annual productivity loss of 6.8% for maize, and 4.3% for cassava. These notional losses have been masked by the continued growth in actual yields due to the intensification of production methods. Thus the results should be read as the estimated underlying decline in productivity, controlling for these other influences.

The final step in the exercise was to relate the productivity declines to farm incomes, worked out for a single year (1985) and capitalised to obtain the present value of future losses (US$484m.). The one-year costs of erosion were c. 4% of the annual value of crop output, about the same as annual recorded growth and the capitalised losses were c. 40% of the annual value of production.

All these data refer to *on-site* losses. In addition, three types of *off-site* effects were considered, the siltation of irrigation systems, siltation of harbours, and sedimentation in reservoirs.

The cost of siltation of irrigation systems was arrived at by estimating how much O & M expenditure was due to silt removal, and scaling this up to reflect a judgement about the minimum 'efficient' outlay to clear silt, estimated at an annual $3-5 per ha. It proved more difficult to estimate harbour siltation costs, because actual spending on dredging was known to be well below what was really needed. Moreover, upland soil erosion accounted for an unknown part of total harbour and channel siltation. Thus, a rough and arbitrary figure of $1.4-3.5 m. on a capitalised basis was arrived at, the precise amount being less important than its relativity to the other siltation and sedimentation costs.

Reservoir sedimentation was the largest quantified item of off-site costs. The study used the key concepts of sediment delivery, trap efficiency and dead storage to determine the extent to which upland erosion reduced the economic functions of reservoirs. The assumptions about dead storage were particularly sensitive for the result - e.g. if the exhaustion of dead storage meant that the

>utlets started to clog up this would hasten the end of the reservoir's economic
ife. It was estimated that the sedimentation of Indonesia's major reservoirs was
reducing output of hydropower and irrigation water by between 0.5% and 2.3%
annually, depending on assumptions about dead storage. Capitalised, these
osses amounted to $16-75m.

The three types of off-site costs of soil erosion considered here amounted to c.
$25-91m. on a capitalised basis, which compared with an estimate of $315 m. for its
on-site costs. The difficulties in measuring off-site effects were partly due to the
attempt to take an aggregate, economy-wide view. At the level of particular
catchments, projects and reservoirs, provided the data are available, somewhat
harder conclusions should be possible.

(iv) El Salvador: Acelhuate River Catchment Management Project (Wiggins and Palma, 1980):

This analysis estimated crop yield loss from soil erosion and benefits from avoiding losses in power generation due to silting of the reservoir. A mixture of catchment management practices such as hillside ditches, live barriers, contour
cultivation, bench terraces, mulching, etc. were appraised.

Method. Soil loss from sheet erosion was estimated, before and after conservation; an expert judgement was sought on likely erosion in a particular area, and
the result was generalised by using the USLE. US data were applied to justify the
assumption of crop yields declining by 2% for each cm. loss in soil. Apart from
preventing this loss in yield, conservation practices would increase soil moisture
and allow more effective use of fertiliser. These effects were considered to be
worth an initial 10% increase in yield. It was estimated that 75% of the eroded soil
would settle in the reservoir within two years, which would reduce its capacity for
power generation, affecting mainly dry-season production. A quarter of annual
power output could be lost in this way.

Results. In the overall CBA, the majority of benefits accrued to farmers. The
avoided loss of power represented a minor part of total benefits. Conservation
was demonstrated to be profitable in both private and CBA terms.

(v) Mali: the on-site cost of soil erosion (Bishop and Allen, 1989)

This study attempted to put a value on the top soil used up in agricultural production. In the absence of an open market for farm land, which would give explicit
values for degraded compared with undegraded land, the authors used physical
relationships to predict erosion and to estimate its effects on crop yields, before
working through farm budgets into money values.

Mali is an African state located in the arid and semi-arid Sahelian zone. Most of the
population depend on various forms of agriculture and livestock, and the signs of

ecological deterioration (reduced rainfall and river levels, loss of forest and pasture, reduced soil fertility and loss of plant and animal species) are potentially very serious.

Method. The basic assumption was that soil loss, in tons per ha, is a reliable predictor of changes in soil nutrient content, soil pH and moisture retention. These three variables accounted for almost all the annual variation in yields of maize and cowpeas. Information about the physical characteristics of land in Mali was obtained from a detailed atlas based on satellite images, containing data on soil, vegetation, rainfall, groundwater and land use on which detailed land categories were established to provide the essential information to the soil loss equations.

The USLE was employed to predict erosion. Most climatic and soil data collected in West Africa during recent decades were intended for use in the USLE and data available in Mali were easily adapted for this. The authors had reservations about the USLE in that it ignored deposition, was designed for small field plots, and that its validity for the tropics was still debatable. Deposition was handled by playing down soil loss on catchments known to receive significant alluvial deposits. The relation between erosion and crop yield was estimated using experimental data from Nigeria. Crop yields were, in turn, translated into farm incomes using farm budgets published by ICRISAT for comparable conditions in Burkina Faso. Farm income forgone from erosion was projected forward ten years and discounted at 10%. Results were grossed up for the whole of Mali.

Results. Soil loss on cultivated land was estimated to be an average of 6.5 t/ha/year for the whole study area, the highest loss being 30 t/ha/year in the southern zone where rainfall is high and the soil more erodible. The mean present value of farm income forgone over ten years as a result of one year of soil loss ranged from CFAF2,000-8,000 per ha (average net annual farm revenues, excluding rice, were c. CFAF9,700 per ha). The sacrifice of future revenues from erosion was 2-9% of current farm income.

These losses were compared with the costs of various kinds of simple water harvesting measures, such as the construction of bunds and ridges which conserve the soil and help conserve rainfall. The discounted total cost of these techniques was in the range CFAF40,000-100,000. The authors indicated where the present value of farm income forgone through erosion was greater than the cost of the cheapest conservation technique.

At a national level, annual discounted losses were estimated to be at least US$31 m. (4% of farm GDP).

This very systematic study used a technique (the USLE) for which local data can be used, and for which erosion-yield relationships and farm budget data were obtained in neighbouring countries. No account was taken of off-site or wider environmental effects (though some adjustment was made for the positive effects of deposition on certain fields). The scale of soil erosion losses is becoming significant to the national economy, and justifies some conservation investment in the worst-affected areas.

4.2. Loss of tropical rain forest

Economic valuation presumes accurate scientific evidence on cause and effect. Some important environmental effects of forests are as yet incapable of such scientific certainty, though their general direction is usually well established. This section will examine the possibility of valuing the various environmental effects of forests as outlined in section 2.3.

a) **Climatic and atmospheric regulation.** The potential effects of deforestation at the local and regional levels are controversial. The removal of forest cover is likely to have effects on the micro-climate, and the new land users may have to introduce measures to compensate, say, for greater local aridity, which would justify the use of the Replacement Cost approach (say, for fertiliser, shade, watering). But this effect cannot yet be predicted with enough assurance at the farm level, and research continues. At the regional level (e.g. the whole Amazon Basin) the climatic effects, and the costs of compensating for them, are too speculative to feature in analysis of individual projects.

Globally, the contribution of deforestation to greenhouse gas emissions is becoming better understood (see section 4.12 for a fuller discussion). In brief, we argue that it is impractical as yet to assign precise responsibility for global and regional climatic effects to particular projects or other specific actions. It is therefore not yet possible, for example, to give precise 'carbon credits' to standing tropical forests, equivalent to the amount of global warming damage that is avoided (Pearce, Furtado and Pearce, 1989).

b) **Watershed effects.** Following sections 2.2 and 4.1, the main watershed functions performed by forests will be taken as: conservation of soil and fertility; regulating downstream water flows; reducing flooding; and controlling sedimentation of downstream water courses, farming systems and coastal fisheries. The direct products of the forest, and its on-site benefits for land use, should also be reckoned in.

Where data are available, certain of these effects can be valued by the use of the Effect on Production and Preventive Expenditure methods (see section 4.1 for examples). In general, though, the difficulty of identifying and valuing these upstream-downstream effects has led recent research to concentrate more on the direct impact of forestry in upstream areas.

In those many areas where tropical forest is the most efficient way of creating biomass from poor soil, its removal to make way for other land uses could reduce fertility. The intensive use of cleared land for annual crops, plantations, or livestock pasture would normally require heavy artificial fertilisation for sustained cultivation; otherwise, on past experience, the yield would rapidly degenerate. With a loss of vegetation nutrients are leached, humus destroyed, soil is eroded and a process of lateritisation starts. There are relatively few examples of sustainable annual cropping or livestock production on formerly forested tropical soils. (For a review of alternative land uses see Fearnside, 1988, and Johnson, Knowles and Colchester, 1989.)

The yield of land under standing forest should be valued as a benchmark against which to compare proposed alternative land uses. This yield should include all its products, whether marketed or not, and any estimates of its wider environmental services. The opportunity cost of the proposed land uses would then be valued using EOP and PE methods. Comparisons of standing forest with alternative land uses should take account of the growing evidence of low and declining yields from crops and livestock on cleared land (Browder, 1988a).

An alternative approach would be to use the Replacement Cost method, costing the artificial fertiliser necessary to maintain yields in subsequent land uses. Farm budgets should include realistic provision for the fertilisation necessary to prevent output collapsing.

(c) **Biodiversity** is important partly because the complex interrelationship of species and ecosystems confers existing benefits to all natural life, which would be reduced if variety were lessened. It is also vital because of the potential value of discoveries yet to be made from species either unknown or inadequately researched. One estimate is that there is a one-in-four chance that the start-point materials for prescribed drugs originate in tropical forests (quoted in Pearce, Furtado and Pearce, 1990). By implication, any loss of biodiversity which affected the supply of unknown or unexploited species could forfeit benefits on a commensurate scale.

None of this is easy to capture in normal cost-benefit analysis. Although there are many telling examples of the commercial value of particular discoveries or advances in biotechnology using wild species (Prescott Allen, 1988), it is impossible to assign firm *ex ante* values to particular conservation actions. Further discussion of biodiversity is postponed until section 4.11.

(d) There are broadly three approaches to valuing **forest products** used in subsistence and not widely traded:

i) To treat them as tradeables, by taking the value of commercial substitutes or the market value of the products if they were traded. Forest products can be viewed as 'import substitutes' for food, medicines, housing and other materials. An inventory of the forest products used by local inhabitants should be made, which would also uncover items with no commercial substitutes. Its value would doubtless exceed any reasonable notion of effective demand by the tribes and aboriginals and would merely indicate the inadequacy of conventional income measures. Valuation of forest products 'as if' they were traded is acceptable where there would be a ready market for the goods, normally only for a minority of products. However, this approach can yield suggestive results, particularly at a national level. The meat of wild animals provides between 20% and 70% of the animal protein intake of people living in the forest zones of Nigeria, Zaire, Ivory Coast and Liberia. In Sarawak it has been estimated that the cost of replacing the meat of wild pigs with commercial substitutes would be $100 m. annually (Myers, 1988a).

ii) The loss of subsistence could entail costs of relocation and provision of alternative livelihoods. Resettling forest-dwellers, for instance in a special reservation, would entail survey and removal expenses. In the Western Ghats of India these were estimated to be 300,000 rupees per family (c. $19,000). In Cameroon's Korup Forest the resettlement and subsequent support of 6 small villages with a total population of 600-700 people was estimated to cost c. £660,000, or c. £10,000 per head. In this case, these were part of the costs of preserving the forest as a nature reserve, rather than allowing continued occupation and subsistence use, mainly for hunting (see section 5.1).

iii) In the last resort, the displaced forest-dwellers might become pauperised, as in the case of Indians displaced by mining in the Amazon. If they were unable to adjust to their changed surroundings, and no alternative arrangements were made for them, they could become a charge on public welfare. These transfer payments could be used as a crude proxy for the real incomes that displaced people formerly enjoyed from the forest. Many forest products are traded, or potentially tradeable, either in local markets or for export. In principle, they can be valued at prevailing market prices.

In one celebrated survey of a hectare of Amazonian forest near Iquitos, 41% of the total number of plants and trees yielded products with commercial value in the local urban market. Using prevailing market prices, net of collection and transport costs, it was estimated that the net present value of the standing forest was almost $9,000. This greatly exceeded the NPV of a managed pulpwood plantation ($3,200) or an Amazonian cattle ranch ($3,000) (Peters, Gentry and Mendelsohn, 1989, quoted in Prance, 1989).

Another study estimated that a managed area of tropical forest could generate wildlife products with a potential annual value of over $200 per ha, $50 per ha. more than commercial logging (Myers, 1988a). This study drew on the experience of people living in the Ecuadorian portion of the Amazon, who harvest the forest wild animals for local consumption (peccaries, deer, tapirs, pacas and agoutis, not to mention birds, turtles and fish) and caimans caught for their hides. Specimens of primates caught for biomedical research also have an export value. A study of the Amazon Delta in Brazil revealed that a single family sold almost $25,000 of products annually in the markets of Belem, all of which were obtained on a sustainable basis from the forest (Anderson, 1988).

Such studies are highly suggestive of the commercial potential of standing forest. Until much more evidence has been accumulated, however, it is dangerous to generalise from studies of single areas to regions with huge variability in structure and productivity. Existing studies have been variously criticised (J. E. M. Arnold - personal communication) for: belittling marketing aspects, especially the ability of markets to absorb the large amount of minor items that would be implied by any major extension of these practices; underestimating transport costs, especially for forest tracts distant from centres of population or transport routes; considering returns to land, rather than labour - which is often the scarce factor; and overlooking the fact that some of the non-timber products are exploited in a non-sustainable way. There is also great variance in the values that emerge from such studies - in one case, producing a value of standing forest below that of shifting cultivation. In general, the higher values are only obtained by substantially modifying the forest, in effect agro-forestry.

'Minor' forest products, considered in the aggregate, can be of considerable local importance. At the national level, the export of minor forest products (principally rattan) from Indonesia amounted to US$238 m in 1987. The corresponding total for Thailand was $23 m. (de Beer and McDermott, 1989). These estimates are illustrative of the possible value of focusing research on representative forest areas, to come up with values useful in appraisal.

Timber is the principal commercial product of tropical forests, and there is evidence that its total value is often underestimated:

Little is known about the potential commercial value of all but a very few of the tropical tree species, so most trees are treated as weeds and destroyed during logging. (Repetto, 1988)

According to one estimate, the value of marketable timber destroyed for cattle ranching in the Amazon over the period 1966-83 greatly exceeded the value of beef produced (Browder, 1988).

(e) Ecological linkages. This is a typical externality. The benefit of bee-keeping for neighbouring fruit orchards is a textbook illustration of external economies. It is possible to have diseconomies too, for instance, where forests shelter wild animals that destroy crops and fences and threaten tame animals.

Where the presence of an adjacent forest can be shown to be essential for a certain production regime (e.g. the cultivation of Brazil nuts) the costs of preserving it can be regarded as part of the total cost of cultivation. However, it will be quite rare to find such strong direct ecological links. A more common situation would be for the disappearance of the forest to have complex ecological effects on neighbouring areas that take time to register. If experience shows that the removal of forest necessitates extra outlays on fertiliser or pesticide, the value of these commercial inputs can be used as a proxy (Replacement Cost) for the environmental services of the natural forest.

(f) Aesthetic, spiritual and existence value. There is little scope for applying economic values to these important, but non-quantifiable, benefits. The aesthetic or spiritual value of a forest cannot realistically be captured by such techniques as TCM or CV because the people immediately affected are wholly or largely outside the money economy.

Local people and outside observers may well differ in their perception of non-quantifiable benefits and costs. Small farmers practising slash and burn cultivation evidently attach little value to the aesthetic aspects of their habitat. Indigenous forest-dwellers would no doubt feel differently, and their views would be important, though they are only one of the interests represented. Urban populations are likely to obtain more pleasure from contemplating trees than people living in the middle of extensive jungle. How should 'existence values' be weighted, even if they can be ascertained from the various interested parties?

The amount of finance available for preserving forests by conservation groups may be one suggestive proxy for existence value. Similarly, the widespread purchase of books and films about tropical forests and their wildlife can be regarded as an environmental surrogate, although it is not easy to use these to estimate values of particular forests at risk. Tourism by wildlife lovers is best regarded as a forest *product* for appraisal purposes (see Korup case study in section 5.2).

4.3. Desertification

The distinction between local 'on-site' and wider 'off-site' environmental effects is blurred in dryland conditions, where shifting cultivation (e.g. using bush fallow) and free-range pastoralism are common. 'On-site' benefits and losses from particular actions may accrue to other people using the same land later. 'Off-site' results may directly affect the perpetrators if they move onto affected land in due course.

In this section we will distinguish instead between 'direct' effects (4.3.1) which are experienced fairly quickly by the perpetrators, and 'ecological' effects (4.3.2), which may take a little longer to be felt either by the people responsible or by others. Eventually ecological effects will start to show up in direct effects, and what started as an externality could rapidly become internalised.

Some of these effects have been discussed more fully in the context of soil erosion and deforestation (sections 4.1 and 4.2).

4.3.1 Direct effects

This category is concerned with valuing changes in products or services as they are experienced by the farmers, pastoralists, or hunters themselves. In practically all cases, the Effect on Production approach can be used, though the valuation of dryland products is not always straightforward.

Changes in the output of **crops** can be valued at either their tradeable or subsistence level. The former method is more straightforward, and where the crops are widely traded it would be appropriate to apply the local traded price to the change in unit output. Although most dryland crops, such as millet and sorghum, are grown for subsistence use, there are normally active markets to handle local shortages and surpluses. Attaching a border price to them is possible (ODA, 1988, p.20) subject to the complication that the typical basic grains of drylands do not feature prominently in international trade. Some subsistence crops, in theory tradeable, are in practice not regularly or widely traded, especially in societies where food self-sufficiency is the norm. The concept of the border price then becomes the 'replacement cost' of subsistence output, in markets that could be thin, irregular and under distressed conditions. Often the marginal supplies would come from food aid. Assigning an objective market or border price to such transactions would not be easy.

Livestock are also widely traded throughout drylands. However, to value pastoral output solely in terms of the marketed offtake of live animals would grossly underestimate their real economic value to herders (Behnke, 1985). Over the lifetime of an animal, the value of milk, dung and traction power needs to be included alongside the value of offspring and the 'residual' value of the animal live or dead. The relative value of this production 'in kind' varies between different societies and tribes. In four different studies of herders in East and Southern Africa, the value of in-kind production was, variously, over 80%, 32·7%, 47%, and 41·7% of the total value of the herds (quoted in Behnke, 1985). This points to the importance of the ways in which subsistence livestock services are valued. Even the value of the animal as meat can be misinterpreted in subsistence conditions:

> Ranching is a predatory system in that it exploits animals by killing them, but does everything possible to insure their well-being up to the time of slaughter. Subsistence herders, on the other hand, live like parasites on their herds in that they rely on the harvesting of live-animal products and treat meat as a residual

benefit to be realized only at the end of an animal's productive career. (Behnke, 1985, p.117)

It is likely that a loss in the amount or quality of pasture would not be reflected immediately in a reduction in livestock numbers, but rather in a decline in the well-being of the animals and in the quality of the milk, dung, traction etc. that they yield. In theory, any change in the lifetime services of an animal, including non-monetary virtues, should be reflected in its market value as and when it is sold. However, this too is not a straightforward matter in pastoral societies. The conventional way to value livestock is to use their sale price, whether at farm gate, auctions, or cattle markets. This could be misleading where only a small proportion of herds are ever marketed, where the animals sold are surplus to requirements, where cash is required to purchase specific items, and/or where there is a 'distress' element in the sale (e.g. during a drought). The use of sale prices to value the entire herd, most of which will not be sold, could seriously undervalue the animals.

It has been argued that the 'use value' of animals to pastoralists is greater than their sale proceeds (Kerven, 1979, 1982, quoted in Behnke, 1985). One obvious reason is that production for home consumption saves purchases at the retail price (including transport), while production for sale only attracts the wholesale price (net of transport). As with subsistence production, livestock held largely for home consumption are best valued at their 'replacement cost'. With regard to herders dislocated by droughts and desertification - 'ecological refugees' - these replacement costs would become actual expenses for agencies responsible for their welfare.

Tree products and fuelwood. The direct services of dryland trees include the following: firewood and wood for charcoal-making; building timber and poles, fodder and browse for cattle, cash products (e.g. gum arabic, myrrh, coconuts), edible products (fruit, nuts, honey, birds, insects, lizards), other useful products (roofing materials, fibres, medicines, resin), and unmeasurable benefits (e.g. shade for household and cattle, protection from wind, sand and dust, aesthetic pleasure). Some of these products have an active market and are produced mainly for cash sale, e.g. firewood, charcoal wood, building poles, gum arabic. Some, e.g. gum arabic, are even exported, and in such cases it would be correct to apply a border price netted back to the 'farm gate'.

Firewood and charcoal can be valued in various ways. Where they are sold for urban use it may be appropriate to use the cost of an equivalent calorific value obtained from commercial fuels like kerosene. In remoter areas where firewood is for local use and commercial purchases are not feasible, the value could be related to the fertiliser value of animal dung which would otherwise be burnt, or to the opportunity cost of the labour necessary to collect it (see Nepal case study, section 4.1).

Other products used for subsistence could be valued at their 'replacement cost' if they had to be bought in. This would be plausible only where there were close substitutes available for these items.

Wildlife. Drylands are the habitats for wild animals, birds, reptiles and fish which provide cash products and subsistence livelihoods to the local people. As with domestic livestock, wild beasts can provide a regular flow of services and products if they are managed and culled on a sustainable basis. Some of these are of subsistence use (eggs, fish, hides, meat) and can be valued either on a replacement cost basis or - where there are active markets - at their market price.

Some products have an international market, e.g. ivory, rhino horn, rare butterflies, crocodile and other skins. Where they are obtained from the natural death of the animal, as a by-product of carefully managed and culled herds, or from hunting at sustainable levels, it is legitimate to regard these high-value products as part of the services yielded by dryland environments, and apply the prevailing market price at the point of origin.

Some of them are obtained illegally through poaching and evasion of international agreements to control or ban such trade. In other cases they may be exploited on a scale greatly exceeding the sustainable yield, to a point where the survival of the species is at risk. In economic terms this is tantamount to increasing current consumption at the expense of depleting capital stocks. The dilemma for the appraiser of dryland projects is how to deal with items that are obtained in such ways. Suppose a dam is proposed that would flood a large dryland area, from which much illegal hunting takes place. What is the appropriate value to place on the products of that dryland? There are at least three possible exits from this dilemma, none of them wholly satisfactory: (i) to avoid any moral stance and take a forward view of the likely income. The present value of that future income stream would incorporate this judgement about declining yields. A decline in stock (e.g. elephants) from illegal poaching might be offset by a rise in unit values (e.g. of ivory), yielding a steady or increasing income; (ii) to value only 'legitimate' income accruing, for example, to government, local communities, and people with various kinds of rights in the area, thus eliminating income going to poachers from outside the region; and (iii) to estimate only the income from 'sustainable yield' and try to bring reality closer to theory by introducing controls or sustainable management systems. The problem with this approach is that the income from the putative sustainable yield would be affected by any illegal or non-sustainable culling which persisted.

The contribution of the dryland environment to tourism can be assessed by estimating national value-added in the tourism sector attributable to the existence of game parks, nature reservations, and managed hunting. Where nature-based tourism is extensive and highly organised - as in Kenya - this benefit could be very large. Certain countries, e.g. Zimbabwe, that control big-game hunting at sustainable levels, find that spending from such legal hunters greatly exceeds all other uses of the land, including poaching. Legally culled elephants may attract US$ 15,000 each (*The Economist*, 1 July 1989). Value-added retained in the host country would consist of net revenue accruing to local airlines and tour operators, the profits of hotels, transport and handicraft ventures, etc. The difficulty of tracing value-added through the many branches of the tourism sector has led to the common use of 'tourism multipliers' based on average tourist spending as a short cut estimator.

'Vicarious tourism', namely the consumption of books, films and TV programmes about wildlife, is becoming an important category of leisure spending in developed countries. Any net spending which accrues locally (film-making costs, royalties, rights, etc.) should be treated as a benefit. Vicarious enjoyment of wildlife is a category of existence value. In principle, it can be assessed using the Contingent Valuation method, in which international public opinion is invited to declare its willingness to pay for species preservation. In practice, there are serious obstacles to using this approach internationally (see section 3.3.6. and Samples, Dixon and Gowen, 1986).

4.3.2. Ecological effects

Using drylands in sustainable ways can yield a variety of 'ecological' benefits. Measures to conserve or restore the condition of drylands can achieve similar benefits.

The reference point for the following discussion will be soil and water conservation methods (Chleq and Dupriez, 1988) or social forestry. The construction of barriers to water run-off, such as earth and stone bunds, and small-scale dams by techniques such as gabions, are recommended ways of conserving moisture, retaining fertile alluvial soil, and reducing flood destruction. Social forestry takes many forms, such as alley-cropping, shelter belts, 'living fences' etc. (see section 5.2).

The EOP, PE and RC methods have greatest value in the circumstances discussed.

Retention of soil and prevention of erosion. Simple soil conservation measures in drylands, such as farm-level bunds, or small dams on rivers, are partly intended to trap fertile soil where it can be cultivated, and prevent it washing away downstream. Social forestry can achieve the same purpose. Trees help to bind and anchor soil through their root system, leaf litter and other detritus; the canopy cover intercepts rainfall and provides shade; a body of trees also protects land from the wind. Thus trees normally help to preserve soil intact, compared with the alternatives, whether annual crops, pasture, or unprotected fallow land. Experiments have shown that the supply of litter is the most important contribution of tree cover to erosion control.

The first step in assessing economic benefits is to form a view about what would happen **without** the project, to provide a benchmark against which the project can be assessed. The views of farmers, extension officers, agriculturalists and soil scientists should be combined to produce such a scenario, perhaps by reference to the loss of farmland in neighbouring or comparable areas. If soil conservation or social forestry can arrest this loss of land, it can be credited with the net value of produce gained or saved. Alternatively, the benefit of minor conservation measures can be regarded as the avoided cost of more expensive works to prevent soil loss or the 'replacement cost' of programmes to bring badly degraded land back into production. The case study below uses both EOP and RC methods to judge how much restoration is worthwhile.

Maintaining soil fertility. Soil and water conservation works assist soil fertility by helping to retain and accumulate fertile elements of soil (alluvions) that would otherwise be washed away. They also help to conserve moisture in the soil that is retained. There are at least three approaches to an economic valuation of this benefit:

(a) The RC approach. Estimate what the cost would have been in artificial fertil-isers of maintaining the same level of soil fertility. (Artificial fertilisers have their own environmental consequences, discussed in section 2.5.) Trapped alluvium or waste organic matter, including animal dung, replaces fertiliser bought for cash. A balanced social forestry regime should also provide enough firewood to avoid the need to burn animal dung as fuel rather than apply it to the land (see Ethiopia case study in section 5.2). The use of dung as fuel is recognised as one of the final twists in the downward spiral of poverty and land degradation.

(b) The EOP approach. Conservation or agro-forestry can be seen as an alternative to periodically returning land to fallow. Many soils need a 'rest period' if they are to be used without fertiliser for annual crops. Over a period of years, their maxi-mum capacity utilisation will be less than 100%, whereas conservation techniques or agro-forestry ought to enable land to approach full utilisation. The difference between the net outputs of these comparative regimes is a proxy for the soil fertility benefit, making due allowance for the extra labour entailed.

(c) If the alternative to conservation or agro-forestry is the decline in fertility of the land under another use, without fallowing or fertilisation, the soil fertility benefit can be captured by comparing net output 'with' and 'without' the project (EOP). Empirical values for the decline in fertility 'without' cannot be confidently pro-vided. One appraisal (Anderson, 1987, see Nigeria case study in section 5.2) took a range of 0-2% for the annual decline in fertility in the 'without' case, but with no firm empirical basis for this assumption. It should be noted that this decline in soil fertility would not persist indefinitely, and would run up against both organic and economic limits, causing an eventual withdrawal of the land from production.

Shelter and crop protection. Depending on their configuration, trees can protect crops from wind and storm damage. Hedges and shelterbelts can also reduce the loss of soil moisture in their lee, though in dry conditions they may compete with crops for available ground moisture. Trees themselves, if they survive to maturity, can normally withstand severe weather conditions better than most crops, though they are vulnerable in their growth phase.

The effect which has been most carefully quantified is the impact of shelterbelts on soil moisture and fertility, and ultimately on crop yield. A large number of studies (reviewed and interpreted in Anderson, 1987) from both developed and develop-ing countries suggest that properly planted and managed shelterbelts can raise crop yields in adjacent fields by anything up to, and even over, 100%. Anderson states '. . . it seems reasonable to expect a 15 to 25 per cent increment in crop yields in shelterbelt areas as the trees approach mature heights'. It is not possible to give equivalent rules of thumb for farm forestry, since the result depends, amongst other things, on the type of trees and their arrangement.

The beneficial effect of shelterbelts is likely to be greatest in drought years. There is empirical evidence that areas with shelterbelts were able to weather drought with very much less damage to crop yield than unprotected areas. In extreme cases, the latter lost the entire harvest. In arid and semi-arid areas with a high statistical probability of drought it would be reasonable to credit shelterbelts with the rescue of a high proportion of the total crop in drought years. Shelterbelts also yield direct benefits in the shape of fodder for cattle, fruit and other products, and building materials.

Shade for crops. Where trees are planted to afford shade to interplanted crops, this effect is best handled by considering the net output of the combined regime, compared with that of the alternatives.

Land stability. Bunds, terracing, mini-dams, gabions and trees help to prevent landslides, soil creep and gully erosion which could engulf or destroy cultivable land lower down. If such measures substitute for other, more expensive, kinds of preventive expenditure, they can be credited with the savings. Where there are grounds for believing that there would be no alternative efforts at soil conservation, they could be imputed with all the benefits of preserving the land intact for crop use.

Control of water run-off. Conservation and tree planting measures intercept and absorb rainfall and surface water and release it more gradually and evenly than fallow land or annual crops. Less soil is washed away, to appear as sediment further down the slope. The causes and effects of sedimentation, and ways of predicting it, have been discussed more fully in sections 2.2. and 4.1. The build-up of sediment can cause flooding, navigation problems, changes in river channels and in-filling of irrigation systems and reservoirs. Remedial action could entail dredging, cleaning and clearing. The longevity of reservoirs and hydroelectric schemes could be drastically reduced. Reduced run-off has potential downstream costs as well as benefits. A lower annual discharge of water, which may be accompanied by reduced low flows, could harm downstream water abstraction for drinking or irrigation. It could also affect river transport and fishing.

Quantifying these potential effects is difficult. Data obtained from particular social forestry plots cannot safely be scaled up to predict effects at the watershed level, which is the most meaningful perspective to take. In the absence of direct evidence on cause and effect, the economist can fall back on Preventive Expenditure. If there are grounds for thinking that social forestry or land conservation would avoid outlays on remedial works, these savings can be counted as benefits. However, they are unlikely to safeguard against flooding resulting from serious storms, and would not therefore dispense with the need for all flood prevention measures. For a reservoir, where continuous dredging is hardly feasible, the benefit would be extending the life of the reservoir/hydropower scheme and obtaining more dry-season power, or avoiding the cost of raising the dam height (and inundating more land) or building new generating capacity (see Morocco case study in section 4.1).

4.3.3. Case studies

There are a number of case studies of conservation projects in developing countries (Dixon, James, and Sherman, 1990), several of which are summarised in section 5.2. Here brief details are given of more comprehensive regional and national estimates of the damage from dryland degradation in Australia which illustrate the recommended approach.

Australia: dryland damage costs in New South Wales (Sinden, Sutas and Yapp, 1990; Sinden, 1990)

Australia is predominantly arid and semi-arid. Over the last two decades there have been a growing number of studies documenting the large-scale land degradation that is occurring, and there is mounting concern over the public expenditure being incurred to arrest it and cope with its consequences.

In New South Wales (NSW) alone, it is estimated that, in the mid-1980s, the following annual sums (in A$m.) were being spent by state government departments and authorities in response to the various aspects of land degradation: Soil Conservation Service: 22.4 for soil conservation; Public Works Department: 6.5 for floodplain management, 3.3 for beach improvement, 3.6 for river management, 2.5 for coastal protection; Maritime Services Board: 1.5 for dredging ports and harbours; Water Resources Commission: 2.6 for urban flood mitigation, 5.6 for floodplain and river management, 3.8 for Murray Valley salinity; Department of Main Roads: 1.2 for road restoration; and Local Government: 16.5 for sediment damage. These outlays are essentially the replacement costs of dryland degradation. Their size implies a high level of public concern about the consequences of degradation. The two studies discussed here attempt a more complete costing of the various effects.

Method and results. A number of effects are distinguished.

(i) Vegetation degradation. Apart from the widespread loss of tree cover to agricultural development, a specific problem has arisen from the uncontrolled spread of the bitou bush, which was originally introduced to stabilise coastal dunes but has turned out to be both ineffective and destructive of native species. Eradication and re-establishment of alternative permanent vegetation is costed at c. A$5,000/ha.

(ii) Soil erosion. A study done in 1975 showed that 90% of NSW's grazing and crop land needed some kind of erosion control works or improved land management. The total cost of implementing this work was put at A$331m. in 1975 prices. Supplementary work on soil erosion suggested, in different studies, that soil losses of 30mm, 75mm, and 150mm resulted in the following declines in wheat yield: 11-39%, 9.5% (protein content 21.5%), 29.1% (protein content 24.2%). The seriousness of these relationships can be gauged by the total value of the wheat harvest in NSW - A$1,079m. in 1984-5.

(iii) Soil acidity. Two million ha of land are believed to be acidic, and the cost of neutralising the acidity with lime applications has been estimated as A$80/ha., or A$160m. in all.

iv) Salinity. In 1982 920,000 ha. of drylands were affected by saline scalding, and a much smaller area by saline seepage. The annual decline in the yield of land from scalding was estimated to be A$2.0 m., compared to the once-and-for-all A$1.5m. that it would cost to restore it.

v) Sedimentation. An estimated A$16.5m. was spent in 1984 by local governments on the removal of wind- and water-borne sediment from roads and culverts, and repairing damage to council facilities and sediment damage to road surfaces. Lake

Macquarie is losing 10-20 ha/year because of sedimentation. Although the costs to fisheries, recreation and ecology were not quantified, the annual cost of removing the sediment would be A$637,000. The costs of sedimentation on estuaries were also believed to be significant for fisheries (risking A$30m./year catch), navigation, ports and harbours. The amounts spent on dredging (A$1.5m./year) were thought to be only part of the real cost of sedimentation.

(vi) Water quality. One specific effect was examined, namely the impact of mining operations which led to the release of heavy metals into water bodies. A$3m. was spent on a single mine to prevent further build-up of heavy metals in Lake Burley Griffin.

This approach mainly employs Replacement Cost, the assumption being that it is worthwhile trying to restore the environment to its original condition. In some instances, e.g. soil erosion, benefits are assessed to indicate the justification of this. As part of the NSW study, a full cost-benefit analysis was done of conservation work on representative farms in the north-west of the state. The underlying question being addressed was, what level of conservation expenditure was justified, and on which farms, in view of the likely benefits of the programme. The first step was to estimate the cost of achieving 'well conserved land', as defined by the Soil Conservation Service. The increase in farm (wheat) yields was also calculated: a production function was constructed which showed that, on average, A$52 outlay on conservation is associated with an increased yield of 0.49 t/ha. In 46 out of the 50 farms in the sample, revenues from the conservation programme were expected to exceed its costs. The entire programme showed a benefit-cost ratio of 1.9:1.0 at a discount rate of 5%.

This pair of studies show the usefulness of complementing values based on RC with benefit estimates from the EOP method. The farm-level part of the study also indicated that, for many farms, RC (i.e. the conservation measures) would greatly underestimate the benefits of the programme as derived from EOP. For a minority of farms, RC exceeds EOP and the programme is not justified.

4.4. Destruction of wetlands

The full range of economic valuation techniques is, in principle, available to quantify the environmental effects of wetlands. Each of the products and functions listed in 2.6 can be valued, most of them in several different ways (Turner, 1988, Pearce and Turner, 1990; Barbier, 1989a, Hufschmidt et al., 1983). Thus, in theory, there are several dozen possible components of a wetland valuation.

In practice, most of these possible 'boxes' will remain empty. Some of the effects will be very small and weak. Some will be uncertain, and depend on further research and long-term observation. In other cases, the empirical values upon which the techniques depend are lacking, and difficult to derive during the appraisal period. As Barbier (1989a) notes:

. . . in many instances the financial and time constraints under which an economic evaluation of wetland conservation must be conducted in developing countries limits the feasibility of sophisticated valuation techniques.

Most empirical values in the literature are obtained from temperate wetlands in developed countries, especially the United States, and focus mainly on environmental services. It is unwise to transfer such data across space (and time) and apply them to non-comparable situations in developing countries, though sometimes the parallels can be illuminating (Turner, 1990). The most practical approach is to draw up a checklist of potential products and functions, and review the characteristics of the wetland in question against it. This would indicate the most important effects and the most fruitful to concentrate on for appraisal. Case study 1 in this section illustrates such a checklist drawn up in Central America.

Using the EOP approach, developing countries are likely to place relatively more weight on the direct products of their wetlands, which are of more immediate importance to the livelihoods of the people who live in or near them, than on the broader environmental services. Nevertheless, the broader perspective should be kept, wetland services should be clearly identified and assessed, and their possible economic effects described, even if valuation cannot proceed very far.

4.4.1 Products

Wetland products are either used or sold. Those that are sold can be valued at the going market price (farm-gate or 'swamp-side') corrected, as necessary, for distortions caused by monopoly or protection. Those that are used for subsistence, and do not enter a market, are more difficult to value. Items like fish, fuelwood or salt, which could be sold if they were not consumed, pose no difficulty, provided there is an active local market. A number of US studies attest to the importance of such products, but also illustrate the enormous range of values depending on the location and richness of the wetland concerned. The annual value of fish, frogs and bait in an acre of wetlands was calculated to be $286 in Michigan in 1979 but only $6 in New York state in 1965 (Danielson and Leitch, 1986). Other items are akin to 'import-substitutes': if they were not available from the wetland, they, or a substitute, would need to be bought in. For products like fuelwood, there is likely to be an active market and a plausible price for the 'import substitute', allowing for the cost of getting it into the hands of the user. In other cases, such as fodder, there is less likely to be a clearly identifiable substitute, or a thriving market in it. There will be a further group of products, like honey, which wetlands people will consume, but which they are unlikely to buy, or could not afford.

Products with no close, or imperfect, substitutes can in principle be valued with reference to 'indirect substitutes' or 'indirect opportunity costs' (Barbier, 1989a). For example, the loss of peat or firewood from a wetland can be valued as the cost of buying in charcoal or kerosene. Or the value of peat could be assessed with reference to the opportunity cost of labour spent in digging and preparing it - but the labour itself would then need to be valued. Where the product (e.g. fuelwood) is substituted by a good which itself is not marketed (e.g. animal dung), the valuation problem is transposed to the latter. (One could estimate the cost of substituting dung by commercial fertiliser.)

Clearly the appraisal of products where there is no active market nor obvious substitutes can entail a very convoluted exercise, with the risk of producing unreal and implausible results. The appraiser is best advised to concentrate on products that are important to the local community, where markets exist, where there are good substitutes, and where the values are obvious and uncontroversial.

Any valuation of wetlands in comparison with their alternative uses should take account of their respective sustainable yields. This comparison will often favour retaining the wetland in its existing use - because much exploitation will be unsustainable, and the costs of converting to other uses is often underestimated. (Dixon, 1989, quotes a Malaysian example of mangrove converted to industrial and housing purposes which is still unused, due, amongst other things, to excessively high unforeseen costs).

Sometimes a particular form of wetland use may be unsustainable too. Excessive harvesting will reduce future yields of the product concerned, and even damage the wetland's ability to fulfil other products and services. This applies particularly to the removal of vegetation, and physical alterations such as digging sand, gravel, and peat. Such non-sustainable development should be clearly flagged to the decision-maker, and should in any case show up in the diminishing future stream of benefits. The device of the 'compensating project' can be considered in such cases, but in practice many products and functions of a wetland will be difficult, and in the case of unique features, impossible, to replace.

The results of the small number of studies of tropical mangroves illustrates the enormous range of values, even for particular types of product like fish and forest items, but also their great potential value relative to other uses. The total annual value of products from a hectare of mangrove in three such studies was US$ 500 in Trinidad (1974), $950-1,250 in Fiji (1976) and $1,550 in Puerto Rico (1973). In Trinidad, recreation and tourism, fisheries and forestry products were the most important elements in total value. Fish, especially shrimps, can show very high values (Dixon, 1989). The study in Chanthaburi, Thailand, in 1982 underlines the importance of considering the *potential* products of a properly managed mangrove, in making comparisons with alternative proposed land uses. When the study was done, the gross income from the mangrove area (in $/ha/year) was 160 (from fisheries outside the mangrove area but dependent on it, on-site fisheries, and charcoal production). This was about the same yield as conversion to rice production. However, it was estimated that the potential yield was almost $600/ha, on the basis of increased charcoal production and the creation of oyster culture. One of the alternative land uses, shrimp farming, also showed a large difference between its current and potential yield, but this latter was dependent on keeping some mangrove as a source of shrimp fry.

In a study of the Philippines in 1983, it was estimated that one ha. of mangrove, used sustainably, would provide the equivalent of a man-year's earnings for a poor fisherman (7,000 pesos), while converting it to fishponds would provide only one month's wages. Products going into this calculation were wood, fish, shrimp, prawns, crab meat, molluscs, sea cucumbers, and the indirect harvest from nearshore fisheries dependent on the mangrove is estimated to be up to 500 kg per ha. of mangrove (World Bank, 1989).

4.4.2. Services

All the usual valuation methods can, in theory, be applied to one or other of the wetland services.

Effect on Production. The presence of a wetland can affect the productivity of agriculture and fisheries. Where rice is grown in swamps and coastal wetlands, the contribution of the wetland *per se* is analogous to the supply of irrigation water, except that in this case it is the rent from a natural resource. A crude estimate of this rent would be the value of the rice minus the cost of inputs and the value of labour.

There is also a symbiotic relation between wetlands and adjacent fisheries (World Bank, 1989). The effect of the disappearance of a wetland on local fisheries is hard to predict, and can only be established after research and monitoring of comparable situations over a number of years. A study of Chesapeake Bay showed that the complete loss of submerged aquatic vegetation could lead to a loss of annual fishing income of $13-14m. (quoted in Turner, 1988). The value of salt marsh systems on the US East Coast for adjacent fishing has been estimated to be about $100 per hectare per year (McNeely, 1988).

Preventive Expenditure/Replacement Cost. These alternative and mutually exclusive approaches apply particularly to water supply and regulation, flood control, coastal protection and transport effects. A number of studies in the United States indicate the scale of water benefits that wetlands can confer. They also exhibit the enormous range of possible values. In a compilation, mostly from the 1970s, the total annual 'social value' per acre (mainly water and flood control functions, plus fish and other living creatures) varied from $20 in New York to $4,070 in Louisiana (Danielson and Leitch, 1986). In Massachusetts the cost of replacing the natural tertiary waste treatment services of marshes has been estimated to be $123,000 per ha. (McNeely, 1989).

RC is sometimes used to value non-commercial species, e.g. of birds or rare fish. In an estimate of the environmental damage of an oil spill in Chesapeake Bay, the replacement cost of birds quoted by commercial breeders and biological supply firms was used, averaging $30 per bird (quoted in Cohen, 1986). There is also a case of $500,000 compensation paid to replant an area of mangrove damaged by an oil spill (from the *Zoe Colocotroni* in 1973, quoted in Cohen, 1986). It is technically possible to create new artificial wetlands ('marsh establishment'), though it is only feasible for lower-order wetlands, and is a long and costly process. Restoration can never fully recreate the original biodiversity, nor compensate for the loss of functions before vegetation grows back.

Travel cost. Inferring recreational values from travel cost data is commonly used in developed countries, but is not a foolproof technique (section 3.3.5). In an extreme case, Turner (1988) cites an important wetland in Eastern England that is inaccessible for most of the year. In developing countries wetlands do not have the same recreational value as they do in some well populated industrial countries. Thus in practice, existence value is likely to be more important, though it is even more difficult to capture in economic values.

Contingent valuation. It is important to consider ways of ensuring that the wider and longer-term features of wetlands are captured in the analysis, and contingent valuation is one such possibility. However, its application to, say, tropical wet-lands, is fraught with difficulties (section 3.3.6). It relies on an enlightened and well-informed reference group, whose 'willingness to pay' answers are credible, and these conditions are not yet evident in many developing countries in respect of wetlands. For sites of international importance, the technique is more meaning-ful. In some cases the most appropriate 'reference group' might be the host government acting in discussion with aid agencies and international conservation groups. This is not to say that the prices actually paid by public agencies to preserve specific wetlands are always a good guide.

It is reasonable to expect that the preservation benefits of wetlands will increase over time (Krutilla and Fisher, 1975, Hufschmidt *et al.*, 1983). This makes it all the more important to take an enlightened, long-term view of values. CV, conducted amongst parties who can take this perspective, is potentially important, though it is easy to show that valuations can be biased (Samples, Dixon and Gowen, 1986).

Opportunity cost. This method can complement the attempt to value benefits by setting a level for the sacrifice entailed in preserving rather than 'developing' wetlands. In theory, the net present value of the best alternative use of the wetland is the 'opportunity cost' of preserving it in its current state, and is the value against which benefits have to be measured, either explicitly (where they can be valued) or implicitly (where they are not fully quantifiable).

It is important to ensure that the alternative development is properly appraised. There is always a risk of hastily conceived projects to 'develop' wetlands turning out to be non-sustainable, in which case the wetland would have been sacrificed too cheaply. In the UK many schemes to convert wetlands to agriculture have turned out to produce negative net benefits (Turner, 1988), which implies that the opportunity 'cost' of preserving them would actually be an opportunity 'benefit'. In any case, the benefits of alternative uses might rest on policies which were distorting or ephemeral. In the UK, much drainage has been in response to the artificial values induced by the EEC Common Agricultural Policy (Turner, 1988). Similarly, in developing countries policies to subsidise crop prices or inputs (such as mechanical equipment), or to offer tax breaks to farm land, would artificially inflate the value of converting wetlands.

Market prices paid for their conversion are one source of data on their opportunity cost. In 1970-71 prices paid by developers for wetlands in Massachusetts varied between $300 and $70,000 per acre (Hufschmidt *et al.*, 1983). Another source of opportunity cost data is the level of compensation that owners of wetlands require not to drain or otherwise alter their land. In 1980 the US Fish and Wildfowl Service paid an average annual amount of $343 per acre for 'easements' on wetland preservation (Danielson and Leitch, 1986).

4.4.3. Case studies

Nicaragua: Ranking of wetland characteristics for appraisal purposes (Barbier, 1989a).

Table 4.2 provides a checklist of characteristics that is a useful first step in apprais-ing proposals to convert wetlands. Components 1 to 5 are essentially 'products', and the remainder 'services', in terms of the classification used in this section.

Table 4.2. A ranking of wetland characteristics: North Pacific coast mangroves, Nicaragua

	Area 1	Area 2	Area 3
Components			
1 Forest resources	High	High	High
2 Wildlife resources	Low	Low	Low
3 Fisheries	Med.	High	High
4 Forage resources	Low	Low	Low
5 Agricultural resources	Med.	Med.	Low
6 Water supply	High	Med.	High
Functions			
1 Groundwater discharge	Med.	Med.	Med.
2 Flood and flow control	High	High	High
3 Shoreline stabilisation	Med.	High	High
4 Sediment retention	High	High	High
5 Nutrient retention	High	High	High
6 Water quality maintenance	Med.	High	High
7 Storm protection/wind break	High	High	High
8 Micro-climate stabilization	Med.	Med.	Med.
9 External support	High	High	Med.
10 Recreation/tourism	Med.	Med.	Low
11 Water Transport	High	High	High
Attributes			
1 Biological diversity	Low	Med.	Med.
2 Uniqueness to culture/heritage	Med.	Med.	Low

Louisiana: The value of coastal wetlands in the protection of property against hurricane wind damage (Farber, 1987)

The study selected one amongst the various functions of wetlands, the argument being that wetlands weaken the force of storms and provide a closed water buffer zone. Hurricanes are fed by ocean heat sources and peter out over land. Wetlands also help to reduce the inland tidal surge associated with hurricanes, but this is excluded from the present analysis.

The study area was the strip of wetland on the Gulf Coast of Louisiana, whose main current functions are for recreation, amenity, commercial harvesting, tertiary waste treatment and coastal protection.

Method. The probability of storms of a certain intensity is first estimated. A storm wind damage function is then specified using historical physical and insurance data from the region and elsewhere. The two are combined to produce estimates of the likely costs of wind damage to property from removing the strip of coastal wetlands.

Results. The loss of a one-mile-long strip of coastal wetland was estimated to expose property to a risk of damage, amounting to $1.1m. in 1980 prices, or $63,676 annually (discounted at 8% over 100 years). This is equivalent to a coastal protection function worth $6.82 per ha. of wetland.

The estimate of the wind damage function is a sophisticated exercise, combining physical relationships and insurance compensation values. The actual values produced need to be related to the circumstances of the study area, which is heavily used for leisure and recreation. Even in this hurricane-prone area, the per ha. value is low. On the other hand, the model omits damage from tidal surges and floods, and leaves out of account the various other wetland products and functions mentioned earlier.

The exercise is of particular relevance to well populated, or well used, coastal areas subject to frequent severe storms - within the developing world this would include the Caribbean and parts of South-East Asia, for example. A number of wetland sites are close to cities, and proposals to convert them for use as housing, commercial development or port expansion need to allow for the risk of damage to high-value property. The actual figures resulting from a rough damage probability exercise, along the lines above but necessarily cruder, could be much higher, and would set useful parameters for any planned preventive expenditure.

4.5. Depletion of fishing grounds

Overfishing damages fisheries, and its costs, namely the difference between the value of actual catches and the sustainable economic yield of the fishery are felt both by its perpetrators and all producers and consumers of fish. This section briefly reviews the notion of sustainable yield fishing and the difficulties of applying it for operational purposes which limits the scope for using economic valuation techniques.

4.5.1. The concept of sustainability

In theory, a fishery can produce a maximum sustainable yield (MSY). As the amount of fishing increases, the yield first increases, then peaks, and finally falls as breeding stock becomes depleted. The MSY indicates the sustainable rate of fishing, before cost factors are considered. Introducing costs qualifies the above schema. On the simplest assumption, that costs rise in proportion to fishing effort, it can be shown that the economic optimum fishing level (the Maximum Economic Rent, or MER) occurs at a fishing level *below* the MSY. Intuitively, this is equivalent to saying that allowing for the costs of fishing reduces the optimum amount of fishing that is done in order to maximise the returns to effort (Pitcher and Hart, 1982).

This simple model can be brought closer to reality. Costs are unlikely to be proportionate to fishing effort. Unit costs - and even more marginal costs - are more likely to vary with the size of boat, size of fleet, and the sophistication of the gear. Likewise, the revenue curve will diverge from the MSY curve where the price of fish increases in response to their growing scarcity. Either of these modifications will alter the MER relative to the biological MSY.

Thus it is dangerous to assume that economic factors will keep fishing down to a level within the MSY. In a fishery with free access, there is every incentive for the numbers and the rate of fishing to increase to the point where the MSY is exceeded, especially if the opportunity cost of fishing is low - as it is in many poor communities. The reaction of fishermen, whether commercial or artisanal, to declining yields may be the perverse one of upgrading boats and gear in order to increase their share of a shrinking catch. Many aid projects have unwittingly contributed to this result.

Communal ownership of fisheries or the creation of a private or public monopoly does not necessarily produce MSY either. The collapse of the Peruvian anchovy fishery happened despite its concentrated management structure. As a general point, fishing effort is very sensitive to the level of discount rate used, relative to the growth of the fish population. At high discount rates, overfishing becomes attractive relative to conservation fishing. Blue whales, which produce few offspring and have a reproductive rate of c. 4% per year, are particularly liable to be exterminated by commercial operators working with conventional discount rates (Clark, 1976).

4.5.2. Other practical difficulties in modelling

Biological models of fish populations are usually in respect of single species. The interrelations between different fish species, especially between predators and prey, complicates the model since fishing changes the species composition of the stock. In recent years overfishing in Peru led to the collapse of the anchovy stock and its replacement by chub mackerel and sardine. Overfishing in Thailand has led to the replacement of large high-value fish by smaller and less valuable species (Dixon et al. 1988). More generally, the sustainable management of the more economically important species is likely to lead to the over-exploitation of other species in the catch.

The simple models described above assume that fishermen are well informed about the economic return to their fishing effort. They also simplify the dynamic effect of their actions on future yields, and the interaction of one party's decisions with what other fishermen do (Allen and McGlade, 1987).

Modelling fish populations is complex and problematic, and MSY is a hazardous basis for fisheries policy (Beddington, quoted in Allen and McGlade, 1987). There are difficulties of measurement, namely ensuring accuracy and precision in sampling a mobile resource in an opaque medium (Gulland, 1983). Modelling is further complicated by changes in the abundance of food, the migration of shoals, and the possibility that fish populations are never in static equilibrium, but always in a state of flux. Biological models used in studies of tropical fisheries are mainly those developed for cool temperate seas. Until more is known, this argues for setting fishing limits well on the conservative side.

In short, the environmental costs of overfishing, in the sense of the shortfall of actual fishing yield from MSY or MER, are very difficult to estimate, for both theoretical and practical reasons. The exercise depends on possessing good historical data on stocks and yields, and making strong and frequently heroic assumptions in order to develop the necessary model. Targets other than MSY have been developed for management purposes, e.g. in the Falklands squid fishery annual survival rates of breeding stock are used as an objective.

One estimate of MSY was made for demersal fish in the Philippines. By comparing the actual depletion of fish biomass in Philippines soft-bottom fishing grounds with a notion of the optimal depletion of the original resource, it was estimated that demersal overfishing cost the economy US$50-90 m. p.a. The clear implication is that a reduction of fishing effort would lead to more fish for everyone

(World Bank, 1989). A similar exercise has been done for demersal and pelagic fishery MSY in Thailand's national waters (ADB, 1986, pp. 109-113).

4.6. Air and water pollution

The various possible effects of air and water pollution can be grouped into six categories for appraisal purposes: human welfare, public services, output, the built environment, amenity, and threats to natural or priceless assets. In all cases, however, valuation depends on clearly establishing cause and effect even though such 'damage functions' or 'dose-response relationships' are difficult to establish and quantify with any scientific or statistical rigour.

For *air pollution* the following are the necessary steps in the logical chain (Kneese, 1984): (i) determine the type and volume of emission. This is relatively straightforward, though there would be problems in collecting data in rapidly growing cities with many individual pollutors (households, small industries, automobiles, etc); (ii) estimate its concentration level at relevant points in the atmosphere. This normally relies on a 'dispersion model' which aims to predict the spread of pollutants from their origin ('point' or 'non-point', mobile or stationary, area or line, etc); (iii) establish the relationship between specific concentrations of pollutant and human health (dose-response studies); (iv) define the population at risk, a matter of estimating population within the pollution dispersal 'plume', which could extend over large distances, with some adjustment for sectors of the population especially at risk.

There are analogous difficulties in establishing links between pollution and health via *groundwater contamination* (Kneese, 1984). It is necessary to: (i) know the source and potency of the sources of contamination (many of which are illegal or uncontrolled); (ii) model the spread of pollutant in the aquifer (a complicated process, shrouded in great ignorance); (iii) estimate the number of people at risk and the extent of their exposure; and (iv) develop dose-response links to indicate the health risks.

Economists should therefore be aware of the weakness of the primary data going into pollution valuation studies.

4.6.1. Methods of valuing the effects of pollution

The principal ways of valuing each of the six effects noted above will now be examined.

(i)*Human welfare*

Although there is growing circumstantial evidence of increasing air and water pollution being associated with growing health problems, it is hard to draw a precise link between a certain kind of pollution (still less from a particular source) and a change in the level of health of a defined group of people.

Even in the OECD countries, where most of this kind of work has been done, the link is far from being scientifically proven. Commenting on dose-response relationships in air pollution and health, Pearce and Markandya (1989) note:

. . . the sophisticated epidemiological data required for such studies are very rarely available outside the United States, and therefore the applicability of this technique in other countries is likely to be rather limited. Attempts to define the statistical relationship between air pollution and mortality in the United Kingdom have not found a demonstrable connection. (p.53)

Clinical and epidemiological research strongly suggests a link between the presence of certain air pollutants at threshold levels (defined as continuing for one hour, one day or one year, depending on the type), and problems of health and excessive mortality among the exposed population. The problem is in defining the relationship in a statistically significant way.

The main responsible pollutants are the following (drawing on Sebastian, 1990 and Kneese, 1984):

Sulphur dioxide (SO$_2$) which mainly affects asthmatics. Where this pollutant is combined with suspended particulates, a wider group is at risk, including children. Decreased lung function can occur, and - at high doses - mortality. A good relationship has also been found between SO$_2$ and early disease in infants.

Hydrocarbons. Some components are known to be toxic, and one -benzine - is a carcinogen.

Carbon monoxide (CO). People with heart ailments are most at risk from the higher levels found in central cities, car parking areas and high altitudes. High CO may bring on angina.

Nitrogen oxide (NOx). Its health effects are not firmly established, though it is suspected of producing respiratory problems in both children and adults.

Particulates. Fine particles are considered to be the most troublesome, but include a variety of substances, some of which are more damaging to health than others. Transported suspended particulates (TSPs) have been linked to certain symptoms, restricted activity days (RADs) and excess mortality, but more accurate links are obtained by considering certain types of particulate. Acid aerosols (especially H$_2$SO$_4$ and NH$_4$HSO$_4$) are the worst, affecting people with asthma and chronic bronchitis, and causing death in some cases. Of all the pollution variables, sulphate particulates are considered the best predictors of mortality. In a major study of 60 US cities, there was also a strong correlation between particulates and pneumonia and influenza.

Ozone. The short-term effects of exposure to high ozone levels are well established on heart and lung functions, and affect athletic performance. It is more difficult to go beyond this, though Kneese (1984) reports a finding from US research that a reduction of 0.01 parts per million (ppm) in ambient ozone would result in 0.65 fewer RADs, on average, per person per year. This reduction amounts to a 50% decrease in average hourly readings in the United States.

The value of these health effects can be inferred using the *Human Capital* approach (section 3.3.3) or cost of risk method derived mainly from wage differentials, which has been favoured in recent US and European work (Kneese, 1984; Pearce and Markandya, 1989). Briefly, this method infers the value of life from the amounts that individuals or governments are apparently willing to spend to save a statistical life, that is, to reduce the probability of death or serious injury. It is customary to value short periods of illness or RADs according to the direct medical expenses incurred and the average loss of earnings.

In addition to the inherent problems of both methods, there are specific limitations in applying either in countries with social and medical backgrounds different from those of high-income OECD nations. Even in OECD countries, it has been concluded:

. . . choosing the 'right' value of life for pollution contexts is not at all straight-forward. At the very least it must take account of the social context in which the risk occurs. (Pearce and Markandya, 1989)

Certain 'environmental surrogates' are widely marketed, and serve as a proxy for the value of the environmental services they replace - an example of RC. The most obvious of these is water, privately sold (in bottles, or from mobile carts) to make up for the inadequate quantitiy and quality of the publicly available product. Private sewerage and garbage collection is also on offer in parts of some cities. For those who can afford them, private swimming and country clubs may suggest the values that users place on clean and safe lakes, parks and gardens (though exclusivity may account for much of their appeal). In such limited markets, citizens reveal the size of their preference for improved environmental services. The cost per unit of these services is usually a multiple of that of the public utility, and effective demand is obviously constrained by income. Thus it is misleading to 'gross up' values obtained in these restricted markets to infer the value of environmental services for the population as whole.

Willingness to accept compensation, both actual and hypothetical, ascertained through CV may also be a pointer to welfare losses. Actual compensation may be awarded for industrial injury or death (e.g. to the victims and their relatives in the Bhopal explosion). These payments are likely to be a poor guide to the victims' subjective value of good health, absence of injury, or life, even where these are clearly formulated, and vary widely depending on the financial strength of the offending concern, the country where the accident happened, and the location of the court making the award. There are hardly any cases of compensation for the more diffuse damage to health from air and water pollution. Hypothetical willingness to accept compensation may also be obtained from CV. In a study of West Berlin carried out in 1983 it was estimated that Berliners placed a total value of $1.6 bn on clean air over their city, on the basis of WTP surveys (Schulz, 1985, quoted in Pearce and Markandya, 1989).

Hedonic Methods have also been used to value air pollution. In a classic study of the South Coast Air Basin around Los Angeles, observed differences in *property values* were combined with estimates of willingness to pay for improved air quality. It was found that the value of clean air from the property comparisons amounted to c. $40 per month, while that from the willingness to pay surveys was $30 per month. However, in San Francisco, with a lesser pollution problem, though with a similar population, the clean air values implicit in both methods were only 15-20% of those obtained in Los Angeles. This shows the difficulty of generalising results (Kneese, 1984).

The same principle is involved in the use of *wage differentials* to infer the values that workers place on occupational safety and health. In theory, workers ought to require a higher wage to work in polluted surroundings or carry out risky tasks. The extent of this 'risk premium' should reflect their valuation of health and safety. The use of the wage differentials variant of HM has very limited application to the labour markets of developing countries (section 3.3.4).

(ii)*Public services*

Environmental conditions cause losses and inconvenience to certain public services, which can be treated as a loss of production (or conversely, if avoided, can be credited as 'avoided loss'). In either event, EOP is relevant. If the damage is anticipated, PE can be used as a proxy for environmental costs. If the damage entails subsequent work to restore the original condition, RC is appropriate.

The decision by the Mexican Government to close schools in Mexico City for several weeks during the winter of 1988/9 because of excessive air pollution is a clear example of interrupted public services. The cost of the lost educational 'output' can be regarded as at least equal to the nugatory spending on teachers' salaries, overheads and caretaking during this period. Other deleterious effects on public services may be more difficult to identify and value - e.g. greater absenteeism, and the effect of respiratory diseases on public employees' morale and efficiency.

Public water sources may become a health hazard if polluted. This may lead the authorities to treat, clean up or otherwise render safe water courses or lakes where these risks arise. The expense of sound-proofing and air-conditioning public buildings is another example of PE.

RC could apply to the public health costs of dealing with an epidemic (while the cost of immunisation would count as PE). Other examples are the costs of dealing with hazardous wastes, and measures taken in the aftermath of an industrial explosion. However, there are few empirical applications in developing countries.

(iii)*Output*

The external environmental effects of urban development may directly affect the output and costs of productive sectors and thus may be handled by EOP. Although industry is the cause of much pollution, it can also be the victim. It may incur extra PE for insulation, air-conditioning, water treatment, etc. due to worsening environmental conditions. Congestion imposes additional cost penalties of transport and distribution. Productivity will be affected by the health of the labour force, absenteeism, and in extreme cases by closure of operations due to excessive air pollution (e.g. in the notorious case of Cubatao, Brazil). Some of these effects may be identified and costed in feasibility studies of the relative costs of different locations.

Intensive farming on the outskirts of cities, and food production from urban gardens and plots, is at risk from air pollution, ozone concentrations, acid rain and water contamination. Further afield, acidification reduces soil fertility (though the precise causes of this phenomenon are still being debated). Commercial forestry can be badly affected by acid rain and 'acid fog'.

Research in the United States has demonstrated a clear negative relationship between ozone concentration and the yield of such crops as soyabeans, wheat, maize, cotton, sugar beet and vegetables. In one study, an increase of 50% in ozone concentrations was associated with a fall of between 3.8% and 17.5% in the value of farm output (Kneese, 1984). Yields of lima beans, celery and cotton were particularly affected.

The reduction in the yield of fisheries downstream from conurbations is well-attested. Uncontrolled effluent, sewerage discharge and industrial smells can also affect tourism and recreation, especially where popular beaches are close to the centre of cities (as in Rio, Bombay, Lagos).

In all these cases, the valuation of lost output or extra costs poses no novel conceptual difficulties, **provided that cause and effect are clear and can be attributed to specific polluters.** The crudest way of valuing output changes is by multiplying the change in yield or output by the prevailing price. This is likely to set an upper limit on economic damage, compared with the results from more sophisticated modelling of supply and demand responses (Pearce and Markandya, 1989; Kneese, 1984).

One theoretical approach to valuing the damage from industrial emissions is to infer such costs from the expense that firms go to (and which their governments require) in order to prevent these emissions. This is based on the logic of the PE approach. The argument is that no country would incur such costs in excess of the benefits (avoided environmental costs) of curbing the emissions. Thus the observed costs incurred by industry, power stations, etc. are taken to be a proxy for the domestic environmental costs of the emissions. The method is applied to inferring the damage from acid rain caused by emissions of sulphur dioxide from power stations in some West European countries (Maler, 1990). The crucial assumptions in this approach are that the polluters concerned (or their regulators) know the size of the environmental damage they would cause, and that the amount of curbing they do is 'optimal', i.e. spending just equals avoided costs. These are strong assumptions in the present state of knowledge about environmental effects, their valuation, and the rationality and power of regulators.

(iv)*The built environment*

This section deals with damage to property and structures which are not unique, historic or otherwise priceless (dealt with in (vi) below).

Most empirical studies have concentrated on the effect of air pollution from sulphur compounds and particulate matter, though the impact of oxidants and nitrogen oxides has also been examined, mostly in the United States and Western Europe. The two principal steps in deriving economic values are estimating the physical effects (the 'damage function'), and applying values to the damage. The latter can be handled by PE or RC, depending on how far the damage is allowed to proceed.

Some common problems in estimating damage functions are that the effects may depend on a 'threshold value' of pollution, they will be influenced by the local climate, and corrosion (especially of metals) may depend on the interaction of several different pollutants. Moreover, no significant work has been done on the important categories of concrete structures, motor vehicles, electricals, plastics and rubber; empirical work has so far only touched part of the spectrum of materials at risk. Translating these physical effects into values depends crucially on assumptions made about maintenance. If 'optimal' maintenance is assumed, then any extra costs will capture the pollution costs, an assumption most easily made for painting, whereas it is very difficult to counter long-term corrosion damage (e.g. to stonework, concrete, machinery) by maintenance as such. Estimates of corrosion damage through air pollution from sulphur compounds and a few other substances in the USA and European countries fall in a range of $3 to $28 per head per year (in, variously, 1982 or 1983 dollars).

In seeking to apply this method to developing countries, certain environmental differences need to be taken into account. Materials may be different - e.g. more use of natural stone, wood, corrugated iron and brick. The ravages of local climate (heat, humidity, wind) and termites are likely to be more extreme. 'Optimal maintenance' is a far cry from what actually happens in most Third World cities. Hence it may be more realistic to work on the assumption of premature replacement, shorter operating lives, and heavier outlays on periodic maintenance.

For discrete projects (e.g. a housing estate, urban flyover, school, public offices) such realistic assumptions can be made in appraisal studies. However, the majority of buildings in developing country cities, and the vehicles and machinery that go with them, are privately owned. The effect of pollution on their fabric, and their owners' response, is uncertain. The kinds of quantification discussed above will give valuable indicators for decisions in the public sector, and for recurrent public costs, but will only capture a small part of the total urban externalities.

There are other possible effects in developing countries entailing damage to property and structures e.g. landslides, explosions etc. These accidents cannot be clearly foreseen. Irresponsible or dangerous developments (e.g. building shanty dwellings on an unstable slope, construction of a hazardous chemical plant near housing) may force others to incur 'defensive' expenditure (e.g. building barriers, thick perimeter walls) which can be regarded as the cost of preserving a safe environment.

(v)*Amenity*

Threats to urban amenity are a cost to psychic well-being, recreation, health and tourism. Parks, beaches, rivers and open spaces have great (but usually unpriced) value to city populations, especially to those unable to afford private facilities (e.g. Rio de Janeiro's beaches, the Maidan in Calcutta, Lumpinee Park in Bangkok).

The two most common techniques for inferring the value of urban amenity are travel cost and contingent valuation. TC bases valuation on the direct expenses and value of time that users incur to visit the facility - their 'revealed preference' for that amenity. (Its application to Lumpinee Park, Bangkok, is described in section 5.4.) Certain weaknesses in the technique were noted in section 3.3.5, and there have been few applications in developing countries and for urban amenities.

Some surveys of this type are extended to cover the willingness to pay of present non-users to preserve the facility. This is an example of CV and is the only way of finding out the size of a facility's option or existence value. A study was carried out of the values that visitors to the Grand Canyon National Park place on clean air, visibility being at risk from existing and projected power stations and smelters. Respondents, both actual visitors and 'arm chair' admirers of the Canyon, were asked to indicate what they would be willing to pay to preserve the visibility. Grossed up for all South West US states, the 'preservation bid' for air visibility was in the range $373-889 m. The largest part of the response was existence value for people who might never see the Canyon in person, rather than user value to actual visitors (Kneese, 1984).

(vi)*Priceless assets*

TC and CV are also applicable to valuing irreplaceable assets such as historic buildings, archaeological remains and famous views which are put at risk by urban development. In the case of tourist attractions there could also be direct *productivity* losses to tourism and visitor income (including entry charges). PE may also be incurred (reinforcing, cleaning, protecting), and demolition, relocation and reconstruction may be a feasible - though expensive - option (RC). In most cases it will be revealing to work out the *opportunity cost* of preserving the asset (e.g. the forgone value of redevelopment, the extra cost of diverting a highway, the added construction cost of shielding historical remains from new construction, etc).

4.6.2. Conclusions on techniques for valuing pollution damage

The basic pre-conditions for using any of the standard valuation techniques in the urban environment are that cause and effect are well established and that costs and benefits are attributable. These conditions rarely hold. The problem is compounded where there are a number of possible contributors to environmental deterioration, and alternative explanations of their impact on the receptors, or where the symptoms of the parties affected may have other possible causes.

These factors limit the scope for serious valuation of the environmental effects of urban projects or even city-wide programmes. Further problems are the plausibility of applying some of the techniques in the cities of developing countries, the absence of, and the costs of gathering, data, and the predominance of developed country cases and priorities in the empirical literature.

Benefit estimation in the urban context may be most useful in the decision to set environmental standards. A number of Third World cities monitor environmental standards, and some have explicit quality targets. Benefit and cost estimators, for all their imperfections and lack of full scientific credence, can provide illustrations of the orders of magnitude of the benefits/avoided costs of setting particular standards. (Even the simple notion of preventive expenditure implies acceptance of some minimum standards.)

Methods of cost analysis have more universal applicability. Cost-effectiveness analysis can provide guidance on the least-cost methods of achieving given standards. The opportunity-cost approach can help in the decision to cancel, postpone, relocate or redesign schemes on environmental grounds.

4.7. Noise

Excessive noise can affect human health, well-being and productive activity. For the purpose of valuation, a useful distinction is that between health and well-being, on the one hand, and commercial activities and public services, on the other.

4.7.1. Effect on health and well-being

The perception of noise as a nuisance is very subjective. Some people positively prefer an environment with some level of noise, and people differ greatly in the noise they can tolerate without discomfort. What follows should therefore be regarded as typical or average experience, which should be reassessed in the light of local circumstances and preferences.

Noise levels in excess of 70 decibels start to become intrusive to the human ear, and at levels of 85 db can damage hearing if the exposure continues for eight hours or more. Regular exposure of more than one minute to more than 100 db risks impairment of hearing. At lower levels of noise, annoyance and interruption of activities can occur, which affect psychic well-being and may have economic costs through defensive expenditures (e.g. relocation, double glazing) or interruptions to output and services. These general statements need to be qualified. People regularly exposed to high noise levels apparently become used to it, and more sensitive to unusual noise than to the high ambient level. The general level of ambient noise is relevant to people's toleration of higher noise levels. Frequency of noise is also important to what is considered tolerable.

Most of the valuation literature has been concerned with aircraft noise, since this is a localised source of great nuisance value. One measure is the Noise and Number Index, which takes account of both average peak noise in perceived decibel levels and the number of aircraft movements. The environmental cost of aircraft noise has been inferred from Hedonic, Contingent Valuation, and Preventive Expenditure methods.

Most hedonic studies have been done in high-income countries, and show a clear negative relationship between noise and property values. In principle, noise nuisance at workplaces could also be picked out by wage differential studies, but there are few such examples that isolate noise, rather than the other factors making for disagreeable and risky working conditions. Differential market values for property omit any consumers surplus that residents enjoy from a noise-free environment, and which is lost when noise intrudes. The Roskill Commission (1971) complemented its hedonic property estimates with those for consumers' surplus obtained from CV surveys. Residents were asked about their willingness to accept compensation for increased noise nuisance, though the method used has been criticised.

Finally, the implicit values that individuals place on environmental noise can be uncovered by examining their actual household outlays to alleviate the problem (PE). In a study of the use made of a public scheme to instal double-glazing in houses near Heathrow Airport in London, it was found that householders were willing to pay £45 to insulate all bedrooms, and £33 for living rooms at 1972 prices (Starkie and Johnson, 1973).

4.7.2. Effects on production and public services

Certain activities particularly sensitive to noise may suffer actual damage (loss of output) or interruption (loss of time). In principle these can be valued directly, though in practice they are likely to be hard to identify and difficult to disentangle from mere inconvenience. A more promising avenue would be to use the PE and RC approaches to identify what the afflicted parties actually spend to relieve the noise effect (e.g. insulation) or to relocate away from it. HM can also be used for commercial premises, to uncover the noise discount (section 5.3). In respect of public services (education, hospitals, community centres) and other social and community functions (religious worship, entertainment, social gatherings), PE and RC are also valid.

4.7.3. Application to developing countries

The gravity of noise as a problem in developing countries is belied by its omission from most lists of crucial environmental issues, and the near absence of noise studies outside the OECD. There are several possible explanations for this.

(i) Many people who are most affected by noise (e.g. shanty town dwellers, those who live next to airports, railways or highways) lack enough effective demand to express their feelings through the market by, for instance, insulation, double-glazing or relocation.

(ii) Noise is often correlated with other disadvantages such as poor sanitation, inadequate water supplies, water and air pollution, and its effect is buried by these other disamenities.

(iii) Whatever the absolute status of noise as a problem, it normally comes below such issues as unemployment, shortage of food, general environmental squalor and poor public services in the majority of poor Third World cities and industrial areas.

(iv) The noise nuisance is likely to have more sources and be more diffuse that in more affluent countries. Air traffic is generally much lighter than in Europe or North America, but street noise and that from industry and power generators could be worse. Noise of this kind is more easily accepted as a constant background and after a while becomes less noticeable. Societies also differ in their tolerance of, or even in their positive fondness for, noise. Values of noise obtained from countries with different income levels and social customs should not, therefore, be transferred uncritically for use elsewhere.

There are also practical problems in carrying out noise studies in developing countries related to the nature of the property market (section 3.3.4), and the perceptions of noise as a nuisance are inseparable from other urban 'bads'. For these and other reasons it may not be very easy or meaningful to put economic values on noise nuisance in developing countries, serious though the problem is.

4.7.4. Case study

Airport noise and property values in Atlanta, USA (O'Byrne et al., 1985)

In this study hedonic price models were developed for the housing market in Atlanta, Georgia, to isolate the effect of aircraft noise on local property values.

Atlanta Airport is long established and has become one of the busiest in the country, with 1,500 daily aircraft movements in 1980. The authors use cross-section data for two periods, 1970 and 1979/80, and develop relationships between aircraft noise (in decibels) and discounts on house values, controlling for a number of other explanatory variables. Combining data for the two periods, they estimate that the sales value of a house is reduced by 0.67% for each decibel increase in noise. This compares with the following results from other studies. In a study of 11 airports using data from the period 1967-76, the mean percentage noise discount was 0.62% per decibel, with a range of 0.4-1.1. In a further group of 6 airports, the weighted mean discount was 0.5% (with Cleveland 0.29 and San Diego 0.74.)

The use of 1960s data for three major airports shows higher values for the noise discount - 2% per decibel. The authors suggest, by way of explanation, that:

. . . the early period of travel by commercial jet was associated with a transitional period of adjustment in residential housing markets.

This could be relevant to circumstances in developing countries where airports are being planned in areas that have not hitherto been exposed to the noise problem. In such cases, higher implicit values for the noise nuisance might be expected.

4.8. Marine pollution and reef destruction

The principal techniques available to value marine pollution and reef destruction are EOP, RC, TC and CV.

Effect on Production. Marine environmental damage can cause clear and direct losses to commercial fishing, seaweed farming, tourism, etc. An oil spill which causes fishing to be temporarily suspended results in a loss of fishing income, which may be long-term if inshore-breeding areas are permanently contaminated. Because oil spills are single dramatic events with highly visible effects, and large companies are usually held responsible, they are usually accompanied by estimates of loss of earnings, which serve as the basis of legal suits.

Compensation payments are therefore one source of estimates of output losses. However, the level of compensation varies greatly according to the case (Cohen, 1986). Using compensation as a proxy for loss of output is a very crude method that needs to allow for variations in the amount of damage, the country of litigation, the legal power of the victims and the attitude of the defendant company. In principle, using the capitalised loss of earnings method can apply to fisheries where there is a clear effect on output and where future catches are predictable - as in the awards to fishermen from in-filling parts of Tokyo Bay (Dixon and Hufschmidt, 1986). The use of compensation is more dubious where the effect of pollution (e.g. from effluent) on fish catches is more tenuous, or where there is evidence of overfishing. In any case, growing concern with environmental damage from oil spillages and the increasing defensiveness of the oil majors is causing an increase in the average settlement (cf. *Exxon Valdez*).

The effect of oil slicks on the tourist industry is also direct and potentially measurable, where it is safe to assume the cessation of visits to the beaches affected. A whole tourist season was at risk in Morocco from the massive *Kharg* 5 spillage in 1989. The effect on tourism of less dramatic pollution, e.g. from algal blooms or local effluent, is more difficult to measure and predict, but potentially serious. The economic effects of pollution in the Northern Adriatic have caused great local concern:

. . . the Emilia Romagna region, at the mouth of the Po, has 130 kilometers of coastline on the Adriatic; this coastal area attracts more than 40 million tourists each year and accounts for 20% of Italian fishery yields. These two industries are now in jeopardy. (World Bank EIB, 1990)

Where the problem is sufficiently serious, trends in visits or hotel bookings in the affected area should give strong indications of the scale of the loss of gross tourist receipts (Hodgson and Dixon, 1988). It is more difficult to quantify the effect of

pollution on local recreation where visitors do not use hotels or commercial estab-
lishments, though the travel cost method may be appropriate - see Ismailia case
study in section 5.4). There is much anecdotal evidence to weigh, e.g. the effect of
locating an abattoir effluent outlet near a prime beach in Mogadishu, which
encouraged sharks, and discouraged swimmers!

Some rules of thumb have been developed from site-specific research relating fish
yields to the loss of reefs or mangroves. It has, for instance, been estimated that a
hectare of mangroves in the Philippines supports on average c. 500 kg p.a. of fish
yield in adjacent waters (World Bank, 1989).

Replacement Cost. Parts of a damaged marine environment may be replaceable,
in greater or lesser degree. Breeding grounds for fish or oysters, or banks used by
migratory birds, may be recreated elsewhere. Oil or chemical pollution can be
cleaned up. Wildlife can be restocked. The cost of these operations can be used as
a proxy for the environmental services that are lost.

As part of the Oosterschelde project in the Netherlands, an artificial lagoon (a *haff*)
was created to replace fishing, ecological, and recreational services forfeited by the
construction of a major dyke across the estuary (this is also an example of a
'shadow' project - Hufschmidt *et al.*, 1983). Plans for the construction of a barrage
across Cardiff Bay in Wales included the creation of new offshore sandbanks for
the use of rare migratory birds, to replace those to be inundated within the
barrage.

Clean-up operations following oil spillages are also examples of RC. Despite the
huge sums involved so far in the *Exxon Valdez* case in Canada, these must be
regarded as minimum proxies for the true losses, since they fail to restore the
environment to its pristine state, they do not compensate for the death and
maiming of wildlife, the solvents used may themselves cause harm, and they do
not reflect environmental sacrifices during the clean-up itself.

Because clean-up efforts are conducted with much publicity with intense moral
pressure on the offenders, it would be unwise to take the actual cost of cleaning,
say, wild animals and birds as society's 'revealed preference' for the value of these
creatures. For instance, the actual cost of cleaning and treating a seabird following
oil pollution in Chesapeake Bay in 1976 was $575, or $1,300 per bird still alive after 2
years. The average cost of saving a sea otter after the *Exxon Valdez* spill in 1989 was
$45,000 (*The Economist*, 26 August 1989).

The danger of using such estimates of RC can be further illustrated from the
Chesapeake Bay case. In one appraisal of the cost of the oil spill the loss of sea birds
was estimated using the cost of buying replacement birds from biological supply
firms and commercial breeders, at an average unit cost of only $30 (Cohen, 1986).
Yet very few species could be replaced 'off the shelf', and those who believe in
animal rights would find the very principle offensive.

Travel Cost is a useful technique where marine pollution damages environmental
assets that are not commercially marketed, e.g. recreation and amenity. The case
study of Ismailia in section 5.4 illustrates the possibilities.

Contingent Valuation has been applied to biodiversity or rare species as the basis
of estimating society's preservation bid for the resource. There are many problems

n applying the technique (section 3.3.6). For instance, in the case of endangered mammals it has been shown that the results of CV enquiries crucially depend on the information provided to respondents about the animal's characteristics and its endangered status. Preservation bids tend to be low if the population size is large enough to assure preservation, or alternatively if extinction is believed inevitable. Bids also depend on the physical attractiveness of the animal and the respondents' views on the efficacy of the preservation method. With these rather damning qualifications, the preservation bid for the humpback whale fell in a range of $36-57 per year (Samples, Dixon and Gowen, 1986).

Human Capital. Where marine pollution affects human health, e.g. where pollutants enter the food chain (through fish or shellfish), effluent causes skin rashes or eye complaints, or untreated sewage leads to intestinal diseases, the loss of earnings and cost of medical treatment provide an estimate of the environmental damage . However, the approach depends on a credible relationship being drawn between certain kinds of pollution and health effects, and the ability to generalise such relationships across different countries. The valuation of ill-health is a subsequent problem. Such case studies as exist in developing countries are often forced to use modified relationships established from developed country experience (e.g. Ismailia case study in section 5.4).

4.9. Soil salinisation, contamination and groundwater problems

Irrigated agriculture is taken as a convenient reference point in discussing these effects, though this does not imply that irrigation is solely or necessarily responsible for them. The main effects to be considered here are soil fertility, water flow and quality, and wildlife and genetic diversity. The discussion of health effects is reserved for the next section. The many positive benefits from intensive farming can be dealt with in the normal framework of cost-benefit analysis and will not be reviewed here.

A decline in **soil fertility** from exploitative or careless agricultural use is the most tangible effect, and can in principle be measured either by EOP, PE or RC methods. Salinisation is now a widespread phenomenon, e.g. in Pakistan, and yield data are available from many of the longer-running schemes. Changes in the underlying soil fertility over time are difficult to estimate, since they are continually being disguised by the application of fertiliser which can even improve soil fertility in the long term. What are required are time-series experiments with fertiliser dosage, with other factors held equal, showing the trend in crop yield for a given application of fertiliser. An alternative approach would be to discover changes in the marginal productivity of fertiliser over time. If it were discovered that increasing amounts were required to produce the same yield, the incremental cost could be regarded as a proxy for the underlying decline in soil fertility.

Alternatively, data are available through the PE and RC routes. There is now evidence from major command areas of the period over which salinisation and waterlogging become critical and begin to affect yield. The massive investment programmes in Pakistan, first in the Salinity Control and Rehabilitation Project, and more recently the Left Bank Outfall Drain, are examples of remedial expenditure, or RC. Their purpose was to try and restore previous levels of fertility by pumping the water-table down via tubewells and conducting the excess water away down a large new drainage canal.

It is important to make estimates of the remedial expenditure necessary to counter waterlogging in irrigation schemes, and to build them into the initial project costs - even though they may be incurred some years into the future. Otherwise, irrigation schemes are approved with a large element in their costs hidden. Discounting will reduce the weight of future costs in the economic appraisal, and it is therefore important for the project's future sustainability that adequate financial provision is made, ideally from income generated during the earlier years of the scheme. If drainage schemes are not considered and appraised at the same time as the irrigation project, there is a risk of treating the original investment as a sunk cost, and all the scheme's benefits are then attributed to the rehabilitation/drainage project, which compounds the original error.

Water flow and quality. Firm cause-and-effect relationships will be difficult to establish *ex ante*. Hydraulic modelling should be undertaken as part of any large scheme, and would indicate the likely effects of diversion on water flows lower down the catchment. In the light of experience, it would be important to make realistic allowance for the waste and seepage of water through the network.

The orders of magnitude produced should be of some value in predicting the size of effect on water users - e.g. the river might shrink to a size imperilling fishing, and could leave water intakes high and dry. In other circumstances, the irrigation system could recharge the aquifer and increase the yield or prolong the life of tubewells. EOP, PE and RC methods of valuation would all have some scope.

Effects on the quality of water to other users should also be broadly predictable, based on relevant experience elsewhere. Quantifying and valuing this impact - through health, crop yield, fishing catch, etc. - is more difficult, and could turn out to be impossible for practical appraisal purposes (though results from comparable situations might be relevant). The use of PE and RC might be more appropriate, where the threat or existence of contamination moves the authorities to construct new water intakes, develop new water sources, or install treatment facilities.

Wildlife and genetic diversity. When an irrigation scheme is first developed, there will be an initial and continuing sacrifice of wildlife on land (forest, wetlands, etc.) cleared for farming. However, in due course wildlife thriving in aquatic surroundings (fish, some birds) will increase. The net effect is hard to predict, as is the impact on household food supply.

The loss of wildlife also reduces the potential for using natural methods of pest control. Chemical pesticides substitute for (and further diminish) natural predators, and do so haphazardly and expensively. Ideally, a comparison should be made between the respective costs of natural (integrated) pest management, and the use of chemical methods with the same efficacy. If the natural methods were cheaper, this would indicate the value of wildlife; the excess cost of chemical pesticides could be regarded as the value of the pest control services of wildlife. The problems in making such a comparison would be, firstly, ensuring the identical efficacy of both methods, and, secondly, allowing for ecological dynamics - growing resistance to pesticides, and the emergence of new pests freed from their former predators. Pure biodiversity is almost invariably reduced by irrigation schemes. The problems of valuing it are further discussed in section 4.11.

4.10 Health problems in irrigated farming

Although this section will concentrate on the negative effects of irrigation on environmental health, its positive effects - on food production, incomes, jobs and even recreation - should be acknowledged as appropriate in the normal course of cost-benefit analysis.

4.10.1. The scope for valuation

The HC approach relies on hard medical evidence of cause and effect, linking the introduction of irrigation with a specific amount of extra morbidity and mortality. In normal circumstances this cannot be predicted with any accuracy. Studies can be done after the event which will yield valid data for decisions to continue the same scheme, or to introduce a similar scheme in comparable circumstances elsewhere. Otherwise, the evidence of fieldwork can only illustrate the possible severity of effects, and decision-makers will have to draw their own conclusions.

The second step - deriving economic values from the observed patterns of morbidity and mortality - is no less problematic. Some of the main diseases concerned - e.g. bilharzia, filariasis - can cause long-term debilitation to their victims. If incurred in infancy, as many diseases are, lifelong mental and physical development may be impaired. The impact of debilitating and disabling diseases on lifetime output and earnings is hard to measure, compared with diseases that lead to short-term losses of output and finite medical costs (less intense bouts of malaria come into this category). In the words of one writer in this area, '. . . studies which attempt to measure the effect of health status on the productivity of agricultural work are quite rare' (Audibert, 1986). Such studies as exist of plantation workers conclude that

> . . . it is difficult to demonstrate the impact of a parasitic infection such as malaria and schistosomiasis on work productivity. It is worth noting that the condition of self-employed peasants has not been studied. (*ibid.*)

Anecdotal evidence can illustrate the scale of the problem. In 1974 20% of the labour force on the Gezira scheme in Sudan were down with malaria, and soldiers and students were drafted in to help save the cotton crop. On the Bura project in Kenya, the malarial deaths of children were one of the main reasons why many of the first settlers abandoned the scheme (Tiffen, 1990).

In one case study (see below) the incidence of schistosomiasis among rice farmers in Cameroon was shown to be clearly associated with reduced output. Such clear relationships are unusual, and even this result depended on unusually favourable research conditions.

Where there is good medical evidence of the link between irrigated farming and health problems, responsible authorities could build counteractive measures into project planning (Service, 1989; Prescott, 1987; Bos and Mills, 1987; Liese, 1986). This would entitle the economist to use PE as a proxy for environmental costs. The costs of design modifications to the irrigation scheme, the provision of safe drinking water, sanitation and sewage disposal, health posts, and public education about safe personal and household hygiene, can be regarded as a proxies for the health risks of the project. Likewise for the more direct measures of disease control, such as immunisation (against Japanese encephalitis), and the various measures of chemical and biological control.

Case study: Irrigation, health and farm output in Cameroon (Audibert, 1986)

This is a study of the Department of Mayo Danai in the north of Cameroon which was the subject of a World Bank-funded irrigation project begun in the early 1970s and extended in 1979. By 1986 12,600 families worked on the scheme, which covered some 6,800 ha. Rice was the predominant irrigated crop, on a typical plot of 0.5 ha. Many farmers also kept on their old farms, based on millet, fishing and livestock.

The irrigation is managed by a public corporation which provides the main farm services, buys the output, and deducts the cost of services from the price - which is fixed by the government. Records have been kept of the output of each grower and the health status of farmers has been examined and recorded. Seasonally-transmitted malaria is endemic to the region. The prevalence of urinary bilharziasis varies from 10 to 60% according to the village.

Method. All relevant determinants of the level of rice production were taken into account in estimating a generalised production function. In principle, the marginal effect of health status was measured by the coefficient of its variation in the estimated function. The output of rice was modelled using as the explanatory variables 'experience' (number of previous growing seasons that a family has taken part in), size of labour force available to the family, prevalence of malaria/bilharziasis, the duration of transplanting, the cultivated area, a dummy variable for the rice variety, and the number of millet fields cultivated (since millet and rice compete for the family's attention at certain times). The most important variables not included were the size of farm inputs - assumed to be the same for all plots, which are mostly of the same size - and the amount of irrigation water and the way it is managed - which is handled by the public corporation. The factor 'farm skills' is difficult to represent, and its differential effect is probably diminished by control and advice exercised by the corporation through its agricultural monitors and irrigation technicians.

Results. There was no significant difference in the prevalence of malaria between rice-growers on irrigated plots and other people. Nor was the prevalence of malaria a significant explanatory variable for rice output. This was probably because malaria was endemic throughout the region. Alternatively, it was not the most severe kind, causing bouts of illness which made people unable to work for short periods. However, schistosomiasis was shown to be more prevalent among people working in flooded paddy fields. This caused debilitation, and was correlated with the duration of transplanting. A 10% increase in the prevalence of schistosomiasis resulted in a 4.9% fall in output. The level of experience of the farm family was also confirmed as a factor in output. This appeared to offset the greater risk that long-serving workers were more exposed to disease.

The findings corroborated the main hypothesis, that poor health affects the area that a family can cultivate - since rice growing is arduous and labour-intensive - and the duration of transplanting of seedlings (the crucial stage, which is best kept short).

This study claims to be the first attempt to relate health to the productivity of self-employed farmers; a few previous studies attempted the same for plantation workers, though with less clear-cut results. The research was carried out 12-15 years after the project started, when trends in health had clearly emerged. (If it had been done earlier its findings would have been relevant to the planning of the second extension.)

Research conditions were unusually favourable, with relatively homogeneous plots, standard farm inputs, and close control and advice provided by the project authority. This enabled a number of crucial variables to be left out of the correlation, whose inclusion in different situations would have greatly complicated the exercise. Even in these 'ideal' research conditions, it was impossible to find a clear effect of malaria on rice output. The finding for urinary schistosomiasis should prove valuable for both this and other planned schemes. Leaving aside the human cost of the disease, an estimate of its economic cost is now available to reinforce the case for improved measures of public health and education

4.11. Loss of biodiversity

Biological diversity has been cited as an environmental issue in all the major habitats. At the same time, the benefits of diversity as such are often elusive, and despite marshalling a full array of techniques, economists have failed to demonstrate plausible ways of capturing its value.

Biodiversity has a more precise meaning than the general term 'wildlife', the valuation of which is discussed at various points in this chapter, depending on the context (e.g. in sections 4.1, 4.3, 4.4, 4.5)

4.11.1. The concept and importance of biodiversity

Biodiversity has been defined by McNeely (1988) as follows:

Biological diversity is an umbrella term for the degree of nature's variety, including both the number and frequency of ecosystems, species and genes in a given assemblage. It is usually considered at three different levels, 'genetic diversity', 'species diversity' and 'ecosystem diversity' . . .

Genetic diversity is a concept of the variability within a species, as measured by the variation in genes . . . within a particular species, variety, subspecies and breed . . .

Species diversity is a concept of the variety of living organisms on earth, and is measured by the total number of species in the world . . . or in a given area under study . . .

Ecosystem diversity refers to the diversity and health of the ecological complexes within which species occur.

Biodiversity differs from 'biological resources' or the looser term 'wildlife'. The nub of the concept is the variety rather than the amount of biological resources. It is possible for biological resources to increase, yet for their diversity to diminish. On a limited scale, resources can diminish but their diversity can be preserved (e.g. by keeping specimens in Kew Gardens, or by targeting the preservation of areas especially rich in species).

Diversity, in its three senses described above, gives a special dimension to conservation. Merely preserving diversity in narrow or artificial surroundings will not achieve true conservation, which requires that species systems be allowed to develop and interact freely, without artificial constraints.

Much discussion, ostensibly about biodiversity, is really about the value of particular natural species. This is legitimate if a reduction in species diversity were to lead to a reduction in the population of the species in question, or even threatened their extinction. But it is easy to conceive of situations where the two concepts are quite distinct, and even antithetical - e.g. where a reduction in the population of the dominant species would increase the diversity of the remaining collection.

Diversity per se is important for at least two reasons, the potential value of biological species as yet undiscovered or unresearched, and the role of diversity in the functioning of ecosystems.

Potential value of species. The overwhelming majority of species likely to exist in the world have still to be discovered. Relatively few even of those that have been identified and classified have been fully investigated for their properties.

> Some 230 years after Linnaeus began classifying the variety of life on earth, we still do not know how many species exist - even to within a factor of ten. Of the estimated 10 million to 30 million species on earth, only some 1.4 million have been named and at least briefly described. (quoted in Reid and Miller, 1989, p.9).

Yet certain wild species have proved to be of enormous importance to agriculture, animal husbandry, medicine and industry. The Green Revolution has been based on the development of high-yielding varieties, but the sustainability of these and other productive strains will depend on periodically infusing new genetic material in order to maintain pest and disease resistance. Wild animals are important to the diet of people in many developing countries, and wild species can be cross-bred with domesticated and commercial animals to good effect. Many medicines in widespread use have their origins in natural ingredients, including some that have marked important break-throughs in the treatment of serious complaints - like the rosy periwinkle in anti-cancer drugs. Traditional societies rely heavily on the natural medicines derived from their habitats. (For many other examples, see Prescott Allens, 1988; McNeely, 1988; Reid and Miller, 1989).

If biodiversity is lost, there is a serious risk that species, which could have been of great human importance, will become extinct, or so rare that they are unlikely to see the light of day.

Diversity and ecosystem functions. An ecosystem is a complicated organism whose functions depend on a dynamic interaction amongst its parts. These interactions are little understood, but the loss of certain component species is bound to affect the overall environmental 'performance' of the system, namely its ability to provide useful services. Species occupy 'ecological niches', depending on others in a complex chain of predators and prey. Remove one, and there could be repercussions on the whole system. The loss of habitat of one species would normally stimulate the growth of species on which the first one preyed. For instance, in Sabah the wild birds in certain commercial plantations keep down the caterpillar population, which would otherwise defoliate the trees (McNeely,

1988). The careless and indiscriminate use of pesticides can upset the natural predator-prey links, and become self-defeating (see section 2.5).

It is appropriate to stress the great uncertainty surrounding this subject. Human activity is constantly disturbing natural processes, and it is misleading to imagine a 'balance of nature' in which the environment is somehow in equilibrium. Even in the absence of human interventions, natural systems are subject to flux and periodic shocks. Biodiversity is not a pristine and immutable condition.

4.11.2. Economic valuation

The economic values of biodiversity can be classified as follows (Flint, 1990):

Use values. (i) direct - the direct consumption of biological resources, e.g. as food, medicine; the use of species in plant breeding; and their role in nature tourism; (ii) indirect - the role of species diversity in ecological processes, e.g. controlling certain pests, assimilating waste, purifying water; (iii) possible future values - the value of keeping an option on these services in future (e.g. the possible value of undiscovered species for drugs, or new crops).

Non-use values. The values that society places on the mere existence of diverse species, or on particular species that would be threatened if diversity were reduced. In other words, the concept of 'existence value', which is unrelated to the direct use made of these resources either now or in the future.

These elements make up the Total Economic Value. Putting economic numbers to these values can be considered under four headings, proceeding in increasing order of difficulty.

(i)*Direct use values*

There are no novel difficulties in valuing known biological resources in actual use. The field studies of biodiverse resources in tropical rain forests (section 4.2), wetlands (4.4), coral reefs (4.7) etc. have generated some data on the products and services of such resources. For instance, the celebrated study by Peters *et al.* (1989) in the Peruvian Amazon discovered 275 species in a one hectare patch of forest, of which 26% of the species and 42% of the individual trees yielded products with a market value in the nearest city. The option of gathering fruit and latex, with selective timber cutting, yielded a sustainable harvest with an NPV of US$6,820/ha., superior to the obvious land-use alternatives. In this example, the implicit choice is between preserving the forest, with most or all of its biodiversity intact, and replacing it with some other land use with few if any of the original species - a clear-cut case for appraising the direct use value of biodiversity as such.

(ii)*Indirect use value*

There are no readily available estimates of the effect of reduced diversity on the performance of ecological functions. It is possible to produce estimates of the value of ecological services due to entire ecosystems, or particular species within them, but difficult to isolate the contribution of diversity *per se*.

(iii)*Possible future value*

The great value of certain genetic discoveries and their successful applications to commercial products has been amply documented. There is clearly some value in retaining enough biodiversity to keep options on doing the same in future. In short, the option value must be positive. But how large should it be?

If past experience is any guide, relatively few species as yet undiscovered or untested will turn out to be of commercial value. Scientists already possess a considerable bank of genetic resources, much of it untested, and biotechnology will doubtless develop a stream of products from its existing sources. Access to species in the wild is still free, and would be difficult to restrict. The overwhelming cost of bringing a product to market is made up of research, testing, and marketing; the economic rent from the product in the wild, akin to the stumpage value in forestry, may be a small part of its total marketed price.

These are all reasons why commercial companies are not willing to pay very much for the conservation of biodiversity. In agricultural research, it has been observed that '. . . the financial value of unresearched exotic landraces at source is very low, even if the potential value of one particular genetic trait is enormous' (Flint, 1990, p. 7).

Likewise in medicine. Novel chemical compounds, whether patented or not, have a low current value as measured by the willingness to pay of commercial companies:

> Few naturally occurring compounds are marketable without an enormous input of costly research and testing - this accounts for most of the value added in drug development. Undeveloped and untested chemicalk compounds are readily available and very cheap for this reason. Even patented discoveries are only worth around £5,000. (Flint, 1990, p. 8)

The above data were used in fieldwork carried out in Cameroon (Ruitenbeek, 1989, see case study in section 5.2) to appraise the value of conserving the Korup Forest. The value per research discovery in the forest was related to the average patent value in the UK, which, at £5,000, was scaled down to reflect the likelihood that only part of this (assumed to be 10%) would be appropriated by the host country. With a further assumption that 10 such discoveries would be made every year, the total appropriable value to the host country of £5,000 was a trivial amount relative to the value of the project.

(iv)*Existence values*

These can only be obtained by CV surveys. The numerous examples of wildlife valuation turn out to be either direct use value enjoyed by actual or potential visitors or CV studies of the preservation of the whole natural resource or of particular species within it. Valuing pure biodiversity is a more subtle matter, and examples are rare.

The heart of the valuation problem is that different groups of people will have different relative valuations to place on biodiversity. It would be a difficult task to obtain a representative average, and to choose a population size to which the sample results could be extrapolated (see section 3.3.6). Local people are likely to place higher values on direct use value, while armchair nature lovers in developed countries would be more likely to appreciate pure existence values, and even then, for the so-called 'charismatic' animals such as elephants, dolphins and pandas. What price for the estimated half million beetle species? As Flint (1990) observes:

. . . the practical contribution of economic valuation [of biodiversity] is limited. The main reason for this is scientific and economic uncertainty, and explains why economists have made much more progress in identifying the types of value than they have in estimating those values - there are a lot of empty boxes, and few numbers. (p. 11)

4.11.3. The role of economics in conserving biodiversity

Economic valuation cannot capture much of the benefit of biodiversity. But this does not mean that economic criteria are irrelevant to decisions to conserve it. Economic analysis is of potential value in the following areas:

(i) stating the types of benefit, and illustrating the size of possible values. This is easiest for direct use values, where representative studies have been done, but even then the figures are best regarded as illustrations, since the value of biodiversity will vary by locality as well as habitat.

(ii) estimating the opportunity cost of conservation, in terms of the net benefits that are forgone if it is decided to retain resources in their current use. This information would be produced by cost-benefit analysis of the proposed project.

(iii) if certain conservation objectives were determined on scientific or political criteria, cost-effectiveness analysis might be helpful in choosing the most efficient way of achieving them.

Further discussion of appraising conservation schemes is contained in section 5.2.

4.12. Global climatic effects

It is now accepted by many, though by no means all, scientists that certain man-made processes are responsible for a rise in global temperatures. Another set of factors is causing the depletion of the earth's atmospheric ozone layer. These are classic examples of externalities, whose perpetrators experience a negligible cost, but which make everyone worse off. At present those responsible for global warming or depletion of the ozone layer, and the consumers of their products, do not directly bear any of the costs incurred by international society from their actions. The issue addressed in this section is whether it is feasible to attribute such costs directly to projects, and if so, how.

Although they are similar in principle to the more familiar localised externalities (e.g. the effect of soil erosion on downstream farmers, industrial air pollution on urban residents), these global externalities possess features which complicate any straightforward attribution. In the first place there is still great uncertainty over the extent of global warming, and even - in some scientifically respectable quarters - about whether it exists at all. Secondly, the incremental effect from new activities is not easy to disentangle from the 'commitment' implied by historical actions, given the natural lags in the climatic system. Thirdly, the distribution of the costs (and benefits) from global warming is very uneven, and important parties may stand to gain by it.

At the time of writing the state of knowledge about these global environmental issues is very fluid, and there is huge momentum behind further research. Meanwhile, international diplomatic efforts are in train to agree preventative actions and the necessary systems of controls, incentives and sanctions.

This section is concerned with both the greenhouse effect and the related but separate problem of the depletion of the ozone layer. Acid rain and other forms of trans-boundary air pollution are geographically more localised problems that have been dealt with in section 4.6.

4.12.1 The phenomena of global warming and depletion of the ozone layer

The greenhouse effect and global warming. The presence of greenhouse gases (technically, Radiatively Important Gases - RIGs) in the earth's atmosphere keep the planet over 30 degrees C warmer than it would otherwise be. These gases are carbon dioxide (CO_2), nitrous oxide (N_2O), methane (CH_4), tropospheric ozone (O_3), and chlorofluorocarbons (CFCs). They allow short-wave visible radiation to enter the atmosphere, but absorb and reradiate (i.e. trap) long-wave thermal radiation, hence the greenhouse analogy.

In theory, past emissions of these gases have committed the earth to a warming of 1 - 2.5 degrees C over pre-industrial levels. In practice, a rise of c. 0.5 degrees C has been observed during the past century, almost half of which has been since 1965. The majority view of scientists is that by 2020 global mean temperatures will have risen to 1.8 degrees C above pre-industrial levels (range 1.3 - 2.5 C), with an increase in global mean precipitation and evaporation of 3%. By 2070 the range of temperature increase will be 2.4 - 5.1 degrees C (best estimate 3.5 C), and precipitation 7% greater. Snow cover and sea ice areas will be smaller (data drawn from IPCC Policymakers' Summary, 1990, and Trexler, Mintzer and Moomaw, 1990). These changes in temperature will be greater in higher latitudes than at the equator, thus North America, the USSR, Europe and China will be more affected than tropical regions.

The most obvious result of such warming would be a rise in sea level due to the thermal expansion of the oceans and melting of some land ice. The sea level is currently rising at 1.6 - 3.3 cm per decade, one quarter of which is due to the thermal expansion of the oceans and the rest to the melting of glaciers and snow-fields. Between now and 2030 it is predicted to rise by c. 20 cm (range 10-32 cm) and by 2070 by 45 cm (range 33-75 cm).

Depletion of the ozone layer. Ozone is present in the atmosphere up to a height of c. 60 km. At lower levels it is one of the greenhouse gases, but at higher levels it is a filter for ultraviolet radiations from the sun. It prevents the most dangerous ultraviolet wavelengths reaching the earth's surface, where they would otherwise cause sunburn, snow blindness, skin cancer, and other effects on plant and animal life. Certain trace gases help to break down atmospheric ozone; these include nitrogen oxides, water vapour, chloroform, methane and CFCs, which are especially important in this process.

The concentration of the trace gases, and in particular the CFCs, in the atmosphere is increasing, mainly as a result of industrial activity. Although the presence of ozone at lower levels of the atmosphere is also increasing, there are signs of some reduction at the upper levels. The most definite evidence of a weakening in the ozone layer comes from observations in the Antarctic, which record a reduction in the amount of ozone by 40% since 1957, most of which has occurred since 1977 (data from UNEP/GEMS, 1987).

There is considerable scientific uncertainty about chemical and physical effects in the atmosphere, and what causes them. Another problem is that CFCs take some time to rise to the level where they damage the ozone layer. Hence there are considerable lags in the process, and by the same token the phenomenon will continue long after the emission of CFCs has been reduced or eliminated.

4.12.2 Causes of global warming

The relative contribution of different RIGs to global warming depends on the rate at which they are emitted, and the lifetime of each gas, amongst other factors. It has been estimated that the cumulative effect of 1990 emissions on 'global warming potential' over 100 years is as follows for the different gases: carbon dioxide 61%; methane 15%; nitrous oxide 4%; CFCs 9.4% in total; others 10.6%. Another way of viewing the relative responsibility of the different gases is to ask what reductions in the current level of emissions would be necessary to stabilise concentrations at current levels. This would be as follows: carbon dioxide 60-80%; methane 15-20%; nitrous oxide 70-80%; CFC 11 70-75%; CFC 12 75-85%; and HCFC 22 40-50% (IPCC, 1990).

The origins of the various gases are as follows (Trexler et al., 1990; Houghton, 1990):

(i) Carbon dioxide: more than 7 billion tonnes of carbon are currently released into the atmosphere every year, with fossil fuel combustion the largest source, with 5.6 bn tonnes. The balance comes from deforestation (either quickly from burning, or slowly from the decay of dead matter), and land degradation.

(ii) Methane: possibly one-third of emissions are due to agriculture, mainly rice farming and cattle rearing. Another source is leaks from natural gas pipelines, oil wells, and releases from coal seams. Burning trees and grass, landfills, sewage treatment, and termites are other sources.

(iii) Nitrous oxide: one-third is believed to originate from fossil fuel combustion, and the rest from the use of nitrogenous fertiliser, forest burning, and change in land use.

(iv) Tropospheric (i.e. lower level) ozone: this is formed from a combination of nitrogen oxides and non-methane hydrocarbons. Fossil fuel combustion is the main cause.

v) CFCs: these gases are manufactured for use in aerosol propellants, blowing agents for plastic foams, refrigerants and solvents. Halons, compounds containing bromine, and used in certain specialised fire-extinguishing systems, are closely related to CFCs and have similar effects.

The contribution to global warming can thus be summed up as follows: energy use (direct and indirect) 49%, deforestation 14%, agriculture 13%, and industry 24% (Trexler et al., 1990). On a geographical basis, emissions of carbon dioxide from burning fossil fuel - the largest single contributor to global warming - are heavily concentrated in developed and industrialising countries: the USA (25%), the USSR (20%) Western Europe (15%), China (10%) and Japan (6%). Developing countries, apart from China, contributed only 15% in 1985. However, this is likely to change rapidly, as developing countries industrialise and increase their per capita energy use - currently only one-sixth that of industrialized countries. One estimate has industrialising developing countries emitting 50% of all carbon dioxide within a matter of a few decades (Trexler *et al*, 1990). These figures leave out of account the contribution of developing countries to CO_2 emissions from deforestation, which is estimated to provide between 20% and 33% of such emissions.

4.12.3 Effects

Global warming. If the temperature changes described in part (i) do come about, they are likely to have the following kinds of effects (Commonweatlh Secretariat, 1989; Trexler *et al*., 1990; IPCC, 1990).

i) A rise in the sea level by a range of 33-75 cm by 2070. Some have put forward higher estimates, 40-120 cm (Trexler *et al*., 1990), while most pessimistic scenarios predict rises of several meters. The worst outcome would be a melting of the West Antarctic ice sheet, which would cause a rise of 7 meters in the sea level. Even the more modest predicted rises would totally submerge some island groups (e.g. the Maldives and some Pacific atolls), erode barrier islands, and inundate many coastal wetlands and estuaries. There would be saline intrusion into groundwater supplies. Low-lying coastal hinterlands, which include many of the world's most productive and densely settled areas, would be lost. The potential impact of a sea-level rise of 1 meter has been described as follows:

> Worldwide, the land area that would be subject to inundation or made vulnerable to salt water intrusion is about 500 million hectares. This is only about 3% of all land area, but it constitutes over 30% of the most productive cropland area. As many as one billion people now live in the vulnerable areas, including some very large cities . . . as much as one-fifth of world market valued assets could be adversely affected (Walter and Ayres, 1990).

A number of the other effects discussed below stem from a rise in the sea level.

(ii) Effects on vegetation. There would be a quickening of the hydrological cycle, leading to a slight increase in global rainfall and changes in the timing and distribution of regional rainfall. The timing and location of monsoons would probably change, and rainfall would probably decline in mid-continental regions and increase in coastal and high-latitude regions. Combined with higher evaporation, this would spell growing water shortages in important food-producing areas. The predicted climatic changes would occur at a much faster rate than historical changes, and it is unlikely that vegetation would have time to adapt smoothly. Some species would be reduced or die out, others would spread rapidly. The growth of some plants wouuld be stimulated by the higher temperatures and greater supply of carbon dioxide, but so also would weeds and insect pests.

(iii) Increased incidence of natural disasters and other extreme events. Hurricanes and typhoons would probably increase in frequency and intensity, since they draw their energy from ocean heat, which would increase. Weather patterns would become more extreme, with more frequent droughts, early frosts, cold periods, storms, storm surges, etc. It is particularly difficult to predict the local distribution of these effects because of the little-understood interaction between the oceans and the climatic zones, and the outcome for major ocean circulatory systems (e.g. the Gulf Stream).

v) Other consequential effects. Amongst the many social and economic effects of the above phenomena are the following:

Energy use would change: in temperate latitudes there would be less need for heating and more for air-conditioning. The net effect would probably be to increase the use of energy and power.

The *fishing* industry would be disrupted by shifts in the boundary between land and sea, the loss of breeding grounds in wetlands and estuaries, and the alterations in species composition due to these changes and the rise in sea temperatures.

The net effect on *food supply* and commercially-important crops is hard to predict, but it is safe to expect a need for major adaptations. Crop zones would migrate by hundreds of kilometers. Forests could be especially at risk as people migrate and adjust to new agricultural systems. Water would become an increasing constraint in a number of important agricultural areas.

Tourism and recreation. Many islands and beaches would be lost and weather conditions would become more unpredictable. Winter sports would suffer.

Wildlife and biodiversity. Many important habitats (wetlands, forests, wildlands) would be lost or invaded. Changes in climate and vegetation, along with population movements, would stretch the adaptation of species up to and beyond their natural limits.

Human settlement. The loss of densely settled coastal lowlands and islands would set in motion migration both internally and to other countries. 'Ecological refugees' would increase in numbers. There would be major needs for new infrastructure - housing, transport, water supplies, health care, education, etc.

Ozone layer depletion. The dangerous part of the spectrum of ultraviolet radiation which is mainly absorbed by the ozone layer is UV-B. If more of this is allowed to penetrate to the earth's surface, there is likely to be more skin cancer and damage to the body's immune system, reduced timber and crop yields, damage to marine algae and possibly fish, and materials corrosion. These effects are enlarged upon below.

(i) Both localised and generalised (melanoma) skin cancer is likely to increase, mainly among white-skinned people living in lower latitudes. One estimate is that a 1% depletion of the ozone layer would increase the incidence of skin cancer by 2%, assuming no change in human behaviour. If CFC emissions could be stabilised, it has been estimated that 1.65 million cases of non-melanoma skin cancer could be prevented (UNEP/GEMS, 1987).

(ii) Increased exposure to UV-B tends to suppress the efficiency with which the body's immune system works. An increased incidence of skin infections might be one outcome of this.

(iii) Plant and tree growth may suffer, since UV-B damages chemicals involved in photosynthesis. Certain crops have been identified as particularly sensitive - namely, cotton, peas, beans, melons, cabbage and soya. Grass and trees may be similarly affected.

(iv) Ultraviolet rays penetrate deep into clear water and threaten single-celled algae. Working through the marine food-chain, this would affect edible fish. There might also be direct effects on fish larvae.

(v) Ultraviolet radiation increases the degradation of many synthetic materials, e.g. paint, glazing, car roofs and plastics used in building, such as PVCs.

(vi) Other possible effects include more eye complaints and more incidence of photochemical smogs.

4.12.4 Costs of global warming

In spite of the great uncertainties about the existence, size and effects of these global phenomena, some attempts have been made to estimate their economic costs. One approach is to estimate greenhouse damage costs assuming no action is taken to control emissions. Another type of estimate is that of the costs of mitigating the effects accompanying global warming, e.g. by raising sea defences. A third type assesses the costs of abatement - i.e. curbing the emissions of greenhouse gases at source.

The first type of study is analogous to taking the Effect on Production approach to economic valuation, while the second and third are akin to the Replacement Cost and Preventive Expenditure methods. In principle, if the values from EOP are less than those from PE/RC, the policy conclusion is that it is cheaper to let the effects happen. Alternatively, if the costs of abatement (PE) are less than EOP or RC, it is rational to curb emissions at source. At a more refined level, the 'optimal' amount of abatement can be estimated, at a point where the cost of abating the marginal unit of greenhouse gas equals the damage that it causes (Nordhaus, 1990). This type of calculation does, however, depend on far greater confidence in the effects, and firmer estimation of their costs, than anyone now possesses.

The case study illustrates the methods used and the scale of costs obtained. It combines estimates of the economic damage from the greenhouse effect (the EOP analogy) and certain defensive measures against sea level rise (RC). There are various other studies, not considered in detail here, which estimate the costs of abatement at source (PE) (notably Manne and Richels, 1990).

Case study: Damage costs from global warming (Nordhaus, 1990, Walter and Ayres, 1990). This is an attempt to extrapolate worldwide from data produced for the United States. The sectors of the US economy are divided into categories according to how sensitive they are judged to be to climatic changes. Agriculture, forestry and fisheries are judged to be most sensitive and contribute 3.1% to GNP, while sectors of 'moderate' sensitivity include construction, water transport and utilities, accounting for a further 10.1% of GNP. Other sectors are taken as largely unaffected by climatic change.

No firm view is taken of the net effect on agriculture, which could be plus or minus $10 bn, according to whether the stimulus from extra carbon dioxide were enough to offset the losses from other factors. The main quantified damage is from the consequences of sea level rise on the need to protect the more valuable property and open coasts by levees and dykes. The total US coastline is taken to be 20,000 km.and the average cost of protection $5m per km. However, there would also be land losses, estimated to be 77 ha. per km. of coastline, or 15,540 sq. km. in total. The lost land is assumed to be worth $5,000 per ha. The coastal defence works ($5.7bn) plus the land losses ($0.48 bn) are converted to an annual equivalent loss of $6.18 bn. The other main quantified damage is from a net increase in the consumption of energy. This results from offsetting the reduced demand for space heating (savings of $1.16 bn.) against the increased demand for air-conditioning ($1.65 bn).

The total economic damage from these two sources is $6.67 bn in 1981 prices, or 0.28% of US GNP. It is recognised that many items are omitted from this estimate, and an upper bound of ten times higher than this is suggested - which would amount to c. 2% of GNP.

These estimates for the United States are scaled up by a factor of 8.1 to illustrate what the effect on global income might be in 2050 if the US costs could be taken as typical (global income is projected to be $26 trillion by 2050 in 1981 prices). On this basis, annual world damages from global warming were projected to be $54 bn in 2050 (most likely) with an upper limit of $520 bn. Related to expected emissions by then of 16.9 bn tons of CO_2 equivalent, a 'marginal shadow emission damage' figure of $3.3 per ton of CO_2 equivalent is derived (or $36.9 per ton in the worst case).

The above figures, grossed up for the world as a whole, are adjusted to allow for a rather greater range of effects (Walter and Ayres, 1990) . Coastal land losses are increased to $2.5 trillion, reflecting the same unit value of land but a much greater hinterland area at risk. Coastal protection costs are estimated to be in the range $2.5-5 trillion, derived from applying a unit cost of $5m per km. to a total world coastline of 0.5-1.0 million km. Some estimate is also made of the cost of resettling refugees, amounting to $0.5-1.0 trillion (250 million people displaced, at $1-2,000 per head, representing direct resettlement costs and lost output for 2 years).

The total costs of the above reworking amount to $5.5-8.5 trillion for the world as a whole, assumed to be spread over 50 years. On an average annual basis they are equivalent to 0.7-1.0% of gross world income - greater than Nordhaus's best estimates, but within his range of error.

The original (Nordhaus) study was prepared as a first attempt to apply cost-benefit analysis to compare the costs of various kinds of abatement actions with the expected greenhouse damage costs, as a means of deciding what kinds of abatement actions were justified. It is hedged about with disclaimers and qualifications, and it is worth stressing some of the limitations.

Both studies rely heavily on effects stemming from sea level rise. Apart from energy use, the many other possible effects of global warming are not treated. It is quite likely, however, that global warming would have its greatest effects on agriculture in developing countries (IPPC, 1990). The global estimates are obtained by extrapolating the US figures to the world as a whole, while assuming the same economic structure and damage pattern in the global economy in 2050 as prevailed in the USA in 1981. It is obviously impossible to predict the state of technology, and therefore consumption patterns, by the middle of the next century.

Although the use of a wide range of values (where the worst case is ten times the best estimate) is useful in suggesting upper bounds on national damages, it is of little help in fixing a shadow marginal damage level per ton of emission. Neither set of estimates does justice to the loss of consumer surplus from reduced enjoyment of environmental services - wildlife, forests, coastlines, etc. - or the possibly irreversible losses to future generations.

In short, the two studies are best viewed as pre-feasibility exercises in assessing the costs and benefits of abatement policies, illustrating the method, the type of data needed, and the orders of magnitude estimates of some of the more easily identified effects. There is clearly great scope for further work in confirming the physical effects involved, and assessing the likely damage costs in economies with radically different features from those of the USA.

4.12.5. Attribution of costs and benefits to projects

The contribution of any individual project or activity to the greenhouse effect is a global externality which is very difficult to quantify at the appraisal stage. In order accurately to ascribe this kind of cost (or avoided cost, or benefit) to a project, the appraiser would need to possess the following information: (i) the likely future effects of global warming; (ii) responsibility for these effects (types of emission, timing, location, etc. The incremental effect of current actions, compared with the commitment to warming caused by past activities); (iii) estimates of the economic cost of the effects in (i), at various future dates, discounted to the present; and (iv) the assignment of responsibility, and thus cost (benefit), to individual projects.

This is a tall order. In the absence of reliable and comprehensive information on the first three items above (see earlier parts of this section), the fourth is impossible. Any valuation method relying on the direct attribution of costs and benefits is unreliable in the present state of our knowledge, since the global environmental costs resulting from a particular project are subject to enormous estimation problems. This is true whether we are considering estimators based on direct effects (EOP, HC, CV), or those based on defensive measures (PE, RC) since the costs avoided by the latter are the same, and equally uncertain.

In present circumstances it is more practicable to consider the attribution problem in a context where a ceiling (or target or quota) for the emission of greenhouse gases is accepted or imposed. This could be at international, national, or local level. To simplify the discussion, assume that a national ceiling is agreed for each country, and that these could be monitored and enforced. (At the time of writing, many countries have accepted such a target for CFC gases, and there is active international discussion of the feasibility of agreeing ceilings for greenhouse gases.)

A proposed project (e.g. a thermal power station) or activity (e.g. continued burning of tropical forest) might use up part of this emissions quota. This would force other sources of emissions to cease, or undertake abatement, either now (if the country was already up to quota) or at some time in the future (if the country was still within its ceiling, in which case the cost would be discounted). In principle, the cost of this abatement action, wherever and whenever it fell, would be the economic cost attributable to the offending project. In other words, within a national emissions ceiling, a project which threatens to increase emissions should be debited with the marginal cost of abating that volume of emissions.

If economic policy-makers were rational, they would try to ensure that the marginal amount of abatement was done at least national economic cost. How this was achieved would depend on the circumstances of each country. In countries where the main emitters were the industrial and power sectors, it might be feasible to create national 'bubbles' for each greenhouse gas, and to allow emitters to trade permits to emit within these ceilings (akin to tradeable permits used in the context of air pollution). This would not be an appropriate solution for countries where a significant part of emissions came from forest or grassland burning, farming, households and vehicles. In some cases a carbon tax might be part of a package of measures, imposed at a level calculated to achieve the national emissions target. This would depend on estimates of the elasticities of demand and supply in the main emitting sectors (see section 4.12.4 for US estimates).

Estimating marginal abatement costs can be done by constructing a 'savings curve', relating the cost of abating a unit of carbon dioxide emission to the volume of abatement, and ranking the various options in ascending order of cost (analogous to ranking sources of electricity generation in merit order). In one such exercise for developing countries, ERL (1990) gave a high cost-effectiveness ranking to fuel efficiency measures in industry, and power station rehabilitation. The management of natural forest and various kinds of reforestation also came out well when their other environmental benefits were taken into account. At the other extreme, fuel switching in power generation was considered a high-cost abatement option.

The determination of the marginal abatement cost can only be done with some knowledge of the feasible alternatives open to each country, and it is unwise to generalise. In some cases, the banning of forest burning would be the most cost-effective course, but only if this were enforceable. Curbing methane emissions by taking land out of rice cultivation is unlikely to be the most feasible or cost-effective option in many rice-producing countries. Whatever the empirical outcome, the cost of national abatement required because of the creation of a project should be included as a 'shadow project' when that scheme is being appraised. It is only by coincidence that this would be equal to the cost of abatement if the project entity had to undertake it itself.

Projects that reduce greenhous gas emissions, or which absorb carbon, have positive benefits equivalent to the avoided costs of abatement in others . The analogy is with energy efficiency and power-saving projects (section 5.3).

Firms and public utilities responsible for greenhouse gas emissions sometimes undertake their own 'compensatory projects' (e.g. thermal power stations and car manufacturers planting trees in other countries to absorb carbon created by their own activities). Although some of these schemes are gimmicks, to the extent that they result in genuine abatement offsets they internalise global costs, and represent shadow projects made real.

Certain activities have national, international and global effects. Industrial and power station emissions cause national air pollution, acid rain in neighbouring countries, and contribute greenhouse gases. Likewise for the burning of tropical forest, and the annual firing of grasslands. Their positive equivalents are projects to control air pollution, etc., which are undertaken for national benefits, but which also have international and global gains.

Provided the incidence of costs and benefits can be sorted out into national and global categories, this is not an insuperable difficulty. A coal-fired power station in India, for instance, would be appraised partly for its national net benefits (a combination of economic and environmental effects) and partly for its effect on greenhouse gas emissions. If India were party to an agreement to limit its national emissions, part of the cost of that power station, to be included as a shadow project, would be the marginal abatement cost imposed on the economy. If this shadow project were very costly, this would influence the decision as to whether to proceed with the project.

The valuation principles discussed in this Guide should help in assessing the respective economic values of national and international environmental effects, which will be important elements in future international environmental diplomacy.

Conclusion

The effects on global climate of the production of greenhouse gases and CFCs are under active investigation. Efforts are intensifying to produce estimates of, respectively, allowing, preventing, and abating these emissions at source. Estimates so far available are interesting illustrations of the scale of possible benefits, but they are incomplete, and offer a wide range of values, which makes them unreliable bases for attributing costs to the responsible projects.

Appraisers are on better ground in a scenario in which national ceilings, targets or quotas are accepted. It is then legitimate to debit projects with the national opportunity cost of their actions, namely the cost of keeping within national ceilings, or the national marginal abatement cost. There is so far little empirical evidence on these costs, but where it is available it should be included as a shadow project in the appraisal. Activities which reduce greenhouse gas emissions should receive corresponding credit, equal to the avoided cost of abatement.

5

Appraising Projects

This chapter is specifically written for economists in an operational role, faced with proposals for projects in the usual variety of sectors. It reminds the reader of the various possible environmental effects of such projects, and draws on relevant parts of Chapters 3 and 4 to indicate what effects can feasibly be valued, and by which methods. Summary case studies are included.

The chapter opens with general guidance on the context and presentation of appraisal results.

5.1. Appraisal in a decision-making framework

Although different offices and agencies have their own procedures, an environmental economic appraisal would normally fit into the following kind of framework:

i) identify **major environmental problems** and their causes in the area affected by the project.

ii) analyse main **potential environmental impacts of the project** (with an Environment Impact Assessment if necessary). Determine whether any impacts constitute a serious risk, and whether these imply redesigning the project or form an absolute constraint. Consider whether the project is 'sustainable'?

iii) review possible **alternative solutions** to meet the objectives of the project, and the costs/sacrifices entailed. Consider whether the project can be redesigned, relocated, or postponed and at what cost, and whether a complementary (or shadow) project should be built in.

iv) **appraise** the chosen project using techniques that quantify costs and benefits so far as possible. Indicate major impacts that cannot be fully identified and measured. Spell out the distribution of costs and benefits between different parties, and over time (using a format such as that in Appendix 2).

v) consider the **financial consequences** of the project for the various parties e.g. direct participants, governments, people indirectly affected.

vi) draw together **implications for policy and institution building**, e.g. regulations, enforcement, tax, pricing, subsidy, etc.

vii) make **recommendations** for decision-maker, in an explicit and intelligible form. Clarify: the method by which the result has been arrived at; the assumptions on which it is based; the alternatives that were considered; areas of particular risk or uncertainty; important non-quantifiable items; the gainers and losers; the duration of the project, and its sustainability; likely implementation difficulties; etc.

The project appraiser has to work both with conventional costs and benefits that can be measured and valued, and with environmental effects, some of which are qualitative. Of those environmental effects that can in principle be quantified, some cannot be valued, and others can be valued wholly or in part. The incidenc of costs and benefits on various parties is also particularly important to trace ii environmental appraisals. For all these reasons, it is useful to draw up a matrix c effects and their distribution, which can be used both as a checklist for use durin; data gathering, and as a way of presenting the final results. A specimen format i given in Appendix 2.

5.2. Natural resources

5.2.1 Agriculture

(i) *Types of project.*

The impact of agricultural projects on the environment is conditioned mainly by the type of habitat, the cropping and input regime, and the system of ownershij and management. Habitats can be classified by climate, altitude, latitude, vegeta tion type, etc. Situations containing particular environmental risks include high rainfall tropical hill farming, the extension of arable farming into marginal dry lands, and any radical change in land use (such as deforestation, draining wet lands, ploughing rangelands, shortening fallow periods, resettlement anc colonisation, etc.).

The cropping pattern is, in practice, crucial to sound environmental use. Certair crops protect the soil better than others, by intercepting rainfall with their lea! cover and binding the soil with their roots. Perennial crops are more protective than annuals, other things being equal, although if the latter are ploughed back ir they can improve soil structure. It is a misconception to think that export cash crops are worse than subsistence food crops; some perennial export crops are very protective of soil, while some annual food crops are very erosive. Much depends on the conditions in which they are grown. Other relevant aspects of the cropping system are whether it is monoculture or mixed, sedentary or shifting cultivation, whether it uses fallow, etc.

The input regime embraces the use of seeds, fertiliser, pesticides, irrigation water, equipment, credit, extension, research, etc . . . The introduction of intensive input regimes (fertilisation, irrigation, mechanisation etc.) can be a source of environmental strain if they are inappropriate or badly managed - though such regimes can be perfectly sustainable, and artificial fertilisation may, for instance, improve the sustainability of otherwise degrading farm practices. Credit pro- grammes can have a generally positive effect, if used to support farm improve- ments, though not if they are used to buy inappropriate equipment or agro- chemicals.

Ownership and management systems determine farming incentives and the skill with which resources are handled. They are vital to explaining why farm systems differ in their sustainable use of the environment. At one extreme, the private family farmer, an owner-occupier, has strong incentives to farm sustainably and improve his/her holding. At the other extreme, the tenant or labourer working the land of an absentee landlord, or workers on a state farm, have little or no interest in long-term conservation or land improvement. The customary or legal arrange- ments between husband and wife may also be important to the way land is cared for.

Among the many forms of ownership are state, co-operative, private commercial (including plantations), private family, tenant, sharecropping, etc. Full owner- ship gives the best assurance of a sustainable regime, but secure leaseholds or usufruct (use) rights can also be helpful. Schemes to settle the landless on colon- isation schemes often have serious environmental consequences. Resettling farmers as part of land reform or redistribution measures can have positive net environmental effects if it relieves pressure on degraded land (e.g. Kenya, Zim- babwe), but the programmes need to be well-planned and supported.

Good management is a key ingredient of sustainability on farms of all sizes. Its absence can have dire environmental consequences on the larger schemes - e.g. irrigation command areas, plantations, resettlement and colonisation schemes. Cost control, cost recovery, regular maintenance, etc. are the humdrum and unsung elements of sustainable farming. Environmental management can be- come an explicit aim of projects, as in soil and land conservation schemes (see Belshaw, Blaikie and Stocking, 1990 for an account of the various types).

The possible environmental effects of processing farm crops should also be con- sidered, whether or not this is part of the project under consideration (see section 5.5).

(ii) *Major environmental effects.*

With due regard to the great diversity of this sector, its major adverse environ- mental impacts can be classified as in the following checklist:

natural vegetation: (changes in predominant land use, e.g.deforestation, bush clearance, shorter fallowing, etc. Include repercussions on displacement, resettle- ment); soil erosion; siltation and deposition; loss of soil fertility;

hydrological: irrigation impact on groundwater levels, river flow, (see also dams and reservoirs, 5.3.); changes in watershed run-off affecting other users; water quality - salinisation, contamination with agro-chemicals;

public health: water contamination and eutrophication; aquatic diseases (irrigated areas); agro-chemicals entering food chain and body systems; vermin, snakes, etc.

biodiversity and wildlife: loss of habitats; interruptions to trails, breeding grounds, migratory routes; introduction of exotic species; indiscriminate use of pesticide and herbicide; hunting, collecting;

amenity: loss of public recreation areas; alterations to natural landscape;

cultural property: archaeological remains; sacred sites; tribal and aboriginal areas;

Obviously not all environmental effects from farming are negative. Schemes to make farming more sustainable and projects to conserve soil and water will have positive effects. Alterations to the habitat will benefit some species, at the expense of others. Improved farming that leads to more income, jobs or food supply is likely to improve the health of farmers and their families, increasing their resist- ance to disease. It is essential, therefore, to compare the environmental effects of farming with those of the land use that it supersedes, especially where the latter is unsustainable.

(iii) *Scope for economic valuation.*

Agriculture can trigger most of the environmental effects reviewed in earlier chapters. However, the case material discussed in Chapter 4 shows a concentration on only a few of these areas. The two most common types of empirical study are on the costs of land-use conversions, and on the effects of soil erosion. In terms of the above checklist, these fall under the first main heading, namely, changes in natural vegetation. There are also a growing number of appraisals of projects with soil and water conservation objectives, which use data on the avoided cost of soil erosion. This section discusses the relevance of this work to agricultural appraisal.

Natural vegetation. Where agriculture involves change in land use there is an opportunity cost, measured by the loss of products and services in the previous use. Obviously, the more drastic the change, the greater the environmental effects, and the greater the opportunity cost. The studies of tropical rain forests have been illuminating, though they have concentrated on the value of minor forest products, and their results are variable (section 4.2).

Work on wetlands has mainly been conducted in the United States and Europe, also with suggestive results, and including both direct products and environmental services - such as sea defence, flood control and water quality. Because of the diversity of wetland ecology between temperate and tropical conditions these results cannot safely be used outside their region of origin. The few studies of wetlands in tropical conditions focus on their value to fishing and aquaculture (section 4.4).

Converting drylands to arable farming, assuming it is sustainable, has an opportunity cost in terms of products, which has been studied in a few cases (4.3), though valuing livestock and their products is problematic.

In all these cases, valuation of products (EOP) has proceeded far ahead of that of environmental services. Where the latter are perceived to be important, PE and RC are relevant, though there are few examples of their use (though see the Australian case study in 4.3). The population that may be displaced from the original habitat may set off a whole new train of environmental effects in their new locations. Ideally, this would be foreseen and their resettlement planned to minimise adverse effects (see Korup case study in section 5.2.5).

Sustainability is an issue both in appraising new farming projects, and in assessing the loss from the previous land use. If a well-planned plantation replaces a system of rapidly shortening fallow in shifting cultivation, the opportunity cost of the change would diminish over time as the shifting cultivation is assumed to lead to land degradation. But the new project should also be sustainable (for an examination of this concept in a farming context, see Conway and Barbier, 1990).

Soil erosion costs are the most common subject for environmental valuation studies. The physical processes at work can plausibly be modelled by the USLE (section 4.1) and for certain regions (e.g. semi-arid parts of West and southern Africa, Indonesia) effects can be traced to the output of crops. However, the most convincing work is that done on *on-site* production, hardly an externality. Work done on off-site effects, principally siltation of reservoirs, is highly suggestive, though not as firmly based in knowledge of the physical processes at work (4.1, 5.3). Siltation of reservoirs can be handled by EOP (the effect on electric power and irrigation water). Otherwise, PE/RC is relevant where the effects are judged serious enough to stem at source or restore afterwards.

The numerous appraisal studies of soil and water conservation schemes commonly use estimates of the underlying decline in soil productivity through erosion, based on specific fieldwork (see Lesotho case study below). This is the 'without' case, to provide the yardstick for the project's benefits. It is also common to include the value of the direct products of the scheme, e.g. fruit, browse, wood. Somewhat rarer are estimates of the avoided cost downstream (e.g. siltation of ricefields in the Korea case study below).

Hydrological effects. Irrigated farming involves major changes to water systems. Where major dams and reservoirs are constructed, the reader is referred to section 5.3. The contamination of used irrigation water from salinisation and agro-chemicals may seriously reduce its value to downstream users (4.9). This would have an impact on output (EOP), or in serious cases require the provision of alternative water supplies (RC). Data on the severity and effects of this problem are unlikely to be available *ex ante*, except where modifications to long-established irrigation systems are involved. Base-line studies and monitoring systems should form part of the project, and a contingency built into costs to anticipate these remedial measures.

The same applies to changes in water run-off from watersheds subject to changes in farm practices. Although the problem is often perceived as a loss of control over run-off, leading to flooding, siltation, etc., the opposite may occur if the farm systems intercept more water than previously, in which case water abstraction lower down would be affected.

Irrigation relying on tubewells will obviously affect the groundwater level. Where the aquifer is intensively used by private farmers, in the absence of controls over abstraction there is a risk of the Tragedy of the Commons being enacted, with farmers lacking an incentive to moderate their use of water. The depletion of the aquifer from the use of an extra well would have effects on the output or pumping costs of other farmers. Such effects have not been well studied, and would depend on hydrological models and field data over a number of years, but this effect also argues for baseline and monitoring data as part of any project.

Public health. Relating irrigated farming directly to local health status is an art in its infancy. The example described in section 4.10 is a rare case where effects on production were derived and valued, but in very favourable research conditions. It would be unusual for the project appraiser to have such data to hand, except as part of an on-going scheme that has been carefully monitored. The same is true of other possible health effects; baseline surveys, monitoring and project contingency provisions would all be part of recommended practice. Some particularly dangerous pesticides and herbicides may need to be banned outright, and the prohibition strictly enforced (ODA, 1989).

Biodiversity and wildlife. Granted the impossibility of valuing biodiversity as such (4.11) the appraiser is obliged to take other approaches. Critical pieces of biodiversity or threatened species may be targeted for conservation (IUCN and other agencies could provide guidance on the relative importance of specific habitats or species), and these actions would imply costs to the project. These would be either the forfeit of the benefits of the scheme if it were abandoned, or the costs of redesigning or relocation, etc.

Cost-effectiveness analysis would also be relevant to choose the most efficient way of achieving objectives. CV could be relevant where the sites or species attracted strong international interest, especially if there were a prospect of an agency making a cash preservation bid (section 5.2.5) The effect on income from nature tourism may also be important (see Korup case study, 5.2.5). Some of the larger animals in East Africa have a price on their heads - namely their estimated contribution to tourist income.

Amenity valuation, by the TC and CV methods, has been done primarily in the more affluent countries. There is little empirical work relevant to developing country agriculture. In exceptional cases where agricultural projects infringe natural beauty or amenity, and there is evidence that this is valued by local people or visitors, TC or CV would be relevant (a simplified version of TC is discussed in section 5.4.3). This might be the case if there were organised tourist visits.

Cultural property. There are many instances of archaeological remains going under the plough and sacred sites being plundered and degraded in rural areas. Estimating their potential tourist revenue is one way of putting some minimum value on these sites, when comparing them with income from agricultural use. If it is decided to protect them, PE is relevant, or RC if they can be relocated (see Goodland and Webb, 1987).

Encroachment on to aboriginal or tribal land is a highly sensitive issue. Given the strength of feeling in many such cases, the role of economics is probably confined to estimating the net benefits forgone from avoiding certain areas, or the costs of resettlement. Compensation - claimed or actually paid - is often a misleading guide to the economic values at stake.

(iv)*Case studies*

Lesotho: Mohales Hoek Farm Improvement and Soil Conservation Project (Bojo, 1987)

This study concentrated on the direct, on-site benefits, and its main noteworthy feature was the estimate of the decline in crop yield from soil erosion that would happen without the project, which comprised a package of measures to reduce erosion in the Lesotho Highlands, including farm inputs, the rehabilitation of terraces, waterways and drainage systems, controlled grazing, afforestation, planting fruit trees, etc.

Benefits were taken as the increase in direct yield of maize, sorghum, fodder and fuelwood resulting from the package, as compared with the scenario in the absence of any project. The 'without' case was specified as an annual decline in crop yield of 2%, based on local agronomic opinion applied to estimates of existing soil erosion. This resulted in an estimated annual decline in the yield of maize of 13.8 kg/ha., and of sorghum of 16.3 kg/ha, in the absence of the proposed conservation measures.

The project yielded a positive economic rate of return, and the adoption of the proposed farm-level improvements was also profitable to the farmer.

Korea: Upland Soil and Water Conservation Project (Kim and Dixon, in Dixon and Hufschmidt, 1987)

The approach taken by this study was to select the most cost-effective method of stemming soil erosion and to demonstrate its superiority to the alternative of letting the damage happen and trying to restore it. The 'without project' case was declining farm productivity on Korean uplands due to the extension of annual cropping, causing soil erosion and the deposition of silt in lowland rice paddy fields. Out of nine techniques for reducing soil loss, mulching was chosen as the most cost-effective form of 'preventive expenditure' in the majority of cases. The cost of mulching, incurred roughly every four years, was compared with the cost of letting the erosion happen and repairing the damage *ex post facto*, or the 're-placement cost' of soil erosion, itemised as the cost of replacing lost soil nutrients with fertiliser, compensation payments from upland to lowland farmers, maintenance and repairs to fields, etc.

The NPV of the project worked out at around half that of the alternative option as defined, indicating the case for preventing erosion. The study did not estimate the positive benefits of either programme, which were implicitly assumed to be large enough to justify the programme's outlay.

5.2.2. Forestry and agro-forestry

(i)*Types of project.*

The main kinds of project likely to be encountered in development are: conversion of forest to other permanent uses, commercial logging, agro-forestry and social forestry, and conservation and natural forest management. Most projects will also involve some institutional strengthening and research, but they will normally be justified on the basis of one or other of the above.

Forests tend to be removed for **conversion** to plantations, cattle ranching, smallholder agriculture, etc., and to make way for settlements, roads, mining schemes, etc. The conversion may be planned, or result from spontaneous colonisation by squatters and small farmers. Sometimes natural forest is replaced by commercial tree plantations - e.g. pine and eucalyptus for timber and pulp, or rubber or coffee trees. The variety of possible conversions makes generalisation difficult. Some of the uses will be sustainable and will minimise environmental damage, while others (e.g. cattle ranching on former rain forest areas) will be short-lived and highly detrimental. The manner of conversion is also relevant - burning the trees releases carbon into the atmosphere, while removal of the wood merely eliminates a potential carbon sink.

Likewise with commercial *logging*. The main distinction is between clear-felling and various kinds of selective or partial logging. Purely exploitative logging of virgin stands is a world apart from carefully managed extraction coupled with replanting. Unrestrained logging is still widespread, whether or not there are statutory controls. The creation of *new plantations* primarily for commercial motives is less common in the developing world than elsewhere. It may arise in temperate countries (e.g. Chile) and where a plantation created previously is available for exploitation (e.g. the large Viphya Forest in Malawi). Replanting and in-filling degraded stands is, however, an active appraisal issue (see below). The creation of new plantations on previously cleared or degraded land has potential environmental benefits, though these depend on the type of timber and the way the land is protected during the growing phase.

Social forestry is concerned with the growth of trees for the direct benefit of local people, whether for their own use or cash sale. The term embraces forestry at farm, village or community level, by or on behalf of small farmers and landless people. It includes both the planting of new trees and the preservation and management of existing ones. In practice, the main kinds of social forestry are: enriched fallows; home gardens; alley cropping; boundary tree planting; community woodlots; private woodlots; interplanting; retaining multi-purpose trees on cropland; using trees as living fences for livestock; trees used as fodder banks in zero-grazing schemes; windbreaks and slope stabilisers; and retaining and managing communal forests.

Agro-forestry cuts across the concept of social forestry, and refers to growing trees on private land. Trees (strictly, any kind of woody biomass) are planted or retained on the same land management unit as crops and/or livestock, in such a way that the trees enhance agricultural output.

Conservation and sustainable yield management (SYM) schemes have explicit environmental objectives. Forests that are particularly rich in biodiversity may deserve to be protected from human encroachment (e.g. the Korup Forest in Cameroon). In other cases, a *modus vivendi* will need to be struck between ecological concerns and the vital interests of the local population. SYM has long been a basic tenet of forest management. In the tropical context, it may entail letting indigenous forest dwellers get on with their traditional livelihoods, and taking due account of their real economic values. But it will usually mean more active management to justify the retention of standing forest (for examples, see Gradwohl and Greenberg, 1988).

The task is forbidding. In a survey of the 828 million ha. of productive tropical forest remaining in 1985, only 1 million ha. was found to be under SYM (Poore *et al.*, 1989). Admittedly, the definition of SYM was strict:

> . . . it should be practised on an operational rather than an experimental scale, and should include the essential tools of management, these being objectives, felling cycles, working plans, yield control and predication, sample plots, protection, logging concessions, short-term forest licences, roads, boundaries, costings, annual records and the organisation of silvicultural work. They must also meet wider political, social and economic criteria without which sustainability is probably unattainable. (Poore *et al.*, 1989)

(ii) *Major environmental issues.*

Different types of forestry proposals invoke different environmental issues, of which the main ones are the following:

Conversion involving global warming from carbon emissions, or loss of carbon store; loss of watershed functions; destruction of biodiversity; diminution of soil fertility and loss of ecological links; micro climatic effects; and loss of products of standing forest. The strength of these factors will obviously depend on the proposed land use. Replanting with perennial trees or other plants will help to recreate the carbon store function, and assist watershed and ecological functions. Depending on the type of biomass, some forest products may also be replaced (timber, fuel, fodder, fruit, etc). Much will depend on how sustainable the proposed land use turns out to be, and how the transition to the new regime is managed (e.g. providing ground cover plants to protect bare soil while new trees grow).

Logging. All the effects associated with conversion are likely to arise with logging, with the one important exception of carbon release through burning. Clear-felling, without any offsetting replanting, is particularly damaging. If cleared areas are left, however, secondary vegetation will return in due course and provide some ground cover, products, and carbon store functions. Careful, selective extraction accompanied by replanting will minimise environmental losses. In practice even selective felling can cause immense damage through building access roads, evacuating the timber (e.g. on skidding trails), and other ancillary activities.

Social and agro-forestry. Most of the effects of these forms of tree culture will be positive, e.g.: soil conservation, prevention of erosion and siltation; provision of useful products (food, timber, browse, fuelwood); ecological benefits for other crops and animals, on- and off-site. However, the use of certain kinds of tree has led to negative ecological effects, particularly when used on the scale of forest plantations. Eucalyptus and certain pines, used in many of India's social forestry programmes, are rapidly growing species popular as cash crops, but which do not provide the range of products offered by indigenous trees. Their thirst for groundwater may also be to the detriment of other crops. Any kind of tree planting programme is likely to lower the groundwater level, compared with the prior land use, and this has caused localised problems for other water users. The introduction of exotic tree species *en masse* also alters the ecological balance in a complex and unpredictable fashion, and indigenous species may suffer.

Conservation and natural forest management. These schemes have benefits which are the obverse of the environmental costs of conversion and logging schemes. Their objectives are to preserve biodiversity, safeguard vital ecological and other environmental functions, and protect the livelihoods and life-styles of forest dwellers. They have no obvious environmental costs. See section 5.2.5 for a further discussion.

(ii) *Scope for economic valuation.*

Proposals for the removal or modification of forest destroy a form of natural capital with an associated income stream comprising its *direct products*, namely, timber and the many kinds of non-timber or 'minor' products. Conversely, a large part of the benefits from conservation projects will consist of retaining this recurrent income stream. There are a growing number of studies (sections 2.3.2, 4.2) documenting the value of these products for both subsistence and marketed uses. Their valuation in subsistence uses is problematic, especially where they have no close marketed substitutes (section 4.1). Where they are traded in local or even international markets it is easier to apply a value, duly netted back to the 'forest gate'. The Korup Project in Cameroon estimated the value of forest use by locals by modifying national average per capita incomes in the light of local socio-economic surveys. In practice, hunting was the largest single use (see section 5.2.5).

Some of the conceptual problems of this kind of valuation are reviewed in section 4.2. There is no satisfactory or credible method of valuing *biodiversity* The role for economic appraisal is reviewed in sections 4.11 and 5.2.5. Similarly, there is no practical method of referring the cost of *global warming* from carbon emissions, or the loss of carbon sinks, back to particular acts of deforestation (section 4.12). Carbon debits and credits have little operational significance. The only sense in which global effects have costs at the project level is where national ceilings or targets are set and observed, in which case projects can have opportunity costs and benefits. This is not yet the case.

The removal of standing timber impairs the forest's *watershed protection* function. This is usually viewed as negative, on balance, where it leads to soil erosion and siltation, but its effect on water flows off the watershed should be carefully assessed. Deforestation is likely to reduce the quality of water flows (through siltation, contamination with agro-chemicals, etc.) and cause greater seasonal peaking in run-off, which might lead to flooding. But the total amount of water flowing off the catchment would probably increase, and this could benefit some water users (a factor noted in proposals for managing the Western Ghats forest reserves in India).

In practice, the watershed effect has been handled by estimating the costs of siltation, especially of irrigation systems and multi-purpose reservoirs (section 4.1 contains examples) and also fishing grounds. Modelling the effect on fisheries of siltation of reefs and coastal breeding grounds is difficult, even though the general cause-and-effect relationships are fairly clear. The Korup appraisal (5.2.5) arbitrarily assumed that all the fishing catch of the mangrove estuary fed by the Korup River would be placed at risk. More systematic research in the Philippines (Hodgson and Dixon, 1988) discovered certain relationships between sediment deposition and coral growth, and between the latter and fish biomass. Certain rules of thumb can be developed (section 4.8) to illustrate the scale of damage.

Among the major appraisal issues raised in **logging** projects are determining the underlying value of the forest as timber, the implications of the notion of 'allowable cut', and the choice of discount rate. Other appraisal questions are discussed in Watt (1990) and Grut (1989).

(a) **Stumpage value.** This is the inherent value of the tree as timber, and it can be viewed as the natural economic rent that a forest bestows on its exploiters. It is normally estimated by taking the border price of the timber, whether exported in raw state or processed form, and deducting all costs of cutting, transport, and processing, with an item for 'normal' profit. It corresponds to the maximum that a concessionaire would pay for the right to cut the tree. The stumpage fee is the price sometimes charged for the privilege of cutting trees, and is usually below the stumpage value.

Stumpage values of the African rainforest have been estimated as follows: In border price terms, and in terms of wood alone, the capitalized value of one hectare of productive and accessible tropical rainforest can be as high as about US$ 2,400 (2 cubic metres per ha/year of merchantable wood with a standing or stumpage value of up to about US$ 120 per cubic metre,; about $10/ha/year for management costs - an average annual output of $239 per hectare . . . (Grut, 1989).

Because stumpage value is derived as a residual, and in typical cases may be 10% or less of the border price of the timber (Watt, 1990), its level is very sensitive to the size of intermediate costs, especially transport and the amount of timber discarded during processing (often very high).

(b) **Allowable cut.** The concept of 'sustained yield allowable cut effect' can be used to justify a replanting programme, where the latter 'releases' existing timber for cutting. The issue arises where a limit has been set on the loss of national timber resources and where that limit has been reached. Replanting schemes are thus justified by the value of old timber that can be extracted, avoiding the delayed returns which are normally a bugbear of planting programmes. This concept was integral to the World Bank's support of Finland's Forest Improvement Project in the 1970s (Grut, 1988). Allowable cut is merely the 'compensating project' in reverse (3.4). Although it helps maintain sustainable forest yield it cannot replace biodiversity, it does not replace forest until the timber is fully grown, and it may substitute different and inferior species for those being cut.

(c) **Discount rate.** The problem for SYM champions is that, no matter how economically attractive their schemes, with a positive discount rate it will always be more attractive to take out merchantable timber in one felling (Grut, 1989). The appropriate response, however, is not necessarily to lower the discount rate (3.4.3) but to add in the various non-wood values of the standing forest. In the well-known study of the Amazon forest near Iquitos, the NPV from gathering fruit from trees on the plot was over ten times higher than sustainable timber harvesting (4.2).

Other ways of justifying forestry projects with a delayed return from timber are: allowing for future increases in the real value of timber, especially tropical hardwoods; reducing costs by making local people responsible for looking after the trees, and allowing them to cultivate around the trees in the meantime; planting in such a way (e.g. in-filling) that many benefits of natural forest can be obtained; minimising transport and processing costs and wood wastage, thereby increasing the underlying stumpage value.

There is a growing collection of studies on the economic justification of **social and agro-forestry schemes,** mostly in semi-arid conditions (Dixon, James and Sherman, 1990, gathers some of these together). Two of these, for Ethiopia and Nigeria, are considered below. They rely for their justification partly on the value of direct products of the trees, especially fuelwood. In the Ethiopian case, this factor was crucial in releasing dung for fertilisation. In the Nigeria study (and also in the study of alley-cropping in Machakos District, Kenya - Kalikander and Hoekstra, 1990) the positive ecological effects of growing trees adjacent to crops were also important benefits.

Conservation projects are considered further in section 5.2.5.

(iv) *Case studies*.

Ethiopia: Afforestation (Newcombe, 1989)

This study argues that afforestation can be justified where the wood is used as a fuel instead of animal dung, releasing the dung for use as manure, thus saving imports of chemical fertiliser. High economic rates of return (35-70%) can be demonstrated for agro-forestry programmes from this element alone. The significance of this case lies in the detailed empirical estimation of dung production and use, its equivalence as fertiliser to chemical products, the response of traditional cereals to the application of dung, and the valuation of dung as a substitute for chemical fertilisers.

In the Highlands of Ethiopia there has been extensive land clearing for agriculture and deforestation to obtain firewood. Dung and crop residues are mainly burned for fuel or sold to urban markets; 90% of the cattle dung produced in Eritrea and 60% of that in Tigrai and Gondar is burnt as fuel. In some towns in these provinces 90% of the fuel burnt by urban households is dung. In areas where most tree cover has been removed, dung has become the main source of fuel and an important 'cash crop'. The land is deprived of organic matter; soil productivity declines, the ability of the land to support cattle falls, and in the advanced stages of the vicious circle the farm is abandoned and its occupants move to the towns. This stage has been reached in some areas.

Method. The annual production of dung from Ethiopia's livestock population is first estimated, allowing for the different kinds of animals. This enables the results to be translated into total annual savings at national and farm levels. Next, the chemical composition of cattle dung is derived, and its nitrogen and phosphorus content compared weight for weight with the equivalent chemical fertiliser. The farm gate value of the latter is estimated, applying a shadow value to the c.i.f. price reflecting the overvalued exchange rate.

Crop responses to the application of nitrogen and phosphorus are taken, the average production of dung per farm household is estimated, and the fertiliser equivalent of this is used as the basis for the crop response calculations. The cost of substituting for dung as fuel is arrived at by estimating the cost of producing wood from agro-forestry or woodlots. Finally, internal economic rates of return are worked out by comparing the costs of planting and growing new trees with the benefits in the form of the net increment in grain production from retaining dung as fertiliser.

Results. Each farm family in the two sampled areas used 2.1-2.5 tonnes of dung as fuel, per year, equivalent to 1.29 to 1.52 tonnes per ha., potentially available for recycling as fertiliser. The crop response data suggested that this rate of application of dung would yield crop increments worth US$84-95, and $120-139, respectively.

A rough estimate of the cost of producing wood from agro-forestry schemes, including administrative overheads, nurseries, civil works, tools, and labour, yielded a value of $1.9-2.9 per cu.m., and $2.9-4.3 per tonne of equivalent dung.

The relative value of dung in different uses was estimated to be as follows (in 1983 US per tonne):

old in Gondar market: 48-115;

substituting for chemical fertiliser: 22;

used directly on farms: 62-43;

burnt as fuel: 2.9-4.3

It was concluded that in rural areas afforestation is justified to substitute wood for the use of dung as fuel. Economic rates of return for afforestation are estimated to be 35% (on the basis that it saves imported fertiliser), 59-70% based on the range of incremental yields from applying the dung to manure the soil, and a worst case of 23% assuming halving the yield and replacing imported fertiliser.

The rates of return show that afforestation projects can be attractive projects if dung is widely used as a fuel at the expense of farm manure. The validity of this result depends on how extensively farmers employ dung as a soil conditioner and fertiliser. Research at the International Livestock Commission for Africa has suggested that it is not widely used in this way because of poor returns to labour (J.E.M. Arnold - personal communication). The method provides a conservative value of afforestation, since it omits many other benefits, both direct and 'ecological'. The Nigerian case study complements this approach by showing how agroforestry schemes can be justified by their 'ecological' benefits.

Nigeria: Shelterbelts and farm forestry (Anderson, 1987)

The study area is the arid zone of Northern Nigeria, with typical annual rainfall ranging from 200 to 800 mm. and with a long dry season. Fuelwood is used for cooking by 90% of the population, at a rate well above the Mean Annual Increment of timber stocks, leading to a sharp decline in farm tree stocks, increased encroachment by farmers on public reserves, and the non-sustainable harvesting of trees in the more humid southern belt. All this is threatening to reduce soil fertility through gulley erosion, loss of topsoil, surface evaporation, reduced soil moisture and the use of dung and residues for fuel rather than nutrients. Storm damage to crops is also becoming more severe.

The study is a cost-benefit analysis of the tree-planting programme already under way in the region. Its two main components are shelterbelts — lines of trees (usually eucalyptus and neem) in 6-8 rows up to 10 km. long — and farm forestry undertaken by farmers on their own land. Typically 15-20 trees per ha. are planted with a view to providing useful products (fodder, fruit, fuel, as well as shelter) for the farm households.

Method. The benefits of the programme are perceived as: halting future declines in soil fertility; improving current levels of soil fertility; the value of the tree products themselves; benefits from increasing the supply of fodder.

A large body of international research is drawn upon to justify the assumptic that shelterbelts can increase the net yield of crops in the vicinity by 15-25% through increasing soil moisture retention, reducing crop losses from wind, ar reducing surface wind speeds. For farm forestry the increased yield is taken to be more modest 5-10%. The impact of shelterbelts is assumed to occur 7 to 10 yea after planting, and for farm forestry 8 to 13 years. These 'with project' benefits a compared with the assumed trend 'without', which is a decline in soil fertility 0-2% p.a. This decline would be halted after 8 years with the project. The value wood and fruit from the new trees is estimated to be $22 per ha. for the shelterbel and $7 for the farm forestry, both net of labour costs.

The major investment costs of the programme are: fencing and planting expense amounting to c. $150 per ha. of protected land for shelterbelts and $40 per ha. fc farm forestry; and the opportunity cost of the farm land occupied by trees, take to be proportional to the area taken up by trees - 12% for shelterbelts, 2% for farr forestry plus other farm forestry costs of setting up seedling nurseries, distribu tion facilities and an extension network.

Results. For shelterbelts, a base case Internal Rate of Return of c. 15% was esti mated. Sensitivity analysis on yield, costs, and underlying erosion produced range of 13-17%, while a consideration of the wood benefits only showed an IRR o 4.7%. The base case for the farm forestry programme was an IRR of 19%, with range of 15-22% in the sensitivity tests. The IRR for wood and fruit benefits onl was 7.4%. The time profile of net benefits is significant. After year 17 net farme income without the shelterbelt programme declined to zero and it is assumed tha land is abandoned at this point. It is also noteworthy that for the first nine years o the shelterbelt programme gross farmer income with the project trails behind tha 'without', because of the effect of taking land out of production to plant the trees.

This was one of the first studies to demonstrate that afforestation *can* be justified according to conventional cost-benefit criteria, despite the lags involved in the appearance of benefits. The assumptions about the benefits of tree-planting on crop yields draws upon existing international research, and the range adopted can be regarded as conservative. Nevertheless, it is worth stressing (as the author also does) that the relationships are highly dependent on local conditions and project parameters, and that results established elsewhere cannot be applied uncritically. The other assumption that is important to the results is the declining trend in soil fertility (0-2% p.a.) which awaits empirical confirmation. The wider validity of the results of this study (as opposed to the soundness of its method) has been chal- lenged: the scheme was at an early stage when it was appraised, and operational data were lacking.

5.2.3. Fisheries

Fisheries are the victims of environmental damage originating in other sectors, as ell as the overexploitation of fisheries themselves. These effects are described in ctions 2.1, 4.5 and 4.8. This section deals with the environmental consequences fisheries projects themselves. The basic distinction to be made from the outset is tween capture fisheries and aquaculture.

id projects in the capture fisheries sector have proved to be especially problemic. A number of special features can be held responsible for the chequered record aid projects, and which are relevant to environmental appraisal. They have en characterised as follows (drawing on Christy, 1986):

high degree of uncertainty. Fish are a mobile resource in a flowing opaque edium, sensitive to environmental variations, and prone to complex interacns between species. This greatly complicates the task of estimating annual elds or catches per unit effort.

mited natural yields. Excessive fishing will eventually lead to a decline in tches, which may be masked by a shift in species composition towards lowerlue fish. The price of fish will tend to rise in the long term, with serious conquences for the lower-income groups who are frequently the target group for heries projects.

ared resources and fishing grounds. Within Economic Exclusion Zones (EEZs), rdly any countries regulate their nationals' access to fishing grounds. As a sult, excessive amounts of capital and labour can easily be devoted to fishing. rtain kinds of fish are also mobile between different fishing grounds, crossing Zs in the process.

any species and products. Fish differ greatly according to species, size, quality, c. This makes it difficult to measure output and makes aggregate tonnage a isleading performance indicator.

quaculture, in contrast, is much more akin to agriculture.

Types of project

apture fisheries. There is an important difference between small-scale (artisanal) d industrial (commercial) fishing operations. Aid to the small-scale sector norally has poverty-alleviating aims, both by creating income and employment nongst poor communities and by improving their diet. The aid package comonly includes the finance for improved gear, vessels, engines, storage, processg and marketing. Environmental effects will usually be localised (including ssible overfishing, waste disposal from the market and processing facility, nflict with tourism over beaches and damage to reefs, etc.).

milar effects are invoked by industrial-scale fishing, but on a potentially more rious scale. Elements of commercial fisheries projects may include the provision patrol vessels, research ships, finance for the purchase or upgrading of fishing aft, provision of on-shore installations such as jetties, cold stores, processing its, transport, etc. In addition to the effects already noted, such projects may use encroachment on artisanal fishing grounds, leading to their further overploitation.

d to both types of project may include 'soft' elements like research, advice, the ation and strengthening of institutions and management, etc. The effect of these seemingly innocuous measures must, however, be judged by their ultimate objectives, e.g. to increase catches, throughput of processing units, etc.

In fisheries that are, or threaten to become, heavily exploited, a further class of project could be attractive, namely disinvestment in vessels, and/or investment in regulation and enforcement. It has, for instance, been estimated that a reduction in the number of trawlers working the west coast of peninsular Malaysia would produce net economic revenues in the region of US$100m. per annum (quoted in Christy, 1986). More generally, investment in regulation (e.g. patrol vessels), and devising fishery management schemes (which may include compensation) would often be attractive, as well as having positive environmental effects.

Aquaculture. Fish farming may occur in inland freshwater bodies or in coastal waters. Inland aquaculture has features in common with agriculture, with which it sometimes competes for the use of land, labour and water. The most common types of fish in tropical aquaculture are carp, tilapia, tropical catfish, giant river prawns and aquarium species. The fishery may be a pond, cage or pen, tank or raceway. Production regimes can be classified as: extensive (where no supplementary feeds are used); semi-intensive (generally using agricultural by-products as feed); and intensive (using high-protein formulated feeds). The semi-intensive regime is most typical of tropical inland aquaculture. Its environmental impact varies greatly according to local conditions and has been less well studied than its counterpart in developed countries (Beveridge and Phillips, 1990). Environmental effects from enclosed ponds and tanks are, for example, generally easier to contain than the use of pens in larger water bodies or rivers, though effluent is a problem when the water is emptied.

Coastal aquaculture uses estuaries, deltas and mangrove areas to produce salt-water species, especially prawns, shrimps, shellfish and lobsters. The use of antibiotics is another growing concern (Brown and Higuera-Ciapara, 1990).

(ii) *Major environmental effects*

Capture fisheries: *overfishing* (resulting in declining catches, reduced yield per effort, increasing proportion of low-value species in total catches); *effect on marine ecology*, coastal erosion/sedimentation of shore installations (e.g. jetties); *damage to reefs and fish breeding grounds* from certain artisanal fishing practices (especially dynamiting, poisoning); *effect on visual amenity* of beaches and coastal areas (e.g. from fishing boats, gear, markets, cold stores, processing plant), affecting visitors and tourists (some positive features, up to a point); *effluent, waste, and smells* from catches, markets, processing units; *in-shore marine pollution* from vessels (oil, waste, effluent).

Aquaculture: *effect on competing land and water uses*: repercussions from use of agricultural land for fish farming (e.g. rice); reduced access to natural fisheries; interruptions to navigation channels; interference with natural fish breeding grounds; *water requirements*: large volumes of fresh water needed for topping up ponds/tanks, and restoring water quality - affecting groundwater supplies, irrigated farming, and natural fisheries; *seed*: use of wild fry to stock ponds can deplete natural fisheries; *construction materials*: construction of pens needs large amounts of wood (bamboo and hardwoods); *chemicals and drugs* to promote growth and control diseases: lime, fertilisers, therapeutants and antibiotics are released into natural water courses, especially when tanks are drained, causing, amongst other things, eutrophication and effects on other lifeforms that are so far little understood. Much depends on the nature of the receiving waters; *impact on host species* from escaped fish (predation, disease, reduced gene pools, disruption); *public health*: creation of new freshwater bodies could increase water-borne diseases such as schistosomiasis, malaria, etc; *effluent from fish processing plants* can cause water pollution, with further hazards to people, cattle, and other fish (though up to a point some natural fish will thrive on certain kinds of waste); *uneaten food, dead fish, faecal and urinary waste* will find their way into water bodies and courses. In excessive amounts that are not naturally dispersed and assimilated they will cause water pollution.

(iii) *Scope for economic valuation.*

As noted earlier, many fisheries projects in developing countries have run into problems because of a failure fully to understand the peculiar characteristics of the sector. The same observation applies with equal force to their environmental impacts. The economist depends on information about physical and biological effects which is rarely available. It has, for instance, been authoritatively stated that:

> There have been no studies of the environmental impact of aquaculture in the tropics. (Beveridge and Phillips, 1990, p.26)

Part of the information gap is due to the great variety of circumstances in which both capture fishing and aquaculture are practised in developing countries - probably much greater than in developed countries. Another factor is that the use of chemicals and antibiotics is a relatively recent development in aquaculture, and its effects have not been properly studied. A third point is that a number of the effects noted above will usually be minor, and not critical in themselves - and therefore have not featured much in analysis.

In these circumstances, economic appraisal should focus on the more important environmental effects. Four of these are considered below.

Overfishing. The difficulty of specifying an 'optimal' level of exploitation of a particular capture fishery was rehearsed in section 4.5. The notion of 'maximum sustainable yield' is a slippery one in practice. Nevertheless, in certain fisheries there is clear evidence of declining yields, whether in terms of the catch of target species, or in decreasing marginal returns to capital or effort. Some allowance clearly has to be made for this in the appraisal of projects that would put further pressure on stocks that are already being heavily fished. This is a simple application of the EOP method, although the actual data used will depend on careful judgement based on scrutiny of historical data (see below) and after taking specialist advice.

In practice, time series data on recorded catches in relation to measures of fishing effort (e.g. trawl hours, or, more crudely, number of trawlers) can give strong indications of where overfishing is happening (the case study on Thailand fisheries in ADB, 1986 is an exercise of this sort). Where there is a strong likelihood of the project achieving its production targets only at the expense of the catches of other parties, this obvious externality should be reflected in a reduction in the project's benefits. In situations of this kind, the project's own yield projections should be treated critically:

the net economic returns from projects implemented where fisheries are al ready fully or over-exploited can be expected to be negative . . . In addition, the open access condition implies that projects cannot earn more than norma profits . . . This suggests that appraisals which have produced high interna. rates of return in a fully exploited common property context have been under-taken with a faulty methodology. (Palfreman, quoted in Christy, 1986)

The externality may fall on fishing activities in the same, or neighbouring, or other waters to which resources are diverted. The Thailand case study referred to reveals that vessels provided under aid intended for deep sea fishing in the Gulf of Thailand and the Andaman Sea were actually converted for use as trawlers in the overfished coastal waters, in direct competition with artisanal fishermen.

Competition for land and water use. Aquaculture is becoming a major factor in the conversion of mangrove areas in South-East Asia and elsewhere. The oppor-tunity cost of using such areas is at least the value of mangrove products and, where data permit, functions. Some estimates of these are discussed in section 4.4.

Land-based aquaculture may compete with agricultural land. In some cases the land is marginal for agriculture, or may serve dual purposes (e.g. the use of rice paddies for fish farming). But in some countries (e.g. Philippines, Indonesia, Taiwan) aquaculture has encroached on good agricultural land, in which case there is an obvious opportunity cost of the land to be reflected in costs of produc-tion. Its water requirements make such aquaculture akin to irrigated farming in certain respects, and the full cost of supplying the water should, in theory, be included in its costs (see 4.9).

Water-based aquaculture may appropriate natural fishing grounds and interrupt navigation. The pen culture industry in Laguna Lake, Philippines has taken over one-third of the lake's surface area, reducing fishing yields and disrupting fish spawning and nurseries - leading to serious social tensions (quoted in Beveridge and Phillips, 1990). The effect on natural fisheries can, in principle, be dealt with by the EOP method.

Conflicts between fishing and tourism/recreation. Artisanal fishing can conflict with tourism and recreation where it occupies or destroys tourist assets such as beaches, picturesque fish, coral reefs, or clear coastal water. Up to a point the two activities may be harmonious, in that fishing can lend some interest to beach life, but they are in competition for the same resources. Diving and snorkelling are particularly sensitive to certain fishing practices.

In the most straightforward case, artisanal fishing may be banned from a certain area of tourist importance (or vice versa where fishing is particularly important for the local community). Estimates should then be made of the resulting loss of fishing income, to balance against the benefits of tourism development. In a more typical situation, the two activities may coexist and it will be much more difficult to attribute their mutual externalities. Some activities may be banned or regulated, imposing extra costs on the fishing sector (though banning certain destructive fishing methods such as dynamiting may be in the long-term interest of the fishing industry too).

Effluent, waste, by-products and public health. There are several problems valu-ing this broad group of environmental 'bads'. Little is known about the effects of residues, chemicals and - especially - antibiotics on other fish, animal, or human life; the effects are very location-specific, dependent on local fish farming technology and practices, the nature of the receiving water system, etc.; certain effects may be beneficial up to a point - e.g. residues of growth hormones and organic waste may promote natural fisheries. Cause-and-effect links will therefore usually be hard to draw. PE is one possible approach. If scientific advice is that certain effects are sufficiently risky to warrant taking preventive measures, the cost of these can be taken as a proxy for environmental costs (e.g. tanks may be lined with concrete, fish farms may be relocated to 'safer' areas, a research or pilot phase can be added to the project). If, say, antibiotics were to be banned in certain areas, the loss of income imposed on the fish farmers (akin to an abatement cost) is a possible measure of environmental costs.

5.2.4. Livestock

Assessing the environmental impact of livestock projects takes the analyst straight into questions of the motives for holding livestock, methods of communal land tenure, whether there is such a thing as carrying capacity, and the measurement of land degradation. Each of these is an immensely complex issue. Taken together, they go far to explain why livestock schemes have had such a mixed record, especially in Africa, and why appraisal often fails to anticipate the problems encountered.

(i) *Types of project*

The variety, and individuality, of livestock regimes cannot be overstressed. One way of categorising interventions is between those focusing on herd management, and those directed at land use and management:

Herd management and improvement: improvement of stock (supply of animals, AI); animal health campaigns (vaccination, etc.); marketing and offtake (abattoirs, processing units); and local watering schemes.

Land-use management: pasture improvement; feed supply (fodder, browse, supplements); grazing rotations, cells; fencing; large-scale water schemes; and conversions from other land use.

In judging how these interventions will affect the environment, it is also important to take into account two other dimensions, the animal types and the production regime. **Animal types** include cattle, sheep, goats, pigs and draught animals. The varieties of **production regime** include intensive, communal grazing, ranching, mixed farming, nomadic herding, and animals kept as supplements to household and small farm units.

This variety argues for caution in generalising about environmental effects. In addition, livestock practices and land usage are notoriously bound by complex and specific social-anthropological factors. Only broad pointers may be given. At one extreme, intensive cattle rearing on a private commercial basis is unlikely to cause land degradation *per se* (though conversion from other land uses should be considered) but it does raise potential risks with effluent and water pollution. At the other extreme, herding on communally-owned land *may* threaten overgrazing and competition with wild animals, but is unlikely to cause pollution. Effects on human health depend on location, the nature of contact, whether the animal products are consumed, how they are slaughtered, the diseases carried by wild hosts, etc.

(ii) *Major environmental effects*.

With all due account of the many local differences, a checklist of the more common effects of livestock projects would include the following: *land degradation*: overgrazing, damage to trees and bushes, soil erosion around water points and along cattle trails, etc); *alterations to the ecological balance*: change in species composition from overgrazing, introduction of new and exotic grasses, conversion of forest, bush and wetlands; *public health*: animals harbour and attract diseases that can affect their handlers and consumers of their meat and milk, e.g. anthrax, brucellosis, malaria from tsetse fly, rabies, etc.; animals may pollute sources of drinking water; offal and effluent from abattoirs can contaminate rivers, etc.; *effect on other wildlife*: habitat may be destroyed to make way for pasture; herders may hunt wild animals; in other cases, domesticated and wild animals may peacefully coexist (e.g. in Masai areas).

The conversions of other natural systems into livestock production have their own set of effects - e.g. forest (4.2) and wetlands (4.4).

Intensive husbandry supported by irrigated or other systems of fodder production brings into play effects associated with arable systems (see above).

The balance sheet is by no means all negative. Animal dung is an important fertiliser in many societies (see Ethiopia case study in 5.2.2) or, in the last resort, a fuel. Income in cash and kind from livestock may rescue poor farmers and households from environmentally damaging behaviour, e.g. removing trees, overcultivation. The loss of livestock or the distress sales entailed by extreme hardship (as in drought) have periodically caused mass migrations to other areas or to cities, with corresponding pressure on other habitats (e.g. in Sahelian states and North-East Brazil.

(iii) *Scope for valuation*.

Environmental effects of livestock projects can most easily be valued through their effect on productivity (EOP), and by preventive expenditure (PE) necessary to avoid some of their costs. In the case of severely degraded ranges, the cost of restoration (e.g. replanting) may be an appropriate proxy for environmental costs. Where livestock production supersedes other ecologically-important natural systems, the opportunity cost of the project is the loss of functions provided by the previous habitat.

Effect on productivity. A livestock scheme can affect the productivity and costs of farmers through its effect on the quality or use of the rangeland, and its impact on arable production. In privately owned farms without communal grazing these effects accrue on-site. Where there is communal grazing or nomadic pastoralism, there is no clear distinction between on-site and off-site effects, and internal effects blur into externalities.

The Botswana fencing scheme case study below is an example of EOP where the costs of the scheme are communally borne, but the benefits accrue to private farmers. Since the effects are on arable production, no unusual valuation problems would arise. Other schemes, to improve the management of land and/or ıerds, are also appropriate to EOP where they improve the returns to factors of ›roduction. Two of the main problems arising concern the valuation of livestock ın pastoral societies and the concept and measurement of carrying capacity.

√aluation of livestock in pastoral economies was discussed at greater length in ;ection 4.3. Suffice it to say that the market price of animals can be a very unreli-ıble guide to their value (Behnke, 1985). These problems would not, of course, ırise in the case of livestock produced on commercial ranches for local or export ;ale.

The carrying capacity of a range is another difficult concept. If a livestock project ˙e.g. animal health, watering, rangeland improvement) leads to a temporary ıncrease in the number of animals it is reasonable to ask whether this would be at :he expense of other rangeland users. This would be the case if that range was at ts maximum carrying capacity. The same issue arises, in reverse, for a project that ıncreases the offtake of livestock (e.g. better marketing, prices), and which may :herefore create 'space' for other animals.

The commonsense notion of carrying capacity has in fact been extensively crit-ıcised by field workers, with the result that it has little operational value (see, for ≥xample, De Leeuw and Tothill, 1990). For instance, in Africa stock is highly mobile over large distances, and can feed off several ecological niches. The pro-duction goals of herders are also a complication, since they may prefer to keep the ;ame number of thinner cattle in preference to killing or selling some. Where land ;ystems are in flux, large livestock owners like to increase their herds even more as ı means of bidding for the use of communal or other land becoming available. There are allied problems in determining whether land is becoming more or less 'degraded' (see 2.4). Consequently, there is no acceptable way of inferring the ≥ffect on the productivity of other rangeland users resulting from changes in ıivestock numbers as part of a project.

Preventive expenditure/replacement cost. Insofar as livestock projects raise ques-tions about the prevention or restoration of environmental damage, PE and RC techniques are appropriate (e.g. Australia case study in 4.3, and the conservation projects in Korea and Lesotho in 5.2.1). Since the link between livestock and human health has been insufficiently charted, PE is appropriate here too, if the effect is believed serious enough (e.g. health care, hygienic slaughtering facilities).

Opportunity cost. The conversion of habitats for use in livestock production entails the loss of their natural functions, some of which can be valued. Sections 4.2 and 4.4 discuss how far tropical forest and wetlands can be valued. Much of Africa's livestock producing area was claimed from tsetse-infested forest. More recently, the conversion of Amazonian rain forest into livestock ranches to take advantage of fiscal and financial incentives has become a *cause célèbre* of develop-ment (see 6.2). It is easier to value the products than the functions of these original habitats. Even the products throw up valuation problems arising from limited markets, high transport costs, non-sustainable use, and the peculiarities of loca-tion (see 4.2). The growth of nature-based tourism is a monetary expression of the opportunity cost of such habitats. Any destruction of the habitats of game ani-mals, e.g. from the encroachment of rangeland, would soon affect income from tourism, though at present only rough rules of thumb are available (e.g. annual tourist revenue per elephant).

(iv)*Case study*

Botswana: collective fencing (Arntzen, 1990a)

Despite Botswana's success in developing mineral exports the bulk of its popula tion depends on the land, where the growth of population and livestock number will demand the utmost care in reconciling production and conservation objec tives. Although cultivated land covers only c. 1% of the country's area, it is a important part of farm systems in many cases, and there is increasing competitio for land between livestock and cropping systems. Individual farmers have starte to erect fences around arable areas in order to reduce damage from livestock, an to provide a basis for better crop and soil management.

This case is a pre-feasibility study of collective fencing undertaken by groups o farmers, either instead of, or as a supplement to, individual fencing. Individua fencing is more effective against cattle, but collective fencing is better agains goats. The author reviews the data that would be necessary to carry out a CBA o collective fencing, but stops short of doing the actual analysis.

Method. Benefits are defined as follows: *Reduction in crop damage by livestock*. Thi saving depends on the number of affected farmers, or the area concerned, the extent of present damage, and the efficiency of the collective fence in excludin cattle during the growing season. In two districts surveyed, 48% and 80% o farmers reported some crop damage, mostly from cattle. *Reduced labour needs fo herding livestock and keeping them off crops*. Surveys suggest that the average sma herdsman spent 114 days per year looking after his animals. *Improved grazin management from rotational grazing*, which has been shown to benefit livestock These benefits could be valued from gains in body weight and meat price. *Bette management of land and water*. Collective fencing is a necessary, though not sufficient, condition for more general improvements in farm practices. Hence i must remain an unquantifiable benefit.

Costs include the material in the fences themselves, and the labour required to con struct and maintain them. There may be incidental costs in altering the location o livestock watering points and resurveying fields. The shadow value of labour is ar important variable, since construction usually occurs during winter when there are few alternative activities. Official estimates of the shadow price of unskilled labou are 50% of the minimum wage, though even lower rates may be justified in some cases. The social opportunity cost of capital is officially put at 6-8%.

The author stresses the importance of including the distribution of benefits in the analysis, since cattle ownership is highly correlated with income. Poor farmers have a greater dependence on cropping and - compared with their richer neigh bours - suffer from the depredations of cattle without enjoying any of its 'benefits' For the sensitivity analysis, the author suggests that the key variables are: the extent of reduction in crop damage, the reduction in herding labour, the applica tion of improved management practices, and the discount rate.

The method proposed is a straightforward application of the EOP technique, wherein costs and benefits accrue purely to the parties undertaking the scheme. No externalities are invoked and all the effects arise in monetary form. 'Environ mental' benefits are confined to those arising directly on the land of the parties to the scheme. Even so, the study admits a lack of data crucial to applying the method - notably the value of attributable crop damage from livestock, and the value of time savings by herdsmen. One could add another key variable - the effectiveness of the fences in segregating animals from cropland (in one survey, 65% of farmers inside the drift fence continued to complain of crop damage by livestock - a worrying statistic). Finally, the shadow value of labour - on both the cost and benefit side - is clearly important to the result.

5.2.5. Nature conservation

The issue of conservation arises in projects in a variety of different sectors, especially those in natural resources. In some cases a project will have an important, though incidental, effect on critical natural resources (e.g. the Kenya road discussed in 5.3.2.). For other projects, conservation will be the main or only motive (e.g. the two case studies discussed below, and the growing number of national conservation programmes being funded by the World Bank and others).

The appraisal of such projects needs to recognise their different motives, and the importance of the conservation issue relative to other project aims. Despite these differences, a common approach is recommended, which would include some or all of the following steps: identify the natural resource in question, the reasons why it is important, whether it is 'critical', and how it would be affected by the project; consider whether the project could be redesigned, relocated or delayed, so as to safeguard the resource; consider whether compensatory projects could be included either as part of the project or as part of the national investment portfolio; use cost-effectiveness analysis to determine the most efficient way of achieving conservation aims; estimate the opportunity cost to the project of accommodating conservation.

The remainder of this section examines the various possible circumstances in which nature conservation is an issue in project appraisal, and discusses appraisal questions, with examples drawn from two case studies.

(i) *Types of project, and scope for valuation*

Soil and water conservation schemes usually have a strong agricultural focus, and are often combined with various kinds of farm development. They can be designed so as to be appraised and justified on normal criteria, with a high proportion of their benefits quantified and valued (see 4.1, 5.2.1, and 5.2.2 for examples). In short, such projects often generate tangible benefits which makes them justifiable in conventional CBA terms.

Protection of major watersheds is important for microclimate, slope stability, regulation of water flow and quality, biodiversity, wildlife, etc. The direct products of the habitat, insofar as they exist and can be valued, would go a certain way to justifying the opportunity cost of retaining the present land use. The environmental functions are more difficult to physically quantify and value. The Western Ghats project in India, Brazil's Atlantic forest, and the Palawan project in the Philippines (v. case study in this section) are cases in point. It is difficult to generalise about such projects; most of them would generate some quantifiable benefits and achieve a positive IRR, but this would often be less than that considered acceptable in other sectors.

Conservation of biodiversity. Preserving natural habitats where biodiversity is the principal motive is a feature of the Kenya case study in 5.2.2 and the Cameroon forest in this section. It is argued in 4.11 that there is no satisfactory way of valuing biodiversity, and the role of economic appraisal is to: clarify the possible benefits and illustrate them where possible; estimate the opportunity cost of preservation; and apply cost-effectiveness analysis to determine the most efficient way of achieving conservation.

There may be a greater role for economics in the larger area of setting conservation policy and strategy (see Flint, 1990).

(ii) *Scope for valuation.*

Of the three exemplary categories mentioned above, the first should pose no insuperable problems for appraisal. Advances made in economic valuation in recent years have allowed such projects to be treated on a similar basis to that of other natural resource projects. The main qualification to be made is that the direct products of such schemes (wood, crops, etc.) have proved easier to value than off-site benefits, which tend to be left unquantified, or under-valued.

The second category is more difficult, since they present fewer opportunities to count in farming or agro-forestry benefits, as compared to the preservation and management of fragile ecosystems. Finney and Western (1986) illustrate the problem of justifying conservation schemes by the same criteria as those used in other sectors. However, it is recommended that the appraisal of such projects proceeds in the normal manner, following the sequence outlined in the first part of this section. If the quantifiable benefits are insufficient to justify costs, at the normal discount rate, the size of the gap should be clearly exposed to the decision-makers. The nature and importance of the conservation benefits which are not captured in the appraisal should be clearly stated, so that they can be weighed against the shortfall in the quantified economic rate of return. The same approach is valid for the third category of project, where there is less prospect of justifying it by the usual criteria.

This approach is preferable to the use of a lower, or zero, discount rate for this category of project. It preserves the usual appraisal disciplines, especially the rigorous scrutiny of supposed benefits and the maximum reasonable effort to quantify them. It ensures that all benefits that can plausibly be measured and valued are treated on the same footing, with the same discount rate. Nor does it introduce distortions from the use of unduly low discount rates, such as favouring capital-intensive solutions. Conservation benefits can, in short, be treated more transparently by this process than by adjusting the discount rate.

This recommended approach is apparently belied by the Cameroon case study below, but on closer examination is consistent with it. The appraisal seeks to justify conserving a bio-diverse forest according to normal CBA criteria, and produces a base case IRR of c. 13% after quantifying many of the relevant costs and benefits. The major contributors to total benefits are sustained forest use, protection of coastal fisheries, flood control, tourism, and the farm output of resettled forest dwellers.

This is an interesting pioneering application of CBA in this area, though it uses strong and often arbitrary assumptions, and its treatment of capital costs is unduly favourable. The substitution of alternative assumptions would lower the IRR, but nevertheless the benefits are clearly stated and enable the decision-maker to visualise the merits of the scheme.

iii) *Case studies*

Cameroon: Korup Forest project (Ruitenbeek, 1989)

The Korup project aims to protect the rain forest in Korup National Park, in the Southwest Province of Cameroon. This is one of the world's oldest rain forests, with a high degree of endemism among its flora and fauna. The forest is at risk of encroachment from small farmers, which is already happening on the Nigerian side. The project was agreed in 1987 by the Government of Cameroon, the World Wide Fund for Nature, and the UK's Overseas Development Administration. It attracted much attention at the time because of its aim of reconciling the needs for conservation with those of the economic development of the region.

The Park comprises 126,000 ha. of rain forest, and an intermediate management (buffer) zone of more than 300,000 ha. The components of the project are: the establishment of the Park, enforcing its regulations, resettling six communities currently based in the Park area, and developing economic activities in the buffer zone (including construction of roads and airstrips).

Method. Conventional CBA is used to demonstrate the economic attractiveness of the project, both to the project management, and the national economy of Cameroon. Such concepts as the opportunity cost of resettlement, the value of the standing forest to its neighbours, its potential value to tourism, the genetic value of its species, its benefits to tourism, watershed protection, flood control and agricultural yields are all quantified and incorporated into the analysis. Table 5.1 summarises the elements of the Base Case.

Among the cost items, only one-third of the roads and other infrastructure is debited to the project, on the grounds that the rest have wider benefits and would be built anyway. There is an opportunity cost of creating the forest park consisting of the forgone income from commercial logging and the forfeit of benefits from the use of the forest by local residents. The labour 'credit' is due to shadow pricing wage costs. The external trade 'credit' arises from deducting externally-financed items from capital costs, on the (debatable) grounds that this aid would not otherwise have been available to Cameroon.

In the list of benefits, 'sustained forest use' comprises the benefits to neighbouring residents from the existence of the forest and buffer zone, managed on a sustainable basis. 'Replaced subsistence production' refers to the livelihoods recreated outside the main forest for those communities being resettled. Tourism benefits are derived from the spending of visitors to the Park.

Genetic value is defined as 'the amount which could be extracted in benefits from industries doing research in this area, were the institutional structures available'. It is assumed that 10 such discoveries are made each year, based on forest materials, and that Cameroon is in a position to appropriate only 10% of the value.

Table 5.1. Summary of Base Case (8%)

	CFAFm.	CFAFm.	Thousand £	Thousand £
Social costs				
Total Capital Costs - excluding roads	-3,849		-7.697	
Total Capital Costs - Roads	-929		-1,859	
Total Long-term Operating Costs	-2,380		-4,761	
Lost Stumpage Value	-353		-706	
Lost Forest Use	-1,310		-2,620	
Labour Credit	1,202		2.404	
Total costs - project		**-7,620**		**-15,239**
External Trade Credit	3,623		7,246	
Total Costs - Cameroon		**-3,997**		**-7,993**
Social benefits				
Sustained Forest Use	1,645		3,291	
Replaced Subsistence Production	489		977	
Tourism	680		1,360	
Genetic Value	240		481	
Watershed Protection	1,888		3,776	
Control of Flood Risk	789		1,578	
Soil Productivity Maintenance	266		532	
Agricultural Productivity Increase	453		905	
Induced Forestry	103		207	
Induced Cash crops	1,608		3,216	
Total benefits - project		**8,161**		16,323
Uncaptured Genetic Value	216		433	
Uncaptured Watershed Benefits	176		351	
Total benefits — Cameroon		**7,769**		**15,539**
NET BENEFIT - PROJECT		542		1,083
SOCIAL BENEFIT COST RATIO		1.07		1.07
RATE OF RETURN		8.3%		8.3%
NET BENEFIT - CAMEROON		3.773		7,546
SOCIAL BENEFIT COST RATIO		1.94		1.94
RATE OF RETURN		13.4%		13.4%

Evaluation Year (Year 0) 1989
Social Discount Rate 8.0%
Exchange Rate: CFAF/£ 500
Shadow Wage Rate 50%
Years of Deforestation 2010-2040
Road Costs Included 33%
[Ruitenbeck, 1989]

Watershed protection is taken to be synonymous with protection of the coastal fisheries affected by the watershed. Korup's share of fisheries protection is taken to be the same as its share of the forest (with Nigeria), and the value of the fisheries is inferred from the value of the catch and per capita incomes of the fishermen. The assumption is that, without the forest to regulate the flow and quality of water leaving the watershed, the whole fishery would be jeopardised.

Flood control functions are valued by making (fairly arbitrary) assumptions about the population at risk (20,000), its per capita income (£785), the share of its income lost during a flood (50%) and the frequency of floods (every 5 years). The soil fertility effect is estimated by the arbitrary assumption that, without the forest, there would be a 10% loss in the value of 25% of the cash crop income in the project area. This is also arbitrary. On the other hand, the 'induced' gains in forestry and cash crops are based on firmer estimates of schemes forming part of the project.

Among the various adjustments made to the basis costs and benefits, the genetic value is reduced to reflect the country's inability to appropriate all of the potential gain, and the watershed benefits accruing to Nigeria's fisheries are also deducted. Shadow wages of 50% are selected in the base case. A number of the cost and benefit items depend on defining a 'without project' scenario. It was assumed that, without the project, the deforestation of Korup would start in 2010, and would be complete by 2040. Degradation of the forest on the Nigerian side is well advanced, and could be complete by 2010 unless measures are taken.

Results. The overall results of the Base Case are shown in Table 5.1. The NPV of the project to Cameroon was found to be positive at a 13% discount rate, and to the project itself at an 8% discount rate. The project is assumed to run indefinitely. Sensitivity tests are performed on infrastructure costs, shadow wage levels, the timing of deforestation in the 'without project' case, and the level of the discount rate.

The contribution of the various cost and benefit items to the overall result is evident from the table. The most important values/assumptions are those concerning the 'external trade credit', the watershed protection (actually, fisheries protection), flood control, and induced cash crops. With the exception of the last mentioned, the treatment of all the major items is debatable. The attempt to value genetic resources is of some methodological interest, though it makes little difference to the overall result. The tourism benefits are based on the conservative assumption that only scientific visitors are likely to be attracted.

Although many of the assumptions underlying the values in this analysis can be questioned, its value rests in quantifying the main environmental effects and incorporating them in a conventional CBA framework.

Philippines: Palawan environmental protection and management (Finney and Western, 1986)

The island of Palawan is mountainous, with a tropical monsoonal climate, and rich natural resources. Two-thirds of the island is forested, and there are good fishing grounds, minerals and rich and diverse flora and fauna, including a number of endemic species. The island is considered very beautiful, and has excellent beaches, reefs, lakes, waterfalls, and wildlife. The population of 300,000 contains some aboriginal people.

However, the rapidly growing population and unrestrained commercial development is causing some environmental degradation. Shifting cultivation, logging and mining are causing serious soil erosion on the upper slopes. causing flooding, siltation, loss of irrigated areas and reliable water supplies, and sedimentation of coral reefs and fishing grounds. Coastal mangroves - rich in biodiversity and important breeding grounds for fish - are also being degraded.

An Integrated Environmental Plan was prepared and appraised. Among its main conservation features were the maintenance of forests on upper watersheds, the replacement of shifting cultivation by settled farming, and the conservation of coastal mangroves. National parks and nature reserves were also included in the IEP which was part of a broader plan including development of productive activities, and the strengthening of 'poles' of development that would reduce pressure on fragile natural systems.

Method. A CBA was carried out of the environmental protection elements in the Plan, making assumptions (the 'without project' case) about continuing degradation in the absence of the project. Activities that did not have a major environmental objective, such as rain-fed agriculture, were not included in the appraisal.

Most of the programme's costs were 100% attributable to the project. Some were partially attributable, e.g. the institutional strengthening of the Bureau of Forest Development, and of Fisheries and Aquatic Resources.

The benefits were classified as follows: agricultural - saving of land that would otherwise be eroded or silted, plus saving of irrigated rice land; forestry - sustainable output from commercial logging (partly offsetting sacrifice of income in short and medium term); infrastructure - avoided damage to bridges and roads from flash floods; fisheries - safeguarding catches by reducing siltation of inshore waters, damage to reefs, and preservation of mangroves; tourism - visitors attracted and retained by preservation of landscape and specific natural features.

Results. The overall Integrated Environmental Plan showed an IRR of 7% on the basis of the above quantified benefits. The mangrove conservation element had an IRR of 8.7%, and the land-based protection schemes 6.1% (the protection and rehabilitation of forests was by far the largest item in costs).

There are several points of methodological interest. First, the elements with a predominantly 'environmental' aim are separated from other parts with a 'development' purpose. Secondly, a number of important benefits are capable of being quantified, using the 'without project' assumptions. Although the authors state a case for using a lower discount rate for the conservation elements of the project, the approach as it stands contains all the information necessary for a decision about the project, along the lines recommended earlier in this section.

5.3. Economic infrastructure

5.3.1. Power and energy

Renewable forms of energy include: solar, wind, waves, tides, hydro, wood and other biomass. The most important *non-renewable* resources are: coal, oil, natural gas, and nuclear materials (excluding breeder reactors). Geothermal energy, obtained from natural underground reservoirs of water or steam, is also non-renewable. These energy sources are transformed into heat and power for human use. The generation of *power* can, in turn, be by thermal, nuclear, hydro, geothermal or non-conventional methods (solar, wind, tidal, etc.).

This section concentrates on energy and power projects of a type likely to arise in the investment programmes of typical developing countries. It will exclude any discussion of *nuclear* energy, on the grounds that relatively few countries undertake such projects, and that they invoke complex political and technical issues which deserve more extended treatment than can be given here. Power generation based on *tidal range and wavepower* will also be excluded since the technology is still being proven, and any projects in developing countries would be on a pilot basis.

(i) *Types of project.*

In the **energy** sector, typical projects are in: hydrocarbon exploration, transport and refining; coal mining; the production of woodfuel and other biomass; and the extraction of peat. Improvement in fuel and energy efficiency is another category, of increasing importance for power generation, industrial heating and processing, and for household heating and cooking. Oil refining is more appropriately treated in section 5.5, and coal mining in section 5.6. Social and agro forestry is discussed in 5.2.

Power projects can be categorised as: hydroelectric; thermal (fired by coal, oil, gas, or biomass); geothermal; non-conventional renewable sources (solar, wind, etc.); and transmission and distribution. Because of the enormous sums at stake in new investment, projects to rehabilitate existing plant, retrofit power stations with 'cleaner' technology, and reduce power losses during transmission and distribution are going to assume great importance in future. Likewise for programmes to improve the efficiency with which power is used by commercial and household consumers.

(ii) *Main environmental impacts.*

The main environmental issues can be considered following the categories set out above.

When energy is burned for heating, it adds to greenhouse gas emissions (especially carbon dioxide), and usually causes some local air pollution (e.g. from nitrous oxide, ozone and sulphur dioxide). These global effects were further discussed in section 4.12.

Oil and gas exploration, extraction, shipping and distribution: marine pollution; reef damage, coastline modification; wetland destruction; disturbance to fisheries; effect on wildlife; loss of amenity; effect on tourism. For land-based exploration/extraction, and pipelines: soil and groundwater contamination; deforestation; threats to wildlands; loss of amenity.

Biomass: (for trees, crops grown for ethanol, e.g. sugar cane, or crop residues used in industrial or power station boilers, see section 5.2).

Peat extraction: release of methane gas; wetland destruction; visual disamenity.

Hydroelectric schemes (dams, reservoirs, generating stations): changed river flows and groundwater levels; less downstream siltation; degraded watershed above reservoir from resettlement; devegetation and erosion during construction; local microclimatic and seismic effects due to reservoir; water and air pollution during construction; visual amenity (positive and negative); loss of wildlife, vegetation and biodiversity from inundation; effects on fisheries (positive and negative); water-borne diseases; loss of cultural property from inundation; noise (of turbines, and during construction). Dams often have flood control objectives, which should be credited with environmental benefits, with due allowance for the loss of fertility in downstream alluvial plains. The use of irrigation water has its own set of environmental issues (sections 4.9, 4.10, 5.2).

Hydro schemes are often the victims, as well as the agents, of environmental damage, e.g.: sedimentation of the reservoir, damage to turbines, intakes; eutrophication of the reservoir water.

Thermal power generation (coal, oil, gas, biomass fuel): air pollution from combustion (NO_x, SO_2, particulates); water pollution (local discharges, ash disposal); noise; visual disamenity.

Geothermal: Marine and freshwater pollution from dissolved chemicals in wastewater; visual disamenity, effect on tourism; loss of wildlands, wetlands.

Solar: visual intrusion (from centralised generation);

Wind: visual intrusion (from large concentrations); noise;

Transmission: devegetation, loss of forest, wetlands along line of wayleaves; visual disamenity; disturbance to wildlife; soil erosion from exposed areas; electromagnetic radiation effects on adjacent population.

Distribution: visual disamenity; health risks from fires and electrocution from unsafe connections.

Rehabilitation, retrofitting, energy efficiency, reduction of generating and transmission losses, etc. are unlikely to have serious environmental costs.

(iii) *Scope for economic valuation*.

Despite the great importance of the energy sector in all countries, and its large share of the typical developing country's investment programme, the amount of hard valuation of its environmental effects has been disappointing. The construction of hydroelectric dams and reservoirs has attracted most attention, because these schemes involve such major alterations to the natural environment, but the increasing attention to their possible effects has not been accompanied by equivalent success in valuation. This is not because of any failure in methodology; the tools have been sharpened, but they are little used.

In other branches of the sector, environmental effects are seen as by-products, though often important ones. Although certain local effects of schemes have been identified and can be valued in principle, there are little empirical data. Little progress has been made on valuing the direct effects on greenhouse gases, or even local air pollution, from thermal power stations for example.

These general points will become clearer after a discussion of the feasibility of valuing environmental effects in six of the typical cases identified above.

a) **Oil and gas.** Exploration and drilling rigs, pipelines and shore installations occupy land and sea areas which have an opportunity cost as environmental resources. Wetlands, reefs, heaths, forests, etc. can in principle be valued, if only partially (4.3, 4.4, 4.8) and the loss of these services is a cost to the project. An example of the *valuation of natural assets* is included in the discussion of dams and hydroelectricity schemes below.

A number of the available valuation exercises have been in respect of the environmental damage caused by *oil spillages* at sea (4.8). The cost of these accidents, however assessed, has been huge. In theory, every project to bring on stream a new source of petroleum increases the probability of a costly accident. But there are many difficulties in the way of attaching this probability as a potential cost to a particular project: major accidents are too infrequent to be statistically predictable; they are likely to occur well away from the source of the petroleum; blame, and legal liability, may attach to the tanker owners or operators; the accidents vary greatly in severity, and in their economic and environmental costs, etc.

In these circumstances, any inclusion of probable accident costs as an international externality in appraising a hydrocarbon project is going to be very arbitrary. It will remain so until there is international agreement on a fair apportionment of these damages among, say, consumers, transporters and producers of the oil, which could result in levying insurance premia on these various parties. In some respects the problem is akin to apportioning responsibility for global climatic effects to a particular project (4.12).

Part of these damage costs will be the loss of wildlife and damage - perhaps irreversible - to fragile ecosystems and wildlands. The building of the Alaska pipeline and the *Exxon Valdez* disaster illustrate the force of public feeling about ecological effects, and the large potential economic costs entailed. However, there are few if any comparable data for the valuation of ecologies damaged in developing country cases, and North American values are unlikely to be appropriate (see the discussion of dams and hydroelectric schemes below).

Localised risks of *seepage, spills, explosions*, etc. are more tractable, and an appropriate contingency should be built into costs to reflect likely environmental damage. The valuation principles discussed in section 4.8 are relevant, provided that appropriate damage data exist from comparable situations.

b) **Dams and hydroelectric schemes.** The environmental effects of dams and associated hydro works have been comprehensively identified, and many of them can in principle be valued (Dixon, Talbot and Le Moigne, 1989, list 11 effects which can be valued by one or other of the techniques discussed in section 3.3). However, a detailed study of six major hydropower schemes concluded:

> Most of the appraisals of large dams reviewed do not quantify the environmental costs in money terms . . . what is done ranges from largely ignoring the environmental dimension, to carrying out a comprehensive environmental impact analysis of the project (Furtado *et al.*, 1990, p. 119).

In practice, exercises in valuation have tended to focus, on the one hand, on the costs of reservoir siltation and the benefits from controlling watershed use and, on the other hand, the value of irreplaceable natural assets that would be inundated by the reservoir.

Reservoir siltation from up-stream soil erosion and landslides is to be expected in many schemes (4.1) and is an example of a project being on the receiving end of environmental damage for which it is partly responsible. It is thus in a different conceptual category from damage for which the scheme is directly responsible, but it is nevertheless an issue to be faced in project appraisal. Siltation shortens the life of a hydro scheme once dead storage is taken up. Beyond this point it reduces the amount of water for power and irrigation sales, and impairs its flood control function. There is also a risk of damage to turbines, intakes and the dam wall itself from, variously, clogging with fine silt and the abrasive action of coarse material. Given reliable data on the rate of sedimentation and the pattern of sediment accumulation, these costs can be estimated (see the Paute case study below).

This is essentially a project for watershed conservation which has been 'internalised' by a power company in its own interests. It can be viewed as a shadow or compensatory project, the cost of which should be included in the original appraisal of the hydro scheme. Alternatively, if conservation comes after the original investment is made, it can be justified by the avoided costs of further sedimentation. Certain extra benefits of such projects, like wood, fruit, and on-farm productivity, should be netted off their costs. Watershed protection may also be carried out to improve the *quality of water* entering the reservoir. In the Nam Pong project in Thailand, a fishing industry that had grown up in the reservoir was threatened by water pollution, amongst other things (Hufschmidt and Srivardhana, in Dixon and Hufschmidt, 1986). This is an example of a 'second generation' project to safeguard one of the scheme's original benefits.

The discussion so far has been concerned with valuation of defensive measures undertaken by hydro schemes. Turning to the costing of their own effects on the environment, one of the best known studies is of the Gordon River Dam in Tasmania, which illustrates an approach to valuing the *preservation of rare natural assets* (discussed in Pearce and Markandya, 1989). The dam would have flooded a valley of particular wild natural beauty and ecological interest, and which had religious importance for aborigines.

The study tackled the question of what development benefits would be forfeited by not proceeding with the scheme - a measure of the opportunity cost of preservation. Estimation of the development benefits calculated the cost superiority of the Gordon River scheme over alternative ways of generating power by coal-fired stations. Strictly speaking, the environmental costs of the alternative should also be included in the exercise. It was then possible to state that, if the Gordon River scheme was not undertaken, society would incur extra costs in obtaining the required power, which (in NPV terms) were represented as the cost of preserving the valley's natural beauty.

In its basic form, this is a straightforward opportunity cost approach to the treatment of non-quantifiables. An important refinement of the method is that the real value of preservation benefits is assumed to increase over time, as the supply of wildlands decreases and the demand for their services increases. This has an equivalent effect to discounting the implicit preservation benefits of the scheme at a lower rate. At this stage of the analysis it is necessary to take a view on whether the preservation benefits would actually be large enough to warrant incurring the extra costs of power from abandoning the scheme. Some preservation benefits can be quantified; net tourism income is an obvious example. TC and CV studies (3.3.5 and 3.3.6) may also be appropriate, though their use in many developing countries is doubtful. In the case in question the extra cost of generating the power elsewhere was low enough to support an intuitive judgement that development should not proceed.

On a more mundane level, the flooding of land that is involved in dam construction destroys timber with commercial value. When the Balbina Dam in Brazil was constructed, the reservoir inundated timber with an estimated sawmilling value of US$138-180 m., and $400 m. including wood not exploited for fuel. If these costs had been included in the appraisal, they would have doubled the cost of electricity generated by the scheme (Gribel, 1990).

It is feasible to value several other environmental effects of dams once they have been established and quantified. The problems are that some effects are not fully predictable when the scheme is being planned, and have both positive and negative aspects. Thus the net benefit is doubly difficult to predict in advance, and much of our information about hydro schemes has been obtained from the *ex post* analysis of existing projects. Since each scheme is different, this is of little help at the appraisal stage.

Fisheries, for instance, are affected both positively and negatively, and the net balance is very hard to predict in advance. In the Nam Pong scheme mentioned above the importance of the reservoir fishery was not anticipated. Dams and reservoirs impede fish migration, reduce downstream water volume, and can increase coastal erosion. But the reservoir itself may become an important fishery (e.g. Lake Nasser). Arriving at a balanced judgement is further complicated by the fact that losers and gainers include different fish species, in different locations, and different groups of people. If these problems can be resolved, the fisheries effect can be valued using EOP.

Dams also deprive downstream land of the fertilising power of sediment. This effect can be valued using the RC approach, based on the cost of applying artificial *fertiliser* to this land. There is a serious practical complication when downstream land use is radically affected by a dam. In Egypt agriculture in the Nile Valley has become much more intensive following the assurance of regular irrigation water from Lake Nasser, and the need for soil nutrients has greatly increased. Only a part of current fertiliser applications can be attributed to the loss of Nile silt from constructing the dam (Abu-Zeid, 1989).

Tourism and recreation are other areas where a balance of gains and losses has to be struck. Hydro schemes destroy previous landscapes, but replace them with new ones, attracting a different type of visitor and recreationist. At the planning stage, the value attached to the prior landscape can be tested by CV and TC methods. This can be compared with net visitor income from the reservoir and dam. Risks to cultural property can be valued using RC, where relocation is feasible (e.g. the Abu Simbel and Philae Temples in the Nile Valley), and using CV and TC methods, where relocation is impossible. In many cases, tourist income would bolster the credibility of TC and CV results.

A balanced judgement of the effects of hydro schemes on *health* would have to take account of the positive effects on nutrition and family income from greater food production, and on lifestyles from greater supplies of electric power. Flood control would have additional benefits. The specific effect of the reservoir on the spread of malaria, bilharzia, etc. may be best dealt with through the PE method, by adding in the costs of vector control and improved health care. HC methods have been little applied in developing countries (though see sections 4.10 and 5.4). As a short cut, an estimate of the value of work lost might be attempted (Furtado *et al.*, 1990).

The resource costs of *resettlement* should also be estimated, as well as any environmental degradation that might be expected as a result of the move.

c) **Thermal power generation**. Although there is widespread environmental concern about the effects of thermal power generation, especially on the production of greenhouse gases and its role in acid rain, there is little to guide the economist on how these effects can be valued for appraisal purposes. This role in this sector is likely to be the less ambitious, though equally vital, one of: describing effects and illustrating their *possible* size for decision-makers; ensuring that relevant data are generated by Environmental Impact Assessments; requiring that baseline studies and monitoring systems adequately cover economic data and the underlying physical relationships (e.g. health, pollution, corrosion) on which valuation can be based; valuing local effects, so far as possible; handling greenhouse gas effects in the context of national abatement policies (see below).

In this context, three important potential effects will now be examined.

(i) **Greenhouse gases**. Section 4.12 argues that it is not yet practical to attribute the effects of global warming to individual projects. The problem is best tackled in the framework of national abatement policies. If the host country accepts a national limit on the emission of greenhouse gases, this gives a context in which to value the costs of an individual project.

At the time of writing, no developing country has accepted such a national limit, or target. Although various schemes have been suggested for setting country quotas for, say, carbon emissions (see Grubb, 1989), these have not been accepted as the basis for discussion, even in principle. However, it is difficult to conceive of the valuation problem except in a national context. In these circumstances, one crude but practical compromise is for governments and their aid donors to act as though they were up against their national carbon emissions 'ceiling'. It would follow that a new project would entail some extra abatement effort, either as an integral part of the project, or imposed on some other emitter.

Section 4.12 argued that the cost of a thermal power station would be the marginal abatement cost imposed on the economy; estimates of this are starting to appear (ERL, 1990) for a few countries. In the case of power stations, abatement of the main greenhouse gas, carbon dioxide, would be impractical except at prohibitive cost, and a truer valuation of marginal abatement costs would have to be sought amongst other projects in other sectors. In some cases, the average 'cost-effective' abatement cost from a variety of projects might be used to indicate the effect of the power station, and this would appear as a shadow cost item in appraisal.

Such data are still rare, and in the typical case all the appraiser could do would be to commission work on comparative abatement costs and meanwhile enter an amount as a shadow contingency against the project in question.

(ii) **Local effects through air pollution**. Air pollution has been linked to damage to health, the corrosion of materials and a fall in productivity of agriculture, forestry and fisheries. Valuing this set of effects rests on the ability to identify the responsibility of particular emitters for pollution, and to establish the link between pollution and the effect concerned ('dose-response' effects) (4.6). These are two giant steps.

The first - assigning responsibility for pollution - is difficult enough, especially where there are a number of agents. It is usually necessary to make strong assumptions about damage being caused in strict proportion to emissions, whereas in practice the location of emitters relative to receptors, the characteristics of the pollution plume, and other local factors would determine the actual responsibilities.

The second step, determining the dose-response data, is equally problematic. There is a scarcity of good epidemiological data on the relationship between air pollution and *public health*. There is a case for setting up baseline surveys and monitoring the impact as it arises, unless there are relevant circumstances elsewhere that would furnish data, in which case they should be surveyed. Once it becomes possible to apportion a certain part of the responsibility to the power sector, health effects can be valued using HC methods, or the short-cut of valuing working time lost (4.6). Even in West Germany, where health data are good, the assignment of health effects to thermal power generation rested on crude assumptions, and produced a wide range of values (Hohmeyer, 1988). In developing countries lacking such data valuing health effects are unlikely to be feasible.

The impact of air pollution and acid rain on *materials corrosion* and *forestry and agriculture* is little understood, even in developed countries (4.6). This is another case where the effects should be closely monitored during the project's implementation. The yields of forest plantations and agriculture are likely to be particularly at risk. As a start, the appraiser could estimate the value of forestry or farm output within the relevant distance of the emission (the area and direction to be determined by the pollution 'plume'), which would set a maximum value to this effect. In the United States, the output of soyabeans, wheat, maize, cotton, sugar beet and vegetables was depressed by amounts in the range 4-17% by a 50% increase in ozone concentrations (Kneese, 1984).

Fisheries are more at risk from water pollution caused by power station effluent. Again, the value of fisheries in the river concerned could be estimated to set an upper limit on damage from this source. Serious pollution has been known to kill all fish life.

(iii) **Amenity values**. Effects on local amenity from the presence of unsightly, dirty and noisy power stations can be captured by versions of the hedonic property method. Where the local property market is sufficiently active and transparent (see 3.3.4) the discount on neighbouring property values can be used as a proxy for the disamenity effects. Once the project is implemented, the property price differential will become apparent, but for *ex ante* purposes the analyst will depend on cross-sectional data from elsewhere.

(d) **Geothermal power**. One of the main adverse environmental effects of geothermal power arises from the disposal of waste fluids. These contain dissolved chemicals in concentrations which can be harmful to other users of surface waters. The temperature of the discharges is also a problem.

In a study of wastewater disposal options for the Tongonan Geothermal Power Plant in the Philippines (Grandstaff and Balagot, 1986), the problem is treated as the choice of the least cost (direct plus environmental) option, after identifying a number of non-quantifiable effects. Seven options are identified, namely reinjection of the waste into the original field, and whether or not to treat waste disposal in each of three different locations. Two kinds of environmental cost are directly estimated, namely the effect on rice farmers and marine fisheries. Other potential effects are identified but not valued - on freshwater fishing, health, domestic water use, and marine ecosystems. The lowest cost option (reinjection) is chosen on the basis of its combined direct and environmental costs, and after making subjective judgements on the non-quantifiable effects of the various alternatives.

(e) **Transmission and distribution**. Of the effects identified earlier, the effect on amenity is most susceptible of valuation (using hedonic property methods for local impacts, and CV and TC for costs to the landscape in general). Other effects are likely to be too diffuse (e.g. on wildlife) or unsupported (e.g. electromagnetic radiation) to justify attaching firm values. However, where health or amenity factors are considered to be overriding - usually in cities, but also to minimise the effect on natural assets or priceless views - extra costs can be incurred in re-routing cables or placing them underground (the PE method).

(f) **Rehabilitation, energy efficiency, etc.** This family of measures has in common the avoidance of major new investments in power generation, with all their associated environmental (and economic) costs (Van Domelen, 1988). They are unlikely to give rise to significant environmental costs in themselves, and, like solar and wind schemes, should be appraised according to the avoided costs of alternative options.

(iv) *Case study*.

The Paute hydroelectric scheme in Ecuador: the benefits of erosion control to a power utility (Southgate and Macke, 1989)

In this instance, INECEL, the Ecuadorian electric power utility, has invested in upstream erosion control in order to preserve its reservoir capacity. The costs of arresting watershed degradation, which arise outside INECEL's boundaries, are being 'internalised' by the utility, in its own interests. This case study illustrates the nature and magnitude of the benefits that can be expected from such actions.

The Paute reservoir was completed in 1983 at a cost of $600 m. Located in the Andean Highlands, its watershed is steeply sloping and heavily populated. It had an initial active storage capacity of 100 million cu.m. and a design lifetime of 50 years.

As in many other hydroelectric schemes, soil erosion in the upper watershed is threatening the viability of the scheme in several ways:

i) reducing the lifetime of the reservoir through siltation and loss of storage capacity. As in other tropical areas reservoir volume is small relative to sediment load, hence the curtailment of its useful life is a more serious factor than in temperate schemes.

i) impairing the thermal energy-saving functions of the hydro scheme. With reduced reservoir capacity, the annual flow of hydro power is reduced in the drier season, requiring additional generation from thermal installations at higher marginal cost.

ii) 'remediation' work is necessary to remove material such as larger stones and boulders that might slough off against the dam or finer silt that would clog the intakes. (In Paute 25% of sediment load is now being deposited within 1500 metres of the dam.) This should be distinguished from ordinary dredging of sediment which is not normally economic. Nor is it normally feasible in a large scheme to flush away sediment.

v) turbine blades and other equipment function less well and require more frequent replacement where a sediment load passes through. The size of these costs can be appreciated from the 'normal' annual allowance for equipment depreciation, which was initially fixed at $20 m.

INECEL has begun a programme of watershed management comprising civil works for keeping eroded material from entering waterways, protection of remaining forests, reforestation and erosion control on farmland on the upper slopes.

Method. The authors develop a simple model which quantifies the first three of the effects above. 'With' soil conservation upstream, the benefits to INECEL are taken to be the increased net value of hydroelectric output from the increased reliability of energy, lower dredging costs and an extension to the scheme's lifetime, compared with the scenario 'without' conservation measures. Modelling the increased reliability of power entails a distinction between 'firm' power which is fully substitutable for that produced from thermal entities, and 'non-firm' power which is too unreliable. The value of firm power is equivalent to the long-run marginal cost of a thermal plant while the value of non-firm power is taken to be the short-run marginal cost. (As a capital-intensive item, the cost of thermal power is sensitive to the discount rate used.)

The cost of 'remediation' in the form of dredging material close to the dam is estimated to be $2.50 per cu.m. of sediment. It is, realistically, assumed that the useful life of the reservoir would cease when its active storage fell below 20% of its initial level. No residual value for the dam is assumed, on the grounds that there could even be a net cost in dismantling the unwanted, and possibly dangerous, structure. Three alternative project scenarios are investigated; first, where the conservation project is fully implemented, and its benefits fully realised; second, where the project is accelerated by four years, and the full benefits are realised earlier; and third, where the project goes ahead on schedule, but the benefits are only half those expected.

Results. All three scenarios show a sizeable Present Value of downstream benefits at an 8% discount rate (conservation costs are not reported, hence a comparison is not possible here). The assumption is that sediment load entering the reservoir would grow at 4% p.a. in the absence of conservation; 85% of the benefits arise from extending the life of the reservoir, compared to which the saving of dredging costs is minor. The 'accelerated' scheme shows significant benefits relative to the base case (PV of $39m. as opposed to $28m.) and even more so in respect of the third scenario (PV $15m.). The results are most sensitive to estimates of the future trend in sediment loads and the value of hydroelectricity. They also rest on the assumption that conservation measures are effective in reducing erosion and siltation, which depends heavily on whether the residents of the upper water-sheds can be induced to change their current farm practices.

The value of this study lies in demonstrating that investing in watershed conser-vation can be in the direct economic and financial interest of a utility company. In this case, savings in dredging costs and the net value of the extra power available from prolonging the reservoir's life can justify the costs of conservation, and help to safeguard the huge initial investment. Investment in conservation can rank favourably alongside other projects for coping with increasing demand for electric power. The analysis can be viewed as conservative, insofar as other possible benefits are omitted, such as avoided damage to turbines and intake equipment, effects on reservoir fisheries, and effects on downstream river users and estuarine fisheries. The authors contrast the problems of a large scheme like Paute with the trend in Ecuador towards the construction of smaller reservoirs (that can be regularly flushed), the location of other reservoirs in the coastal plain, away from steep watersheds and the development of 'mini-hydro' schemes. The problems of sedimentation are clearly recognised in the design of new schemes.

5.3.2. Roads and railways

These two surface transport modes can be considered together insofar as many of their environmental effects are similar. The construction of fixed tracks and routes causes some alteration to the landscape, and improved transport is the agent of far-reaching socio-economic change, which has a further impact on the environ-ment. The construction phase will also have a major temporary impact.

(i) *Types of project*

Roads. At one extreme are major national trunk roads, which have important effects on geographical activity. Their consequences are particularly serious where they cross virgin areas, and induce new settlement patterns (e.g. Brazil's Trans-Amazon Highway). At the other extreme are the construction of access roads or tracks to connect households or farmers to an existing road network. The effects of the latter will be principally on personal mobility, social services, and farm incentives. If roads help to improve farm incomes, they could help farmers to become better environmental conservers - but this depends on the type of crop, the way the land is farmed, and the tenurial arrangements.

Roads also feature as minor components of projects in other sectors, such as agriculture, logging, mining and as temporary access to any major construction project. It is often such road-building, undertaken with far less planning and care than is usual in road schemes *per se*, that causes the worst environmental damage.

Maintenance of existing roads will have less environmental effect than the con-struction of new ones. However, restoring a road network to something close to its initial state will normally increase traffic usage and speeds compared to the 'without' case of continued deterioration. The construction or maintenance works will have their own impact on the environment. Upgrading existing roads (e.g. grading earth roads, gravelling, bitumen sealing, local improvements, bridge construction) will also have environmental impacts, both local and regional. Improving a road may cause traffic to divert on to it, thus increasing noise pollution and danger to local inhabitants (but reducing these dangers on the alternative routes). Improvements that cause an increase in the average speed of travel may result in more accidents, unless extra safety features are included.

Vehicles. The supply of motor vehicles or programmes to rehabilitate existing fleets will have an impact mainly through increased usage of existing routes - pollution, noise, safety, and indirect socio-economic changes. However, replacing old and inefficient vehicles will often improve fuel efficiency and reduce pollution.

Systems improvement. Some projects entail the offer of 'software' - advice, management systems, regulations, etc. - enabling an existing system of vehicles and routes to function more effectively. In urban transport such measures include better traffic control, segregation of vehicles and pedestrians, installing traffic lights, changing speed restrictions, creating bus lanes, licensing private taxis and other carriers, etc. Some large cities have introduced measures to shift the balance between public and private transport (in Singapore by a road pricing scheme, in Mexico City by allowing private cars to enter the centre only on alternate days, etc). Many of these measures will have positive environmental effects - e.g. reduced congestion causing less noise, dirt and fumes.

Railways. The construction of new railways is a comparatively rare event in developing countries, and it is more common to find projects to upgrade existing permanent way, improve the operating system, and supply new or upgrade existing locomotives and rolling stock. In the urban context, a number of developing cities have established mass rapid transit systems based on rail.

Railways built to serve individual mines or industrial plants are likely to have a limited effect on permanent settlement patterns, but can lead to great environmental damage during their construction. For instance, the construction of a railway to link a large iron mine in Northern Brazil to the coast caused much localised deforestation, but had nothing like the permanent impact of the major highways through the Amazon. A passenger railway, with frequent stations, would have a much greater impact on settlement, and therefore the environment.

Projects to restore existing railway systems are unlikely to have major direct environmental impacts. In most developing countries the frequency of rail services is low, and the problems of noise, vibration and pollution (from coal and oil fumes) will be tolerable. The main indirect effect, which will be generally positive, will be the diversion of traffic from roads.

Urban rail systems, including underground metros, are generally built to improve environmental conditions by relieving road congestion and air pollution. However, in the course of construction they usually make local environmental conditions very much worse.

(ii) *Major environmental effects*

The main environmental effects of a road or railway project can be considered under various headings (ODA, 1988; TRRL, 1988).

Vegetation. Apart from the devegetation that occurs along the track, which may extend far enough back to reduce fire risk, there is often considerable degradation during construction for fuelwood, fencing, etc. and as a result of the other activities of construction gangs. The existence of roads is also a potent cause of further deforestation by new settlers, firewood collectors, etc.

Hydrological. Roads may interfere with *surface drainage*. A properly-designed road should contain features to mitigate these effects, such as drainage channels, culverts, bridges, for which adequate provision should be built into costs. However, a poorly designed, or cheaply executed, road system may cause serious siltation and congestion in rivers and off-shore waters that does major damage to fisheries, and risks flooding. As Pereira (1989) points out:

> Mountain roads act both as collecting surfaces and as hillside cut-off drains that intercept surface flows. When intense tropical rainstorms occur, roads concentrate water so that the culvert discharges have dangerously erosive energy.

Jeep tracks on tropical hill ranges can have similar effects. Roads that cut off or damage *wetlands*, either directly or through the excavation of construction materials, damage a particularly sensitive environment.

Geotechnical. Railway cuttings and embankments, and badly built roads and roads built across slopes can destabilise the land and lead to landslides and soil erosion. Vegetation removed above the road, or for the cut, can have the same effect, and add to soil erosion above and below, and run-off and deposition further down. Timber required for railway sleepers and fuelwood used during construction, or for fires by construction gangs, can cause local degradation. Some of the most convincing evidence of the geotechnical damage done by roads has been of roads that were unplanned, or cheaply-built minor components of other schemes, such as logging, or as temporary access to construction sites.

Land use. Road construction causes, and is usually associated with, drastic changes in land use such as the regrouping of population along the route, settlement of farmers in the vicinity, etc. Roads may complement developments already planned, such as construction of a new town, opening up a mine, relocating a port. In such cases, it is more satisfactory to consider the environmental impact of the whole development. These effects will be especially striking if the development occurs through a previously unsettled area. As TRRL (1988) note: '. . . indirect effects are often more potentially damaging than the project itself' (p. 11).

Socio-economic. The above environmental effects work through to local human populations. The fact that settlements in developing countries are attracted to roads and railways is evidence of the benefits they are perceived to bring, but settlers bring environmental costs down on themselves, as well as the indirect problems caused by changes in land use.

In rural areas where road and rail traffic is light, noise, pollution, vibration and visual amenity are unlikely to be seen as major problems by those affected. These issues will obviously weigh more heavily as traffic increases, as in inter-urban highways or suburban railways. Health problems could be more serious, from the greater passage of people and animals, from water contamination, from malarial areas caused by changes in surface water flows, flooded borrow pits, etc. Transport routes into virgin or lightly-populated areas are likely to bring major changes into the lifestyles of aboriginal or tribal peoples, which many of them will find hard to cope with.

Wildlife is affected in various ways by road building and its consequent traffic. Trees and plants are destroyed during construction. Air pollution, interruptions to drainage, fires, etc. have a continuing effect. The agriculture which often follows in the wake of improved transport will lead to further clearing and the introduction of foreign species.

Animals will suffer from the loss of shelter and habitat, interruption to migration trails and breeding grounds, and the death toll from passing vehicles.

(iii) *Scope for valuation*

For the typical transport project, it is unlikely that most of the above effects could be valued. Many will be too elusive, or too small, to value with any confidence. In practice, economic appraisals will be obliged to concentrate on one or two important effects that can be predicted and valued with some confidence, and base the case on these. Thus, economic appraisal will usually undervalue the aggregate environment effects of the project. However, it is wiser to stake the economic appraisal on a convincing analysis of part of the impact than to make an implausible attempt at a comprehensive assessment.

It is important to include effects from the construction (and maintenance) phases as well as those from operation. Because roads are such important agents of development it is also advisable to take a wide-ranging view of their potential impact, allowing for their many possible indirect effects (e.g. on settlement, farming practices, personal mobility).

The potential *environmental benefits* of transport modes should not be ignored. These might include: relocating a route to by-pass a town or village, relieving congestion, noise and pollution; local works to improve safety and amenity; replacement of old, inefficient and polluting vehicles with more environmentally friendly ones; improving the competitiveness of a railway *vis-à-vis* roads, thus relieving congestion, pollution, etc.

A possible framework for carrying out an economic appraisal is to draw up a matrix, such as the one in Appendix 2 (see DOT, 1979). This approach focuses the analysis on the *distribution* of environmental benefits and costs, which supplements the usual economic and financial analysis. At the extremes, certain roads (fast trunk roads with limited local access) impose costs on their vicinity without bringing much obvious gain. Others, such as rural access roads, will confer a more favourable balance of benefits and costs on the local community.

Some benefit and cost categories would appear in monetary terms (e.g. value of time savings), some in absolute amounts (reduction in accidents), others in the form of judgements about their relative importance (severe, or mild). The categories involved might include the following (drawing upon UK practice in DOT, 1979): travellers (motorists, passengers, pedestrians, other modes); residents (householders, tenants, visitors); productive activities (trade, farming, artisans, tourism, etc.); various levels of government; other interested parties. Some account should be taken of the incidence of costs and benefits over time. Costs associated with the construction programme would not be expected to persist. Some costs would get worse over time, as traffic built up. Others might diminish, e.g. as an earth road is eventually sealed, dust will become less of a problem.

Although there are many Environmental Impact Studies of road and railway projects, there are few exercises in environmental valuation, mainly because effects are usually spread over several different habitats, and invoke a variety of processes, with the result that overall impact is diffuse and rarely critical in any specific effect. There is nevertheless some scope for valuing the following effects.

(a) **Soil erosion, siltation, landslides**. Some localised risk is to be expected from road and rail construction in humid, hilly terrain. The effect on output (using EOP) is unlikely to be very large or predictable. Hodgson and Dixon (1988) studied the relationship between erosion from logging roads and the reduced yield of fisheries and effects on tourism from the resulting sedimentation. There are few comparable studies. A more plausible approach is to use PE. The physical works should include design features aimed at minimising erosion and landslides (retaining structures, gabions, proper drainage, etc.). The extra cost could be justified either by the scale of avoided losses to output, or by the avoided costs of rehabilitating the road following landslips (which happened soon after the opening of the Dharan-Dhankuta road in Nepal).

(b) **Destruction of wetlands, forest, wildlands, etc.** The natural resource at risk may be susceptible to valuation of some of its products and functions (see section 4.4 for wetlands). However, in developing countries it will be easier to value the direct products rather than its environmental functions. In any case, the road or railway is only likely directly to take up part of a wetland or forest, leaving the rest intact, though indirectly at risk. It will be difficult to assess the project's impact on the whole natural resource, still less the long-term impact of greater traffic.

If the route entails the loss of biomass (secondary forest, bush, scrub of no great ecological value) it may suffice to create a compensatory project to replace the lost vegetation by planting elsewhere. Temperate wetlands can even be replaced (4.4) though this is unlikely to be satisfactory in tropical conditions with richer and more diverse ecology. For natural resource habitats of great rarity or beauty, containing great biodiversity, rare species, etc., the preferred option may be to conserve the resource by abandoning the project, or postponing, modifying, or relocating it. In such cases conservation has a cost represented by the forfeit of benefits from such actions (see discussion of the Gordon River scheme in 5.3.1).

(c) **Pollution, noise, contamination**. Except on heavily travelled routes, problems from the passage of traffic are likely to be diffuse and difficult to correlate with local health problems. There will, however, be evidence from *ex post* studies of transport impacts in comparable situations elsewhere which will provide pointers to the scale and type of health problems likely to arise (malaria from changes in surface water flow, intestinal disorders from groundwater contamination due to the relocation of population, bronchial complaints from traffic fumes, communicable diseases from the movement of tourists, lorry drivers, etc.). A well-planned project would anticipate these problems by including health-care provisions, safe water supplies and sanitation. Segregating the road from existing villages will reduce the impact of noise, dust and air pollution. The construction of barriers and sensible design of junctions will reduce the chance of accidents (see TRRL, 1988). These facilities require adjustments to the cost of the project, internalising some of the potential external costs (an example of PE).

The prediction and valuation of health- and pollution-related damage from roads can be taken further in the context of heavily trafficked routes through well populated areas. Studying similar roads in comparable areas elsewhere may generate data on pollution-induced health problems, or 'defensive expenditure' by householders, factories or offices to protect themselves against noise, dust or fumes (see sections 4.6, 4.7). In more affluent areas with well developed property markets, the benefits and costs of transport projects may be partly reflected in changes in property values (3.3.4).

d) **Biodiversity and wildlife**. In appraising effects on fauna and flora it is useful to distinguish between biodiversity as such, and particular animals and plants actually at risk. Section 4.11 argued that it is not feasible to expect to capture much of the benefits of biodiversity in economic valuation. If it is decided that the biodiversity at risk from a project should be preserved at all costs, the project will have to be amended, and there will be an opportunity cost. In certain cases, the 'existence value' of the natural resource will find expression in effective demand, such as in a cash offer from an international conservation group. Otherwise, there is no direct way of valuing the resource. Where the fauna and flora have commercial or other use value to local people, their loss has some market value. Common species of animals can even be bred and introduced into the wild. Alternatively, the costs of the project can be increased to include defensive or compensatory measures such as replanting, restocking, design amendments, conservation measures, etc. (PE). The case study below is an example of a rural road project incorporating conservation elements.

(iv) Case study: Kenya: the Molo-Litein Road

This project, approved by the ODA in 1988, illustrates the potential impact of a road on a forested watershed, the tension between the interests of local farmers and environmental concerns, and ways in which the design of the project can minimise its environmental harm.

The project is located in a fertile upland area in North-West Kenya with a mixture of smallholder, estate, and livestock farming. The original proposal was to upgrade an existing earth road traversing a forest of major environmental value. Following negotiations between the government and ODA, the project was redefined to exclude the segment of road actually in the forest, for both economic and environmental reasons.

The declared purpose of the road was to reduce transport costs, improve access and stimulate the economy of an area of good agricultural potential. The growth of the rural population was leading to some encroachment onto forest land. A project was eventually approved for upgrading the existing road outside the forest boundaries to all-weather bitumen standards. The project showed positive quantified NPVs based on cost savings to existing and generated traffic, plus economies in road maintenance. A number of conditions were attached to the project to minimise any damage it might cause to the environment. It is noteworthy that the road would probably have gone ahead sooner or later, with or without the stringent environmental conditions that were imposed.

Environmental risks included the following factors: (i) The blossoming of the local economy following upgrading of the road was expected to lead to growing pressure on the forest perimeter, and even settlement within it. (ii) The forest is the largest of its type in East Africa, and one of the largest indigenous forests left in Kenya. A number of unique and rare species of fauna and flora had been identified, and more could be expected from a thorough inventory. The improved road through the forest would mean greater traffic, some settlement, loss of vegetation, and the consolidation of the road as an artificial barrier to species dispersal. This would threaten biodiversity, and could lead to the loss of rare species. (iii) Any serious loss of forest cover would affect its functions as a catchment for a major river, serving rural communities and a large nature reserve. The most likely result would be to exaggerate the peaks and troughs of stream flow, with a longer dry season and more severe flooding.

During negotiation of the project, the following design features and conditions were agreed:

i) the impact of the construction work entailed in upgrading the road would be mitigated by: using as much of the existing alignment as practicable; control of surface water discharges; full rehabilitation of quarries and camps after completion; and a limit on the number of detour roads provided during construction. Some of these measures would raise construction costs and possibly reduce user benefits.

ii) the government accepted the principle that measures should be taken to control access to the road once it had been upgraded.

iii) before any eventual work started, there would be a full ecological assessment of the forest in conjunction with a social anthropological survey of its importance to neighbouring populations. Measures might then be necessary to redesign the project which would have cost penalties, and reduce user savings.

iv) the Forestry Department would be strengthened in the districts concerned and the funding agency would offer advice on conservation and management; the Government would commit itself to respecting and protecting existing forest boundaries; farmers would be encouraged to take up agro-forestry, and there would be 'enrichment planting' of trees on areas that had been degraded.

As it happened, the decision not to fund the upgrading of the road through the forest was justifiable on economic grounds - the conventional savings on user costs and maintenance were inadequate. Had this not been the case, and if the forest road could not have been ruled out on economic grounds, there would have been an environmental dilemma. The appraisal might then have taken the following form:

a) from the ecological and social anthropological surveys conducted as part of the project preparation phase, identify the environmental risks from development, and areas where damage would be serious and irreversible (e.g. extinction of rare species, loss of watershed functions, reduction of biodiversity). Indicate design modifications helpful to the environment.

) calculate the ostensible 'costs' of the environmental modifications to the project:
i) the effect on the NPV/IRR of the project modifications and conditions - e.g.
extra construction cost, loss of some user savings; (ii) where the surveys presaged
unacceptable environmental risk, the opportunity cost of not proceeding with
part or all of the scheme.

c) identify, measure and value - to the extent possible - the environmental benefits
of the proposed modifications, including, in the extreme case, halting the project.

d) offset these quantifiable benefits against the extra costs, the remaining cost
being the opportunity cost to development of complying with the environmental
safeguards. This cost would be weighed against the identified, but unmeasurable
and unquantifiable, benefits, as well as wider political, social and economic factors, in reaching a view on the project.

5.3.3. Ports, harbours and coastal structures

This section deals with various kinds of structures at the interface between sea and
land. Although most of them are involved in maritime transport, many other
coastal developments are not, e.g. sea-walls, housing, tourist buildings and structures, promenades, coastal roads, etc.

(i) *Types of projects*

The environmental impact of coastal developments depends on a variety of factors, which can be simplified as scale, location and function. Scale is vital. At one
extreme, major ports are sizeable industrial settlements in their own right, or else
vital parts of large cities, and their environmental impact is hard to disentangle
from that of the whole metropolitan area or industrial estate. At the other extreme,
individual wharfs or jetties serving local or specialised functions will have effects
limited to their immediate vicinity, and involving such local issues as coastal
stability and amenity. Location is also vital. Certain specialised ports (e.g. for
minerals or oil) are located well away from major population centres, whereas
others are in downtown areas (e.g. Bombay, Rio de Janeiro). A given environmental effect (e.g. pollution) is a graver risk if it occurs in proximity to large settlements. Another important distinction is between ports located in estuaries, and
those in bays. The former tend to affect a wider range of economic activities, such
as artisanal fisheries, salt reclamation, aquaculture, dredging of sand and gravels,
mangrove exploitation, as well as tourism. Ports in embayments, on the other
hand, tend to have fewer such activities, and are less susceptible to siltation and
industrial water pollution (Vandermeulen, 1990).

Functional aspects are also important factors. Terminals for the export and import
of petroleum and refined oil products carry a different set of environmental risks
from those of, say, grain terminals or general cargo wharfs, and give rise to a
different pattern of storage and transport in the immediate hinterland. They are
also associated with a different type of ocean vessel.

The largest projects are those to create new ports, either to cater for the development of new products in new areas (e.g. oil, minerals, phosphate) or to relieve

congestion in existing sites (e.g. the development of Port Qasim near Karachi, or Nhava Sheva near Bombay). Estimating the net environmental impact of such new ports is complicated by the need to take account of effects on existing ports (e.g. relief of congestion and pollution). In practice, there are often strong pressures to keep the previous ports in operation for as long as possible!

The major environmental effects will obviously arise during the course of putting the basic infrastructure in place. Recurring environmental effects will arise mainly from dredging, discharges, spillages and waste from visiting ships, and any water pollution from the port activities or associated industrial processes. Compared with these, the effects of many aid projects will be minor, e.g. provision of port equipment, transport, storage, organisational improvements. Some schemes may even have environmental benefits (e.g. operational efficiency leading to fewer ships waiting offshore, less waste or pollution, less area taken up with containers, goods in transit, etc.).

Non-port coastal structures are a large category that takes in a variety of residential, commercial, transport, touristic and amenity developments. All involve modifying the natural coastline in various ways and increasing the intensity of its use. The creation (or destruction) of amenity, the increase in household or municipal effluent and other water pollution, and interference with reefs, cliffs, mangroves, beaches, etc. are all likely to be relevant environmental issues.

(ii) Major environmental impacts

The main effects can be classified as: land-use conflicts, interference with natural processes, and man-made pollution. Certain problems may *appear* in port areas, but be due to agents elsewhere, e.g. industrial effluent, household sewage. Certain effects will be more prominent during initial construction than during subsequent operation (e.g. land-use conflicts, as opposed to pollution).

Land-use conflicts: interruption to fisheries, fish breeding grounds, aquaculture; displacement of sand, aggregate mining; pre-empting wetlands; disruption of tourism and recreation; interference with traditional shipping.

Interference with natural processes: effects on beach material, longshore drift, siltation; destruction of reefs, sandbanks; river-bed shifts; altered configuration of sea-bed; loss of original vegetation, e.g. rare flora; destruction of natural habitats for birds, fish, animals; excavation of construction materials, e.g. sand, landfill.

Pollution: petroleum and chemical spills from vessels and shore-based operations; risks from storage of hazardous materials; discharges from vessels.

(iii) Scope for economic valuation

The effects listed above can be handled in appraisal mainly by EOP, PE and RC methods, though the TC and CV approaches are relevant to the valuation of wildlife and recreation.

(a) **Land use**. Ports occupy areas with actual or potential benefits in other uses. The income, or other benefit, forgone is the opportunity cost of using the land for ports. Thus, ports in both temperate and tropical areas have made serious encroachments on wetlands. To the extent that the benefits of the latter can be valued (see 4.4) the loss of these services is a cost to the port project. Likewise for osses to fisheries, aquaculture, construction materials, and tourism. Ports either completely displace, or seriously affect such alternative activities, and the costs can be measured using the EOP method.

Loss of recreational areas can, in principle, be tackled using TC and CV methods, though there are few if any examples of these techniques being used for this purpose in the context of tropical ports or coastal projects. Certain coastal structures may have positive amenity benefits - e.g. the creation of promenades along seawalls or reclaimed areas, and the construction of piers. TC and CV methods are equally applicable in appraising their benefits (see case study of Bangkok in 5.4.1).

b) **Interference with natural processes.** Very few coastal regions are in a pristine state, and even 'unspoiled' coastlines are subject to great natural changes in the long run (more often, where they are prone to violent storms and hurricanes). Hence man-made interventions have to be placed in context. It should also be recognised that there are gainers as well as losers from given changes (e.g. some kinds of marine life thrive on organic wastes; some sea birds will lose from the disappearance of sandbanks while others will gain from extra nutrients resulting from human activity and the passage of shipping; and one man's siltation is another man's beach).

Some environmental effects of coastal works can be rectified by remedial measures. Thus, the coastal protection function of reefs, sandbanks and wetlands can be restored by building seawalls, etc. (see 4.4). Changes in navigation channels or new patterns of siltation can be corrected by extra dredging. In developed countries entire wetlands may be replaced, after a fashion, as in the 'off-site' wetlands developed and enhanced as 'mitigation credit' by port authorities in Southern California, following in-filling of natural wetlands (Vandermeulen, 1990). Sandbanks and shallow-water areas can also be engineered to replace habitats for seabirds and other threatened wildlife. In all the above cases, RC is an appropriate proxy for the value of original environmental services lost by development. Several of them also exemplify the use of the 'compensatory project' alongside the original environmentally-damaging one.

c) **Pollution.** It is unlikely that there will be sufficiently firm cause-and-effect evidence linking marine pollution from port activities to damage to public health or marine life. In these circumstances, it is for the public health authorities to judge the gravity of various kinds of pollution, and indicate which are becoming excessive, and which should be absolutely prohibited. This would set port authorities and port users standards to aim at, or comply with, and the level of PE that is imposed on them is one measure of environmental damage.

5.3.4. Airports

(i) *Types of projects*

Within the air transport sector a spectrum of investments ranges from the construction of a new international airport to improved radio communications for a grass airstrip. The former would have a huge environmental impact, the latter very little. Appraisers conditioned to think of airport investments as necessarily large and environmentally intrusive should be aware of the many possible forms, and options, for investment in this sector.

Proposals for *new* airports can be expected to have the maximum environmental impact. But there would also be effects from the rehabilitation, upgrading and re-equipment of existing ones if they permitted greatly increased movements of aircraft and passengers, or if they allowed night landings, for example. Likewise, spending on training, software, and advisory services could have similar effects to that of investment in hardware and buildings if it leads to the increased use of the airport.

The total environmental impact of an airport would have to allow for its role virtually as an industrial town and a gateway for tourism. Sections 5.5 and 5.7 should be consulted where relevant.

The various kinds of airport investments include (following Bridger and Winpenny, 1987):

Landing strips, taxiways and aprons. These take up large areas of flat land - in some hilly areas often the best farming land. The need for clear approaches precludes buildings and other infrastructure some way beyond the perimeter. Major earthworks are entailed, in some cases extending into the sea, with serious interruption to surface and groundwater patterns. The search for construction materials could also leave its mark on surrounding areas.

Terminals. Apart from the terminal buildings and their associated vehicles and services, car parks and approach roads have to be built or enlarged. The environmental 'catchment' of a large airport extends over large areas, altering traffic flows and the pattern of commercial activity.

Instrumentation. Approach and navigation aids, instrument landing systems, airport lighting, etc. will all have the potential effect of increasing aircraft movements, and/or altering their daily or seasonal pattern. Their impact on aircraft noise, amenity and wildlife may be particularly serious.

Aircraft. The purchase of additional aircraft, new or second-hand, or their replacement with newer and different versions, will also tend to increase traffic, and alter its pattern. There will be obvious effects on noise and air pollution - though there could be benefits if quieter and more fuel-efficient versions are introduced. The introduction of even light aircraft into remote or undeveloped areas could have profound cultural, social and economic implications. Amphibians, still used in some countries, will have an impact on fishing and the ecology of shallow lagoons. The noise nuisance of supersonic aircraft is of a totally different kind from that of ordinary aeroplanes.

(ii) *Major environmental impacts*

Vegetation: conversion of natural landforms (wetlands, bush, forests); devegetation around perimeter and on aircraft approaches.

Hydrological: changes in natural drainage pattern (damming, drainage, diversions, creation of large impermeable concrete areas, quarrying and in-filling, etc.).

Marine: in-filling of sea for coastal airports; destruction of coral and beaches for construction material.

Noise: from aircraft movements and passenger traffic.

Air pollution: aircraft fuel; passenger traffic and other commercial activities.

Public health: air pollution and noise; risk of introduction of exotic diseases from travellers and cargo.

Biodiversity and wildlife: loss of habitat; effects on animal behaviour from noise and unaccustomed movements.

Tribal and indigenous people: cultural shock; loss of habitat.

Cultural property: removal of buildings and other artifacts of historical, religious or aesthetic interest.

iii) *Scope for economic valuation*

Most environmental valuation of airports has been concerned with noise, and to a lesser extent general amenity, wildlife and cultural property. The Report on the Third London Airport (Roskill, 1971) illustrates the preoccupations of airport planners at the time. This bias reflects the concerns of the general public in the developed societies in which the major part of airport investments occur.

In developing countries a much wider range of issues are at stake, which have been neglected in environmental appraisals. Although aircraft noise is a clear disbenefit in such societies, it is often occluded by more pressing concerns. Competing land uses, the destruction of habitats, water pollution, and threats to biodiversity, wildlife and indigenous people, will be closer to the top of the agenda in many countries. It follows that there is little comparative empirical data available to the airport appraiser in developing countries, and his/her role is to identify and attach priorities to the range of possible impacts, where possible set maximum values to the effects, and introduce baseline and monitoring systems to generate data useful for subsequent future investment or modification. With all due allowance for the variety of circumstances in developing countries (Bangkok's problems are closer to those of Chicago than to those of Tuvalu), the following discussion offers some pointers to how important effects can be tackled.

(a) **Changes in land use**. Where the airport entails the conversion of natural habitats with clear environmental products and services, the value of the latter can, in principle, be estimated and entered as a cost to the project. This might arise if, for instance, coastal wetlands were drained to extend a runway, or tropical forest removed to make way for jungle airstrips. In practice, it is easier to value products than services (see sections 4.2, 4.4) .

(b) **Hydrological effects**. The clearest effects of disruption to surface or groundwater flows are on water supply and quality. If the civil works result in the loss of a river used for fishing or agriculture, the loss can be valued using EOP (with due allowance for any gains from the creation of a water body elsewhere). Otherwise, new water supplies may need to be developed for farming or domestic use, especially if the water becomes contaminated. RC is then the appropriate basis for valuation.

Any damage to coral or beaches to produce construction material (common in the Caribbean, Indian Ocean and South Pacific), or in-filling of the sea to extend the landing strip, may affect the fishing industry and tourism. The value added from these respective sectors in the affected zones can illustrate the maximum cost of these effects.

(c) **Noise** is likely to be most important where the airport is adjacent to large settlements, and the flight path crosses densely populated areas. In such cases, many residents will be affected, and the most commonly used measure of this cost is the effect on their property values. This cost is attested by a growing number of empirical studies, mostly in OECD countries (4.7). Establishing an effect that is statistically reputable is, however, fraught with problems, and a major undertaking (see Roskill, 1971). The full exercise would not be worthwhile in most cases, though crude proxies might be obtained from the local property market. It might be warranted in middle-income countries where there is a perception that noise is a serious problem, with busy airports close to dense settlements, and with an active free property market. In addition, if the airport is close to housing, schools, factories and other activities sensitive to noise, the cost of necessary insulation can be included as an imperfect and minimum proxy for the loss of environmental quality (an instance of RC).

(d) **Public health**. The effects of air pollution on health, though clear in general, are not established to the point where they can be attributed as a cost to specific polluters (4.6). In any case, aircraft and vehicle movements in airports are likely to be only one contributor among many others to pollution in large metropolitan areas. Valuation is not, therefore, feasible in this instance. The risk of introducing exotic diseases can be reduced by proper screening, equipment, buildings, quarantine facilities, etc. The project should include the cost of such facilities.

(e) **Other non-quantifiables**. Loss of biodiversity cannot be valued (4.11) but, if it is judged important enough, steps can be taken to protect it, at a cost to the project. Relocation is one option - obviously not easy for a major airport, but possible for light airstrips if it were important to protect a rich piece of biodiversity or the habitat of an endangered species. Alternatively, a wildlife sanctuary could be created. These are examples of RC.

Relocation of airstrips, or resettlement of indigenous peoples, are also ways of shielding tribal and aboriginal people from contact with air traffic for which they are culturally unprepared.

The valuation of cultural property turned out to be a major issue in the Roskill Report (1971), in the shape of the Norman church standing in the way of the proposed runway; the decision to use its fire insurance value proved controversial. In developing countries, it seems most sensible to relocate important artifacts, where this is feasible, and for sites of major importance to seek an alternative airport location. While this decision will ultimately be taken on non-economic criteria, it could be helpful to estimate how much tourism and recreation hang on preserving the sites concerned, using direct tourist receipts, TC or CV valuation methods.

5.4. The built environment and social infrastructure

This section introduces some of the appraisal issues involved in urban projects, and deals specifically with housing, water supply, sewerage and sanitation.

5.4.1. Urban projects: general

Environmental appraisal of urban projects is rarer in developing than in developed countries. It is also less common than for rural projects. This is partly because there are fewer such projects: aid agencies have traditionally regarded urban projects as less deserving, and have taken the view that many such schemes lend themselves to private financing. But some of the general problems of applying environmental appraisal are magnified for projects when they appear in an urban context.

(i) *Types of projects*

Many 'urban' projects are schemes that could equally well be undertaken in rural areas, but which happen to be located in towns. Examples include: housing (especially low-income settlements, and upgrading schemes); water supply and sanitation; garbage collection and disposal; industry and trade (including small-scale industry and commerce); road construction and transport services; electric power generation, transmission and distribution; clinics, primary health care.

Other schemes are more typical of urban development, viz.: rapid transit systems; traffic engineering (e.g. bus lanes, traffic signals); creation of amenity (parks, reviving run-down areas); large hospitals (e.g. for teaching, specialised units); telecommunications (telephone and other services); public buildings and monuments (e.g. government offices); central sewerage systems. In some of these sectors the immediate environmental dimension will be slight, e.g. telecommunications. In others, environmental effects will be seen as significant by-products to their main purposes, e.g. electricity supply, hospitals. In others, however, improving the local environment is a major motive of the scheme, e.g. housing, water supply, sewerage, garbage collection, traffic engineering, parks and amenity.

There will be many instances where projects are introduced to compensate for failures of policy and planning (e.g. squatter upgrading, instead of the planned provision of site and services). Taking a longer-term view, authorities may be better advised to rectify policies rather than rely on 'fire-fighting' projects. Usually, however, the provision of urban services lags far behind the demand, a product of rapid urbanisation and rising expectations. Many projects for improving urban services can therefore claim environmental benefits with reference to a prior situation where such services are either absent or provided privately.

In practice, it is rare to find a total absence of services, even where no public provision occurs. Users, and private intermediaries, often improvise some form of supply, e.g. private garbage collection, water carts, even illegal tapping into public power lines. This has several implications. It affords evidence of the values that people place on certain environmental services, such as safe water (purchase from a water cart is an environmental 'surrogate' for reliable and safe piped supplies). It is unwise to assume a complete absence of such services in appraisal, i.e. the project benefits may not be as large as is sometimes assumed. The 'without project' case might consist of a growth in private provision, which gives a yardstick against which putative benefits should be measured. It should not be assumed that private provision is automatically superior to public services, or vice versa. Private services may be feasible only for the wealthy few, or they may be provided at high cost. Public provision may be the most efficient solution, especially if widespread coverage is desirable.

'Environmental improvement' is often invoked to justify public action against low-income settlements and the informal sector. Public health risks have often been used as reasons to demolish and clear squatter housing, informal markets and small-scale backyard industry. Sometimes these concerns are justified, but in other cases they may conceal other motives. In any case, such decisions involve difficult trade-offs between the environment, on the one hand, and income and jobs, on the other. It is desirable for projects involving the destruction of settlements or occupations to contain provisions to rehouse and relocate the people affected.

(ii) *Major environmental impacts, and the scope for economic valuation*

The list of possible urban projects is so large that a detailed checklist of their environmental effects would be inappropriate here. It is more useful to concentrate on a typical group of urban effects that cause particular problems in appraisal, namely, air and water pollution, noise, amenity, and public health. The remainder of this section offers some general guidance on the relevance of the various valuation methods to these effects, drawing on sections 3.3, 4.6 and 4.7, and finally describing an exercise to value urban amenity in Thailand.

The notion of opportunity cost is relevant where projects pre-empt environmental resources such as open space, parkland, or sea views. If it is not possible, or sensible, to value these assets directly (see below), and if there is a predilection for preserving them, it may be illuminating to estimate what would be sacrificed by abstaining from development. This is the opportunity cost of keeping environmental resources in their present use. In the Bangkok case study below, the opportunity cost of preserving Lumpinee Park in its present use is the net benefit of property and commercial development being forfeited.

The difficulty of specifying the 'damage function' is a serious obstacle to using the EOP method. The effect of air and water pollution or noise on output of, say, industry, farming, tourism or public services is difficult to establish except by lengthy and extensive research.

The PE/RC method is rather more useful where environmental quality is deteriorating, and where people and firms can be observed to spend money on defensive or substitute measures. Such items as private wells, water purifiers, and purchases from water carts are common ways of coping with poor water supplies or quality, while in wealthier circles private sewerage systems provide crude proxies for 'willingness to pay' for sewerage. The problem to be faced in appraisal is how far such 'environmental surrogates' can be considered representative of the groups affected, rather than the habits of better-off consumers. Estimates of willingness to pay for improved services, e.g. for improved sewerage in the Bogota case study in section 5.4.3, rest on firmer grounds when they can relate to the existing use of environmental surrogates.

HC is not of wide relevance as a method of valuing the effects of pollution on human health and loss of earnings (for reasons spelled out in 3.3.3). However, a short-cut method is illustrated in section 5.4.3 below, though it depends on transposing epidemiological data into a different, and arguably inappropriate, context. Despite the presence of active property markets in the cities of the Third World, it is also argued (3.3.4) that HM are of little applicability in inferring the value of urban environmental quality. However, the comparison of property rents and prices in otherwise comparable areas, with and without, or before and after, environmental changes can provide rules of thumb for valuation purposes - which is useful in slum upgrading schemes, for instance.

The Bangkok case study exemplifies the use of TC and CV in valuing urban amenity. The use of TC in the urban context is unusual and has limited applicability where the enjoyment of an amenity does not involve paid transport and occurs in leisure time (3.3.5). However, estimates of willingness to pay or to accept compensation based on CV techniques are relevant in urban circumstances, where there is usually an appreciation of the benefits of the amenity and the majority of users are used to monetary valuations. The Bangkok example does, however, illustrate the problems of 'grossing up' the results of the sample. Specifically, how large is the population assumed to be interested?

Case study: Lumpinee Public Park, Bangkok (Grandstaff, Dixon and Eutrirak, in Dixon and Hufschmidt, 1986)

Lumpinee is a public park in the centre of Bangkok. No charge is made for admittance. The opportunity cost of retaining it for recreation is high and rising because of its potential value for commercial development. By the same token, its importance for recreation, health, and air quality is also increasing. This is one of the few studies in developing countries to estimate the recreational value of an open-access urban park, using a mixture of travel-cost and hypothetical valuation (CV) methods.

Method. Surveys were carried out amongst both users of the park and other people living in different parts of the city to infer the values they placed on keeping the park in its present use. The techniques used were:

i) **travel cost:** A representative sample of visitors were asked how long they took to get to the park and how much they spent in so doing. Their answers were calibrated according to which of various zones of the city they came from. This made it possible to conceive a demand curve for visits to Lumpinee, relating frequency of visit to total 'cost' (comprising time and money expended on the visit). Since the facility is free, all the area under the demand curve is 'consumers' surplus'. The axiom underlying this method is that the cost in time and/or money spent travelling to a free recreational site reflects an individual's valuation of it. The sum of these amounts for all visitors represents society's valuation of that resource.

ii) **contingent valuation:** Residents in various zones of Bangkok were asked about their willingness to make annual payments to keep the park in its present use. The sample included actual users of the park and those who did not actually visit it, but who valued its existence and the opportunity to visit it in future - a kind of 'option value'.

Results. Grossing up the results from the sample interviews, three possible bases of valuation for the park emerged (in 1980 Baht): (i) based on travel cost admitted by actual users: 132m.; (ii) based on hypothetical willingness to pay by actual users: 130m.; (iii) based on hypothetical willingness to pay by both users and present non-users (so-called 'social value') 1,166m. The striking feature of these results is the coincidence of the first two measures, and the difference between them and the third. Clearly, the inclusion of the 'option value' greatly increases the valuation of the facility.

5.4.2. Housing

Most people in developing countries build their own houses. Their governments, and aid donors, tend to become involved in this sector mainly through the provision of services to existing housing, or by upgrading the housing stock.

(i) *Types of project*

Building completed new dwellings is usually done as part of the construction of new towns or capital cities (Belmopan, Islamabad, Brasilia, Abuja) or to provide housing for workers in industrial, mining or agricultural projects in remote or newly opened up areas. In many bureaucracies the provision of a government house is a condition of service. Large-scale new housing estates may take up virgin forest or previously undeveloped land, with drastic effects on wildlife and aboriginal peoples. In contrast, the provision of a few new houses for key staff as part of a new plantation or mine would have little extra environmental impact compared with the larger scheme of which they form a part. The quality of housing for unskilled workers in plantations and mines is often criticised for being cramped and insanitary (e.g. workers 'lines' on tea plantations), but it is fair to compare them with workers' alternative housing conditions.

Since building complete new houses is an expensive way for governments to meet a growing housing shortage, the provision of 'sites and service' plots or 'wet cores' is somewhat more common. The essence of such schemes is that residents are allocated sites on planned estates, with foundations and minimal services (usually piped water, various kinds of sewerage, and occasionally electric power). A rudimentary plumbed kitchen and bathroom may also be provided. The resident is expected to build the remainder of the house, usually with financial help and technical assistance. Such schemes, being planned and equipped with minimal services, are usually kinder to the environment than unplanned and spontaneous settlements. Although an eyesore to begin with, they can mature into pleasant neighbourhoods.

Finally, the provision, or improvement, of services to existing settlements (slum upgrading, squatter improvement, etc.) should have clear net environmental benefits. Although projects may entail some demolition incidental to building service lines, or in the interest of layout and amenity, the main point of these projects is the preservation and upgrading of existing housing investment. Often insecurity of tenure affects the incentive to improve properties, as well as the will of local government to lay on services. Granting *de facto* or *de jure* tenure (which would probably involve survey and registration) is usually a pre-condition of upgrading schemes.

In judging the net environmental impact of housing schemes the residents' own reactions are crucial. The housing may not be used in the way anticipated by planners; it may be used to conduct petty trade and small businesses, and the plots may support livestock or food cultivation. New accommodation is often provided at considerable distance from sources of work and income, which puts great strain on transport services. In extreme cases, residents may divide their time between the new dwelling and the old location close to their workplaces - which partly defeats the purpose of the scheme (Winpenny, 1977 and 1982).

(ii) *Major environmental impacts*

Virtually everyone has some kind of housing, even if it is only a tent or packing container. Hence housing projects invariably entail substituting new or improved accommodation for whatever was there before. This often involves relocating people's accommodation. A complete assessment of the environmental consequences of housing schemes therefore involves analysing their effect on previous habitats. With due regard to the diversity of housing programmes, the following is a brief checklist of their possible environmental effects (the same effect can be either positive or negative, depending on whether the project causes a new problem or relieves problems caused by previous housing arrangements):

Land use: encroachment on farmland, forestry, wetlands, etc.; pre-empting open spaces and sources of amenity; loss of recreational areas; occupation of unsuitable sites, e.g. unstable slopes or waterlogged ground.

Effects on informal settlements: creation of spontaneous, unserviced, satellite towns; creation of 'temporary' settlements of construction workers; opportunities to demolish and relocate dangerous squatter areas.

Local air pollution: household fires, small-scale industry, incinerators, traffic.

Noise:

Water pollution: (from unserviced settlements); raw sewage discharge; garbage accumulation and seepage; contaminated stormwater run-off; household sullage (from serviced settlements): downstream pollution from overloading existing water courses and sewage treatment units; concentrated run-off, e.g. from stormwater drains.

Public health risks: water-borne diseases; local air pollution; insanitary and crowded living conditions; close proximity of animals; dust from construction, small-scale industry, passage of vehicles and animals.

Construction materials: effect of cutting wood for poles, timbers, frames; brick-making (sources of materials, fuel, air pollution); sources of sand, gravel, stone.

Urban fuel: effect of increased demand for woodfuel and charcoal on hinterland.

Water demands: impact of wells on local groundwater; wider repercussions on hinterland of search for new water sources.

Amenity: effect on scenic attractions in urban area and vicinity; character of neighbourhood/estate itself.

(iii) *Scope for valuation*

The effects of housing schemes on the environment, both positive and negative, should be signalled through the workings of property markets. The growth of a squatter camp on the hillsides overlooking a middle-class neighbourhood should in theory depress property values in the latter. Upgrading a slum area by providing piped water, sewerage, electric power and storm drains should increase property values in that area. The values of houses on a new estate ought to contain an element reflecting environmental quality as perceived by the residents.

The problem is in disentangling environmental values from the other elements affecting property values. Hedonic methods (3.3.4) are designed to separate the environmental factor from others, but are difficult to apply to the housing markets of developing countries. In the cases mentioned above, the squatter settlers not only worsen the perceived physical environment of the middle-class house-holders, they may also increase the fear of crime. Upgrading slum areas will have a disproportionate effect on property values if it confers greater legal recognition or security of tenure to residents. The value of new houses or serviced sites is likely to contain an element reflecting superior position, size or quality of services, as well as 'environmental' quality. In all these cases, it is difficult to infer environmental values from property values taken alone.

The following discussion separates new housing, including serviced sites, from upgrading schemes, and concludes with a brief treatment of externalities.

(a) **New housing and site and service plots.** The 'output' of new housing schemes consists of an underlying stream of housing benefits which, in a free market, is reflected in the size of rents or the capital value of the property - as compared with their costs of production. This may understate benefits, if residents enjoy a consumers' surplus - that is, if they would have been willing to pay more for the same housing. Some idea of the size of this surplus may be gleaned from surveying their previous housing conditions.

In theory, it is reasonable to expect the value of environmental improvements to be eventually 'internalised' in the value of new housing, assuming no rent controls or other artificial impediments to market forces. The problem for appraisers is to predict the values at which the market will settle; experience on other comparable estates may provide guidance. It is common for authorities to restrict the sale of public housing or serviced sites until a certain number of years have elapsed, in order to prevent the units falling into the hands of non-targeted groups. Even in this case, rentals may give pointers to the underlying capital values.

(b) **Upgrading schemes.** Neighbourhood upgrading schemes are now very common. In theory the environmental improvements that they create will find expression in the enhanced value of the property concerned. If these schemes are widespread in a city, it should be possible to measure the trend in property values in areas with and without, and before and after, the upgrading to provide rough incremental values for appraisal purposes. The fact that the residents are not the owners of the property - a common occurrence - does not affect the principle. In fact, landlords are often quick to raise rents in the wake of upgrading schemes - which may even price the poor target group out of the area.

(c) **Externalities.** An efficient property market should eventually incorporate the external impact of the project on the value of housing in other areas. Thus, resettling refugees or squatters in decent housing, or upgrading a slum, should enhance property values in adjacent areas. The difficulties of appraisal arise where there is no 'market' for the effects concerned. Three examples can be given:

i) encroachment on undeveloped land. Such land, often regarded as worthless for productive use, is likely to have some opportunity cost equal to the value of its products and environmental services. Estimating these values in the specific cases of forests and wetlands is discussed in sections 4.2 and 4.4.

ii) occupation of areas of public amenity, e.g. parks, hillsides, river banks, open land used for recreation. TC and CV methods have evolved to value these unpriced assets (see the Bangkok case study in 5.4.1). In practice both methods require a great deal of data and have other limitations. In more typical cases, crude short-cut approaches will be necessary in estimating values held by the general public. Examples include the results of appeals and voluntary donations to community recreation schemes, the cost of travel to alternative facilities, the cost of providing football pitches elsewhere, etc. None of these proxies are very good indicators of the real social value of public amenities, but they serve to indicate that these assets are not 'free' to developers.

iii) air and water pollution from settlements. As discussed elsewhere (4.6) it is difficult to attribute effects on output, building fabric or health to specific sources of pollution. However, such effects can be anticipated at the planning stage, and, if they are considered serious enough, measures can be taken to curb pollution (e.g. proper household sanitation, building a sewage interceptor, enlarged sewage treatment units, public collection of garbage, safe location of waste incinerator, etc.).

5.4.3. Water supply, sanitation and sewerage

This section considers the appraisal of proposals to improve the supply of water and the disposal of household and municipal sewage. Industrial effluent is dealt with in section 5.5.

(i) *Types of project*

Proposals can be divided into those concerning improved water supply, household sanitation, and the collection, treatment and disposal of sewage.

Water supply. The most common proposals are the following (Bridger and Winpenny, 1987):

a) the development of new or improved sources of supply. These may be from groundwater sources (e.g. from springs or wells), surface flows (rivers), the creation of storage reservoirs (by damming or bunding rivers), or desalinating salt or brackish water. Apart from the last mentioned, these developments all entail major changes in local hydrology, and in the case of dams trigger a full range of environmental impacts. The transport of water, e.g. by pipelines or canals, can be another source of environmental impact.

b) treatment. There are various levels of treatment - storage, screening, sedimentation, chlorination, aeration, etc., with generally minor local environmental effects (except when accidents in chemical treatment result in contaminated supplies to water users). Recycling waste water involves a higher degree of treatment, and the use of chemicals and disposal of waste materials are potentially hazardous.

c) distribution and reticulation to consumers is generally a low-profile activity involving some local storage reservoirs or tanks, underground pipes and household connections or public standpipes. Their environmental impact has to be judged against that of the system they are replacing.

d) improvements to the efficiency of an existing system. This class of project may include repairs, rehabilitation, installation of meters, introduction of new water charges, reforms to the public water utility, etc. Insofar as they reduce waste and losses in the system, and induce more careful water use, these measures ought to have positive environmental effects.

e) rural water supply. This is a special category of project, usually involving the development of low-volume water sources for the benefit of populations in their vicinity. Springs, open wells, tubewells, and small tanks and reservoirs are common features of such programmes, and are often accompanied by public health advice and facilities. Well conceived and maintained schemes, which are complemented by more hygienic domestic use, should lead to benefits in public health as well as improved productivity in activities using water (e.g. cattle rearing, small industry). However, there are many situations where such benefits will not be realised, and there could even be adverse effects from pollution of the new sources and erosion around the new water points.

Sanitation. The safe disposal of excreta is now possible using a variety of low-cost techniques - e.g. dry, pour-flush, Ventilated Improved Pit, or conventional WC latrines linked to pits, septic tanks or mains sewers. Provided they are properly installed, used, emptied and serviced they would normally score environmental benefits over the systems they replace. These qualifications are, however, important and often not realised. Leaks into groundwater and freshwater systems are a perennial hazard in areas of high population density. Programmes of advice and education on household hygiene are usually necessary to get the full benefits from sanitation projects.

Sewerage projects can be divided into those involving collection, treatment and disposal of sewage.

a) collection. Septic tanks are serviced and emptied by fleets of vehicles, with minor environmental disturbance. The construction and operation of underground sewers can, on the other hand, entail major disruptions during construction, and thereafter have potential effects on groundwater movements and quality. Leaks and temporary overflows can cause localised risks to public health, and damage to agriculture.

b) treatment. There are various degrees of treatment, depending on the volumes, the human environment, and whether the water is to be recycled. Sewage treatment works are invariably intrusive, and damage local amenity, though these effects need to be offset against those of the system they replace, especially the disposal of untreated sewage into the sea or inland water bodies, or the use of human waste as fertiliser.

c) disposal of the treated waste water and residual sludge may pose problems for public health, agriculture and fisheries, though again such problems have to be compared with those from alternative systems of disposal.

(ii)*Major environmental issues*

The above effects may be grouped and summarised as follows:

Water supply. *Benefits*: public health, from greater volumes, and better quality and reliability; productivity of water-using activities (food production, livestock, small industry) and time savings from improved access to water sources. *Environmental costs*: effects from construction of major dams and reservoirs (see 5.3.1) depletion of groundwater sources, saline intrusion (affecting existing water users, stream flows); effects on surface water flows (other water users, intakes, fisheries, agriculture, navigation); negative effects on public health and productivity (if new supplies run ahead of sewerage provision); damage to amenity (and wildlife, tourism, fisheries) from depletion of natural lakes and rivers; specific problems of desalination plants (hazardous effluents, concentrated brine, noise, some air pollution, amenity, etc.).

Sanitation. *Benefits*: public health; local amenity. *Environmental costs*: leakage from pits and septic tanks into freshwater sources; (other effects unlikely to be significant).

Sewerage. *Benefits*: public health; productivity (avoided costs to agriculture, fisheries, other activities using the water - such as power stations, other water intakes -, gain of land for housing and other development, etc.); amenity (recreation, wildlife). *Environmental costs*: public health risks from leaks, overflows, and groundwater contamination, hazards to sewage operatives, and contamination from sludge disposal; amenity losses from location of sewage treatment works; productivity losses in agriculture, fisheries, tourism from sludge disposal.

(iii) *Scope for valuation*

It is not feasible to value all the effects listed above, but a number of studies demonstrate the scope for valuing some of the more important of them: namely, public health, output, and amenity. The use of cost-effectiveness analysis is also potentially applicable to all projects. The methods are illustrated in relation to actual case studies from Egypt, China and Colombia.

Where water is supplied as part of an integrated hydroelectric scheme involving major damming, the reader is referred to section 5.3.1.

(a) **Public health**. Human health is placed at risk from drinking, cooking, or washing with contaminated water, from contact with raw or partially treated sewage or from eating contaminated produce. In theory, health effects can be captured by the Human Capital, Preventive Expenditure/Replacement Cost, or Contingent Valuation (Willingness To Pay) approaches.

An application of the HC method is illustrated in the Ismailia case study below. The link between water pollution and the incidence of certain water-borne and water-related diseases, which is reasonably well established in general, has been hard to translate into firm relationships useful for CBA (see 4.6 and 4.10). The Ismailia case study uses a relationship established in the United States for one particular disease - enteric illness due to faecal contamination - and adapts it to Egyptian circumstances. A relationship was also postulated for viral infections, using local medical advice. Loss of earnings and medical costs are estimated from local parameters, with a WTP assumption for viral diseases that did not lead to absence from work. The results are strongly suggestive, though care should be taken in extrapolating them to other countries, since they have already made one transatlantic crossing.

PE and RC are also applicable. If authorities judge the public health risks from bad water and untreated sewage sufficiently grave, they can relocate populations or declare certain areas out of bounds (though such measures tend in practice to be easily avoided by poor squatter communities). Private households can also take steps to treat their water by filtering or simple chlorination, and in the last resort move to safer areas (relocation is a special case of RC). There are few reliable studies of these costs. The Bogota case study below sweeps up these effects, with others, into a WTP assumption based on what the average household might be willing to pay for safe water and sewerage. The choice of 5% in this case was rather arbitrary, and would have been on firmer ground if supported by surveys of what households currently spend on water supplies - a case for commissioning baseline surveys.

(b) **Output**. The use of contaminated water for irrigation, livestock or fishing can be shown to affect yields, and if it leads to the presence of an unacceptably high element of dangerous chemicals (e.g. heavy metals) or other pathogens, could risk loss of the entire output (e.g. if it is banned or shunned by consumers). Tourism and recreation income is also put at risk. These effects can be captured by the EOP method. Benefits to agriculture and fisheries are illustrated in the Bogota case study.

Alternatively, benefits of water improvement schemes can be regarded as the avoided costs of remedial action that would otherwise be taken by activities sensitive to water quality. Both the Beijing and Bogota case studies detail these costs for the power and irrigation sectors. Recycling treated sewage saves the cost of investment in new water supplies for irrigation. Better quality water used for cooling in power plants increases the plant's thermal efficiency, saving or delaying new capacity. The Beijing case study also illustrates the value of safely treated sludge as fertiliser, replacing spending on chemical compounds.

Where such effects cannot be directly valued, a WTP estimate can be applied to farmers and other commercial water users in an attempt to capture some of the assumed benefit.

(c) **Amenity**. A good, safe water supply, the presence of hygienic sanitation systems, and proper treatment and disposal of sewage will enhance the attraction of a neighbourhood or village for residents and visitors. However, providing such improved systems may itself cause offsetting damage to amenity value. The excessive abstraction of water from an attractive lake, the construction of desalination plants in prominent positions, or locating a sewage works close to settlements are obvious examples. The Travel Cost method can be used to value the unpriced benefits enjoyed by visitors and recreationists. The Ismailia case study illustrates a simple application to recreationists on Lake Timsah, using minimal data.

In the more general case where improved water and sewage systems improve the general quality of a neighbourhood, either willingness to pay (e.g. Bogota) or the use of increased property values (e.g. Ismailia) would be appropriate. Care should be taken to avoid double-counting of other benefits which would already be reflected in WTP or property values. One form that an improvement in amenity could take would be to increase the supply of property suitable for development (e.g. land alongside a badly polluted river - Bogota).

Finally, cost effectiveness is likely to be commonly applicable, where a particular requirement for water supply, quality and waste treatment is given, and where benefits are elusive. The appraisal of disposal of wastewater in the Philippines (Grandstaff and Balagot, 1986) by various options is one such case study. The problems arising where different options satisfy the set standards to different degrees feature in the Beijing case study. Two criteria are combined in this last mentioned appraisal - one based on the NPV of identified net benefits of the various options, and the other according to how well they satisfy water quality standards. Ranking the options in the light of their scores on the two criteria requires some subjective judgement.

iv)*Case studies*

Egypt: Waste water treatment in Ismailia (Luken, 1987)

As part of its preparations for Phase II of the Canal Cities Water and Wastewater Project, USAID commissioned an appraisal of the proposed wastewater treatment plants in Ismailia, Port Said and Suez, and a water supply project in Port Said. The case study summarised here is the project for Ismailia.

Ismailia is located on the shores of Lake Timsah, half way along the Suez Canal. At the time of the appraisal, its population was estimated to be over 300,000, and was expected to grow to 470,000 by 1995 as a result of implementing the Ismailia Master Plan and the Tourism Development Plan for the Suez Canal Zone. The Lake is used for recreation by local people and visitors from Cairo, and there is some commercial fishing. The existing wastewater treatment plant discharges untreated waste into the lake. Although the overall quality of the lake water is good, there are several areas in which faecal contamination exceeds the WHO standard for contact recreation. If unchecked, this can only get worse with the planned increase in population.

Method. The CBA divides benefits into three categories - recreation use, recreation-related illness, and amenity value. There is only a limited amount of commercial fishing in the lake and it is not expected that fishing would be significantly harmed by pollution in the absence of the project.

i) recreation use. If the Lake remained relatively unpolluted annual visitor-days were projected to rise to 1,500,000 by 1995. On the other hand, if the Lake became seriously polluted, this would fall to 500,000. A simple TC model was used to estimate the consumers' surplus obtained from use of the Lake. Visitors from Ismailia were assumed to have no travel costs, whereas the larger number of day trippers coming from Cairo were assumed to have £E11-12 per user (£E4-5 for transport and £E6 for the value of time).

Following standard TC theory, the recreational value of the unpriced natural asset was derived from a demand curve obtained by relating the observed visitation rates in Cairo and Ismailia to the respective travel costs to the lake. A 'distance-decay' function was estimated, with a 'choke price' at which no visits would be made. The area underneath this demand curve is taken as a measure of the consumers' surplus from enjoyment of Timsah, the assumption being that people enjoying the facility free of charge would be willing to pay something nearer to the actual travel cost of visitors from further afield. On this basis, the consumer surplus of the Lake without the project was estimated to be £E7 per visit, and with the project £E11.

This approach was complemented by applying estimates of the consumer surplus from recreational fishing obtained from the United States, scaled down to reflect the lower incomes in Egypt. There is evidence that a day of water-based recreation (whether fishing or swimming) is valued at $US 25 - 35, which is 10.5% of the weekly gross earnings of the average worker. Applying the same proportion to average Egyptian earnings yields a value of £E 6.10, which is in the same range as the figures derived from the travel cost method.

No account is taken of the non-user recreational benefits, namely the recreational facility for people not currently using it (option, existence, or bequest value).

ii) recreation-related illness: It was first necessary to estimate the incidence of water-contact diseases, and then apply an economic cost to it. In both stages data developed in the USA were used, modified for Egyptian conditions. Two kinds of disease were examined: acute gastro-intestinal (AGI) symptoms such as vomiting, diarrhoea, stomach ache and nausea related to enteric diseases such as typhoid, paratyphoid, hepatitis and dysentery. Secondly, viral diseases such as skin rashes, and eye, ear and nose complaints. Relationships obtained from US data implicating faecal contamination with enteric diseases were adapted for Egyptian conditions. It was also assumed that all recreation visits in 1995 would involve water contact recreation. The relationship between water contact and viral diseases does not have the same scientific veracity as that for bacterial diseases. Local advice was taken, and an attack rate of 10/1000 exposures was used.

The cost of illness was calculated comprising three elements: loss of earnings for one week, unquantifiable pain and suffering, arbitrarily assumed to be worth the same again, and medical expenses. The same calculation was made in respect of viral diseases, except that no allowance was made for loss of earnings since it was assumed that the victims would not miss work.

iii) amenity values. A simple version of the hedonic property value method was used to infer the amenity value of Lake Timsah. By the year 2000 24 million people are projected to live within 150 km. of the Lake, and it is assumed that 1 million households will take vacations and weekend trips there. It is further assumed that one per cent of these households would maintain second homes on the Lake. A market value is placed on these properties, and the rental income is taken to be 10% of that.

It is then assumed that, in the absence of the project, these housing units would lose 10-25% of their rental value.

Results. The benefit estimates are displayed in Table 5.2.

The range of benefits in the table compares with an annualised total cost of £E18.54m. Since the mid-point of the benefit estimates slightly exceeds the costs, calculated on a conservative basis, the project is taken to yield a positive NPV.

This is an example of what can be achieved from a relatively short piece of field work, using a methodology and relationships developed mainly in the United States and adapted to local conditions. Most of the benefits are from recreational use of the Lake, estimated from a very simple TC model with minimal data. Estimates of the cost of illness are based on reasonably good US data on health relationships, applied to Egypt in the absence of alternative local information. Possibly the least satisfactory part of the study is the estimation of amenity values from property prices, which are significant in relation to total benefits, but based entirely on a tissue of assumptions.

Table 5.2 Ismailia wastewater treatment plant; annual benefit estimates

(with project)	(without project)	(difference) £E m.
recreational use		
user days 1.5 mn	0.5 mn.	
£16.5m.	3.5	13.0
) recreational illness		
negligible	10,000 AGI, 5,000 viral	
£2.1m	—	2.1
ii) amenity value		
full increase in rental income for 5-10,000 units	10-25% reduction in rental income for 5-10,000 units	
£12.5-25.0	11.25-18.7	11.25-6.3
Total		16.35-21.4

China: Water pollution control options in Beijing (Hufschmidt et al., 1986)

This compares various ways of tackling surface water pollution in a southern suburb of Beijing. The water system formed by the North Canal, the Tong Hui River and the Liang Shui River receives heavy pollution from residential, agricultural, power, and industrial water users in the shape of wastewater, sewage, storm run-off, irrigation return flows, and effluent. The main needs are clean water for drinking and industrial uses, and facilities for sewage disposal.

Method. A detailed technical model is built up of the entire surface water system to measure and predict pollution and water quality at a number of points within it. This is then used to measure the effects on water quality, and the associated costs and benefits, of various physical control measures in different combinations. These include: eliminating sewage overflow from the treatment plant, separating part of the clean water from the sewage mix, primary treatment of sewage for irrigation, etc. The many permutations are reduced to seven main alternatives.

Economic benefits are considered to be threefold: (i) recycling clean water for industrial use. The benefits consist of the avoided cost of providing clean water from an alternative source. (ii) use of treated sewage for irrigation. Untreated sewage has long been used for irrigation, but at the cost of some crop contamination, outbreaks of diseases among children, and pollution of groundwater. The benefit from using treated sewage is regarded as the avoided cost of developing alternative irrigation sources, and the savings from avoiding use of chemical fertiliser. (iii) improvements in the quality of water used for cooling in the power plant. These savings are based on increases in the plant's thermal efficiency, leading to an increase in energy generated.

Results. Each option was evaluated in two ways: first, on the basis of its net present value after comparing costs with the measures of benefits described above; second, on the basis of water quality measured by biochemical oxygen demand and dissolved oxygen. The two yardsticks need not necessarily converge. Options were ranked on each criterion. The alternative giving the highest overall score was chosen, which in this case was a combination of the separation of clean water from the sewage mix, recycling clean water, cutting off the sewage inflow from other systems, and the primary treatment of sewage for irrigation use.

Colombia: Bogota sewage treatment project (ODA, 1990)

This was a proposal to install sewage treatment facilities on one of the four main feeder rivers entering the Rio Bogota, which skirts Colombia's capital city. At present raw sewage is discharged into the river, the water from which is used for irrigation, hydroelectricity and fisheries. The city has a well-developed system of piped water supply and sewage collection, but no sewage treatment. The proposal was appraised by several sets of consultants, and a decision was taken not to proceed in the form suggested (though some sewerage project will undoubtedly take place). The attempt to quantify benefits is of wider interest.

Method. The problem that the proposed scheme would take care of only part (30%) of the projected sewage flow into the Rio Bogota was overcome by basing benefits on the assumption that all the sewage would eventually be treated, and pro-rating these to the project - equivalent to a 'time-slice' approach. Amongst the benefits to be valued were the following:

a) health, amenity and convenience of households connected to the improved sewerage system. This was captured in an assumed willingness to pay for water and sewerage, taken to be 5% of average household income in the area. One-third of this was ascribed to sewerage.

b) the value of new land released for development - the increment in amenity value of land adjoining the polluted river. It was assumed that a belt of land close to the river would be developed for low-income residential, commercial and industrial purposes. The increase in values were based on comparable data in Medellin.

c) improved water quality for irrigation. The benefits were assessed in terms of the increased capacity to produce irrigated products safe for human consumption.

d) recreation. No attempt was made to value the non-pecuniary gains to visitors to areas adjacent to the river, but it was assumed that 200 additional tourists are attracted to the Sabana area, each spending an additional net amount of $60.

e) power generation. It was assumed that the reduction of organic matter, suspended solids, hydrogen sulphide and other pollutants in the river would lead to cost savings and other benefits to hydro power generation. Specifically, these would include less wear and tear on turbines, pumps and casings, more efficient pumping, a lower rate of reservoir siltation, and reduced damage to concrete pipes and tunnels from sulphuric acid corrosion. The saving is estimated by assuming that the project avoids having to replace one major turbine every ten years, and that the life of concrete pipelines is increased from 50 to 80 years.

f) avoidance of fishing losses in the Rio Magdalena. The benefit of purer river water was estimated on the basis of a study of the impact of dissolved oxygen content on the yield of certain edible fish. No account was taken of the effect of other pollutants such as pathogens, ammonia and heavy metal.

Results. The values of benefits identified above amounted to: household willingness to pay $41m.; new land for development (one-off) $85.9m.; irrigation $16.0m. per year; recreation $0.6m. per year; power generation $4.3m per year; avoidance of fishing losses $0.9m. Other benefits, used in the original, are not given here, since they depended on the flood-control components rather than sewerage *per se*.

This shows the importance of the methods used to estimate benefits to two main categories: householders, on the one hand, and gains to property values, on the other. The use of WTP proxies for household benefits from sewerage, as part of a water services tariff, assumes that households are fully apprised of the likely benefits, which is not always the case. The use of WTP and property values also requires care not to double-count certain benefits (e.g. amenity, public health) which may be reflected in those measures.

5.5. Manufacturing and processing industry

Industry surpasses any other sector in the variety of its potential impacts on the environment. This is partly because of its own inherent diversity, and partly because of its many indirect effects - through, for example, its demands for raw materials and energy, and the ways in which its final products are used and disposed of. This section is a brief introduction to a large and complex subject.

(i) *Types of projects*

The sheer variety of activities included in the manufacturing and processing sector frustrates any generalisation. Instead, some of the main factors determining the likely environmental impact of a project can be identified, as follows:

Scale. Size has various facets - the land area occupied, the volume of throughput and output, the number of workers employed, etc. Large plants have a heavy and concentrated impact, but - if they are well managed and use 'clean' technology - their aggregate environmental impact need be no worse than several smaller plants producing the same total output. However, the waste and pollution resulting from a dispersed pattern of production is normally easier to assimilate through natural receptors (dispersion by air and water bodies) than one that is concentrated. Other things being equal, a plant with a large labour force carries a greater risk of accidents and occupational health hazards than one with capital-intensive technology. Integrated iron and steel works, heavy chemical complexes, and large engineering works are likely to have particularly great environmental impacts.

Location. Geographical position is important, first because location relative to raw materials, on the one hand, and markets, on the other, influences the nature and length of transport systems - themselves having major environmental effects. Secondly, proximity to population centres directly affects the number of people at risk from pollution or subject to accidents, noise and other nuisances. Thirdly, location affects the use of natural receptors for waste disposal (air basins, prevailing wind, rivers, lakes, oceans, etc.). There may be environmental trade-offs between various locational factors, e.g. a location more distant from population centres may reduce the incidence of pollution on public health but increase the project's impact on wildlife and nature reserves.

Process. The nature and degree of transformation that takes place in the industrial process governs the use of energy and water and the generation of by-products and waste; all important environmental pointers. The vintage of the technology and the care with which it is maintained and operated are also influential.

Materials. Materials differ in the extent to which they can be safely handled, processed and disposed of. Agricultural produce is not normally a problem for handling and processing, though its wastes can be responsible for the spread of disease and water pollution. Inorganic materials, especially metals and chemicals, are more hazardous at all stages. Toxic chemicals, most of which are generated by the chemical, paper products, primary metal, petroleum refining and textile industries, pose particular risks. Certain hazardous substances are practically impossible to destroy or assimilate by natural processes (e.g. DDT, radioactive material, heavy metals). Another important distinction in discussions of sustainable development is between exhaustible and renewable materials (though consumption of the latter may also be at an unsustainable rate).

Products. Products differ in the extent to which their use has environmental effects. The product of the motor industry is likely to have more drastic environmental effects than the output of a factory producing office equipment. Products built to last will, *ceteris paribus*, have less environmental impact than those with built-in obsolescence. Capital equipment may be sold to other industries, which themselves will give rise to environmental effects, and so on. Producers of pesticides, explosives and newsprint, to take three random examples, can hardly turn a blind eye to the environmental impact of their products when they are used or discarded.

Pesticides illustrate the naiveté of assuming that products are invariably used strictly according to manufacturers' instructions. The packaging of an item also has major environmental consequences, e.g. through the production of the packaging material (paper, glass, polystyrene, plastic) or problems of waste disposal (waste paper, cans, bottles, plastic bags).

Waste. Industrial processes differ greatly in the extent to which they generate waste, in the degree to which this is hazardous, and in the ease and cost of its safe disposal. Within a particular industrial branch and for a given product there is often a choice between technologies with more or less waste production (e.g. 'low waste' and 'no waste' techniques, 'clean' technology, recycling). In turn, waste reatment can be handled through radical changes to the design of the process, or hough 'end-of-pipe' treatment. Residual wastes may be in the form of air and water pollution, solid wastes, and hazardous waste. The latter, in turn, can be divided into toxic chemicals, flammable materials, explosives, and infective/biological substances (UNIDO, 1990).

(ii) Major environmental impacts

It is important to take a broad and imaginative view of the environmental effects of industry since its operations tend to have wider repercussions than those of other sectors. For instance, a firm may side-step environmental problems by sub-contracting some processes to others, but this merely displaces the problem to other parties. Although most of the effects listed below arise in the locality of a project or its immediate hinterland or region, certain effects will be felt at some distance (e.g. acid rain, river and marine pollution, the mining or farming of raw materials). An extreme case is that of global climatic effects from the emission of industrial greenhouse gases and CFCs; industry is thought to be responsible for about one-quarter of the production of greenhouse gases.

It is therefore important to specify the *distribution* of environmental costs and benefits. Some will be internal to the project (e.g. workers' health), others will affect the vicinity or hinterland, others will be felt in neighbouring countries (acid rain, river pollution), and some will be of global concern (greenhouse gas and CFC emissions).

Ideally, checklists should be developed for each specific industrial sub-sector (see World Bank, 1984; UNIDO, 1988, also contains useful lists of sensitive substances, processes and wastes).

Construction: land clearing and preparation (levelling, clearing, devegetation, erosion, siltation); access roads and temporary construction villages; health risks (dust, fumes, dangerous machinery, explosives, poor construction safety standards, hazardous materials); nuisance (noise, vibration, dislocation, unsightliness); waste, refuse disposal, resettlement of displaced people, housing for workers; effects on hydrology (interruption of water courses, damming, diversion, waterlogging, water pollution); ecological damage (loss of habitats, breeding areas, polluted air and water); aesthetic loss (ruin of natural beauty, unsightly plant and buildings).

Raw materials and other recurrent inputs: use of fuel (coal, oil, etc.) and power (see 5.3.1); water requirements; extraction of materials (see 5.2, 5.6); transport by road, rail, air or water (see 5.3); handling and storage (health, occupational risks, water pollution, visual amenity etc.).

Operations: noise, vibration, dust, smell; emissions; liquid waste; airborne waste (gases, particulates, causing local or regional pollution, or adding to global climatic effects); solid waste; toxic waste; health and safety (hazardous machinery, processes, materials; transport (materials, products, workers).

Use of final products (capital goods, intermediate industrial materials, or manufactured items going into final consumption): risk of abuse or misuse (e.g. pesticide, fertiliser, explosives); effects of further processing (e.g. metal fabrication); danger of accident during transport to user (e.g. chemicals); problems with final disposal (vehicles, tyres, plastics, toxic waste, etc.).

(iii) *Scope for valuation*

Major industrial projects implicate other sectors, each with its own environmental effects. Heavy industrial plants often require new transport links, e.g. iron and steel works with captive rail systems. Metal processing has linkages with iron and copper mines. Edible oils depend on oil palm plantations. Large labour forces have to be accommodated in new settlements. Paper industries are massive users of water, and aluminium of electric power. The appraisal of such projects will involve reference to sections respectively on transport (5.3.2), mining (5.6), agriculture (5.1.1), housing (5.4.2) water (5.4.3) and power (5.3.1).

It can be assumed that most major industrial schemes, certainly those funded by aid agencies, will be subject to an Environmental Impact Assessment which will highlight major impacts and provide a basis for ranking them in order of severity. Many effects will be minor, and the appraiser will only have time and resources to concentrate on major impacts. The more important of these will be discussed below.

Industry is everywhere one of the most highly regulated economic activities, and is often obliged to conform to certain public environmental standards. The more far-sighted industrialists will anticipate future legislation by adapting their current technology and operations as if they were statutorily required to do so. It is therefore likely that a number of environmental effects will be controlled, entailing preventive expenditure incorporated in money costs. The costs of such environmental controls, whether or not they are actually adopted, might be taken as a proxy for the damage costs in question (e.g. for air pollution, effluent discharge, safe disposal of solid waste, noise abatement). This is an example of the use of PE.

The scope for valuation can be illustrated with reference to the following issues.

(a) **Pre-emption of natural resources**. The creation of a factory or plant occupies land and pre-empts natural resources with environmental value. This is most clearly seen when the factory is sited on converted wetlands, or an area cleared from forest or reclaimed from the sea. The use of such land has an opportunity cost consisting of the environmental products and services which are lost to society (see sections 4.2 and 4.4 for forests and wetlands).

The provision of raw materials, power, water and transport to industrial projects may have the same end result, and can be handled in a similar way. For instance, an aluminium works or pulp and paper mill is likely to require, variously, plentiful electric power or water, necessitating building a dam and creating a reservoir. Growing sugar to provide the material for a sugar mill will entail creating large plantations. The iron mine and railway to serve a steel works may be the most environmentally damaging part of the operation.

(b) **Air pollution**. The effects of industrial air pollution on output, public health, and materials corrosion are not sufficiently well established to be valued at the project level. Scientific evidence is usually unsatisfactory, other polluters are also involved, and the symptoms may have other causes (4.6.2). There will be cases where specific studies have been done, whose data can be valued using EOP or HC methods. But in the more common situation such data will be absent, and for major projects there is an argument for setting up baseline studies and monitoring the effects of pollution. The cost of complying with regulations (PE) may be a valid proxy for environmental costs.

(c) **Water pollution**. The problems of attributing the costs of water pollution to particular industrial projects are similar to those in the case of air pollution, but less severe. If an industrial plant is the largest single cause of pollution in a river, which has clear identifiable costs to fisheries or other downstream water users, such costs can be attributed to the project. This is the situation discussed in the Thailand case study below.

The EOP method is suitable for measuring the costs of water pollution on fishing (see case study). Where the level of pollution in drinking or irrigation water is considered potentially injurious to health, the cost of treatment or the creation of new water supplies illustrates the scale of the environmental costs (the PE/RC method - discussed in the case study of the Indonesian palm oil processing mill in ADB, 1986).

(d) **Waste disposal**. Industrial effluent can be considered in the context of water pollution, discussed above. Other major industrial residues are solid and toxic waste. In many countries of North America and Europe sharply rising environmental standards have outlawed previous forms of waste disposal, and the cost of disposing of solid and toxic waste has greatly escalated. Although few countries outside the OECD implement such rigorous waste controls, the trend will undoubtedly spread to other countries as they experience the true costs of inadequate disposal.

US experience is a pointer to what is likely to become a more general trend. US car factories formerly buried paint sludge in the ground. It must now be treated, and solidified or burned - hence disposal of a barrel of paint sludge now costs $250. Toxic waste disposal typically costs more than $200 per ton, thanks to tighter regulations and a growing shortage of landfill space (*Economist*, 8 April 1985). In short, waste disposal is becoming a significant cost of production, (UNIDO, 1990, contains a useful checklist of the main types of waste generated by various different industries.)

There are various ways of incorporating these costs in appraisal. The most obvious is to include the cost of treatment or safe disposal where it is required by law. Where it is not, the cost of 'best practice' or 'state of the art' disposal can be estimated, either from consultants' reports, or by observing practice elsewhere in the same country, or in a similar country. This is a straightforward use of the PE method. The exercise is complicated where the waste problem is tackled by recycling or the redesign of plant to use 'low waste' or 'no waste' technology. Ideally, the cost difference between operations with and without, or before and after, such changes will indicate the cost of prevention.

The use of landfills for waste disposal has an obvious opportunity cost. The casual burial of heavy metals, toxic waste, solvents, etc. may effectively prevent the safe use of that land for other purposes over very long periods. In certain cases it will directly damage human health (e.g. that of children playing on asbestos waste dumps in South Africa (Durning, 1990). In such cases medical expenses, loss of earnings, or compensation may indicate environmental costs (the HC method).

(e) **Global climatic effects**. Industrial plants are major generators of greenhouse gases and CFCs (see section 4.12). In this respect they elicit the same appraisal issues discussed for thermal power stations (5.3.1). In the absence of reliable measures of their global environmental costs, industrial projects responsible for such emissions cannot be directly attributed with these costs. Until they can be, the exercise is best conducted in the framework of national emissions targets (which at the time of writing have no legal status). In principle, the 'cost' of greenhouse gas and CFC emissions can be regarded as the cost of abating that amount of emission, either by the offending firm, or by the most efficient form of abatement elsewhere in the country. Sections 4.12.5 and 5.3.1 discuss this method further.

Case study: Thailand: effluent from sugar mills (Phantumvanit, 1982)

Sugar mills on the Mae Klong River west of Bangkok release contaminated water into the river which diminishes catches of fish and shellfish, and which is damaging to agricultural and domestic water users. The effluent is of two main types - waste water used for floor cleaning, and water used for cooling condensers. The quality of effluent released into the river causes serious pollution, especially in March and April when the river is low. During the 1970s the problem worsened, leading in 1976 to the government banning the creation of new sugar mills, and requiring existing ones to install water treatment systems. This attempted to estimate the damage costs from water pollution, compare them with the cost of abatement, and indicate an appropriate standard for water treatment.

Method. The author considered, and rejected, using real estate values as a proxy for the loss of amenity along the river, since there was no established real estate market in the area. Likewise for willingness to accept compensation, an unfamiliar concept to the subsistence producers involved, and who lacked full access to litigation procedures. He decided to try to estimate the damage function directly, using a combination of scientific evidence and direct questioning of the parties involved.

Various kinds of damage from water pollution were estimated:

a) effect on cockle farming. A field survey carried out during 1970 revealed that up to 81% of cockles were lost in the sampled area, and the remaining clams were substandard in size and could not be marketed.

b) the loss of shrimp production was also estimated from official records and discussions with local fishermen.

c) effects on agriculture and domestic water consumption proved more difficult to estimate, because the area is flooded annually. Residents adjusted to the recurring pollution by digging additional groundwater wells, and by storing more water. Estimates were made of these costs, plus costs from odour and skin diseases.

The relationship between water quality and the above damage costs was estimated. A model of water quality was built up for the various portions of the river, to predict the biochemical oxygen concentrations and dissolved oxygen profiles associated with various conditions over the course of a year.

Results. The total damage cost was estimated to be 45.5 m. Baht (1976 prices) which it is assumed applies to zero concentration of dissolved oxygen. It was concluded that the critical level of dissolved oxygen was 4 mg/l. Above this level, it was assumed there would be no damage costs. Within the range 0-4 mg/l the damage cost was assumed to decline in a straight line function of the increase in treatment level. For each given level of water quality the damage cost was added to the cost of treatment. The composite cost curve was minimised at a 75% level of treatment. Since the existing treatment level at plants was over 96% it was concluded that there was no point in continuing to ban new sugar milling capacity.

5.6. Mining and extractive industry

The scope of this section will be defined to include quarrying, the production and processing of precious, semi-precious and base metals, and coal mining. The exploration, extraction and processing of hydrocarbons (oil and natural gas) have been treated in section 5.3.

Few activities can rival mining in its potential physical impact on the environment. Its plans and activities come under the closest scrutiny from environmental groups, and many governments have enacted legislation controlling its activities and stipulating preventive, compensatory or restorative work. The mining industry works under close environmental controls in most countries, and the worst problems arise from illegal operations or parastatals able to evade regulation. One consequence is that major proposals in this sector are normally accompanied by an Environmental Impact Assessment drawing attention to the main potential effects and how they can be mitigated. These EIAs are obviously important sources of information for economic appraisal. It is, however, important to understand the motives of people commissioning EIAs, the results of which may be angled to support the positions of parties in a negotiating process (Pintz, 1987).

(i) *Types of project*

The sector spans a wide range of activities, each bringing into play a different, but overlapping, set of environmental effects. Various types of *material* are extracted. The *method of extraction* is a more important variable for environmental purposes. Open-pit methods are normally more damaging than strip mining, in which overburden is replaced behind the mining operation. There are also various methods of underground mining, not to mention alluvial and underwater methods, and recovery from spoil heaps.

The method of *processing* is a further important factor, e.g. size reduction (comminution), simple screening and washing, extraction, metallic reduction, concentration and refining using physical, thermal, and chemical processes. These in turn may be on-site or elsewhere. The list of factors could be lengthened to include the amount of *waste* generated, how it is disposed of, and the method of *transport* of the ore or material.

The *location* of the project will govern which of the effects are considered most serious; a mine close to existing settlements is potentially more disruptive to the social environment than one in a remote and thinly populated area. Likewise, mines that induce *associated activities* using the material will tend to have a greater total environmental impact than enclave projects destined for the export market.

There is always a risk of major projects for mining precious and semi-precious metals and minerals spawning an active '*informal*' and sometimes illegal sector on the fringes, working discarded spoil heaps, alluvial deposits, etc. In Brazil gold miners pollute rivers and poison fish with mercury that they use illegally to process their output. This sector is very hard to control, and working conditions and local environmental pollution can be very bad.

A similar case is that of the setting up of small-scale smelters to process iron, the mining of which may be subject to exemplary environmental standards. The Carajas iron mining project in Brazil, which is often invoked as a model project for its observance of environmental safeguards, has given rise to several dozen uncontrolled pig-iron smelters, which will lead to large-scale deforestation in their search for fuel (Goodland, 1988; Gutierez, 1990).

An increasingly important category of projects is the *rehabilitation* or mechanisation of mines begun in a less fastidious age. Mine safety schemes are one example. Likewise projects for the *restoration* of land to something near its previous condition, and reduction of the environmental costs of spoil, etc. Such projects are specifically aimed at securing environmental benefits, or mitigating previous and future costs.

(ii) *Major environmental effects*

Mining can affect the environment through extraction, processing, storage, transport, and through its supporting infrastructure. Indirect effects through consumption (e.g. burning coal) are not considered here.

Extraction

Land degradation: removal of soil and rock, loss of fertile topsoil; devegetation; soil erosion from exposed surfaces; deposition of spoil and tailings; subsidence from underground mining; slope instability, causing landslides.

Hydrological effects: disruption of groundwater (abandonment of wells, saline intrusion, etc.); pollution of surface water and seas with tailings, chemicals, acid drainage; release of large amounts of water used in mining process to surrounding water system; flooding (e.g. in abandoned mines); creation of waterlogged areas; sedimentation of rivers and reservoirs.

Coastal areas and wetlands: deposition of tailings in river estuaries and inshore waters; deposit of overburden on surrounding land; water contamination; dredging sand, coral and rock for construction.

Wildlife and biodiversity: loss of habitats; poisoning with chemical pollution; deterrence from explosions, unaccustomed human activity; loss of river and inshore fisheries and reefs.

Public health: diseases, occupational hazards, accidents to workers; chemical pollution of water used for drinking, irrigation, fishing, etc.; dust (with or without toxic elements), dirt, noise; exotic diseases introduced amongst indigenous peoples; problems from resettlement or growth of shanty towns which are unplanned, or with inadequate social and health provisions.

Amenity: unsightly open-cast areas and mine structures; noise, explosions, dirt.

Processing

Many of the above, plus: air pollution (e.g. fumes from smelting, fossil fuel burning); disposal of toxic and solid waste; water pollution from heavy metals used in processing.

Storage

Land taken up with stored material prior to transport (e.g. coal); seepage into soil and water systems of chemical elements from stores and dumps; intrusion into landscape of spoil and slag heaps.

Transport

Railways, roads and airstrips to serve remote mines are themselves major agents of environmental change (5.3.2); jetties and ore terminals affect coastal areas and marine life (5.3.3).

Supporting infrastructure

Townships (5.4); power stations (5.3.1); hospitals, schools, sports facilities, etc.; provisions for displaced population elsewhere.

Not all these effects will be negative. The land subsidence and waterlogging that may accompany underground mining may create new wetlands. Some of the landforms that are the by-products of mining can, with modifications, become recreational facilities, especially in well populated areas short of other land (e.g. lakes, artificial hills, slopes). Abandoned mines, provided they can be made safe, may be interesting to pot-holers and cavers, as well as offering storage for anything from foodstuffs to hazardous waste. In countries with strict regulations, the landscape following restoration may arguably be more attractive than before mining began.

(iii) *Scope for economic valuation*

The increasingly common requirement for EIAs to support mining proposals would normally ensure that the main potential effects were identified, and their severity assessed - either in physical relationships or through qualitative judgements. On the other hand, there are apparently few cases of the economic valuation of these effects in developing country projects. There should therefore be scope for applying certain of the valuation methods, but so far there is little comparative data to guide the appraiser.

In view of the predominant environmental concerns in developing countries and the nature of projects coming forward for finance, the most feasible valuation methods are the Effect on Production, Preventive Expenditure, and Replacement Cost variants. The Human Capital method is potentially applicable if health effects can be satisfactorily measured and ascribed, but in the absence of such data this effect is best dealt with by regarding essential health safeguards as an example of PE.

(a) **Effect on Production**. The effect of mining on the output of fisheries, agriculture and forestry, and power generation can in principle be captured by EOP. There are several examples in Papua New Guinea (Jones, 1988, Pintz, 1987). In the Ok Tedi project the main problem turned out to be the disposal of mine waste into the river. Up to 1987 14 million tons of tailing fines and several million tons of eroded construction spoil had been released into local rivers. The larger part of this material eventually found its way to the river delta. The authorities defined an area of river 70km. downstream of the mine within which pollution and damage to fisheries was permissible (the 'mixing zone'), but not beyond. This area was fixed with reference to local settlements, and the importance of fisheries to them.

In Misima the mine is located on a small island, with a steep submarine slope and deep water close offshore. Tailings are reduced, diluted and discharged into the ocean 100 meters offshore. In theory they flow down the submarine slope and are trapped in a deep ocean trench. They severely affect coral within 500 meters of the dump, and damage the small local fishery.

Farmland is directly lost, either temporarily or permanently, to open-cast mining and submerged by spoil heaps. The coarse material from the Bougainville copper mine has covered 2,500 ha. of the floodplain. Attempts are now being made to revegetate this area with lime treatment. The removal of overburden to create open-cast mines and quarries often leads to the loss of topsoil which is difficult to recover during the subsequent process of restoration - effectively an irreversible loss. In dry conditions some of the waste material may form dust, and settle on farm land, which is particularly serious in areas that are intensively farmed (e.g. phosphate mining in the Nile Valley, lead/zinc mining in India).

In a study of the Yongping opencast copper mine in China's Jiangxi region, it was estimated that the levels of copper in the surrounding farmland would be unacceptably high within 10 years, due to the percolation of acid discharges into the irrigation system (Wang Hua Dong, 1985). In a similar manner, the effect of phosphate mining in Egypt may expose soil to the risk of saline damage through the impact of mine drainage on the quality of irrigation water.

The Carajas iron mine in Brazil is indirectly causing large-scale deforestation through the activities of its associated pig iron smelters. It has been estimated that 56 tons of pig iron requires 1 ha. of forest to produce the necessary charcoal. There are various estimates of the annual rate of deforestation implied by the production targets of the mine, ranging from 48,000 ha. to 152,000 ha. In 20 years, total deforestation would be close to one million ha. on the *minimum* estimate (Gutierez, 1990). (See sections 5.2.2 and 4.2 for the valuation of tropical forest.)

(b) **Preventive Expenditure and Replacement Cost**. Mining ventures are increasingly required to comply with local environmental regulations, and observe the appropriate safeguards. In other cases similar actions are necessary to deflect public or shareholder criticism. In some countries, especially the United States and Canada, mining concerns are required to take every reasonable measure to restore the original condition of the site, once mining ceases.

All such actions amount to internalising some of the environmental costs. They are the balance-sheet expression of the PE and RC valuation methods and it is an easy matter to include them on the cost side of the CBA. These costs are sometimes large. Between 1981 and 1985 the Companhia do Vale do Rio Doce spent US$54m. to mitigate the environmental impact of the Carajas mine, mainly on land reclamation, creating offsetting protected natural reserves, and promoting environmental awareness and training (Maher, 1989). Similarly, in the Ok Tedi scheme the company spent $25m. on a waste rock retention structure and $40m. on a tailings dam. However, some elements of PE, such as the cost of neutralising residual cyanide in tailings and of maintaining waste rock dumps, were very hard to predict in advance and could even be regarded as a contingent liability (Pintz, 1987).

Certain effects whose impact on productivity or health are difficult to measure may be best treated by PE. The effect of siltation on river navigation or reservoirs could be approximated by the cost of dredging (e.g. at Bougainville). The potential damage to health caused by dust, fumes, water pollution, etc. could be approached by estimating the costs of obvious preventive measures (e.g. protective clothing, regular medical inspections, screening dangerous emissions, relocating outflows, etc). Insofar as these measures did not completely remove the hazard, they would provide only minimum estimates of environmental costs.

Human capital and other techniques. Although actual studies are lacking, the use of HC methods can be envisaged where there are robust data on the link between mining activities and health. Data on the health status of miners are accumulating (the Bolivian tin miners being a well-known example) as a first step towards valuing their loss of earnings and medical expenses. Other techniques such as CV, TCM and HM, which come into their own for valuing amenity, recreation, and biodiversity, have rather less obvious application where these issues are not viewed as paramount, and in any case examples of their use in this sector in developing countries are lacking.

A number of the recent mining projects in developing countries are located in relatively isolated areas, and their most obvious impact has been on primary production. Most mines are now under some obligation to take measures to safeguard or restore their environment. These considerations lie behind the emphasis here on EOP and PE/RC valuation methods. In other situations, where there is a much greater direct impact on adjacent populations, or where there are severe threats to amenity and wildlife, there is a better case for commissioning TC, HC, or CV studies, but there are few if any examples of them so far.

5.7. Tourism

International tourism rivals oil as the largest item in world trade. For many countries tourism is the most important economic sector and source of foreign exchange. Domestic tourism is no less important than its international equivalent measured by spending, although the main focus of this section is on the international version.

In the environmental context, tourism has a number of unusual features:

a) The tourism 'product' (i.e. the services being sold to visitors) is highly sensitive to environmental quality. Tourism suffers acutely from environmental damage caused by other sectors, but may also spoil its own environment. In the long run the tourist industry has a strong interest in environmental management and preservation. It often leads to the preservation and enhancement of key natural resources, buildings and monuments, where they would otherwise be exploited, plundered or neglected. It also helps to preserve local customs and crafts (though it may cheapen and 'commoditise' them in the process).

b) Tourism illustrates some of the same problems as other common property resources. Visitors are attracted to 'unspoiled' areas; as numbers increase the area's attractiveness falls, but no visitor has an incentive to stay away. The tourist resource can become seriously congested or degraded before any remedial action is taken.

c) The fact that tourist services are consumed in the country of supply means that their social and cultural impacts are particularly strong.

d) In many cases the growth of tourism has accelerated the decline of traditional occupations like agriculture, which creates 'second order' environmental consequences.

e) Tourism often provides the first experience of modernity to sheltered or aboriginal societies. Its 'culture shock' can be very great, though not necessarily any worse than that of other sectors such as mining or plantation agriculture.

(i) *Types of project*

The multiplicity of types of tourism can be reduced to three for the purpose of illustrating environmental impacts: namely, coastal resort, nature-based, and cultural tourism. There are of course many others, e.g. sporting, business convention, entertainment- or gambling-based, etc. However, the above three stereotypes exemplify the importance, on the one hand, of the habitat in which tourism occurs and, on the other hand, the principal motive for the visit.

Coastal resorts. The common feature of this kind of tourism is its dependence on beaches, sea, or other water bodies for recreation and relaxation. It is thus highly sensitive to water quality and the cleanliness and appearance of beaches, and there is a risk of uncontrolled and careless development spoiling those very assets on which it depends. The main environmental issues are likely to be marine pollution, reef destruction and degradation, the alteration of coastal landforms, the accumulation of garbage and waste, and the general decline in visual amenity. Resorts built in previously undeveloped areas will also destroy and threaten wildlife habitats.

Nature-based tourism. The common element in the various kinds of nature-based tourism is enjoyment of scenery and wildlife, and includes walking, trekking, climbing, canoeing, safari, organised hunting, fishing, etc. The impact on the environment is double-edged. On the one hand, a growing number of visitors provides an incentive to preserve and enhance natural assets through the creation of nature reserves, protecting wild animals, etc. On the other hand, the very growth of numbers can threaten that same wildlife and upset the balance of nature. The main issues likely to arise are threats to wildlife and biodiversity, cultural shock to aboriginal peoples, localised instances of erosion and pollution, etc. Some kinds of nature-based tourism infringe 'unspoiled' areas that are particularly sensitive. In general, however, this tourism can provide a strong commercial motive for caring for the natural environment, as well as increasing environmental awareness and enjoyment by visitors and local people.

Cultural tourism. The 'cultural' tourist tends to be a more discerning visitor, exploring the history, arts, and cultural identity of the host community. Much of this type of tourism is urban-based, centring on major national monuments, buildings, churches, temples, museums, etc. Although many individual cultural tourists are sensitive to local *mores*, the growth of this tourism *en masse* causes congestion, pollution, and damage to the fabric of buildings, as well as changing the character of many cultural sites and affecting the relations of local people to them. Against this, cultural tourism provides motives and funds for preservation, restoration, and enhancement of national cultural assets, and can help to sustain local traditions. The main environmental issues are thus congestion, pollution, uncontrolled garbage and waste, damage to cultural property, and the effect on national self-esteem of what has been called 'commoditising ethnicity' (Swain, 1990).

Apart from the above factors, the environmental impact of tourism depends on:

a) the stage of development of the host society, the gap in economic and social levels between locals and visitors, and the resilience of local society to cope with, and benefit from, the influx of tourists. The West Indians and Thais are, for instance, well able to cope with tourism, compared with the Kalahari Bushmen or the Amerindians of Brazil.

b) whether tourist development is concentrated or dispersed, and whether tourists are encouraged to mingle with local people, or stay apart from them.

c) whether the tourism is for mass markets or for selected groups. The former will normally be more intrusive, though it may be possible to confine its effects to certain localities.

(ii) *Major environmental impacts*

Tourism may be a major factor in the development of airports, roads, coastal structures, etc. Its growth may also stimulate other sectors (e.g. fishing, handicrafts) and discourage others (often, agriculture). Where these inter-sectoral linkages are important it would be appropriate to examine the environmental impacts of the induced development also.

The main possible environmental effects of tourism are summarised in the following checklist. The accent is on possible negative effects, since its purpose is to highlight potential environmental threats. However, projects should be given credit for positive impacts, where they exist. Some of these are listed at the end.

Coastal landforms: loss of wetlands, dunes, lagoons; destruction of natural coastal defences - cliffs, reefs, shallows, sandbanks; interference with beach formation, longshore drift; beach erosion from building in active beach zones, quarrying for sand and coral.

Marine pollution: oil spillage from motor boats, marinas; discharge of untreated sewage; disposal of litter, other waste.

Land degradation: localised devegetation for hotels, campsites, nature trails, etc.; erosion from hill tracks and paths; fire risk.

Wildlife and biodiversity: destruction of habitat, migration trails and sites, breeding grounds; disturbance of natural habits; overfishing, e.g. for lobsters; reef destruction - removal of coral, shells, for souvenirs.

Local public services: overstretching water supply, sewerage, power, garbage collection services; development of new water and electric power sources.

Public health: risk of infection spread by visitors; spread of drug-taking, and dru
dealing.

Amenity: loss of views, scenic attractions from hotels and related buildings; noise
smells, traffic; alteration of local 'character'; congestion, air pollution.

Cultural property: damage to buildings, monuments, etc.; debasement of loca
culture and traditions.

Indigenous people: impoverishing aboriginal and tribal peoples, e.g. by changing
the use of natural resources on which they depend, bans on hunting, etc.; trivialis
ing their culture; introduction of disease.

Some of the *positive* environmental impacts of tourism are as follows:

a) improvement of local infrastructure and services (sewerage, safe water sup
plies, electric power, health care, waste collection and disposal, beach cleaning
etc.).

b) beach cleaning and protection.

c) introduction of measures to protect reefs, fish, wrecks, etc.

d) incentives to protect animals that would otherwise be hunted and poached, o
whose habitat would have been degraded.

e) generates funds for conservation, nature reserves, etc. and improves awareness
of nature and cultural heritage.

f) rescues, preserves, enhances buildings and cultural property.

(iii) *Scope for valuation*

Case studies of the valuation of the environmental effects of tourism are rare
However, tourist projects can have effects analogous to those of other projects and
can be handled in a similar way. For instance, locating a new tourist village in a
former wetland entails the loss of wetland products and services, the valuation of
which is discussed in section 4.4. Building a marina or sea-front apartments can be
dealt with using methods discussed in the context of coastal structures (5.3.3). The
development of specialised nature tourism may go hand in hand with conservation projects, discussed in section 5.2.5.

(a) **Opportunity cost of environmental resources**. As with all other projects,
tourism pre-empts land and resources with environmental value in their alternative uses, and the loss of these services is an opportunity cost of the project. In
practice, this could apply particularly to wetlands and fisheries. Safari lodges may
also involve the removal of crucial forest areas.

(b) **Public services**. Taking a wider view, tourist projects are likely to entail public
services, which themselves have environmental impacts. The need to provide
new safe water supplies and electric power brings into play their specific environmental effects, discussed in 5.4.3 and 5.3.1 respectively. On the other hand, if a
large new hotel requires investment in sewage collection and treatment for the
whole locality, the benefits of that scheme (5.4.3), as well as the costs, should be
included in the hotel appraisal.

(c) **Preventive Expenditure and Replacement Cost**. Where a tourist development
is likely to destroy an important natural function PE or RC methods may be

plied. In coastal situations the loss of natural sea defences such as reefs, cliffs and shallows to make way for tourist structures may lead other parties, or the local authority, to build artificial sea defences, or reinforcements for buildings at risk. The loss of the water purification function of a wetland may require investment in water treatment plant. If the project disturbs an important wildlife habitat (estuary, mangrove, etc.) the project may include the cost of replacing it elsewhere (a compensatory project).

This type of preventive expenditure or replacement cost may be imposed on tourist developers by law where they infringe environmental standards. This would apply to water pollution, beach cleanliness, noise, waste disposal, etc.

d) **Amenity and cultural property**. Most types of tourism involve trading on amenity or cultural property. Projects may preserve and enhance natural or cultural assets for visitors to enjoy, but the converse is that they may also degrade and destroy such amenity by excessive or insensitive development. Both positive and negative aspects of the problem can be treated by the TC or CV methods. TC essentially evolved as a means of valuing recreational assets. It is particularly relevant for measuring the enjoyment of amenity and cultural property by tourists whose time and travel costs have clear monetary values. Willingness to pay, ascertained by CV methods, is also highly relevant for valuing amenity from tourist assets. The Bangkok case study in section 5.4.1 illustrates the use of both methods to value urban amenity. The approach is easier in the case of commercial tourism where these values can be directly observed, instead of being merely inferred.

e) **Non-quantifiables**. A number of issues arising in tourism are not capable of measurement and valuation. Effects on indigenous people, biodiversity, and wildlife are, for instance, best handled by non-economic criteria, though cost-effectiveness or opportunity cost methods may be useful in reaching decisions in these difficult areas. The discussion in section 4.11 is relevant.

6

Policy Appraisal and Adjustment

It is a commonplace that good projects will fail if they are subverted by bad policies. Careful design at the project level will be undone if wider economic incentives and institutions are tugging the project in the wrong direction. Farmers will not plant environmentally friendly tree crops in conservation projects if the export price for tree products is set too low. A model industrial project that treats its effluent and limits its air pollution will suffer if it competes against other firms that are not compelled, or have no incentive, to follow suit.

Project planners therefore need to understand the policy context of their actions, and which policy variables are most likely to affect the performance of their projects. Armed with this understanding, analysts have several choices. They may insert conditions into project agreements aimed at removing policy obstacles (e.g. the removal of a state monopoly of seed distribution as a condition of support for a small-farmer project). Obviously some of these conditions encroach on sensitive policy areas, and analysts need to understand the wider repercussions of the proposed policy changes, and in negotiations be in a position to convince the recipient of the importance of the changes.

In many cases it will be unrealistic to expect the desired policy changes to happen at once, in time to incorporate into project agreements. It might then be appropriate to take a longer view, entering into 'policy dialogue' with the recipient, perhaps involving the exchange of information at a professional or technical level, setting up research programmes, offering consultancies or long-term advisers, etc. Sometimes the dialogue would occur in the framework of more general economic reforms, as in Structural or Sectoral Adjustment Programmes. Where the environmental problem to be tackled is pervasive, and the influence of policy particularly strong, it might be concluded that the project-by-project approach would be ineffectual or insufficient. In that case, the whole weight of influence wielded by the donor or lender might be thrown behind policy reforms, and the appropriate instrument would be sectoral or programme aid rather than project finance.

Policy reform might consist of measures that are explicitly 'environmental' in their aims, e.g. carbon taxes, tradeable pollution permits, the prohibition of the use of certain pesticides, subsidies for the use of kerosene rather than woodfuel, etc. Alternatively, the government may prefer to adjust policies already in existence which serve more general purposes. One possibility would be to take advantage of impending macroeconomic or general economic reforms to 'fine tune' for environmental aims. This chapter gives some indication of the scope for doing this in the context of Structural Adjustment Programmes and other economic policies. Naturally, such reforms will be undertaken mainly with non-environmental objectives in view, and it will be important to analyse any trade-offs, or costs to the other objectives. If, for instance, a devaluation is under consideration, and it is roposed to levy offsetting export taxes on a crop of particular environmental alue, a case might be made for reducing the tax in that instance.

he chapter proceeds on the assumption that governments wish to manage the se made of the environment under their jurisdiction. The first section discusses 1e general scope for policy measures to contend with such deep-seated forces as overty, population and the prevailing distribution of assets and income. Section .2. deals with the broad types of available policy options under the headings of ersuasion, regulation, use of property rights, targeted economic instruments nd indirect economic measures. Separate sections follow on the latter two op- ions, and the impact of structural adjustment on the environment is the subject of ection 6.5. The discussion is related to a number of specific habitats in section 6.6, o illustrate how policies have contributed to current environmental problems, nd what kind of reforms would be desirable. Finally, 6.7 contains some general eflections on the choice of policy mix appropriate for developing countries.

.1. The limits of policy

Governments are not universally wise, altruistic or omnipotent. Even if they vere, they would have to contend with powerful natural and historical forces vhich seriously limit the scope for policy interventions. Three of these forces, in varticular, act as serious constraints on state action - population, the existing distribution of assets and income, and poverty.

Where there is heavy population pressure on natural environments (e.g. in Haiti, 3angladesh, the Nepal Hills) the scope for policy to affect environmental relief is eriously curtailed. The growth in the numbers of poor people often outstrips the idaptive capacity of their productive systems. Hence populations spread into 'cologically unsuitable areas, or try to milk unsustainable yields out of existing and, forests or pastures. In the urban context, inward migration and natural eproduction swell the numbers of the poor faster than the authorities can supply uitable housing, water, sewerage and refuse facilities, hence pollution grows. The demands of growing urban populations reach out to cause over-exploitation of woodfuel resources, and add to pressures on marginal food-producing land.

Likewise where environmental degradation results from a highly uneven dis- ribution of assets, income and power (e.g. Brazil, Mexico), policy measures alone will have limited effect. Few governments have shown a willingness to tackle land reform or income distribution, despite signs that the lack of secure land tenure, on the one hand, and poverty, on the other, can interact with drastic results for the environment.

Questions of distribution also directly affect political will. There is an obvious link between policy making and the distribution of economic and political power. It is commonly and conveniently assumed that governments are rational, benign, and act in 'the public interest'. This is to view most governments through rose-tinted spectacles.

There is little reason to expect undemocratic governments to behave in the inter- ests of the majority of their people. Even in nominal democracies, it should not be assumed that governments are able and willing to act in the wider national inter- est if political power rests on a seriously unequal distribution of wealth. As Foy and Daly (1989) point out:

The probability of policy makers abandoning the general welfare in favour of private interests is positively linked to the degree of economic inequality in the country.

The relative importance of these factors in a particular situation will obviously differ between countries, and in the same country at different points in time. There are countries where population pressure is arguably dominant (Haiti, Nepal Hills). Elsewhere, the distribution of assets and income and 'policy failures' are probably more important explanations of environmental abuse (e.g. the Brazilian Amazon).

Poverty is also an important factor in the way people use their environments. The visible coexistence of poverty and environmental deterioration has led many to infer a causal relationship:

> In many marginal, rural areas inhabited by growing numbers of poor people, it is inevitable that the poor may face the need to degrade the environment just a little more each day in order to make ends meet. (Leonard, 1989)

The apparently immiserating behaviour of poor people has been related to the higher than average discount rates they apply to future costs and benefits. They are less interested in future gains in income if this means present sacrifices; conversely, they place a heavy discount on future losses resulting from present actions. Their ability and willingness to respond to incentives and goads is diminished if this entails risk, investment or any other forfeit of current income, because they are so close to subsistence levels, and a bad outcome could tilt them into starvation and destitution.

One does not need to subscribe to this general theory to recognise that it clearly applies in many serious cases. The poor are not necessarily more shortsighted or feckless than other people. Indeed, there are many examples of productive systems that have been painstakingly evolved by poor communities, and which are models of 'sustainable' resource management. But such examples are matched by many circumstances where the environment is being ravaged at an unsustainable rate. The normal careful husbandry of the poor tends in practice to be overturned by any of several compelling forces - population growth, natural and other disasters, and the various factors that propel poor people on to the margins of cultivation and the edges of cities. These forces are magnified by poor people's frequent absence of property rights in the natural resources that they use.

This lack of property rights can explain some aspects of poor people's behaviour. Lacking a secure legal or usufructory claims on land or other resources, the poorest have no incentive to take a long view, and can rarely borrow without fixed assets as security. A woman working on her husband's land has little incentive to practise conservation. Open access areas are a special case where users have no ability to exclude others from exercising their rights to use a resource, and the result is general over-exploitation. This situation (the archetypal 'Tragedy of the Commons') is not to be confused with communally managed resources, where communities are able to enforce sustainable management practices on users even in the absence of formal property rights.

In short, the poor are not irrational *per se*, nor are they condemned to degrade their habitats. But development often takes a form which pushes them into the front line of environmental degradation, made worse by population growth, natural and man-made disasters, and legal and institutional factors. One persuasive view is that the role of poverty in environmental degradation is indirect, and is mediated by the policies and institutions in which the poor find themselves (Jagannathan, 1989).

In practice, the relief of poverty and conservation of the environment are part of the same problem and call for consistent solutions. Policies to promote growth in ways that relieve poverty can be fully consistent with environmental care.

6.2. Policy options

The policy choices open to a government wishing to take action to manage its environment can be simplified as regulation, persuasion, the use of property rights, the use of targeted economic instruments, including market creation, and finally adjusting indirect economic policies that do not have environmental care as their prime purpose.

Regulation. 'Command and control' regulation is still the predominant method of controlling environmental abuse. Laws govern the amount of, say, air and water pollution that is allowed, or elephants that can be shot every year, and offenders are fined or imprisoned. Regulation forces all parties to comply whatever their circumstances, and whatever their compliance costs. Laws are normally based on typical, or 'best practice' technology available when they were passed. Once a firm, or individual, has adjusted to meet the legal requirement, there is no further incentive to improve the use of the environment.

A number of countries have enlightened regulations on their statute books but a poor record of enforcement and compliance. Effective regulation obviously needs strong political will, active public involvement, and the support of industrial and other producer groups. All too often regulations are ineffective owing to weaknesses of monitoring, administration and enforcement, as well as corrupt evasion.

Persuasion. This includes exemplary behaviour by public figures, exhortation by leaders, campaigns and propaganda. The power of persuasion is often overlooked, especially in countries whose rulers carry legitimacy and strong influence. Official campaigns and propaganda may have some effect if they are backed by the moral authority of a popular government, ruler, public figure, or local community leader. Persuasion may be exercised by popular movements independent of governments or even directed against them. In many countries, citizens, consumers and shareholders have emerged as very powerful forces urging improved environmental use on companies and public authorities (e.g. the campaign against logging in Thailand in 1988). It is unlikely that persuasion alone could prevail against powerful forces tugging in the opposite direction, or in the absence of other measures. But it can be an effective reinforcement of other measures.

The use of property rights. The creation or restoration of property rights is now seen as vital in resolving environmental problems in many areas. Tenants, labourers and squatters have little direct financial interest in conserving and improving the land they use, in contrast to owners and owner-occupiers. Security of tenure usually improves access to other key inputs, like credit (Lutz and Young, 1990). Forests that are nominally owned by the state are less likely t be looked after by local people than forests owned by the local commmunity, c those where clear user rights (usufruct) exist. Likewise for fishing grounds. Pos ible solutions may be found in land reform, restoring community rights usurpe by the state, creating leasehold and user rights, and other means of giving alier ated resource users incentives to conserve.

Privatisation is not feasible for genuinely public goods such as the atmospher(the high seas, biodiversity, etc. However, a similar result can be achieved t endowing citizens with rights to a certain level of environmental quality. If thes are infringed, the victims can claim compensation. This is similar to the priva owner of an environmental resource, like a river running through private proj erty, claiming damages from a company releasing effluent into the stream. Th approach relies on enacting enlightened environmental laws, providing a basis fc civil rather than criminal suits.

The next two sections discuss the use of targeted economic instruments an indirect economic policies in somewhat more detail.

6.3. Targeted economic instruments

Economic instruments address two of the weaknesses of command and contrc methods. So long as pollution is taxed, or permits to pollute cost money, firms wi continue to try and improve their environmental record because of the continuin savings they would make. Economic incentives are thus 'technology forcing leading to constant pressure to improve ways of reducing pollution (Helm an Pearce, 1990). They also lead to abatement being carried out by firms best able t do it, and so tend to minimise the aggregate cost of compliance.

The most efficient firms, which might include those with the newest technolog or those about to invest in state-of-the-art plant, will tend to originate most of th abatement. Older firms, or those unable to comply except at very high cost, wi pay taxes and charges, but may nevertheless survive because of other competitiv advantages (e.g. fully written-down plant). The selection of the least-cost con pliers is carried to its limit in tradeable permits (see below).

Thus economic instruments could deliver the same environmental standards a regulation, but with less overall cost of compliance, and without forcing firms ou of business. Compared with regulation, they also provide a source of revenu through taxes, charges and licence fees and are easier to manipulate since they d not require amendments to legislation.

Economic instruments include the following types of measure (OECD, 1989):

Charges and taxes can be levied on 'users' of the environment, with the object c persuading them to change their behaviour, or to defray the cost of cleaning u after them, and administering the regulations. Effluent charges, for instance, ar levied on industrial discharges, and can be used as an incentive for installin control or purification methods by the polluter. The charge can be made at th product level, where the item is considered noxious and the intention is to reduc consumption. Tax differentiation is another example (e.g. differentiation betwee leaded and lead-free petrol). Tax changes do not have to increas the overall tax burden. The public reaction to a tax increase on environmental grounds could be mollified by some equivalent reductions elsewhere, to preserve revenue 'neutrality'.

Subsidies, in the form of grants, soft loans or tax allowances, can be used to soften the blow to polluters forced to introduce costly new techniques (e.g. emission control devices, wastewater treatment). Alternatively, they can help persuade consumers to switch to products kinder to the environment (e.g. kerosene and bottled gas in countries where the use of woodfuel and charcoal is leading to serious deforestation) .

Deposit refund schemes are intended to encourage the safe disposal or recycling of polluting products. A surcharge is levied on the sale price, which is refunded when the used product is returned or safely disposed of. In some developed countries it is applied to bottles and cans to discourage litter and avoid injury to people and animals. In poorer developing countries (e.g. Bangladesh) there is already an active market in the collection and re-use of such materials (as well as paper and other useful items) which could easily be extended. There is a good case for using the scheme on motor vehicles, to discourage the abandonment of old vehicles on roadsides and public spaces where they cause congestion, obstruction, and are a danger to children. Likewise for batteries and other latent sources of toxic waste. The scheme could be operated by the public authorities as an extension of garbage collection, e.g. by having reception centres for the rubbish, or it could be left to the firms and traders who sold the goods, or sub-contracted to the private sector (who are already, in effect, heavily involved in garbage disposal and recycling).

Market creation allows polluters themselves a voice in how the costs of complying with environmental regulations are shared. The best-known area is the market for emissions trading practised in the United States. The US Environmental Protection Agency set oil refineries a quota of lead for use in petrol, reducing over time, which they could trade with each other. Areas falling short of air quality standards have been allowed to 'pool' emissions from different industrial sources for the purpose of complying with the target - and firms which had bettered their limit can sell their unused quota to firms falling short. A recent proposal is to reduce sulphur dioxide emissions by creating tradeable permits for electricity utilities.

Among the refinements used in the US are: 'netting' (allowing an individual firm to increase emissions from one part of its plant so long as there is a corresponding decline in another part); 'offsets' apply to 'non-attainment' areas and allow new polluting sources only if, and to the extent that, existing sources reduce their pollution; 'bubbles' allow existing sources to raise or lower their emissions, provided the overall level of emissions conforms to the target; and 'banking' permits firms that reduce current emissions to carry forward these 'credits' to allow them to increase pollution in future (Pearce et al., 1989).

A variant of emissions trading would be to auction permits to pollute, the revenue going to the government. This would raise funds for the authorities, and penalise heavy polluters, though it would not be as flexible as the trading system.

One misconception is that such schemes legitimise pollution. In fact, trading permits to pollute takes place within the overall ceilings implied by national standards, and there is no reason why these ceilings should not fall over time. What trading systems achieve is the attainment of given standards at least economic cost, since low-polluting firms create the headroom for the heavier polluters to continue, and receive a financial reward in the process. Under a system where each polluter was required to meet the same emissions standard, the older, less efficient plants would be forced into costly investment and modifications, and might even have to close down.

The creation of such markets is not a substitute for regulation. Indeed, the system requires ceilings to be set for each polluter, and for emissions to be closely monitored. It is easiest to operate where one pollutant is involved (e.g. suspended particulates, sulphur dioxide, CFCs) from a manageable number of emitters (e.g. power stations, oil refineries, a few large firms). It is not a practicable system for controlling emissions from a mass of small industries, still less households. Even in the United States, the home of market systems, emissions trading has a sizeable administrative cost, and to work well it requires good records of emissions (Tietenberg, 1990).

Market creation can also include spontaneous **exchanges** of the right to use scarce natural resources. In California, farmers who are entitled to buy irrigation water at a very cheap rate have agreed to sell their entitlement to urban consumers. Both parties profit, and avoid costly and environmentally-damaging schemes involved in tapping new water supplies (Stavins, 1990).

Although they are not usually included in the menu of targeted economic instruments, at least in the OECD context, the conscious use of prices under state control can have the same effect as taxes and subsidies. Energy pricing is one of the most crucial market signals affecting the environment. Much environmental degradation has been caused by the use of artificially cheap energy - petrol (gasoline), coal, oil - or low prices of goods and services incorporating such products (electric power, steel, chemicals, public transport etc.). Correcting these distortions will not be easy, since often whole economic sectors have developed around cheap oil products (Mexico, Iran) or coal (East Europe, China). The usual economic arguments against artificial prices can be powerfully bolstered by the environmental case for fixing *at least* the economic price for polluting energy sources.

The price of natural resource products (e.g. maize, rice, fuelwood) is also commonly under direct government control, whether through guaranteed purchase prices, or the application of price controls. Fixing these prices has the same effect as imposing taxes or offering subsidies in the way they discourage or encourage the production of the products concerned.

To sum up, at present virtually all countries, including OECD members, incline heavily to the use of regulations rather than economic instruments to control environmental pollution. A recent comprehensive study of their use in developed countries concluded that: 'The incentive impact levels of the economic instruments are quite low in general' (OECD, 1989). This is partly due to the levels at which they were set. In most countries economic devices are used mainly to raise the revenue necessary to finance administration and enforcement, so it is not surprising that they have a muted impact on polluters' behaviour.

The developing world so far contains few examples of the purposeful use of instruments to control environmental use. It is worth stressing that the use of economic instruments like taxes and market creation does not reduce the need for information and monitoring. The US schemes for emission trading, which are widely cited as models for market solutions to pollution, evolved from a highly developed system of command and control measures, and continue to depend upon detailed monitoring and approval by pollution control authorities (Tietenberg, 1990).

5.4 Indirect economic measures

Monetary policy. Through the direct printing of money, setting official interest rates, and the various techniques of regulating the banking system and money markets, governments can influence the two key variables of the price level and interest rates.

The rate of inflation affects the form in which people choose to hold their wealth, and their preference between current consumption and future income of uncertain real value. Where inflation is endemic there will be a loss of confidence in the currency and in all assets not indexed to inflation. This could lead producers to minimise their cash balances and move as much as possible of their investment and working balances into physical goods and natural assets such as land. The choice of land or forests as an inflationary hedge is not necessarily bad for the environment. But when other financial incentives favour forest or bush clearing the flight of capital into land can be damaging to the environment, as the case study of the Amazon in section 6.6.3 illustrates. Coping with rapid inflation can also induce an excessive preoccupation with the short-term outlook, and divert resources towards managing financial balances and speculating in currencies. Brazilian industry in the 1980s exemplifies this syndrome. It is not conducive to investing in projects with a delayed return, such as energy efficiency or pollution control. Uncertainty about future government policy in conditions of hyper-inflation further paralyses normal decision-taking.

A widespread loss of faith in the currency will undermine the efficacy of market-related instruments. If farmers receive depreciating money for their crops, and are uncertain whether prices will be maintained in real terms, they are likely to shift towards produce that can be bartered, or into subsistence production.

The rate of interest, adjusted for expected inflation, affects the cost of capital, and thus the number of projects that go ahead, the rate of natural resource depletion, and the design of selected projects (in particular, how capital-intensive they are and the profile of their future costs and benefits). A high real rate of interest will discourage all kinds of investment, which will reduce the use of environmental resources, other things being equal. However, it will also discourage conservation projects and other environmentally desirable projects with delayed returns, and put a premium on rapid exploitation of depletable resources. High interest rates will favour investment solutions that have lower initial costs, but lower future benefits, as compared with projects with the opposite features. This affects the choice between thermal and hydro electricity projects, for instance.

On the other hand, high interest rates also discourage capital-intensive solutions, which would penalise inappropriate farm mechanisation, but also the adoption of certain kinds of pollution control equipment. Interest rates that are kept artificially low will suppress the development of capital markets, with a different set of consequences (see below). Thus the level of interest rates can have a number of environmental effects, which need to be carefully worked through in each case, and which prevent sweeping *a priori* generalisations.

Fiscal policy. The government's overall fiscal stance, the ways in which it raises revenues, and the directions of its spending, also have environmental repercussions which are complicated and defy easy generalisation. For example, efforts to reduce a budget deficit can cut both ways: they may reduce spending programmes and subsidies that are harmful to the environment. The elimination of Indonesia's pesticide subsidies and Brazil's ranching subsidies had their origin in fiscal pressures (Panayotou, 1989). But the axe may also fall on conservation programmes, the salaries of forestry guards, etc.

If taxes are raised, and the burden falls on imports and the use of natural resources (the common bias in poorer countries), there could be a positive environmental outcome. On the other hand, higher import duties on pollution abatement or energy-efficient equipment, or kerosene to replace local woodfuel, would discourage their use, while export taxes on tree crops could lead to their substitution by annual crops that are more conducive to soil erosion.

The prerequisite for analysts is a set of specific fiscal proposals on both the revenue and spending sides, without which no generalisation is possible.

Exchange rates. The rate of exchange of the local currency governs the attractiveness of exports and import substitutes compared with sales in the domestic market. If the exchange rate is allowed to become overvalued this will discourage export crops with environmental benefits (such as gum arabic - see 6.6.4), and swing the balance of advantage towards potentially eroding crops (e.g. certain edible root crops and cereals). However, not all export crops are from perennial bushes and trees, and not all crops sold domestically are environmental hazards. Moreover, some export crops have undesirable side-effects, e.g. tea production uses much woodfuel for the curing process, while the expansion of rubber production on to steep slopes in Thailand contributed to landslides and floods.

Insofar as export crops are perennials providing good ground cover and soil stability (e.g. coffee, cocoa, rubber), and the alternatives are annual field crops (e.g. cotton, groundnuts, maize, sorghum, cassava) then there is a presumption that devaluation will have positive environmental effects (Panayotou, 1989). But there are many exceptions, and local circumstances should be carefully considered. As Repetto (1988) notes:

> . . . there are substantial differences among crops and land uses in underlying soil erosibility, but to the extent that there is any association between erosion and production for exports, it is that most export crops are more protective of soils than subsistence food crops.

In the industrial sector, overvalued currencies have shielded the growth of import-substituting industries many of which have caused serious environmental pollution. A more export-oriented policy, encouraged by devaluation and other incentives, could stimulate more labour-intensive activities with fewer costs to the environment (see below). On the other hand, a lower exchange rate would also make state-of-the-art technology imports more costly, which would penalise energy saving and pollution control.

Foreign investment. Foreign private investment is mainly attracted by the size of the local market, the prospects for its growth, or the attractions of using the country as an export base to the regional market. Economic and industrial policy can have some effect on these factors in the long term. A government has more direct scope for influencing the kind of inward investment and the terms on which it happens.

Certain countries have consciously sought to attract polluting industries that are increasingly being shunned by countries with higher environmental safety standards (Leonard, 1988). Whether by choice or not, many poor industrialising countries have found a new comparative advantage in the production of goods by processes which impose heavy environmental costs, as a result of the need to provide incomes and employment. Countries at different levels of development will continue to exercise such a trade-off, which is rational so long as environmental costs are identified and internalised so far as possible.

On closer analysis, the problem is the nature of the product and process, rather than the fact that finance is provided from external sources. Once a decision is taken to produce, say, bulk chemicals, the choice of a domestic source of production under import-substituting programmes might well be more environmentally damaging than attracting a foreign company to perform the same function. This is because the local company or parastatal might not have the same access to finance and state-of-the-art technology as the multinational. Sometimes a country will import plant and equipment which has become obsolete in the developed world because it cannot meet stringent environmental controls. Or else the local producer will be allowed to operate under a more protected or otherwise laxer regime giving little incentive to take environmental safeguards. Often, the financial position of local producers rules out investment in pollution control measures (Kosmo, 1989).

In short, a government concerned with environmental quality can act to attract foreign investment in certain product areas rather than others, it can require certain environmental standards of its foreign partners, and can facilitate the import of state-of-the-art technology and pollution-control equipment by adjusting tariffs on those items or by other promotional devices like cheap credit.

Capital markets. Many governments suppress the development of free markets for capital and credit by capping the level of interest rates and controlling the resulting scarcity of capital through administrative allocation. As a result, savings are discouraged, and finance does not necessarily go to those who could make the most productive use of it.

The outcome is potentially serious for natural resource use and conservation. Although farmers fortunate enough to obtain credit and investment funds pay less than the market-clearing rate of interest, the majority of potential borrowers are unable adequately to finance long-term improvements, or long-gestating crops. Conservation is one of the victims of the artificial scarcity of finance and its distorted allocation. According to one authority:

> The liberalisation of the capital market is critical to land improvements, reforestation investment, resource conservation, agricultural intensification and the growth of the rural industry. (Panayotou, 1989)

Labour markets. Government attempts to regulate labour markets, often with the best intentions, may indirectly affect environmental use. Policies to guarantee employment are a case in point. Using the public service as the residual source of employment may assist the rural environment if it siphons excess population off the land. At the other extreme, programmes to create rural work (e.g. the Indian National Rural Employment Programme) help to stabilise the rural population and discourage migration to cities, which relieves potential urban problems at the expense of rural habitats. Fixing minimum wage levels could reduce total employment in the sectors concerned, forcing disappointed workers to remain on the land or to move into other activities with a higher potential for degradation. On the other hand, active attempts to upgrade the quality of labour through education and training (as in Singapore) are likely to help the environmental cause if they lead to the growth of service and high-technology industries at the expense of agriculture and heavy polluting sectors.

Debt. Foreign debt can affect environmental use in various ways, but it is useful to distinguish three separate kinds of decision that a debtor country can make: whether to become more indebted, i.e. to borrow more; whether to service existing debt wholly, partly or not at all; and how to create the export surplus in order to effect the foreign transfer payments.

It is erroneous to blame foreign debt for environmental problems. Much depends on what the debt was incurred for in the first place. If it was used to finance productive investment and relieve some poverty then it is no more guilty of harming the environment than the same development financed from internal sources, and arguably better than if development had been 'financed' from inflation. At the other extreme, debt which is incurred effectively to finance consumption, current debt servicing, capital flight or wasteful investment imposes a future repayment burden without providing any useful asset from which such transfers could be financed.

The choice of whether to service existing debt in full, to build up arrears, to impose a limit on the amount of payment, or to default, has more complicated potential effects on the environment. The decision may reduce the amount of new money available from, say, multilateral aid agencies or private investors for uses that could favour the environment. It could also affect the debtor country's ability to attract normal commercial credit to finance trade. It might also tilt a country more towards an inward-looking economic policy with environmental effects that are hard to predict *a priori*. The crucial factor, however, is how the export surplus would be, or would have been, generated.

Suppose a debtor is forced to deflate in order to generate the required export surplus. This reduces aggregate demand in the economy, and would release some pressure on environmental resources. However, it might also increase poverty and the associated degradation. As part of the adjustment to create the exportable surplus, for instance by a devaluation, there would be some encouragement of export and import-substituting sectors and discouragement of non-tradeable output. The net impact on the environment is impossible to predict, without knowledge of what these sectors are and the demands they place on environmental resources. The popular stereotype of a debtor country forced to cut down its forest to repay its foreign debts is a caricature of a set of very complicated effects.

Industrial strategy. The choice between an export-oriented and import-substituting industrial strategy has important environmental implications. It is often the case, though not a universal rule, that export industries are less polluting because they make more efficient use of their materials. However, there are many cases of heavy polluting industries (steel, chemicals, shipbuilding, smelting, etc.) being set up to serve export markets, often with export incentives, particularly in the newly industrialising countries. It is therefore more meaningful to focus on the sectoral implication of industrial strategy rather than just whether it is inward- or outward-looking.

In a study of Egypt, Yugosalvia, Algeria and Turkey it was found that the influence of general industrial policies predominated over specific anti-pollution measures. Subsidies for inputs like water, energy and other raw materials aggravated pollution in the Mediterranean. Controls over the prices of output (e.g. cement, fertiliser and chemicals) discouraged product recovery and recycling. The poor financial position of state enterprises makes it difficult for them to finance resource recovery and investment in pollution abatement. The absence of incentives for good performance blunted the motive for the efficient use of inputs. In three of the countries negative real interest rates encouraged capital-intensive projects, which happened to be heavy polluters (Kosmo, 1989).

Urban or rural bias. A systematic pro-urban bias has been discerned in the policies of certain governments in such areas as public investment and recurrent spending, the location of activity and infrastructure, food prices, etc.(Lipton, 1976). Its extent has been questioned (Satterthwaite, 1991) but where it does exist it may simultaneously add to rural poverty and magnify the growth of cities. Its most direct effect on the environment is likely to be through its influence on the location of infrastructure, settlements, and productive activities.

The opposite syndrome is also visible in many countries, where farmers are a powerful political force. Agriculture, and the larger and more powerful farmers in the sector, commonly receive input subsidies and tax relief, which often is designed to offset the effect of unduly low crop prices. Some of the most degrading practices - inappropriate mechanisation of marginal land, pesticide abuse, conversion of forest to pasture or crops, and the wasteful use of irrigation water - are abetted by lavish subsidies. Logging is over-stimulated by the government's (often deliberate) failure to capture the full stumpage value of the trees.

Energy policy. Countries that are rich in fossil fuels tend to subsidise their use. The plentiful coal in parts of China, India and Eastern Europe is available to local households, industry and utilities at a low price, which has promoted its heavy use and led to serious local air pollution and disfigurement of the landscape.

Likewise the low price of petrol in oil-producers like Mexico, Nigeria and Indonesia has stimulated the growth of motor transport, causing both urban congestion and air pollution.

In such cases the argument for raising fuel prices to their market levels is strongly supported by environmental considerations. This would also improve the competitive position of other energy sources such as wind and solar power, and generally make fuel efficiency a more attractive investment option. (Some alternative sources, such as nuclear power and peat have their own environmental costs, however.) Raising the price of electricity to economic levels would also promote economy in the use of coal and oil, and lessen the need for building new hydro and thermal stations.

In poorer countries where wood is the predominant source of energy the balance of use between fossil fuels and wood is a more delicate matter. At the margin, raising the price of coal and oil could increase the use of woodfuel by small industry and urban households, and hasten deforestation. Ideally, the price of fuelwood and charcoal should reflect its replacement cost or any environmental costs of its extraction, but it is rarely possible to enforce this precept. A more promising line would be to subsidise the use of kerosene by urban households.

To sum up, a number of the major macroeconomic policy devices available to governments have potentially important effects on the environment. Very often these will overwhelm the impact of more specific measures at the project or sector level. In every case they are likely to affect a far larger number of environmental users than can be reached by specific projects.

However, it is not possible to generalise about the impact of any of these policies on the environment without studying the context in which they will operate. A measure that would be helpful in one context could be harmful elsewhere, where a different crop, product or process was involved. The aim of this section has been to outline what the possible effects might be, and the most promising lines of enquiry in tracking down the many ramifications. A government concerned to safeguard its environment should be aware of the great number and variety of levers that are to hand.

The opportunity to make changes in some of these 'indirect' economic policies commonly arises in the course of Structural or Sectoral Adjustment Programmes carried out with the support of the World Bank and other donors. This is the subject of the following section.

6.5. Structural adjustment and the environment

Over the last decade much policy reform in developing countries has been carried out in the name of 'structural adjustment'. Structural Adjustment Loans (SALs) are made typically by multilateral aid agencies (especially the World Bank and the Asian Development Bank), often complemented by aid from bilateral donors, for mutually agreed programmes of economic reform. The aid is offered for a range of eligible imports, rather than for specific projects.

SALs have three main purposes (Mosley and Toye, 1988): i) to provide the financial resources for coping with debt servicing and balance of payments deficits over the medium term; ii) to produce macroeconomic adjustment, by bringing aggregate demand into better balance with supply, in order to provide the conditions

r non-inflationary growth; and iii) to improve supply-side performance by re-
oving distortions in specific markets, especially foreign exchange, energy, pub-
c utilities and agriculture.

hese objectives entail far-reaching interventions, often into sensitive parts of the
conomy like the civil service, the price of food, and such sacred cows as the
ational railway or steel works. In contrast, IMF stabilisation programmes tend to
cus on the exchange rate, monetary policy and the budget.

he various policy conditions of a SAL can be related to each of its main objectives.
n the realm of *trade policy* common measures include the removal of import
uotas, the reduction of tariffs, and improved export incentives. The aim of
source mobilisation is most frequently served by fiscal and budgetary reforms, the
reater use of interest rates in allocating capital and credit, better control over
xternal borrowing, and improvements in the finances of public enterprises. On
he supply side, the more *efficient use of resources* is assisted by a set of measures
ncluding: revised priorities in public investment, changes in agricultural prices, a
educed scope for state marketing boards, reduced farm input subsidies, revision
n energy prices and promotion of energy conservation, and an overhaul of indus-
rial incentives. Finally, *institutional reform* typically includes measures to improve
he design and implementation of public investment and support for the product-
ve sectors. Reforms in the bureaucracy and privatisation may form a part of this
ub-set of measures.

t is clear that a number of these measures can have important unintended effects
n the environment - e.g. energy and farm price changes, tax reforms, changes in
he priority of different public investment projects. In order to clarify their en-
ironmental impact, the various SAL programme measures can be grouped in a
nore illuminating way, as follows. (The following discussion draws upon the
eviews of a large number of SALs by the World Bank and Asian Development
3ank, discussed in Sebastian and Alicbusan, 1989, and Hansen, 1990.)

Agriculture. SALs affect output and input prices in a major way, for instance by
hanges in prices directly offered by marketing boards, changes in subsidies and
export taxes, new price controls, fees and royalties for natural resource use, and
changes in the exchange rate. A more liberal trade policy that fostered import
competition and gave export incentives could have profound effects on the shape
of domestic agriculture. The input prices chiefly affected are those for pesticides,
herbicides, fertilisers, farm equipment and spares, credit and irrigation water.
Trade policy and exchange rate changes can also affect input prices, e.g. by raising
he price of imported fertiliser and making spare parts more readily available,
even though more expensive.

Energy. Production costs and sale prices of energy are affected by reforms that aim
o bring the prices of petroleum, coal and natural gas closer to their import parity
evels and/or their long-term marginal costs. Consumer prices are similarly affected by reductions in subsidy, adjustment of electricity tariffs, changes in fuelwood prices, and manipulation of the differential between diesel and petrol
prices. The promotion of energy efficiency is influenced by public programmes for

further research and development in hydro and geothermal sources, and other non-conventional energy programmes and in a range of energy conservation measures.

Trade and industrial policy. Import liberalisation, a common theme in SALs, takes the form of a reduction in quotas and other non-tariff controls, and a reform of the tariff system. Export promotion is targeted through devaluation, provision of fiscal incentives, reduction of bureaucratic obstacles, etc. The encouragement of private enterprise works in the same direction.

The environmental effect of these measures is not self-evident. If they stimulate export industries that are major polluters, or if import substituters cut corners in order to stay competitive, the environment will suffer. But if, as a result of lower tariffs, the import of state-of-the-art equipment and pollution abatement systems becomes easier, this would be an offsetting factor. It should be recalled that enterprises, especially parastatals, tend to be influenced by general trade and industrial measures rather than more focused attempts to shape their environmental impact (Kosmo, 1989).

Public expenditure. SALs usually entail reducing and reordering public recurrent and investment programmes. This involves scrapping, postponing or scaling down capital projects, promoting maintenance and rehabilitation ahead of new construction, etc. In some SALs, conservation has benefited from the revision of priorities. On recurrent account, fiscal problems have often been the impulse for reducing subsidies, including some with serious environmental costs. However, insofar as welfare payments and wages are also reduced, poverty will increase, and this may place offsetting strains on natural resources.

Institutional reform. SALs invariably specify changes in the balance between the public and private sectors, and improvements in the efficiency of interventions. The clearest environmental impact is in natural resource sectors, where the most common elements are reforms in marketing boards, the system of farm credit, the regulation of forestry and reforms in land tenure and use.

To sum up, SALs have not so far had the environment in the forefront of their policy conditionality. It is only recently that their power to affect the environment has been appreciated, and their positive environmental potential recognised. Two major reviews of SALs and their environmental impact come to suitably guarded conclusions, but stress their positive impact in many cases:

> Far from being a major source of environmental degradation in developing countries, adjustment policies appear, on balance, to have a bias in favour of the environment. With adequate complementary measures to make sure they are implemented correctly, the policies can be manipulated to achieve environmental as well as economic objectives. (Sebastian and Alicbusan, 1989, p. 28)

And,

> Experience with adjustment programmes has shown that, if there is political will, targetting for clear objectives of income distribution and of environmental protection is possible, even when a general budget cut is enforced. (Hansen, 1988, p. v)

Designing a SAL with positive environmental features, or with minimal environmental disturbance, is an art still in its infancy.

6. Policies in a sectoral context

This section relates the previous discussion of general policy measures to their effects on particular sectors.

6.1. Marine environments

The problems of overfishing, marine pollution and the loss of marine biodiversity are examined here in two contexts - coastal and inshore fishing and open sea fisheries.

Coastal and inshore fishing. Inshore waters, those within about three miles of the coast, are of major interest to their adjacent populations, for income, jobs and food. They are usually capable of being fished by small-scale artisanal methods. Many are, or threaten to become, overfished. Fish are a vital source of protein to many growing coastal populations. In some countries overfishing results from population pressure. Traditional agriculture is unable to provide full-time work to all workers, some of whom turn to fishing to earn supplementary income. To many marginal fishermen the imperative of survival colours their view of the future, which they tend to discount in favour of present gratification. This combines with the problem of controlling access to imply that they would continue fishing even if they knew this was jeopardising future catches. Sometimes there is competition between locally-based artisanal fishermen and long-range fleets of vessels using industrial methods. Both outside encroachment and excessive numbers of local fishermen arise in the absence, or breakdown, of local powers to control access to the fishery. Fish stocks can also be reduced by destructive fishing techniques and marine pollution. Perversely, many aid projects aimed at improving the fishing industry have been inappropriate, and have had the effect of reducing the returns from fishing a finite local resource (DANIDA, 1989).

Clearly some of these causes are more susceptible to policy influences than others. The fact that in some countries fisheries are a residual occupation for the dispossessed or unemployed points to larger problems that will not be solved by measures confined to the fisheries sector. The price of fish is a basic variable, but is not something that can usefully be manipulated. Fish caught in inshore waters are normally sold in free markets, and it would be difficult to control the price, even if that would serve any purpose - which is not obvious. There may be greater scope for removing subsidies to major capital inputs - boats, nets, gear, motors - which often only encourage inappropriate development and increase pressure on limited fish resources. Pollution can be tackled by a mixture of regulation, fines and fees (see section 6.3).

One of the more promising policy interventions would be the creation of local property rights over fisheries, with systems of management and incentives. Exclusive user rights would be vested in local fishermen, who would have the incentive to conserve and manage their resource and police it against outside encroachment or internal violations. Co-operatives in Mexico control the exploitation of the spiny lobster, and individual fishermen can trade their patches with each other or with new entrants. In the Philippines, Marine Management Committees have been set up in a few areas with the task of conserving and managing their respective resources for the benefit of the local community. In effect the local people have exclusive use of the managed reef fisheries (McNeely, 1988). In New Zealand fishing quotas for certain inshore waters are initially auctioned, and subsequently tradeable.

Open sea fishing. The creation of 200-mile Exclusive Economic Zones amounts to forming property rights within countries' waters, which they can either exploit or lease. This is a necessary, but not a sufficient, condition to control overfishing, and needs to be complemented by fixing quotas comfortably within sustainable yield (where this can be confidently estimated - but see section 4.5) and rigorously policed. These quotas could be auctioned, or the payment could be related to actual catches.

Activities in open seas beyond the 200-mile limit cannot be so regulated, and there is little alternative to international conventions governing undesirable fishing practices (e.g. drift gill nets), catching endangered species, and the dumping of hazardous waste. It is possible to foresee the evolution of international agreements on the design and operation of oil tankers, with financial penalties imposed collectively on violations in international waters.

6.6.2. Watersheds

Short of undertaking specific watershed management programmes, or eschewing risky projects such as dam and reservoir construction, governments can - consciously or unwittingly - influence what happens to watersheds at various policy levels. These influences can be illustrated by examining the forces that make farmers settle on marginal, erodible land and pursue cultivation practices that lead to land degradation. Equally, farmers are susceptible to incentives and disincentives to carry out conservation practices.

The small farmer is the prime agent of degradation in some areas (e.g. Nepal, Java). But the role of the larger, sometimes absentee, landowner responding to commercial rather than subsistence incentives is important elsewhere (e.g. cattle ranching in the Amazon, cash crop production in Indonesia). Timber extraction (sections 2.3 and 4.2) is an important source of deforestation (e.g. logging in Burma and the Philippines), while firewood collection for urban use (widespread in Africa) responds to another set of incentives. In the discussion that follows, the variety of possible circumstances should be borne in mind.

A number of forces push farmers to the fragile edges of cultivation. Population pressure is a widespread factor in countries where the density of settlement is already high. Anything that changes the capacity of existing farmed areas to hold population and offer employment will also expel farmers to the marginal limits. The development of large-scale farming systems (e.g. by subsidies and tax incentives) and the substitution of capital for labour in agriculture (e.g. by tax incentives and artificially cheap imports of machinery) will have this effect (Southgate, 1988).

Degradation is often prevalent in frontier conditions. Clearing land of its original vegetation is usually the surest way of staking claim to it and is thus a more profitable way of securing cultivable land than investing in conservation measures on existing plots (Southgate and Pearce, 1988). More generally, the small farmer often finds it difficult to get access to good land in 'safe' ecological areas, because of a lack of cash, credit, or local political connections. Hence the people forced on to erodible slopes are frequently those least able to take the longer view entailed in carrying out conservation measures.

Sometimes farmers find themselves on erodible land as a result of government settlement and colonisation policies (e.g. the South African 'Homelands' policy, Zimbabwe's post-Independence small farmer settlement schemes, transmigration in Indonesia, the colonisation of the Amazon in Brazil). Road construction into virgin territory is a potent source of agricultural settlement, much of it 'inappropriate' (e.g. Brazil). It is also possible to invoke wider factors having their roots in national and even international political economy to explain why people are poor, and why they behave as they do (Blaikie, 1988).

Another set of factors seeks to explain why farmers, having settled in an area, follow practices leading to erosion. Whether or not potentially erosive crops (maize, cassava, tobacco, etc) are grown on slopes rather than products less liable to cause erosion (tree crops, terraced rice, managed pasture, etc.) will depend heavily on their relative prices. These in turn will depend on official price-fixing, import controls, and (in the case of exports or import substitutes) the exchange rate (Barbier, 1988).

For farmers to pursue conservation measures on their land depends on their perceiving the benefits of the investment exceeding the initial costs, which include the opportunity costs of labour and the sacrifice of alternative crops. Security of tenure is an obvious precondition of farmers taking the necessary long view. Tenant farmers are unlikely to make long-term investments in their land. Open access land is especially liable to be over-used and eroded, and one option would be to grant local people property rights to its use (Southgate, 1988). Better-off farmers, with access to credit and markets, are potentially more receptive to the conservation message, though equally they are more prone to 'degrading' behaviour if market incentives point them that way. Farmers' attitudes also depend on the initial depth and fertility of the soil, and on the cost of fertiliser to compensate for erosion and loss of nutrients (Barbier, 1988).

Labour used for conservation work (e.g. terracing, bunding) usually has an opportunity cost, either in the value of crops and livestock it could have produced, or in the off-farm wage employment it could have obtained. Where off-farm employment is plentiful, interest in conservation measures tends to be less, other things being equal. However, if farmers come to rely on off-farm jobs on a long-term basis, they may become more interested in less labour-intensive techniques on their own farms, which would pave the way for perennial crops.

The scope for using official policies to influence these various behavioural factors will vary. Serious rural population pressure, or a determination to settle virgin areas, would nullify the best-intentioned policy measures. The field of forces bearing on the farmer in marginal areas is quite complex and some policies can be double-edged. The government's research and extension services need to support market incentives. In badly eroded or vulnerable areas, the only effective long-term solution might be to encourage out-migration.

For all these qualifications, macro policies can influence environmental behaviour. Commenting on Java, a densely farmed island with a high degree of commercial penetration, Roche (1988 p. 32) asserts:

Manipulation of selected non-staple prices would be a cost-effective means of encouraging more profitable and sustainable upland farming to complement stronger programs for research, extension and credit. Continuation of restrictive import policies for perennial fruits and animal husbandry products will spread agro-forestry and forage systems. Price support or buffer stock schemes for tradeable crops such as cloves and coffee would also have a positive impact on soil conservation.

There is clearly room for policy-makers to improve their understanding of the reasons why farmers and settlers behave as they do, and adjust pricing, credit, fiscal, and other policies to improve signals for environmental management.

Some policy options for managing the environment in Nepal are illustrated in the following case study.

Case study: Environmental degradation in the Hills of Nepal (ERL, 1989)

The degradation of the Himalayan foothills has enormous potential consequences for the people living in them, and equally for the many millions in the plains of Northern India and Bangladesh at risk from flooding and siltation. Degradation results from the individual actions of millions of people, many of whom exist outside the cash economy and who cannot be reached by many of the normal instruments of regulation and policy. This makes the task of policy-makers particularly daunting.

Causes of pressure on the natural environment. A growing number of very poor people are forced to live in an area which is naturally subject to degradation. The situation is aggravated by specific kinds of resource use, institutional features, and exogenous factors such as tourism and border disputes with India.

i) *natural factors*. The Himalayan range is relatively young by geological standards, and the Hills are naturally liable to landslides and the loss of surface soils. 'Many experts believe that natural processes cause even more degradation of productive land and sedimentation of rivers than farming practices do' (ERL, 1989). Only 5% of hill land is 'good' for agriculture (Class I and II): 38% needs terracing, 45% is only good for forest, and the rest is totally barren.

ii) *population growth*. The national population has been growing at c. 2.6% annually, and even with heavy out-migration to the Terai (lowlands), the net population of the Hills has been increasing at 1.35%. The easily cultivable land has long been settled, and the increment of population is forced onto more and more marginal hillsides. Private farm units are very small and fragmented, requiring intensive farming - but without the commercial inputs that would permit sustainable increases in productivity.

iii) *poverty*. The Hill-dwellers of Nepal are some of the poorest people in the world. In 1987 the *national* average income per head was only $160, and that of the rural population would be less (with all due allowance for the problems of estimating living standards for subsistence farmers). This poverty, and the lack of cash incomes, severely limits ability to buy substitute resources from outside the Hills - such as food, fertiliser, or commercial fuel. In any case, the poor transport links limit the penetration of such goods, and provide an inducement for the exploitation of resources in close proximity.

v) *growing demand for food, fodder and fuel.* Food deficits have started to appear in some areas, leading to the more intensive exploitation of marginal land. Fodder of all kinds is becoming scarce, especially where the poorest farmers graze their animals on common land. Likewise the consumption of fuelwood has its most damaging effects where the poorest households, lacking their own land, use common forests.

*) *property rights.* The government holds the property rights to forest and pasture land. Nationalisation of forests occurred in 1957, and management by local users has been discouraged until recently. (Now around one-third of forests are informally managed by local user groups.) The Community Forestry Programme has covered only 1% of national forest, and has had little success in its avowed aim of involving local people in management.

vi) *tourism.* Trekking and mountaineering, the major foreign-currency earners, add to the local demand for fuelwood, often in areas with a severe shortage. The frequent passage of trekking parties adds to the depredation of fragile landscapes.

vii) *transit difficulties with India.* In 1989 problems in renegotiating the Trade and Transit Treaties with India led to the closure of the border between the two countries to trade, and Nepal was unable to import basic goods from almost any source. The inability to obtain kerosene for use in towns or national parks temporarily increased the demand for fuelwood.

Possible solutions. Any lasting solution to environmental problems in the Nepal Hills will need to: reduce the pressure of demand of hill farmers on natural resources; increase the productive capacity of all land, private and public; reduce the net growth, and change the distribution, of the population; relax some of the socio-economic constraints on the supply of key natural products, and improve 'institutional delivery mechanisms'; reduce and control the impact on the resource base of tourism and infrastructural development.

ERL's conclusion is that the usual panoply of taxation and price measures can have little effect on household and farmers' behaviour. Prices for agricultural produce have to remain on a rough par with those in India across the (usually) open border, hence taxes or subsidies lose their force. Most activity in the Hills escapes the cash economy and very little tax falls on productive incomes.Family planning is an important endeavour, but is unlikely to make much difference to population growth over the next generation, bearing in mind the low current uptake of the programmes. There is unlikely to be enough aid available to fund the import of products, to cover the resource deficits and relieve local pressures.

In agriculture, programmes are under way to substitute chemical fertiliser for compost, and improve the efficiency of composting itself. Villagers are being encouraged to improve their management of livestock and reduce their holdings of large animals. There are first-class research stations, dealing with the specific problems of rain-fed hill farming. Substitutes for fuelwood are being researched and developed, though without much success to date. Within the forestry sector, initiatives are frustrated by the small proportion of public land that is properly managed, and by difficulties put in the way of user groups wishing to manage public land. One encouraging sign has been the increasing use of private land for planting fodder and fuelwood.

In the energy sector, while there is great potential for developing hydro-power, the bulk of rural users are too poor to buy commercial substitutes for the biomass that they now use. Per capita consumption is very low, which limits the scope for savings, and most energy is for domestic use. In urban areas, however, the use of (subsidised) kerosene and electricity is gaining ground.

Soil and watershed management features in a number of projects and integrated rural development schemes. It usually includes physical measures such as check-dams, the stabilisation of stream banks and slopes, gully control, terracing, and the protection of grasslands.

In a nutshell, the proposed measures involve changes in regional policy - specifically the more intensive development of the Terai lowlands and resettlement of the hill population most at risk - encouragement of non-farm income, via the promotion of cottage and small industry, urbanisation, strengthening of user groups, increasing private sector distribution of goods and services, greater control and taxation of tourism, and control of infrastructure development via Environmental Management Units.

6.6.3. Forests

How far the process of deforestation, and the effects it sets in motion, can be halted or reversed by policy measures varies from place to place. Removing trees to accommodate population pressure and the expansion of subsistence agriculture is a deep-seated trend, although it is susceptible to policy influences (section 2.3). Where farmers and settlers are pressed or enticed into encroaching on virgin forest this is often a sign of a failure of agricultural strategy. It points to the need to rethink a complex of tenure, pricing, credit and other issues that lie behind the presence of farmers at the cultivable margins.

Likewise where deforestation is primarily for fuelwood. In Africa 90% of households use wood for cooking, and in the poorer countries household consumption of energy from fuelwood is up to ten times that of commercial energy (Anderson, 1986). The collection of fuelwood on a non-sustainable basis (i.e. which destroys trees or stunts their growth) will continue until its price rises to exceed that of commercial substitutes, by which time very few trees will be left. The relative contribution of fuel-efficient technology, social forestry, and subsidies for the use of 'commercial' substitutes for firewood and charcoal will differ from country to country, but the role of policy, rather than direct, measures is likely to be important.

The depredations of livestock are due to deep-seated causes and will be difficult to reverse. Much of the problem arises from uncontrolled grazing on open-access areas (not to be confused with communal grazing land, where some form of common control is often present). There is no ready solution. Fencing, zero-grazing schemes, conversion of state-owned or open-access land to community or private plots, may all be appropriate in different cases.

The destruction of forests for commercial logging and ranching has little to do with population pressure, and is largely a product of government concessions and incentives. Remedies lie mainly in the realm of policy and enforcement.

Policies affecting forestry can be divided into general economic measures and policies specific to the forestry sector.

General economic measures need to be interpreted very broadly. It has been asserted that: '. . . economic stagnation and poverty inevitably accelerate deforestation' (Repetto, 1988). If this is accepted, any of a wide range of policies which impoverish vulnerable groups, especially those on the margins of cultivation, could be held responsible. Such people are commonly forced into a short-term outlook towards production and investment. More specifically, agricultural programmes involving the extension of the cultivated area, such as for plantations or state farms, often encroach on forest. Programmes for settling people from overcrowded areas into virgin lands have the same effect. The construction of major infrastructure projects entails direct forest clearance, and seondary depletion as settlement or shifting cultivation follows. Mining can have a drastic effect both on-site, and through transport infrastructure, settlement, and use of charcoal for smelting (as in the pig iron smelters in Carajas, Brazil).

Farmers' behaviour responds to a mixture of incentives, all susceptible to policy changes. Farm pricing policies can cut both ways. On the one hand they can encourage the production of particular crops, at the expense of forest (e.g. plantation crops in Malaysia). On the other hand, 'urban bias', endemic in many countries, can squeeze farmers' incomes and tilt them towards non-sustainable forest exploitation.

Land tenure lies at the heart of much forest abuse. Many countries grant title to land only when claimants can demonstrate that they have cleared it of trees. If settlers have property rights to a forest they have some incentive to look after it. But often these rights are lost or overridden, as in the nationalisation of forests. This may be done in order to protect the trees, but its effect is often to accelerate the degradation of the forest, since management is neglected, and encroachments go unpunished. Nationalised forests all too often become open-access areas, and degradation is inevitable.

Fiscal and credit incentives to ranchers and large farmers may make large-scale forest clearance inevitable (see case study of the Brazilian Amazon below). The gloomy conclusion of a major survey of forest policy in ten countries is: 'Economic policies affecting the forest sector have exacerbated deforestation in almost every country investigated' (Repetto, 1988).

Forest sector policies are no less injurious. The terms of timber concessions are often highly advantageous to the concession holder and offer strong incentives to cut down trees. The stumpage value of a tree - the value of standing timber before any cutting, transport or processing costs are incurred - is a form of economic rent. Only rarely do forestry revenue systems appropriate anything near this rent, so heavy exploitation continues to be profitable. The structure of royalties usually encourages concessionaires to 'high-grade' their tracts, extracting only high value timber but devastating the rest to get to it. Concessions of limited duration, less than the natural regeneration cycle, deprive timber companies of any incentive to take a longer view and harvest their tracts on a sustainable basis. Protecting local wood-processing industries often leads to faster deforestation, not least because the protected industry makes very inefficient use of the timber and enjoys favourable terms for timber extraction.

To state these various policy influences is to hint at the shape of reforms. The forces leading to deforestation are strong and ubiquitous, and policies affecting forestry are often perverse in their impact. Against this background, foresters and others are actively exploring the scope for 'sustainable yield management' of remaining forest tracts (see section 5.2.2).

This concept is 'timber-oriented', and the final qualification above is important. The forest is a source of many non-timber products and services, and a broader conception of SYM ('multiple use management'or MUM) may be more appropriate where the local community has strong interests at stake. MUM would entail recognition of the interests of local people, preserving the resource base that yields non-timber products, helping the local collection and marketing of these items, and involving the locals in decisions affecting the forest.

The most satisfactory way of recognising the interests of the local community is to grant them formal legal rights to occupy and use the forest. The decision of the Colombian Government to confer legal property rights over 18 million hectares of the Amazon forest on indigenous Indians is an important precedent. The failure adequately to recognise the interests of forest dwellers when planning development projects can have serious social and political repercussions (Anderson and Huber, 1988).

The effect of policy measures in inducing deforestation is well illustrated by the Brazilian Amazon.

Case study: Deforestation in the Amazon

The Amazon region of Brazil is a striking illustration of the perverse effects of government-inspired development and settlement policies, backed up by a range of fiscal and credit incentives. Even judged against their own objectives, these policies have been unsuccessful. Their impact on the environment through massive deforestation has been disastrous.

By 1988 the deforested area in Amazonia as indicated by satellite images was 600,000 sq. km., 12% of the region, an area larger than France (Maher, 1989). The rate of deforestation has increased sharply during the 1980s, and is currently equivalent to an area the size of Belgium each year. Much of the original forest is burned, a process which impoverishes the soil by destroying organic matter, and which adds to the build up of carbon dioxide in the global atmosphere. A large proportion of the cleared land is converted to pasture for livestock, and much of this rapidly degenerates, with a permanent loss of fertility.

Deforestation is due to a variety of agencies, the relative importance of which varies in different regions. In Rondonia settlement by small farmers, partly under official colonisation schemes, is largely responsible. In Southern Para and Northern Mato Grosso large-scale commercial cattle ranching is the principal agent. In Maranhao uncontrolled mining activities are the main culprits. Everywhere, spontaneous settlement along major new highways has made deep inroads into forests.

The following discussion draws heavily on the formidable critiques of Maher (1989), Binswanger (1989), Hecht (1989) and Prance (1986), which are unanimous about the seriousness of the environmental damage and agree on the main factors, though differ on their relative weights.

Since the late 1960s a succession of partly overlapping programmes have been in operation with the aim of developing and exploiting the region. These gave rise to various new institutions, and an array of incentives, some of them common to all programmes. In 1966-7 Operation Amazonia was launched, comprising the construction of the Belem-Brasilia Highway, related agricultural colonisation, and tax incentives and credit subsidies for industry and agricultural enterprises. A regional development agency (SUDAM) and a regional development bank (BASA) were set up. This was followed in 1970 by the National Integration Programme (PIN), the centrepiece of which was construction of the Trans-Amazon East-West Highway and associated planned settlement. Although geo-political motives were important, this initiative was also seen as a solution to poverty in the overcrowded North-Eastern coastal states.

On the south-western frontier, Rondonia started to be opened up in 1968 with the construction of the Cuiaba-Porto Velho Highway, which led to partly planned, partly spontaneous settlement mainly by small farmers. An important stimulus to this migration was the modernisation of agriculture in Parana state, linked with incentives for mechanisation and diversification out of coffee, which greatly reduced employment.

Between 1974 and 1987 POL-AMAZONIA operated as a programme for the creation of growth poles through the development of infrastructure and the offer of fiscal and credit incentives to private enterprise. The programme was a policy response to Brazil's macro-economic difficulties and its basic aim was to increase exports of minerals, timber and farm products. The mining potential of Eastern Amazonia was a specific target, and the Greater Carajas Project emerged as the principal scheme. One of its components was the Carajas Iron Ore Project, involving the development of a huge iron mine and construction of a railway to the coast. Although the project was scrupulous in its attention to environmental impact, development outside the project boundary was uncontrolled. The combined effect of migrants, squatters, construction workers and, especially, pig-iron smelters and charcoal producers, has been to deplete forests over a wide area. Finally, in 1981 the North-West Brazil Integrated Development Programme - POL-ONOROESTE - had the laudable aim of rationalising land use and management in Rondonia and part of Western Mato Grosso, in the hope of creating sustainable land use. So far, however, it seems to have made little difference.

Certain common threads of policy run through all the above programmes. The Brazilian Government made generous use of tax incentives, credit subsidies, and rules on land acquisition in developing the Amazon region. Each of these policies encouraged deforestation.

i) *Fiscal incentives*. Income from agriculture in Brazil has enjoyed virtual tax exemption and agriculture has become a tax shelter. This has increased the demand for land, already running at a high level as a hedge against inflation, especially from larger buyers, and shows up in large encroachments on virgin forest at the margin of cultivation, partly because sizeable areas of land are still available there, and partly because the rise in price of 'intra-marginal' land pushes small, poorer, farmers into settlement at the frontier. In practice, a more specific tax credit, available for investment in 'approved' projects, has been largely responsible for the creation of big cattle ranches in the Amazon. The scheme allows corporations to offset up to 25% of their tax liability against investment in such schemes, which include all those approved by SUDAM. Up to 75% of investment in these projects can be financed in this way, and it is estimated that the government forfeited over $US 1 billion in tax on this programme between 1975 and 1986 (Binswanger, 1989).

In view of the low financial opportunity cost to the investor, many projects have been embarked on with a low financial return and many ranches, possibly the majority, are intrinsically uneconomic (Browder, 1988a, 1988b). Once established, their owners have a further incentive to overgraze the land to obtain quick returns, abandon the pasture and move on. Only a minority of SUDAM-approved livestock investments have been completed, and even these have fallen short of expectations (Maher, 1989).

Cattle ranching has been described as 'the worst of all conceivable alternatives' for the Amazon because of its potential for degrading the soil (Goodland, quoted in Maher, 1989). The overall result is that: 'The environmental damage associated with cattle ranching (including operations not benefitting from fiscal incentives) may account for as much as two-thirds of the deforestation of the region' (Maher, 1989). The 'progressive' land tax is a further stimulus to deforestation. The tax rate varies according to the degree of land use. Forested land is considered unused, and attracts the highest rate. This measure has its greatest impact in settled areas where the tax is effectively enforced, and gives owners an incentive to convert any remaining forest to pasture or cropland.

ii) *Credit subsidies*. In the 1970s official credit was made available to agricultural borrowers at interest rates that were substantially negative in real terms. (After 1980 the volume of such credit was drastically reduced, and in 1987 the subsidy was completely removed.) Farmers, especially ranchers, in the Amazon were among the beneficiaries of this preference for agriculture over other sectors. Credit was only available to farmers with full title to their land, a provision which in practice favoured the larger operators, who went in for capital-intensive operations. This factor, together with the inequitable impact of the subsidy and unequal access to land title, tended to push small farmers into virgin forests. Although it is impossible to apportion responsibility precisely between credit subsidies and other factors tending in the same direction, it has been concluded: 'The availability of subsidised rural credit undoubtedly facilitated the acquisition and deforestation of large tracts of land in Amazonia, particularly during the latter half of the 1970s' (Maher, 1989).

iii) *Land tenure practices*. In most states in the region, virgin land can be acquired by squatting, clearing the forest, obtaining the right to use that land (usufruct), and in due course getting legal title to a multiple of the cleared area. By an irony, deforestation is accepted as evidence of land 'improvement' in the adjudication of claims. Although this system has benefitted small settlers, especially in Rondonia, in other states most public land has been allocated to ranches or large companies, mainly because, in the 'land rush', the larger operators have the resources to build access roads into virgin areas. There are no absolute ceilings on land holdings, and huge areas have been allocated (e.g. 8.4 million ha. in ranches). Although the average size of a ranch is 24,000 ha., there are several larger than 100,000 ha., and one is over half a million ha.(Maher, 1989). This system has led to rapid and indiscriminate land clearance, on both good and bad soils. Many of the investors have little interest in the permanent sustainable development of the land in question, and are attracted mainly by the prospect of speculative gains in land values.

The main impact of these fiscal and financial subsidies has been on a few hundred very large commercial operations. However, there are over 50,000 livestock operations in Amazonia. Although many of these also benefit from incentives, for the majority clearing forest for livestock pasture has deeper attractions, bound up with the role of cattle in land speculation (Hecht, 1989). Some of these attractions are: i) the possession of land and animals is a hedge against inflation, and in addition can be bought with loans at negative real rates of interest; ii) cattle help to reduce the risks in farm operations. They provide income in cash or kind from their products and offspring, and can be sold at any time; iii) cattle can occupy large areas of land, with little labour requirements; iv) cattle ranching gives access to subsidies, safeguards against future expropriation, and gives the option to title on a larger area of land, whose value increases in real terms. One view is that the majority of ranchers are motivated by land speculation, rather than the intrinsic value of their farming:

> What drives land speculation now are high inflation rates, the relatively low entry costs of acquiring land in Amazonia, the clear commitment to infrastruuctural development by the Brazilian Government, colonisation programmes, the threat of expropriation of uncleared land, and the concerted promulgation of doctrines of national security, national integration and national destiny which justify continued infrastructure expansion. (Hecht, 1989)

Possible reforms. The deforestation and occupation of Amazonia, mainly for cattle ranching, has acquired a momentum which will not be halted by the removal and correction of financial incentives to large companies. There are powerful political vested interests in the current trend, and the forces fuelling land speculation originate deep in Brazil's present economic and social situation. Nevertheless, policy reforms would take some of the force out of the motives to deforest. Some of the reforms proposed would be applicable to comparable problems elsewhere. Others involve correcting specific national policy distortions. Different approaches are needed for planning the development of virgin forest as compared with land which has already been allocated and cleared.

Existing forested areas which remain inaccessible and 'undeveloped' could ideally be approached with the aim of leaving them undisturbed or developing forest-based activities in which the region has a comparative advantage. Active development would be postponed until a land-use survey was done, which would enable the land to be divided into agro-ecological zones. Land with little agricultural potential could either be kept as forest/biological reserves or devoted to other forest-based activities like rubber tapping, brazil nut gathering, tourism or sustained-yield logging. No land title would be issued for areas with poor soil, and as a general principle preference should be given to people proposing sustainable and environmentally-sound land uses. Where there is a large Indian population their rights to occupy and use forest areas should be legally recognised. Any of these solutions would depend on greatly improving forest protection services and incentives for forest guards.

It must, however, be recognised that: 'Projects cannot succeed in the presence of massive distortions' (Binswanger, 1989). The more distortionary tax policies would need to be changed. Tax credits available for livestock development in the Amazon are unjustified on any development criteria, as well as being environmentally damaging. For 'approved' projects it should be possible to use fiscal incentives more discriminatingly, and there would be a case for halting incentives for projects, such as those in Carajas, which rely on environmentally damaging charcoal production. The abolition of rural credit subsidies should be maintained. Finally, the land tax should be restructured to allow land left under the original forest to qualify for the lowest tax rate.

At the time of writing, certain of the tax incentives for livestock production have been abandoned.

6.6.4. Drylands

The purpose of this section is to identify those causes of desertification which appear to be caused by 'policy', loosely interpreted, and which therefore are potentially remediable by changes in those policies. The task is difficult in that environmental problems in drylands are not well understood, and their causes are disputed. As Warren and Agnew (1988) point out, '. . . drylands are probably the least well understood environment on earth'.

Most of the serious reports on drylands conclude with a long research agenda. For the foreseeable future, any proposed 'solutions' in the realm of policy must be regarded as tentative.

Some policies are easier to change than others. Where policies are distortionary because policy-makers failed to foresee their full implications (e.g. incentives for mechanised farming), a change can at least be contemplated. Where policies result from deep-seated social and political pressures - e.g. resettlement to relieve population growth - changes would be more difficult. A basic distinction is between policies that encourage unsustainable farm practices and inappropriate project interventions.

Various kinds of policy have the effect of **encouraging unsustainable practices**:

a) *Resettlement schemes* are sometimes introduced to relieve population pressure (e.g. the Mahaweli scheme in Sri Lanka), to accommodate people displaced by war or drought (e.g. in Somalia, Ethiopia, Sudan), or as a land redistribution policy (e.g. Zimbabwe after Independence). Another motive may be to create new social groupings for political reasons (e.g. Ethiopia, or Tanzania's *ujamaa* experiment). Unless these movements are carefully planned and backed up with advice and inputs they can easily lead to unsuitable land use such as intensive food cropping which quickly depletes soil fertility.

b) *Mechanisation* is often seen as a 'quick fix' to food shortages or export promotion, and as a way of introducing modern farming methods to underutilised areas (e.g. Zambia's state farms, Sudan's 'business farmers'). Such techniques as public loans on easy terms, the subsidised import of machinery at heavily overvalued exchange rates and tax incentives on farm income have led to large areas of dryland being ploughed up, farmed for a few years, and then abandoned in the face of declining soil fertility (Pearce, 1987b; Barnes and Olivares, 1988).

c) *Price-fixing* is a powerful influence on the balance of crops grown in an area. It is the composite of domestic support prices, price ceilings, export or import prohibitions, subsidies, and the level of the exchange rate. The general injunction to 'get prices right' for the purpose of efficient export promotion, import replacement or static resource allocation is too crude a guide for the sustainable management of drylands. Raising prices for certain kinds of annual crops could encourage their expansion at the expense of long-term soil fertility. Squeezing crop prices too much, on the other hand, might lead to the neglect and decline of land uses which have important environmental benefits, especially if they are tree products. As Pearce (1987a) warns: '. . . there is a potential dilemma for some crops between high-incentive prices and sound resource management'.

There is no clear-cut maxim available to guide policy-makers out of this dilemma. In one particular case - the gum arabic belt of Sudan - some combination of policies is required which encourages cultivation on existing land, discourages the expansion of farming on to unsuitable land, and encourages the continued growth and care of the acacia trees that furnish gum arabic (Pearce, 1987b).

d) The *'commercialisation'* of agriculture in places like the Sahel bears a share of the responsibility for dryland degradation (ODI, 1987). Farmers have been growing export crops (cotton, groundnuts, etc.) to meet the cash needs of their households. Apart from any direct effects such cultivation has on the soil, it also reduces the scope for dry-season grazing, with its valuable manuring.

e) *fuelwood pricing* usually encourages the continued cutting of trees for wood and charcoal, compared with alternative fuels that are less environmentally damaging. Fees and charges levied on firewood and charcoal traders hardly ever cover the real cost of replacing and managing the forest resources. In most countries the prices of firewood and charcoal stubbornly refuse to signal their eventual long-term scarcity, which is concealed by periodic wood bonanzas as new areas are opened up. The economic case for taxing firewood and subsidising substitutes like kerosene is more often turned on its head, with firewood subsidised and kerosene taxed. If the budget cannot support the strain of subsidising substitute commercial fuels, a revenue-raising alternative would be to impose a tax on the transport of firewood into urban areas (Stryker, 1989).

Apart from policy reforms implicit in the above discussion, three general kinds of measure could help the cause of environmental conservation in drylands. First, the stimulation of alternative livelihoods for marginal farmers, either on- or off-farm, would help to reduce degradation that is born of sheer desperate poverty, and which rapidly makes their plight even worse (Jagannathan, 1989).

Second, the development of credit programmes should help to avoid the immiserating behaviour which farmers may fall into when they are pressed for ready cash. Such programmes would be difficult to mount, and would almost certainly require subsidies, but their justification would be the powerful externalities from arresting further degradation.

Third, moves to restore powers of land management and control to local communities, which might include vesting them with property rights over current open-access land, would put some discipline back into the use of common resources. This particularly applies to water, where the restoration of the powers of local authorities, including charging where appropriate, would put back a sanction on its use and abuse.

The script for the Tragedy of the Commons is often written by governments (sometimes taking a leaf from their colonial predecessors) seeking to replace local controls and customs with central management and directives. This may be well-intentioned, but often causes a breakdown in sustainable resource usage.

Inappropriate Projects. Drylands contain great human poverty, and occur in some of the world's poorest countries. It is not surprising that they have witnessed many well-intentioned aid projects. Very few of these appear to have been sucessful: 'The contribution of previous development initiatives in semi-arid areas . . . has been negligible' (DANIDA, 1988). Again: 'In more than two months of travelling the Sahel I did not find a single major success story' (Ellis, 1987, quoted in Nelson, 1988). Large-scale irrigation schemes, afforestation, ranching, and large-scale pastoral improvement projects have, in general, been strikingly unsuccessful outside a few showpiece projects (ODI, 1987). There are practically no agronomic packages available which are both attractive to the dryland farmer and capable of widespread replication (Nelson, 1988).

The best that can be said of unsuccessful projects is that they are wasteful. Unfortunately, some of them have been harmful to the environment as well. An earlier generation of rangeland and pasture improvement projects led to the devegetation of land from cattle concentrations around watering points. The universal provision of free water from government wells is a revolutionary idea that has wrested control of water use from traditional communities and caused much local degradation. Many veterinary campaigns also got in the way of the necessary Malthusian adjustment between herd size and land carrying capacity. Large irrigation systems in dryland areas have, with some notable exceptions, failed to provide sustainable improvements to their users and at worst have tied down recurring government subsidies and reduced the long-term productivity of the soil (Repetto, 1988). The promotion of settled farming ('sedentarisation'), with the admirable intention of resettling drought-struck pastoralists and improving food security, does them no service if it interferes with familiar ways of adjusting to periodic droughts.

A more modest menu of dryland interventions is now being canvassed, which emphasises local needs and management and much more research on all aspects of desertification. Some of the favoured actions are small community-managed irrigation schemes, social forestry, water harvesting, restocking ex-pastoralists, seed banks, etc. There is increased scope for NGOs in implementing these actions.

Case study: Desertification in Western Sudan

Although the extent of desertification in Sudan has not been precisely established, and its causes in different locations have not been clearly determined, there is evidence of widespread natural resource degradation in the giant Western provinces of Kordofan and Darfur. Observations confirm reduced vegetation cover, growing problems of fuelwood supply, an increase in permanently abandoned areas, and clear signs of localised desertification. The problems are typical of other Sahelian zones. A survey of the region notes:

> Devegetation, shortening fallows and falling crop and herd productivity resulting from increases in the human and cattle populations have been accentuated by the 20 year period of below average rainfall . . . . Population pressure and overstocking are already acute in certain localities and the Zone appears increasingly vulnerable to drought and land degradation (LRDC, 1987).

The two main types of occupants of Kordofan and Darfur are sedentary farmers and nomadic pastoralists. The former, numbering 4.2 million in 1983, own livestock and practise shifting agriculture around watering points, based on millet, groundnuts and sesame, with an important income from tapping gum arabic from *acacia senegal* trees. The nomadic pastoralists, mainly from the Baggara peoples, numbered 1.3 million in 1983, and migrate over large distances in pursuit of water supplies and pasture, and to avoid cattle pests (LRDC, 1087, Pearce, 1987b).

Current problems have arisen from a mixture of natural, human, institutional and policy-based causes, which are not in contention, even if their relative weights are disputed.

i) *Natural causes*: By historical standards, there has been a secular drought in this part of the Sahel since the 1960s. Although it is not clear whether this is part of a permanent change in climate, it is capable of inducing patterns of natural resource use which are for practical purposes irreversible (ODI, 1987).

ii) *Population pressure*: Assessments of population growth are complicated by migration and refugee movements both from other countries (e.g. Chad, Ethiopia) and between different parts of West Sudan (mainly from North to South in the current decade), superimposed on the normal migrations of the pastoralists. The net result is likely to have been a sizeable growth in the number of people living in Kordofan and Darfur since the last Census of 1983 (Pearce, 1987b). This has been at a time of continuing drought and land degradation. A specific result of urban population growth, both regionally and further afield, has been some localised loss of vegetation to urban charcoal and woodfuel demands. Compared with these undoubted extra pressures from people, it is a matter for dispute whether there has been an 'excessive' growth in livestock numbers.

iii) *Institutional and land tenure factors*: Land tenure in Sudan is complex, and recent legal changes have caused confusion. The traditional system under which local leaders had a large measure of control over land use was modified in 1970 and again in 1984 in an attempt to vest more control with regional and central government bodies. The 1984 Act is understood to be under revision. It is important to establish the ownership and, particularly, the control, of land use to avoid the

Tragedy of the Commons in respect of grazing, shifting cultivation, and tre
harvesting. Cultivators of intensive settled farms need some assurance of the
rights (e.g. usufruct) before they can be expected to spend money on land im
provements or bear the delayed returns from growing trees.

iv) *Policy factors*: There are obvious limits to the ability of the central government t
influence affairs in Darfur and Kordofan through pricing, fiscal and monetar
measures. The distances involved are large, the country is very poor, and it
administration is thinly stretched. The population concerned is scattered over
large area, many of its members are migratory, and most produce largely fo
subsistence. Relations between central and local authorities have been tenuous
and often uneasy. Data supplied by the Regions have sometimes been suspecte
of serving political purposes. In any case, the central government has previousl
been unwilling to acknowledge famine conditions, or admit food security to be ;
serious economic and social issue.

The measures with the greatest potential influence on natural resource use are th
administered prices of the main cash products, groundnuts and gum arabic, an
to a much lesser extent sesame (Hunting and MacDonald, 1976). Groundnut is th
main export cash crop, and at the time of the last comprehensive economic survey
of the area represented the best returns to both land and labour. However, i
requires the land to be cleared, and the whole plant is harvested. Hence it ha
potentially degrading effects on the environment.

Gum arabic is an important cash crop in the two provinces, raising almost $US 8(
m. in export revenues in 1984/5, of which about half went to the producers them
selves. Until prices were raised in 1986, there was a long period when the rea
returns to producers declined, and led to smuggling of the crop through neigh
bouring countries. Except in the long term, when new planting is possible o
when unproductive old trees can be removed, changes in the prices of gum have
their main effect on the amount of gum *collected*, rather than changes in the
number of trees. The *acacia senegal*, which exudes gum arabic, has considerable
environmental value. It stabilises soil, protects against wind erosion and the
encroachment of sand dunes, and encourages the growth of crops and grasses in
its vicinity. Its direct products include animal fodder, fuelwood (mainly from old
trees) and the gum itself (Pearce, 1988). From every point of view it is highly
desirable to encourage the planting, preservation and care of these trees. The offer
of a purchase price for the gum linked to, and a high proportion of, the export
price is the single most important way of doing this. Another necessity is that the
individual responsible for the trees has recognised usufruct over them.

Solutions. The natural resource degradation of Western Sudan is happening
because increasing numbers of poor people are interacting with an increasingly
harsh environment in ways which will eventually impoverish themselves as well
as destroying their habitat. The eventual aim should be to raise living standards
and break the vicious circle which makes poverty compound itself.

More foreign aid along previous lines is unlikely to be helpful. In recent years aid
volumes have exceeded the Region's ability usefully to absorb it. There has been
duplication of effort and repetition of previous mistakes. Donors have usurped
the normal functions of government without offering permanently viable solutions to the Region's increasingly serious problems (Adams and Hawksley, 1989,

Wallach, 1989). On the other hand, foreign aid redirected to sensible development priorities would play a crucial part in any set of solutions.

There are differences of opinion on the appropriate balance of strategy. One approach would seek to maximise agricultural development on land already settled, and discourage the extension of the frontier of cultivation into fragile environments. The main stress of policy, on this view, would be on tenure and institutional reforms, backed up by direct enabling measures (e.g. extension, water) and price and credit reforms (Pearce, 1987b).

LRDC (1987) have a somewhat different emphasis, based on opening up unused or under-used land through water development, and encouraging an integrated package of agronomic measures to raise productivity. Adams and Hawksley (1989) lay their emphasis on improved infrastructure - especially better roads within the region and with Khartoum - and on a long-term commitment by the government and donors to appropriate agricultural research. Wallach (1989) rests his case on promoting indigenous research.

The Government of Sudan is under-resourced for the task of managing a huge, poor country, and distracted by natural calamities, internal unrest and foreign refugees. Solutions that call for a large increase in government functions and budgets are implausible.

The following threads can be unravelled from the tangled skein of possible actions:

a) Clarify the arrangements for land tenure and land-use control. The aim would be to cede greater responsibility to local communities for the management of commons, and to give some security to farmers prepared to invest in land improvement and conservation (e.g. tree planting). This could be part of a wider attempt to recreate some of the former institutions of local government (e.g. fire control) which have been taken over or allowed to wither.

b) Adjust crop pricing policy to encourage crops and trees that are good for the environment (e.g. gum arabic) and avoid overstimulating crops that can deplete the land (e.g. groundnuts). The power of prices differs in the two cases. For gum arabic, any effect on the trees themselves will only take effect in the long term. For groundnuts, the effect on land use is much more direct, but the profitability of this crop is such that relatively large changes in prices would be required.

c) Improved food security, by such means as more local storage, could help to abort the vicious circle of poverty and degradation that sets in during and following a drought.

d) Improved transport and communications would help both food security and farm incentives. It would also undermine the local monopolies of merchants and usurers.

e) The development of rural credit systems would also help to finance sustainable land-use practices (e.g. tree planting and conservation measures) which at present have a high opportunity cost in food and income forgone. Such schemes would be inherently unprofitable, but the potentially heavy environmental payoff would justify a degree of subsidy.

f) Diversifying rural sources of income, for instance by encouraging off-farm income and employment, would help the problem in two ways. Firstly, it would reduce the compulsion to extend cultivation onto unsuitable land. Secondly, it would enable individuals to take a longer view (lower their personal discount rates, cf. Pearce, 1987b) and provide them with investible resources to back up that view.

g) The revival of long-term agricultural research under a suitable institutional structure and with assured funding. The stress would be on appropriate and realistic solutions to the perceived needs of the Region's inhabitants.

6.6.5. Irrigated areas

The factors responsible for the unsustainable features of irrigation can be broadly divided into those resulting from the design of the particular scheme, and those which are a consequence of general political and economic policies. A search for solutions can start from this basic distinction. Economists and agriculturalists disagree over the weight to be placed on financial and economic factors and design and management features, respectively, though there would be agreement on the importance of including both sets of factors in any programme of amelioration.

Project-specific features. There are a number of areas in which projects could be improved:

a) *Design*. Due attention to drainage, canal lining, field levelling and other aspects of on-farm development would reduce the waste of water, seepage, and waterlogging, and help farmers to have more control over application of their water.

b) *Funding*. Schemes that are properly funded, with cost recovery adequate at least for operation and maintenance outlays and eventually for drainage measures, are less likely to suffer problems caused by neglect and damage. This implies a degree of financial autonomy for the irrigation sector.

c) *Maintenance*. Even with sufficient funding, schemes need an adequate maintenance capability, preferably with some responsibility devolved to the users.

d) *Management and control*. Any scheme needs a balance between central direction and control, on the one hand, and the involvement of farmers and communities, on the other. The larger the scheme the more important, and difficult, it is to get the balance right. The tension would not normally arise in privately owned schemes, and small schemes are easier to manage than larger ones.

e) *Farming practices*. It is safe to assume that irrigated farmers are rational in their choice of crops, inputs and water application, given the design of a scheme, their own geographical position in the command area, input prices, and the prices of alternative crops. However, their actions may have undesirable consequences for their neighbours, or even their own long-term welfare. Project authorities can influence farm practice through extension services, the issue of irrigation and leaching schedules, the supply of certain kinds of inputs (e.g. safer pesticides) or the stipulation of certain kinds of crop.

f) *Public health measures*. Aspects of public health care such as provision of clean water, safe sanitation, rural health centres, education in personal hygiene, can be projectised rather than left to the central government authorities. Likewise the various possible measures for disease vector control.

g) *Care in relocating and resettling communities* that are displaced by or attracted to irrigation schemes could anticipate some adverse social and environmental consequences. The planned provision of housing and other infrastructure is normally better than allowing them to be added after the problems have arisen.

General economic policy measures. In irrigation national political, economic and institutional factors have a very close bearing on how schemes are operated. Five examples can be quoted:

a) *National groundrules for the respective roles of private and public sectors in agriculture.* In South Asia most large command area schemes have been developed in the public sector, for cogent technical, social and economic reasons. Tubewells lend themselves more easily to private finance and ownership (e.g. in Bangladesh). Where there is a choice, as in parts of Africa, experience has shown the value of allowing private schemes to develop alongside or instead of public ventures. This has implications for the planned size of schemes, where there is a choice - since the larger the scheme the more likely it will be to involve the public sector.

b) *Centralised or decentralised control and management.* The optimal balance of central and local management and control will vary according to the scheme. Some large schemes require strong central control of water management. However, where technical factors permit, experience indicates the value of allowing local or co-operative involvement in operations, provided this does not allow the schemes to be hijacked by powerful local interests.

c) *Financial autonomy for irrigation authorities.* Cost recovery from many irrigation schemes is very low, but even where it is adequate, the revenues are often creamed off for the central government budget. This is understandable in a poor country with pressing fiscal needs, and it is not necessarily economically efficient to earmark charges or taxes to particular uses. However, where diverting irrigation revenues away from schemes causes them to underperform (e.g. where authorities are left with insufficient to cover operating and maintenance outlays) more revenue should be allowed to remain at the local level. In an ideal world, irrigation authorities would be financially autonomous, recovering the full costs (including capital) of their schemes, and able to finance all subsequent development, such as drainage. In practice, most public schemes are a long way from this ideal position (see below).

d) *Charges and cost recovery from irrigation water.* All over the world irrigation water is heavily subsidised. This is ultimately a sop to the political power of farmers, though in poor countries it is also justified as a way of keeping down the price of food (which benefits urban consumers as well). The low price of water is one among several reasons why it is wasted and over-applied by many farmers, which in turn causes salinisation as well as public health problems. Increasing charges, relating water costs to usage, and improving collection would reduce the financial incentive to this abuse. If it were desired to continue subsidising food prices, or helping farmers, it would be more economically (and environmentally) efficient to do this directly (e.g. out of the savings from no longer subsidising irrigation water).

e) *Subsidies on harmful agro-chemicals*. In the long run the environment would gain by a reduction or elimination of the use of harmful pesticides and by phasing in more natural methods of pest control (Integrated Pest Management). There is little justification for continuing subsidies on harmful pesticides. On the other hand, it would be irresponsible to rely solely on the market (e.g. prices and taxes) to curb the use of dangerous agro-chemicals, and outright bans might be more appropriate in these cases.

6.6.6. Wetlands

Threats to wetlands arise from a variety of causes. Some are the unintended results of development elsewhere. Others follow from the deliberate exploitation or destruction of the wetland in the belief that it is a free or low-value resource. The attitude that wetlands are practically worthless, which lies behind much of their 'development', will only disperse as knowledge of their functions becomes more widespread and attempts are made to place economic values on them.

A country with wetlands needs to build up enough information about these resources to determine their value and the scale of threats against them. Certain wetlands of particular value will need to be targeted for conservation. Others can be subject to various kinds and levels of policy instruments. The choice is basically threefold (following Turner, 1988):

i) *Public ownership and management*. Purchase of the site by a public authority (or charitable body) may be appropriate for a wetland of particular significance. This would not apply in many developing countries if it would cut local people off from the site, destroy local informal control and management, and could not be adequately funded or managed. The option of public ownership and private/co-operative lease and management could be applied where the state lacked money and skills. This would have the advantage of increasing the authority of the government to impose use conditions.

ii) *Regulation of the 'internal' and 'external' use*. 'Internal' uses are those performed in the wetland area itself, and should normally be easier to detect and police. They include site-specific controls over tree-cutting, major alterations to land use, commercial fishing in fish-breeding zones, commercial cutting of mangrove, major excavation of material, etc. These controls would be difficult to enforce in many developing countries, unless property rights or usufruct were vested in a responsible local body.

The 'external' use of wetlands describes the effect of activities outside the area which affect the wetland through water pollution, siltation, permanent or temporary changes in water levels, etc. These effects would be easier to check and control where they emanate from a few large sources (factories, infrastructural works) than where they are caused by many smaller actions (e.g. farmers, householders). Individual projects of a minimum size should be required to identify these effects through an Environmental Impact Assessment, and a growing number of international agencies are binding themselves to 'wetlands standards' in their project planning.

It is, on the other hand, most unlikely that, in poorer societies, pollution controls would be introduced specifically to help wetlands. On the other hand, the problems caused to wetlands would be further ammunition for those wanting to introduce more general controls on water pollution, etc. The long-term salvation of wetlands lies in such general improvements in standards, though the other measures discussed here will also be necessary.

iii) *Incentives and charges*. Many of the devices available to developed countries for preserving wetland functions are not plausible for poorer countries. Subsidies to 'compensate' landowners for not developing the land, for instance, cannot be widely used in countries with serious budgetary difficulties. Entry fees and hunting licences may be fine for certain well-endowed conservation areas, especially if visited by tourists, but would not be appropriate for others. Tax incentives are powerless to encourage conservation where taxes are widely evaded.

In developing countries, the most hopeful start may be to force potential developers of wetlands to pay a price that reflects their full economic value. This would choke off much development, which would cease to be profitable. As an alternative, if there were a strong case for development, the buyers could be required to set aside funds for the purchase and restoration of degraded wetland elsewhere. (In the United States this 'wetland mitigation banking' is carried out by a public agency, which holds a 'bank' of wetlands, and can restore them in a coherent manner.) (Turner, 1988).

6.6.7. Industrial and urban conurbations

Urbanisation and industrialisation are deep-seated trends in developing countries, and are projected to continue in most cases. Existing large cities can, however, choose to make their future growth kinder to the environment than in the past. Governments of countries at an earlier stage of urban concentration have the additional option of a more dispersed and manageable pattern of urban and industrial growth.

Underlying causes of growth. The size and character of cities partly reflect historical and geographical factors over which the present generation of authorities has no influence. Other factors are more amenable to human control. Population growth has fuelled the growth of cities, both because of the expansion of people already there, and as a factor behind the heavy in-migration from the rest of the country.

Rural migration occurs with the expansion of jobs and incomes in cities, as compared to rural opportunities. In some cases it is exaggerated by 'urban bias' in the allocation of investment and public services, and in distorting the terms of trade between agricultural and industrial products. Inflexible land tenure arrangements frequently deny the growing rural population a stake in the land. Certain kinds of agricultural modernisation displace rural populations and economise on labour. The magnetic force of cities has rarely been cancelled out by purposeful regional and locational policies.

Industrialisation has been promoted by a range of policies such as protection against competing imports, financial subsidies, credits, subsidies for imported materials and equipment, discrimination in government procurement, the formation of state corporations, etc. The developing countries find themselves as a result with a spectrum of industries that includes some of the worst polluters (mining, iron and steel, heavy chemicals, heavy engineering, oil refining). Other industries which are not inherently a risk to the environment (textiles, vehicle assembly) have become so because of the technology and standards adopted (partly because low costs are paramount and workers' safety is an afterthought).

Much of the industry that has developed in these conditions has become dependent on continuing protection and subsidy, and inefficient and unprofitable. It is ill-equipped to incur the expenses entailed in emission controls, waste recycling, water purification, or workers' protection. Some of the worst polluters are large employers and major providers of government revenue (and patronage). Changing the environmental practices of existing industry is not, therefore, a soft option for developing countries. More can perhaps be achieved in respect of new industrial developments, especially where foreign investors or donors can bring influence and funds to bear.

Available and necessary measures. Certain measures are fundamental to improving the urban environment, and there is a range of management actions to choose from. There are also a number of possible economic instruments to influence environmental behaviour.

a) *Information*. An understanding of the quality of the urban environment, and the way it is changing, is a basic precondition. While such monitoring is normally done by government, there is a role for private environmental groups to keep their own records to supplement official data. As a minimum, air and water quality needs to be regularly sampled and measured, and it is desirable to check noise levels too. The measurement of ambient conditions (e.g. of air) should be complemented by checks on the exposure of receptors. The care involved in setting up a reliable and representative system of environmental monitoring should not be underestimated (Brady and Bower, 1981).

b) *Public awareness*. Changing environmental behaviour often carries short-term costs, whether to industry or households. A public consensus on the need for measures is vital. This must start with an awareness of the environment as a political issue (e.g. the formation of 'green' parties, or acceptance by the major political parties of the environment as an important part of their platforms). The public may respond to campaigns, where the issue is urgent and widely experienced (e.g. the campaign to clean up Lagos). There is great scope for public education and exemplary behaviour by prominent figures and leading firms. However, the foundations of environmental awareness are laid in schools. Personal, household, and community environmental health should feature in the school curriculum.

c) *Setting standards*. Appropriate standards should be set for air, water, noise, toxic waste disposal, allowable discharge limits, etc. Some countries may also wish to set standards for specific sub-sectors, such as electric power, chemicals, motor vehicles. Setting standards is a difficult exercise that needs to take into account the state of the environment, local requirements, and what can realistically be enforced. It is rarely appropriate to adopt standards set in other countries, without modification to suit local conditions. Economic analysis can assist in standard setting in two ways - by quantifying some of the benefits that can be obtained by setting the standard at a particular level, and by estimating the economic costs from compliance with standards set at different levels.

d) *Institutional arrangements.* The arrangements for monitoring and enforcing environmental standards need to be clearly set out to avoid confusion and overlapping responsibilities. Where possible, existing procedures should be used and modified rather than new systems and agencies created (e.g. in Thailand, compliance is checked in the course of re-issuing annual industrial licences to firms).

Most countries rely on regulations ('command and control' systems), enforced by inspection, with the sanction of fines or imprisonment for offenders. As a variant of fines, performance bonds could be levied from potential offenders, which are repaid when compliance is proven. Fines could be either fixed, or vary according to profits obtained from not complying ('non-compliance fees').

e) *Planning.* Strategic urban planning has had a chequered record, and few cities have been able to control their size and growth. But it is self-evident that the careful planning of the crucial parts of a city (especially the location of industry, housing and open spaces, and the provision of strategic services like water, sewerage, power and transport can help to reduce environmental stress. At the project level, Environmental Impact Assessments should be an automatic requirement for all proposed major public and private investments, and for other programmes or decisions with large potential environmental consequences. The economic valuation of economic costs and benefits should also be adopted where practical.

f) *Urban management.* City management entails deciding on many issues important to the urban environment. They include revenue raising, zoning, the provision of public transport, the regulation of private traffic, the preservation of open areas and public recreation, and above all, the provision of satisfactory public services to a majority of the population. Safe water, sewerage (or a safe septic tank service), sanitation, and waste disposal are minimum requirements.

The sheer scale of Third World urbanisation, allied to the shortage of city finance, leaves no choice but to aim at 'appropriate' (i.e. cheap and cost-effective) standards of provision. Providing serviced sites and upgrading existing squatter settlements are likely to have greater environmental benefits than a programme of housing aiming at higher standards but achieving only a fraction of the coverage. Programmes to improve the efficiency of existing services (e.g. traffic management rather than new urban roads) are likely to be more cost-effective than new investments.

g) *Economic instruments.* The various methods of using prices and market devices to alter people's behaviour towards the environment (6.3) would apply in an urban or industrial situation. They can be used independently of, or in support of, 'command and control' methods.

Regulation is a feasible approach for pollutants coming from a few large sources. In these circumstances, it is also feasible to consider employing market creation to improve the efficiency of compliance. But pollution from many small sources (households, automobiles, small industries) lends itself to control by the various economic instruments discussed in section 6.3, especially prices, taxes and subsidies.

Charging motorists for entering central city areas is often canvassed as a solution to congestion and air pollution, though there are few actual examples (e.g. Singapore). The manipulation of petrol prices is a more plausible instrument, though it depends on a measure of political will which is rare in practice (see Harris and Puente, 1990, for discussion of Mexico City's problems).

6.7. Conclusion: the choice of policy mix in developing countries

The aim of the previous section was to help project analysts gain an appreciation of the role of policy factors alongside project design and other non-policy issues. This final section recapitulates the policy mix open to developing country governments, and what is likely to influence choice of options. If persuasion is best viewed as a complement to other types of intervention, the effective choice before developing countries is between four types of measure, or, realistically, a mixture of them.

Regulation is the common starting point. Command and control is still the overwhelming preference of environmental policy-makers in all countries, and a sound regulatory structure is the essential base from which market creation schemes take off. The absence of a sound data base and monitoring capability is a serious limit on tradeable permit schemes even in developed countries, and applies even more in developing ones.

Countries differ in the extent to which environmental regulations are in place. Some, including several East European countries with a poor environmental record, have extensive regulations on their books, but they are little enforced. Some developing countries have adopted standards based on those of developed countries, which are inappropriate. The enforcement of these laws is difficult in the face of political indifference and administrative weaknesses.

The adjustment of *property rights* to improve incentives for environmental use is a promising avenue in many cases. Sometimes it is an acknowledgement of the weakness of central power, and part of the delegation of decisions to local communities or individuals better able to make them. In Nepal, the nationalisation of forest lands has had the paradoxical result of weakening collective control over their use, and the restoration of local rights seems overdue. There are a growing number of instances of vesting rights in environmental users, to encourage sustainable use (McNeely, 1988).

At the same time, policy-makers should beware of stereotypes. Despite the Tragedy of the Commons, Botswana's attempts to increase private tenure and user rights over rangeland through the award of leases has had little impact on the problem. Likewise the *de facto* privatisation of rangelands around boreholes has not shown itself to be greatly superior to the previous forms of common property management (Arntzen, 1990).

Fine-tuning *macroeconomic policies* for the purposes of environmental management is one of the most promising challenges for the leaders of developing countries. Evidence of the potential effects is growing (Hansen,1990). Such policies can reach users who are beyond the pale for regulation, targeted devices, or projects - such as marginal hill farmers, artisans and small industry, peripheral urban squatters, etc.

However, in the present state of the art, macroeconomic policy is an opportunity rather than a blueprint for environmental management. Its use requires a thorough grasp of the possible ramifications of each policy tool, allied with a good knowledge of local circumstances in order to predict how economic agents will respond to certain changes. It also calls for a judgement of the possible trade-offs involved - e.g. should a measure called for on macroeconomic grounds, such as a reduction in public spending, be dropped, modified or offset if there are good environmental reasons?

There are other hazards. What seems desirable in one case (increased export price for a certain crop which gives farmers an incentive to invest in conservation) might be ill-advised in other circumstances (where the crop is produced in potentially degrading conditions). There are glaring gaps in our knowledge of how producers might respond to changes in the price for their products (e.g. livestock owners in Botswana - Arntzen, 1990). There are often local constraints to obvious policy moves - e.g. Nepal's need to keep basic prices in line with those in India (ERL, 1989).

Nor will administrations that are reluctant to enforce regulations or use targeted instruments leap to apply macroeconomic policy any more purposefully, except as a less transparent way of achieving their objectives. The Mexican government already has at its disposal a powerful policy lever - the price of oil and petrol - but does not use it for environmental management. In Botswana, where the government controls important price variables like the price of meat and various livestock subsidies, it has so far used them with perverse effects on the environment.

Targeted economic instruments are no less susceptible to problems in poorer countries. Leaving aside market creation devices, which have been briefly touched on, the purposeful use of taxes and subsidies would depend on major improvements in the way public finances are planned and administered. Taxes are widely evaded, while environmental subsidies are not feasible in the face of many more pressing claims on public coffers (though some undesirable subsidies have been removed in the name of reducing the budget deficit - e.g. to livestock ranchers in Brazil, and on the use of pesticides in Indonesia).

In Eastern Europe, and other countries with major state ownership of industry (e.g. India, Brazil, Turkey, Algeria) any changes in prices, taxes or subsidies would fail to evoke the desired response in enterprises lacking the profit motive and able to pass changes in costs back to the government. The incorporation of full environmental costs into the price of a good would entail widespread public tinkering with prices, which would go against the grain for countries embarked on economic liberalisation and market-oriented reform programmes.

The most fruitful use of targeted instruments in developing countries could well be to concentrate on a small number of key products widely produced or consumed, and whose prices the state has power to fix, tax or subsidise. Depending on the country, these could include energy and power - oil, petrol, electricity, coal, wood and charcoal (where feasible), kerosene, etc.

In natural resource sectors, such key prices would include the exchange rate, the level of export taxes on different products, the guaranteed price for the main crops, meat, fish, etc., the terms for logging concessions, the prices of irrigation water, fertiliser and pesticides, etc. In mining and hydrocarbons, export taxes and the terms of concessions offer scope for manipulation. In industry, key variables include the tariff, the cost of power and energy, and the prices charged by parastatals. In many cases, radical changes to a few of these basic price variables would make a major difference (coal in East Europe, irrigation water in Pakistan, petrol in a number of oil-producing states).

Liberalising the economy, and returning to market disciplines, is often advocated as a step towards better management of the environment. There are obviously situations where artificially low prices (e.g. for energy, forest exploitation, water, pesticides) have encouraged degradation and pollution and where market prices would be closer to the true economic price incorporating environmental costs and benefits. However, it is only by coincidence that the market price is 'green'. Removing a pesticide subsidy, and allowing the price to settle at market levels, would not be enough; environmental pricing would require a tax as well.

It is equally fallacious, and for the same reason, to argue that reforming economic policies through removing distortions in exchange, product, factor and capital markets would promote growth *and* favour the environment. Countries that score well on removing economic distortions, which have enjoyed above-average growth, and which are usually quoted as a tribute to the working of the market (Agarwala, 1983) include some that are experiencing serious environmental problems (e.g. Taiwan, Korea, Thailand, Philippines, Hong Kong). One fundamental reason for this is that the market has not internalised environmental costs.

'Internalising' environmental costs in prices would require intricate adjustments to taxes, subsidies and administered prices which it is unrealistic to expect in most cases, given the present state of our knowledge and the unwillingness of governments to grasp this nettle. In short, 'prices should tell the truth' (Weizsäcker, 1990). However, far more is involved in applying this maxim than letting prices find their market clearing levels. Although often brandished by free-market enthusiasts, this precept is actually a recipe for massive public tinkering with prices.

In theory, only when all environmental costs and benefits are internalised in prices will production and consumption be optimal from the environmental point of view. Until government policies are able to achieve the full internalisation of environmental costs in *actual* prices, the kinds of adjustments discussed in this book will continue to be necessary.

Appendix 1

Bibliographic References and Further Reading

Abu-Zeid, Mahmoud (1989) 'Environmental impacts of the Aswan High Dam', *Water Resources Development* 5(3), September.

ACE (1989) 'Solutions to global warming: Some questions and answers'. Association for the Conservation of Energy, London.

ADB (1986) *Economic Analysis of the Environmental Impacts of Development Projects,* prepared by John A. Dixon et al. Asian Development Bank Economic Staff Paper No. 31, Manila.

Adams, Martin E. and Hawksley, Elizabeth (1989) 'Merging relief and development: the case of Darfur', *Development Policy Review* 7(2).

Agarwala, R. (1983) *Price Distortions and Growth in Developing Countries.* World Bank Staff Working Paper No. 575, Washington, DC.

Ahmad, Yusuf J. (ed.) (1982) *Analysing the Options: Cost-benefit Analysis in Differing Economic Systems.* UNEP, Nairobi.

Ahmad, Yusuf J., El Serafy, Salah and Lutz, Ernst (eds) (1989) *Environmental Accounting for Sustainable Development.* World Bank, Washington, DC.

Allen, P.M. and McGlade, J.M. (1987) 'Modelling complex human systems: a fisheries example', *European Journal of Operational Research* 30.

Anderson, A.B. (1988) 'Use and management of native forests dominated by acai palm (*Euterpe oleraceae*) in the Amazon estuary', *Advanced Economic Botany* 6.

Anderson, Dennis (1986) 'Declining tree stocks in African countries', *World Development,* July.

Anderson, Dennis (1987) *The Economics of Afforestation: a Case Study in Africa.* A World Bank Occasional Paper, Johns Hopkins University Press, Baltimore, MD.

Anderson, Dennis (1989) 'Economic growth and the environment'. Unpublished paper.

Anderson, Robert S. and Huber, Walter (1988) *The Hour of the Fox: Tropical Forests, the World Bank, and Indigenous People in Central India.* University of Washington Press, Seattle and London.

Arntzen, J. (1990a) 'A framework for economic evaluation of collective fencing in Botswana' in Dixon, James and Sherman.

Arntzen, J. (1990b) 'Economic policies and rangeland degradation in Botswana', *Journal of International Development,* October.

Audibert, Martine (1986) 'Agricultural non-wage production and health status', *Journal of Development Economics* 24.

Barbier, Edward B. (1988) *The Economics of Farm-level Adoption of Soil Conservation Measures in the Uplands of Java.* Environment Department Working Paper No. 11, World Bank, Washington, DC, October.

Barbier, Edward B. (1989a) 'Economic evaluation of tropical wetland resources: applications in Central America'. Unpublished report for the Centro Agronomico Tropical de Investigacion y Ensenanza and the IUCN, May.

Barbier, Edward B. (1989b) *Economics, Natural Resource Scarcity and Development.* Earthscan Publications Ltd, London.

Barnes, Douglas F. and Olivares, José (1988) *Sustainable Resource Management in Agriculture and Rural Development Projects: a Review of Bank Policies, Procedures and Results.* Environment Department Working Paper No. 5, World Bank, Washington, DC, June.

Barrett, Scott (1988) 'Economic guidelines for the conservation of biological diversity'. Paper prepared for IUCN General Assembly, Costa Rica, February.

Behnke, Roy H. (1985) 'Measuring the benefits of subsistence versus commercial livestock production in Africa', *Agricultural Systems* 16.

Belshaw, D.G.R., Blaikie, P.M. and Stocking, M.A. (1991) 'Identifying key land degradation issues and applied research priorities' in J. Winpenny (ed.) *Development Research: The Environmental Challenge.* Overseas Development Institute, London.

Beveridge, M.C.M. and Phillips, M.J. (1990) *Environmental Impact of Tropical Inland Aquaculture.* Proceedings of the International Conference on Environment and Third World Aquaculture Development, ICLARM, Manila.

Binswanger, Hans P. (1989) *Brazilian Policies that Encourage Deforestation in the Amazon.* Environment Department Working Paper No. 16, World Bank, Washington, DC, April.

Bishop, Joshua and Allen, Jennifer (1989) *The On-site Costs of Soil Erosion in Mali.* Environment Department Working Paper No.21, World Bank, Washington, DC, November.

Blaikie, Piers (1988) 'The explanation of land degradation' in J. Ives and D.C. Pitt (eds) *Deforestation: Social Dynamics in Watersheds and Mountain Ecosystems* (A case study of Nepal). Routledge, London and New York.

Blaikie, Piers (1989) 'Explanation and policy in land degradation and rehabilitation for developing countries', *Land Degradation and Rehabilitation* 1(1).

Bojo, Jan (1986a) *A Review of Cost-benefit Studies of Soil and Water Conservation Projects.* Report No. 3 of SADCC Soil and Water Conservation and Land Utilization Programme, Maseru, Lesotho. (A review and comparison of 18 studies).

Bojo, Jan (1986b) *An Introduction to Cost-benefit Analysis of Soil and Water Conservation Projects.* Report No. 6 of SADCC programme, Maseru.

Bojo, Jan (1987) 'Cost-benefit analysis of the farm improvement with soil conservation project, Mohale's Hoek, Lesotho'. Internal paper of the SADCC Co-ordination Unit, Lesotho, First draft January.

Bojo, Jan, Maler, Karl-Goran and Unemo, Lena (1990) *Environment and Development: an Economic Approach.* Kluwer Academic Publishers, Dordrecht.

Bos, R. and Mills, A. (1987) 'Financial and economic aspects of environmental management for vector control', *Parasitology Today* 3(5).

Bowers, John (1990) *Economics of the Environment: the Conservationists' Response to the Pearce Report.* The British Association of Nature Conservationists, London.

Brackley, Peter (1988) *Energy and Environmental Terms: a Glossary.* Gower Publishing, Aldershot.

Brady, Gordon L. and Bower, Blair T. (1981) *Air Quality Measurement: Quantifying Benefits.* Research Report No. 7, East-West Environment and Policy Institute, Honolulu.

Brent, Robert J. (1990) *Project Appraisal for Developing Countries*. Harvester Wheatheaf, Hemel Hempstead.

Bridger, G.A. and Winpenny, J.T. (1987) *Planning Development Projects. A Practical Guide to the Choice and Appraisal of Public Investments*. HMSO, London.

Briones, Nicomedes D. (1986) 'Example of estimating the costs of erosion in the Lower Agno River watershed in the Philippines' in K.W.Easter, J.A.Dixon, and M.M.Hufschmidt (eds) *Watershed Management: an interdisciplinary approach*. Westview Press, Boulder CO. Reproduced as Annex 3 to FAO (1987).

Brooks, K.N. et al. (1982) 'Economic evaluation of watershed projects - an overview methodology and application', *Water Resources Bulletin*, April.

Browder, J.O. (1988a) 'The social costs of rain forest destruction: a critique and economic analysis of the "hamburger debate"', *Interciencia*.

Browder, J.O. (1988b) 'Public policy and deforestation in the Brazilian Amazon' in R. Repetto and M. Gillis (eds) *Public Policy and the Misuse of Natural Resources*. Cambridge University Press, for World Resources Institute.

Brown, Jennifer (ed.) (1989) *Environmental Threats: Perception, Analysis and Management*. Belhaven Press, London, in association with ESRC.

Brown, J.D. and Higuera-Ciapara, I. (1990) 'The use of antibiotics in shrimp culture'. Unpublished paper, Institute of Aquaculture, Stirling University, Scotland.

Brown, Lester R. et al. (1990) *State of the World*. Worldwatch Institute Annual Report. W.W.Norton & Co., New York and London.

Brundtland (1987) *'Our Common Future'*. Report of the World Commission on Environment and Development. Oxford University Press, Oxford.

Burke, Tom (1989) 'Why the quality of life has yet to be priced accurately', *The Independent*, 23 August 1989.

Campbell, Tim (1989) 'Environmental dilemmas and the urban poor' in Leonard et al.

Chambers, R. and Leach, M. (1989) 'Trees as savings and security for the rural poor', *World Development*, March.

Chester, P.F. (1988) 'Major projects and the distant environment'. Paper delivered to the Conference on Major Projects and the Environment, organised by the Royal Geographical Society and the Major Projects Association, London, November.

Chleq, Jean-Louis and Dupriez, Hughes (1988) *Vanishing Land and Water: Soil and Water Conservation in Drylands*. Macmillan, London in association with Terres et Vie.

Christy, F.T. (1986) 'Special characteristics of fisheries important for development planning and project identification and preparation'. Paper prepared for EEC Fishery Development Donor Consultation, Paris, October.

Clark, Colin W. (1976). *Mathematical Bioeconomics: the Optimal Management of Renewable Resources*. John Wiley & Sons, New York and London.

Cohen, Mark A. (1986) 'The costs and benefits of oil spill prevention and enforcement', *Journal of Environmental Economics and Management* 13(2), June.

Commonwealth Secretariat (1989) *Climate Change: Meeting the Challenge*, a Report by a Commonwealth Group of Experts. Commonwealth Secretariat, London.

Conway, G. and Barbier, E. (1990) *After the Green Revolution: Agriculture for Development*. Earthscan Publications, London.

Covello, Vincent T. (1987) 'Decision Analysis and Risk Management Decision Making: Issues and Methods', *Risk Analysis* 7(2).

DANIDA (1988) *Environmental Issues in Dryland Agriculture*. DANIDA, Copenhagen.

DANIDA (1989) *Environmental Issues in Fisheries Development*. DANIDA, Copenhagen.

Danielson, Leon E. and Leitch, Jay A. (1986) 'Private versus public economics of prairie wetland allocation', *Journal of Environmental Economics and Management* 13(1), March.

Dasgupta, Parthe and Maler, Karl-Goran (1990) 'The environment and emerging development issues'. Paper produced for World Bank Annual Conference on Development Economics, Washington, DC.

De Beer, Jenne and McDermott, Melanie (1989) *The Economic Value of Non-timber Forest Products in Southeast Asia*. Netherlands Committee for IUCN, Amsterdam.

De Boer, A. John (1989) 'Sustainable approaches to hillside agricultural development', in Leonard et al.

De Leeuw, P.N. and Tothill, J.C. (1990) *The concept of rangeland carrying capacity in Sub-Saharan Africa - myth or reality?*. ODI Pastoral Development Network Paper 29, London, May.

Dixon, John A. (1989) 'Valuation of mangroves', *Tropical Coastal Area Management* 4(3), Manila, December.

Dixon, John A. (1991). 'Economic valuation of environmental resources' in J. Winpenny (ed.) *Development Research: The Environmental Challenge*. Overseas Development Institute, London.

Dixon, John A., James, David E. and Sherman, Paul B. (eds) (1990) *Dryland Management: Economic Case Studies*. Earthscan Publications, London.

Dixon, John A., Talbot, Lee M. and Le Moigne, Guy J-H. (1989) *Dams and the Environment: Considerations in World Bank Projects*. World Bank Technical Paper No. 110, World Bank, Washington, DC.

Dixon, John A, and Hufschmidt, Maynard M. (eds.) (1986) *Economic Valuation Techniques for the Environment: A Case Study Workbook*. Johns Hopkins University Press, Baltimore, MD and London.

DOE (1987) *Digest of Environmental Protection and Water Statistics*. The UK Department of the Environment, HMSO, London.

DOT (1979) *Trunk Road Proposals - a Comprehensive Framework for Appraisal*. Standing Advisory Committee on Trunk Road Assessment, HMSO, London.

Durning, Alan B. (1990) *Apartheid's Environmental Toll*. Worldwatch Paper 95. The Worldwatch Institute, Washington, DC.

El Serafy, Salah (1989) 'The proper calculation of income from depletable natural resources' in Ahmad, El Serafy and Lutz.

Ellis, William S. (1987) 'African Sahel: the Stricken Land', *National Geographic*, August.

Elwell, H.A. and Stocking, M.A. (1982). 'Developing a simple yet practical method of soil loss estimation', *Tropical Agriculture* 59.

Environment Resources Ltd/MacDonald Agricultural Services Ltd. (1989) 'Natural resource management for sustainable development. A study of feasible policies, institutions and investment activities in Nepal with special emphasis on the Hills'. A consultancy report for the World Bank and the Overseas Development Administration, London, August.

Environment Resources Ltd (1990) 'Assessing the cost-effectiveness of selected options to reduce CO_2 emissions in developing countries'. Report to the Overseas Development Administration, London, February.

Falconer, Julia (1989) 'Agro-forestry and household food security'. Paper presented to Commonwealth Science Council's Workshop on Agro-forestry for Sustainable Development, Swaziland, April.

FAO (1978) *Forestry for Local Community Development*. FAO Forestry Paper No.7, Rome.

FAO (1987) *Guidelines for Economic Appraisal of Watershed Management Projects*, by Gregersen, Brooks, Dixon and Hamilton. FAO Conservation Guide No. 16, Rome.

Farber, Stephen (1987) 'The value of coastal wetlands for protection of property against hurricane wind damage', *Journal of Environmental Economics and Management* 14(2), June.

Fearnside, Philip M. (1988) 'An ecological analysis of predominant land uses in the Brazilian Amazon', *The Environmentalist* 8(4).

Finney, C.E. and Western, S. (1986) 'An economic analysis of environmental protection and management: an example from the Philippines', *The Environmentalist* 6(1).

Fischhoff, Baruch et al. (1981) *Acceptable Risk*. Cambridge University Press, Cambridge.

Fisher, Anthony C. (1981) *Resource and Environmental Economics*. Cambridge University Press, Cambridge.

Fleming, W.M. (1983). 'Phewa Tal catchment management program: benefits and costs of forestry and soil conservation in Nepal' in L. S. Hamilton (ed.), *Forest and Watershed Development and Conservation in Asia and the Pacific*. Westview Press, Boulder, CO.

Flint, M.E.S. (1990) 'Biodiversity: economic issues'. Unpublished paper for the Overseas Development Administration, London.

Flowerdew, A.D.J. (1972) 'Choosing a site for the Third London Airport: the Roskill Commission's approach' in Layard.

Foley, Gerald and Barnard, Geoffrey (1985) 'Farm and community forestry'. ODI Social Forestry Network Paper 1b, Winter.

Foy, George and Daly, Hermann (1989) *Allocation, Distribution and Scale as Determinants of Environmental Degradation: Case Studies of Haiti, El Salvador and Costa Rica*. Environment Department Working Paper No. 19, World Bank, Washington, DC, September.

Freeman III, A. Myrick (1979) *The Benefits of Environmental Improvement. Theory and Practice*. Johns Hopkins University Press for Resources for the Future Inc, Baltimore, MD and London.

Furtado, José dos Remedios et al. (1990) *Development Assistance and Integrated Management: Large Hydropower Dams in the Tropics*. A Report to the Overseas Development Administration, London, March.

Goodland, R.J.A. (1988) 'Environmental implications of major projects in Third World development'. Paper presented to Conference of the Major Projects Association and the Royal Geographical Society, London, November.

Goodland, Robert and Webb, Maryla (1987) *The Management of Cultural Property in World Bank-Assisted Projects*. World Bank Technical Paper No. 62, Washington, DC.

Gradwohl, Judith and Greenberg, Russell (1988) *Saving the Tropical Forests*. Earthscan Publications, London.

Grandstaff, Somluckrat and Balagot, Beta (1986) 'Tongonan geothermal power plant in Leyte, Philippines' in Dixon and Hufschmidt.

Gribel, Rogerio (1990) 'The Balbina disaster', *The Ecologist* 20(4), July/August.

Grubb, Michael (1989) *The Greenhouse Effect: Negotiating Targets*. Energy and Environmental Programme, Royal Institute of International Affairs, London, December.

Grut, Mikael (1988) *Issues Arising in Economic Analysis of Bank-Financed Forestry Projects*. AFTAG Division, World Bank, Washington, DC.

Grut, Mikael (1989) 'Economics of managing the African rainforest'. Paper for Thirteenth Commonwealth Forestry Conference, September.

Gulland, J.A. (1983) *Fish Stock Assessment. A Manual of Basic Methods*. John Wiley & Sons, New York and London.

Gutierez, Maria Bernardette (1990) 'The Carajas Iron Ore Project: an integrated assessment'. Unpublished thesis, University College, London.

Hamilton, L.S. (1988) 'Forestry and watershed management' in J. Ives and D.C. Pitt (eds) *Deforestation: Social Dynamics in Watersheds and Mountain Ecosystems*. Routledge, London and New York.

Hansen, Stein (1988) 'Structural adjustment programs and sustainable development'. Paper for Committee of International Development Institutions on the Environment, Washington, DC, June.

Hansen, Stein (1990) 'Macroeconomic policies and sustainable development in the Third World', *Journal of International Development* 2(3), October.

Hardin, Garrett (1968) 'The tragedy of the commons', *Science*.

Hardoy, Jorge and Satterthwaite, David (1989) *Squatter Citizen: Life in the Urban Third World*. Earthscan Publications, London.

Harris, Nigel (1989) 'Urbanization and economic development'. Paper read to Lille International Meeting on 'Cities: a motor for the economic development of developing countries', November.

Harris, Nigel and Puente, Sergio (1990) 'Environmental issues in the cities of the developing world: the case of Mexico City', *Journal of International Development*, October.

Heathcote, R.L. (1983) *The Arid Lands: Their Use and Abuse*. Longman, London.

Hecht, Susanna B. (1989) 'The sacred cow in the green hell; livestock and forest conversion in the Brazilian Amazon', *The Ecologist* 19(6).

Helm, Dieter and Pearce, David (1990) 'Assessment: economic policy towards the environment', *Oxford Review of Economic Policy* 6(1).

Hicks, J.R. (1968) *Value and Capital*. Clarendon Press, Oxford, (2nd edition).

Hodgson, Gregor and Dixon, John A. (1988). *Logging versus fisheries and tourism in Palawan*. East-West Environment and Policy Institute, Honolulu. Occasional Paper No. 7.

Hohmeyer, Olav (1988) *Social Costs of Energy Consumption: External Effects of Electricity Generation in the Federal Republic of Germany*. Springer-Verlag, Berlin.

Houghton, R.A. (1990) 'Tropical deforestation and emissions of greenhouse gases'. Paper from the Woods Hole Research Center, USA, presented to the Tropical Forestry Response Options Workshop of the Intergovernmental Group on Climate Change, Sao Paulo, Brazil, January.

Hufschmidt, Maynard M. et al. (1983) *Environment, Natural Systems and Development: an Economic Valuation Guide*. Johns Hopkins University Press, Baltimore, MD.

Hunting Technical Services and Sir M. MacDonald and Partners (1976) 'Savanna Development Project, Phase II'. A consultancy report. March.

IPCC (1990) 'Policymakers' summary of the scientific assessment of climate change', Report of Working Party I of the International Panel on Climate Change.

Jagannathan, N. Vijay (1989) *Poverty, Public Policies and the Environment*. Environment Department Working Paper No. 24, World Bank, Washington, DC, December.

Jahnke, Hans E. (1982) *Livestock Production Systems and Livestock Development in Tropical Africa*. Kieler Wissenschaftsverlag Vauk, Kiel.

Johansson, Per Olov (1990) 'Valuing environmental damage', *Oxford Review of Economic Policy* 6(1).

Johnson, Craig, Knowles, Richard and Colchester, Marcus (1989) *Rainforests: Land Use Options for Amazonia*. Oxford University Press and WWF UK, Oxford, in association with Survival International.

Jones, S.G. (1988) 'Environmental aspects of mining developments in PNG', Preprint series of the Society of Mining Engineers, 88-155, January.

Kalikander, F. and Hoekstra, D.A. (1990) 'Dryland management: the Machakos District, Kenya' in Dixon, James and Sherman.

Kneese, Alan V. (1984) *Measuring the Benefits of Clean Air and Water*. Resources for the Future Inc., Washington, DC.

Kneese, Alan V. and Russell, Clifford S. (1987) 'Environmental economics' in J. Eatwell et al. (eds) *New Palgrave Dictionary of Economics*. Macmillan, London.

Kosmo, Mark (1989) 'Economic incentives and industrial pollution in developing countries'. Paper produced for the Environment Department, World Bank, Washington, DC, July.

Krutilla, J. and Fisher, A.C. (1975) *The Economics of Natural Environments: Studies in the Valuation of Commodity and Amenity Resources*. Johns Hopkins University Press, Baltimore, MD.

Layard, Richard (1972) (ed.) *Cost-benefit Analysis*. Penguin Books, Harmondsworth.

Leach, Gerald and Mearns, Robin (1988) *Beyond the Woodfuel Crisis: People, Land and Trees in Africa*. Earthscan Publications, London.

Ledec, George and Goodland, R.J.A. (1986) 'Epilogue', in D.A.Schumann and W.L.Partridge (eds) *The Human Ecology of Tropical Land Settlement in Latin America*. Westview Press, Boulder, CO.

Ledec, George and Goodland, R.J.A (1988) *Wildlands: Their Protection and Management in Economic Development*. World Bank, Washington, DC.

Leonard, H. Jeffrey (1988) *Pollution and the Struggle for the World Product: Multinational Corporations, Environment and Comparative Advantage*. Cambridge University Press, Cambridge.

Leonard, H. Jeffrey et al. (1989) *Environment and the Poor: Development Strategies for a Common Agenda*. Transaction Books for the Overseas Development Council, New Brunswick and Oxford.

Liese, B. (1986) 'The organisation of schistosomiasis control programmes', *Parasitology Today* 2(12).

Lipton, Michael (1976) *Why Poor People Stay Poor: Urban Bias in World Development*. Temple Smith, London.

Little, Ian M.D (1982) *Economic Development: Theory, Policy and International Relations*. Basic Books Inc. for Twentieth Century Fund, New York.

Little, I.M.D. and Mirrlees, J.A. (1990) 'Project appraisal and planning twenty years on'. Paper prepared for World Bank Development Conference, Washington, DC.

LRDC (1987) *Sudan: Profile of Agricultural Potential*. Land Resources Development Centre, Overseas Development Administration, London.

Luken, R. (1987) 'Economic analysis: Canal Cities Water and Wastewater Phase II'. An unpublished report for USAID, Cairo.

Lutz, Ernst and Young, Michael (1990) *Agricultural Policies in Industrial Countries and their Environmental Impacts: Applicability to and Comparisons with Developing Nations*. Environment Department Working Paper No. 25, World Bank, Washington, DC, February.

McNeely, Jeffrey A. (1988) *Economics and Biological Diversity: Developing and Using Economic Incentives to Conserve Biological Resources*. IUCN, Gland.

Magrath, William and Arens, Peter (1989) *The Costs of Soil Erosion on Java: a Natural Resource Accounting Approach*. Environment Department Working Paper No. 18, World Bank, Washington, DC, August.

Maher, Dennis J. (1989) 'Government policies and deforestation in Brazil's Amazon region'. A World Bank pamphlet, Washington, DC.

Maler, Karl-Goran (1990) 'International environmental problems', *Oxford Review of Economic Policy* 6(1).

Maltby, Edward (1986) *Waterlogged Wealth: Why Waste the World's Wet Places?*. Earthscan Publications, London.

Manne, Alan S. and Richels, Richard G. (1990) 'CO_2 emission limits: an economic cost analysis for the USA'. *The Energy Journal*.

Markandya, Anil and Pearce, David (1988) *Environmental Considerations and the Choice of the Discount Rate in Developing Countries*. Environment Department Working Paper No. 3, World Bank, Washington, DC.

Medvedev, Zhores A. (1990). 'The environmental destruction of the Soviet Union'. *The Ecologist*, January/February.

Mishan, E.J. (1971) *Cost-benefit Analysis*. George Allen & Unwin, London.

Mishan, E.J. (1972) 'What is wrong with Roskill?' in Layard.

Molion, Luiz Carlos B. (1989) 'The Amazonian forests and climatic stability', *The Ecologist* 19(6).

Mortimore, Michael (1989) *The Causes, Nature and Rate of Soil Degradation in the Northernmost States of Nigeria and an Assessment of the Role of Fertilizer in Counteracting the Processes of Degradation*. Environment Department Working Paper No. 17, World Bank, Washington, DC.

Mosley, Paul and Toye, John (1988) 'The design of structural adjustment programmes', *Development Policy Review* 6(4), December.

Myers, Norman (1988a) 'Tropical forests: much more than stocks of wood', *Journal of Tropical Ecology* (4).

Myers, Norman (1988b) *Natural Resource Systems and Human Exploitation Systems: Physiobiotic and Ecological Linkages*. Environment Department Working Paper No. 12, World Bank, Washington, DC, November.

Nelson, Ridley (1988) *Dryland Management: the 'Desertification' problem*. Environment Department Working Paper No. 8, World Bank, Washington, DC, September.

Newcombe, Kenneth J. (1989) 'An economic justification for rural afforestation: the case of Ethiopia' in Gunter Schramm and Jeremy J. Warford (eds) *Environmental Management and Economic Development*. Johns Hopkins University Press for the World Bank, Baltimore, MD.

Nordhaus, William D. (1990) 'To slow or not to slow: the economics of the Greenhouse Effect'. Unpublished paper, February.

O'Byrne, P.H. et al. (1985) 'Housing values, census estimates, disequilibrium and the environmental cost of airport noise: a case study of Atlanta', *Journal of Environmental Economics and Management* 12(2).

O'Loughlin, Colin L. (1985) *The Effects of Forest Land Use on Erosion and Slope Stability*. Report of a Seminar, East-West Center, Hawaii, May.

O'Riordan, Timothy (1988) 'On the greening of major projects'. Paper presented to a Conference on Major Projects and the Environment" mounted by the Royal Geographical Society and the Major Projects Association, London, November.

ODA (1988) *Appraisal of Projects in Developing Countries: A Guide for Economists*. HMSO, London.

ODA (1989) *Manual of Environmental Appraisal*. HMSO, London.

ODA (1990) 'Bogota sewage treatment project'. An unpublished report of the Overseas Development Administration, London.

ODI (1987) *Coping with Africa's Drought*. A Briefing Paper of the Overseas Development Institute, London, July.

ODI (1990) *Environment, Markets and Development*. A Briefing Paper of the Overseas Development Institute, London.

OECD (1989) *The Application of Economic Instruments for Environmental Protection*. OECD Environment Directorate, Paris.

OECD (1990) *The Economics of Sustainable Development: a Progress Report*. OECD, Paris.

Panayotou, Theodore (1989) *The Economics of Environmental Degradation: Problems, Causes and Responses*. Harvard Institute for International Development, prepared for USAID, December.

Pearce, Andrew J. and Hamilton, Lawrence S. (1986) *Water and Soil Conservation Guidelines for Land-use Planning: Report of a Seminar-Workshop*. East-West Center, Hawaii. (A concise set of practical guidelines).

Pearce, David and Helm, Dieter (1990) 'Assessment: economic policy towards the environment' in *Oxford Review of Economic Policy*, 6/1.

Pearce, David (1987a) 'Economic Values and the Natural Environment'. Discussion Paper No.87-08, Department of Economics, University College, London.

Pearce, David (1987b) 'Natural resource management in West Sudan'. An internal document of the World Bank's EAPNA, World Bank, Washington, DC, July.

Pearce, David (1988) 'Natural resource management and anti-desertification policy in the Sahel-Sudan zone: a case study of gum arabic', *GeoJournal* 17(3), Kluwer Academic Publishers.

Pearce, David and Markandya, Anil (1989) *Environmental Policy Benefits: Monetary Valuation*. OECD, Paris.

Pearce, David, Markandya, Anil and Barbier, Edward B. (1989) *Blueprint for a Green Economy*. Earthscan Publications, London.

Pearce, David, Furtado, José dos Remedios and Pearce, Susan (1990) 'Economic values and tropical forests', in Jeremy Warford and David Pearce (eds) *Environment and Economic Development in the Third World*. Earthscan Publications, London.

Pearce, David and Turner, R.K. (1990) *Economics of Natural Resources and the Environment*. Harvester Wheatsheaf, Hemel Hempstead.

Pereira, H.C. (1989) *Policy and Practice in the Management of Tropical Watersheds*. Westview Press, Boulder, CO. and Belhaven Press, London.

Peters, C.M., Gentry, A.G. and Mendelsohn, R. (1989) 'Value of an Amazonia rain forest', *Nature*, 339.

Pezzey, John (1989) *Economic Analysis of Sustainable Growth and Sustainable Development*. Environment Department Working Paper No.15, World Bank, Washington, DC, March.

Phantumvanit, Dhira and Liengcharensit, Winai (1989) 'Coming to terms with Bangkok's environmental problems', *Environment and Urbanization* 1(1).

Phantumvanit, D. (1982) 'A case study of water quality management in Thailand' in Ahmad.

Pintz, William (1987) 'Environmental negotiations in the Ok Tedi Mine in Papua New Guinea' in Charles S. Pearson (ed.) *Multinational Corporations, Environment and the Third World*. Duke University Press, Durham, NC, for the World Resources Institute.

Pitcher, Tony J. and Hart, Paul J.B. (1982) *Fisheries Ecology*. Croom Helm, London, and AVI Publishing Co. Inc., Westport Conn.

Poore, Duncan et al. (1989) *No Timber Without Trees: Sustainability in the Tropical Forest*. A Study for ITTO. Earthscan Publications, London.

Prance, Ghillean T. (1986) 'The conservation and utilization of the Amazon rain forest', *Revista de la Academia Colombiana de Ciencias Exactas, Fisicas y Naturales*, Bogota, November.

Prance, Ghillean T. (1989) in J.M. Browder (ed.) *Fragile Lands of Latin America*, Westview press, Boulder, CO. 'Economic Prospects from Tropical Rainforest Ethnobotany'.

Prance, G.T., Balee, W., Boom, B.M. and Carneiro, R.L. (1987) 'Quantitative ethnobotany and the case for conservation in Amazonia', *Conservation Biology*, December.

'rescott, N.M. (1987) 'The economics of schistosomiasis chemotherapy,' *Parasitol-gy Today* 3(1).

'rescott-Allen, Robert and Christine (1986) *The First Resource: Wild Species in the North American Economy*. Yale University Press, New Haven, Conn.

'rescott Allen, Robert and Christine (1988) *Genes from the Wild*. Earthscan Publications, London.

Reid, Walter V. and Miller, Kenton R. (1989) *Keeping Options Alive: the Scientific Basis for Conserving Biodiversity*. World Resources Institute, Washington, DC, October.

Repetto, Robert (1985) *Paying the Price: Pesticide Subsidies in Developing Countries*. World Resources Institute, Washington, DC, December.

Repetto, Robert (1986) *Skimming the Water: Rent-seeking and the Performance of Public Irrigation Systems*. World Resources Institute, Washington, DC, December.

Repetto, Robert (1988a) *Economic Policy Reform for Natural Resource Conservation*. Environment Department Working Paper No.4, World Bank, Washington, DC, May.

Repetto, Robert (1988b) *The Forest for the Trees? Government Policies and the Misuse of Forest Resources*. World Resources Institute, Washington, DC.

Repetto, Robert et al. (1989) *Wasting Assets: Natural Resources in the National Income Accounts*. World Resources Institute, Washington, DC.

Repetto, Robert and Pezzey, John (1990) 'The economics of sustainable development'. Paper prepared for the UNECE/USEPA Workshop on the Economics of Sustainable Development, Washington, DC, January.

Roche, Frederick C. (1988) 'Java's critical uplands: Is sustainable development possible?', *Food Research Institute Studies*.

Roskill (1971) *Report of the Commission on the Third London Airport*. HMSO, London.

Roy, Peter and Connell, John (1989) '"Greenhouse": the impact of sea level rise on low coral islands in the South Pacific'. Occasional Paper No.6, Research Institute for Asia and the Pacific, University of Sydney, Australia.

Ruitenbeek, H.J. (1989) 'Social cost-benefit analysis', Appendix 13 of *The Korup Project: plan for developing the Korup National Park and its Support Zone*. Ministry of Plan and Regional Development, Cameroon, with support from WWF, EEC and ODNRI.

Saha, B.K., Kaul, S.N. and Badrinath, S.D. (1989) 'Environmental Economic Appraisal of Command Area Development Projects', *Asian Environment* 11(1).

Samples, Karl C., Dixon, John A. and Gowen, Marcia M. (1986) 'Information disclosure and endangered species valuation', *Land Economics* 62(3), August.

Sandford, Stephen (1983) *Management of Pastoral Development in the Third World*. John Wiley & Sons, Chichester, in association with Overseas Development Institute, London.

Satterthwaite, David (1991). 'Urban and industrial environmental policy and management' in J. Winpenny (ed.) *Development Research: The Environmental Challenge*. Overseas Development Institute, London.

Schteingart, Martha (1989) 'The environmental problems associated with urban development in Mexico City', *Environment and Urbanization* 1(1), April.

Sebastian, Iona (1990) 'Internalizing the social costs of air pollution - the recent experience'. An unpublished Background Draft Discussion Paper from the World Bank's Environment Department, January.

Sebastian, Iona and Alicbusan, Adelaida (1989) *Sustainable Development: Issues in Adjustment Lending Policies*. Environment Department, World Bank, Washington, DC, October.

Service, M.W. (1989) 'Rice, a challenge to health', *Parasitology Today*, 5(5).

Shepherd, Gill (1985) 'Social Forestry in 1985: lessons learnt and topics to be addressed'. ODI Social Forestry Network Paper 1a, Winter.

Shepherd, Gill (1989) 'The reality of the commons: answering Hardin from Somalia', *Development Policy Review* 7(1).

Sinden, J.A. (1990) 'The costs of soil degradation on the northwest slopes of New South Wales, Australia' in Dixon, James and Sherman.

Sinden, J.A., Sutas, A.R. and Yapp, T.P. (1990) 'Damage costs of land degradation: an Australian perspective' in Dixon, James and Sherman.

Southgate, Douglas (1988) *The Economics of Land Degradation in the Third World*. Environment Department Working Paper No.2, World Bank, Washington, DC, May.

Southgate, Douglas and Pearce, David (1988) *Agricultural Colonization and Environmental Degradation in Frontier Developing Countries*. Environment Department Working Paper No.9, World Bank, Washington, DC, October.

Southgate, Douglas and Macke, Robert (1989) 'The downstream benefits of soil conservation in Third World hydroelectric watersheds', *Land Economics* 65(1) February.

Starkie, D.N.M. and Johnson, D.M. (1973) 'The valuation of disamenity: an analysis of sound attenuation'. An unpublished paper of the Department of Geography, University of Reading, 1973. A book-length account of this research appeared as *The Economic Value of Peace and Quiet* (Heath, Lexington, 1975).

Stavins, Robert N. (1990) 'Innovative policies for sustainable development in the 1990s: economic incentives for environmental protection'. Paper for UNECE/ USEPA Workshop on the Economics of Sustainable Development, Washington, DC, January.

Stocking, Michael (1984) 'Erosion and soil productivity: a review'. Consultants' Working Paper No. 1, Soil Conservation Programme, Land and Water Development Division, FAO, Rome.

Stocking, Michael (1986) 'The cost of soil erosion in Zimbabwe in terms of the loss of three major nutrients'. Consultants' Working Paper No. 3, Soil Conservation Programme, Land and Water Development Division, FAO, Rome.

Stocking, M., Bojo, J. and Abel, N. (1989) 'Financial and economic analysis of agroforestry: key issues'. Paper produced for the Workshop on Agroforestry for Sustainable Development - Economic Implications, organised by the Commonwealth Science Council, Mbabane, Swaziland, April.

Stryker, J. Dirck (1989) 'Technology, human pressure, and ecology in the arid and semi-arid tropics' in Leonard et al.

Swain, Margaret Byrne (1990) 'Commoditizing ethnicity in Southwest China', *Cultural Survival Quarterly* 14(1).

TRRL (1988) *Overseas Road Note 5: a Guide to Road Project Appraisal*. Overseas Unit, Transport and Road Research Laboratory, Crowthorne, Berkshire.

Tickell, Crispin (1989) 'Environmental refugees: the human impact of global climatic change', the NERC Annual Lecture, National Environment Research Council, UK, June.

Tietenberg, T.H. (1990) 'Economic instruments for environmental regulation', *Oxford Review of Economic Policy* 6(1).

Tiffen, Mary (1990) *Guidelines for Intersectoral Cooperation to Improve Health Aspects of Irrigation*. World Health Organisation, Geneva.

Trexler, Mark C., Mintzer, Irving M. and Moomaw, William R. (1990) 'Global warming: an assessment of its scientific basis, its likely impacts, and potential response strategies'. Paper delivered at UNECE/USEPA Workshop on the Economics of Sustainable Development, Washington, DC, January.

Turner, R. Kerry (1988) *The Environmental Effects of Market and Intervention Failures in the Management of Wetlands*. Report to the Environment Committee Group of Economic Experts, OECD, Paris, November.

Turner, R. Kerry (1990) 'Economics and wetland management', *Ambio*.

UKCEED (1986) *The Use of Market Mechanisms in the Regulation of Air Pollution*. UK Centre for Economic and Environmental Development, London.

UNEP (1988) 'Reducing profits from poison', *UNEP News*, August.

UNEP/GEMS (1987) *The Ozone Layer*. UNEP/GEMS Environment Library No. 2, Nairobi.

UNIDO (1988) *First Guide for UNIDO Officers in Evaluating the Environmental Impact of Industrial Projects*. UNIDO, Vienna, April.

UNIDO (1990) 'Industry and the Environment', Chapter III in the UNIDO 1990 Annual Report, *Industry and Development*. Vienna.

USEPA (1988) *Guidelines for Preparing Regulatory Impact Analysis. Appendices A, B, C, and D*. Office of Policy, Planning and Evaluation, US Environmental Protection Agency, Washington, DC, March.

Vandermeulen, J.H. (1990) 'Environmental developments'. Paper presented at a Conference on Ports as Nodal Points in a Global Transport System, Pacem in Maribus, Rotterdam, June.

VanDomelen, Julie (1988) *Power to Spare: the World Bank and Electricity Conservation*. Osborn Center, for World Wildlife Fund and the Conservation Foundation, Washington, DC.

Wallach, Bret (1989) 'Improving traditional grassland agriculture in Sudan', *Geographical Review* 79(2), April.

Wang Hua Dong (1985) in *The Mining Magazine*, July.

Walter, Jörg and Ayres, Robert (1990) 'Global warming: damages and costs'. Paper presented to the IPPC, January.

Warren, Andrew and Agnew, Clive (1988) 'An assessment of desertification and land degradation in arid and semi-arid areas'. An IIED Paper, IIED, London, November.

Watanabe, Tatsuya (1989) 'Research and training needs in environmental management and reforestation in Asia-Pacific'. Paper for EADI Workshop on Environment and Development, Rome.

Watt, G.R. (1990) 'Techniques and issues in the design and appraisal of commercial forestry projects and programmes in developing countries'. Paper prepared for the Overseas Development Administration, London.

Weizsäcker, Ernst von (1990) 'Global challenges and environmental tax reform'. Paper for International Conference on Economic Instruments for Environmental Protection, Institute for European Environmental Policy, Rome, January.

White, Sue (1989) *The Technical Costs and Benefits of Agroforestry to the Catchment as a Whole. Upstream-downstream Relationships*. Hydraulics Research, Wallingford, UK, 1989.

Wiggins, S.L. and Palma, O.G. (1980) *Acelhuate River Catchment Management Project, El Salvador. Cost-benefit Analysis of Soil Conservation*. ODA Land Resources Development Centre, UK. (A pioneering study of great technical and economic interest).

Winpenny, J.T. (1977) 'Housing and jobs for the poor'. A monograph issued by the Development Planning Unit, University College, London.

Winpenny, J.T. (1982) 'Housing the poor' in P.J. Richards and M.D. Leonor (eds) *Target Setting for Basic Needs*. International Labour Office, Geneva.

World Bank (1984). *Environmental Guidelines*. Office of Environmental Affairs, Washington D.C.

World Bank (1989) *Philippines: Environment and Natural Resource Management Study*. World Bank, Washington, DC.

World Bank/EIB (1990) *The Environmental Program for the Mediterranean*. World Bank and European Investment Bank, Washington, DC, and Luxembourg.

WRI/IIED (1988) *World Resources, 1988-89*. A Report by the World Resources Institute and the International Institute for Environment and Development, in collaboration with the United Nations Environment Programme. Basic Books Inc, New York.

Yudelman, Montague (1989) 'Sustainable and equitable development in irrigated environments' in Leonard et al.

Appendix 2

Specimen Format for Project Appraisal

The format is illustrated in Table A.1 for an imaginary road project in a developing country (a more elaborate version is used by the UK's Department of Transport in trunk road appraisals, see DOT, 1979). The conclusions to be drawn from this format are:

i)   On a conventional CBA using vehicle cost savings, time savings, and savings from maintaining the previous road surface, total benefits of £16 m. just exceed the investment and recurrent costs of £15 m. (all on an NPV basis).

ii) Various environmental effects can be valued: a tree-planting programme to replace local forest lost by the road construction, £1 m.; the loss of fishing catch in the local river from heavy siltation caused by soil erosion due to the road, £1.5 m.; and the cost of creating a wildlife sanctuary to protect a rare breed of monkey whose habitat borders on the road, £1.0 m. This last mentioned cost is shared between central and local government, and is net of a donation from the World Wildlife Fund. The sanctuary will have some tourism potential.

iii) These environmental effects amount to negative benefits of £3.5 m., which reduce total project benefits to below total costs (a deficit of £2.5 m.).

iv) Central government contributes all the investment cost, and two-thirds of the maintenance. It meets half the costs of tree-planting and the wildlife sanctuary. It captures all the benefit from maintenance savings on the previous road (for which it was wholly responsible). It also benefits substantially from reduced congestion, and vehicle cost and time savings, though these were not costed at the time of the appraisal.

v)   The finances of local government are likely to be strained by the project since it must find the funds to meet its share of tree-planting and the creation of the wildlife sanctuary, and the only offset is some savings from vehicle costs and travelling time for its officers. On the other hand, local residents who directly use the road stand to gain substantially from user cost savings, which exceed the likely losses from fishing, an important part-time occupation and dietary supplement. This may offer some scope for the local government to raise more revenue from its community.

vi) The major local non-quantifiable effects are the greater number of fatalities from the higher average speed of traffic, increased pollution and noise in the village along the route, and a slight reduction to biodiversity which affects collectors of forest products, but there is some gain from reduced congestion.

(vii) Traders, operators of commercial vehicles, and the tourist industry appear to be clear net gainers from the road, and indicate the scope for revenue raising.

(viii) The decision-maker should be briefed that there is a negative NPV of £2.5 m after certain environmental costs have been reckoned in. The main effects that are either non-quantifiable or have not been quantified for the appraisal concern tourism, agriculture, safety, pollution, noise, congestion and biodiversity. The decision-maker may wish to postpone a decision pending further study of the impact on tourism and agriculture, and may wish to commission a redesign of the road to reduce the accident rate for local residents.

Table A.1. Format for displaying results of environmental appraisal: a road

Effects/Parties	Travellers					Government		Total
	Local	Commercial	Tourist	Residents	Agriculture	Local	Central	£mn
User cost savings:								
Vehicles	3.0	6.0	2.0	+	+++	+	++	11.0
Time	0.5	2.0	0.5	++	++	+	++	3.0
Maintenance savings							2.0	2.0
Safety (3)		10		4				
Pollution				—				
Noise (4)				—				
Congestion			++	+++			+++	
Natural habitats (5)						(0.5)	(0.5)	(1.0)
Soil erosion (6) &								
slope stability			(1.0)			(0.5)		(1.5)
Biodiversity		—				—		
Wildlife (7)			+++			(0.5)	(0.5)	(1.0)
Greenhouse effect, CFCs								
Investment costs							(12.0)	(12.0)
Recurrent costs						(1.0)	(2.0)	(3.0)

Notes

(1) Final column in net present value terms
(2) Negative values (costs) shown in brackets e.g. (0.4)
(3) Reduction in *number* of fatalities (from TRRL study)
(4) % Increase in noise incidence for roadside dwellings
(5) Tree planting programme cost
(6) Loss of fishing catch from pollution of river
(7) Cost of creating wildlife sanctuary as compensatory project
(8) Size of benefit +++ or cost — (the more signs out of 4 the greater the effect).

Author Index

Subject Index

Printed in the United Kingdom for HMSO.
Dd.0294687, 5/93, C10, 3397/5, 5673, 244381.